# The Creation of Monuments

# The Creation of Monuments

## Neolithic Causewayed Enclosures in the British Isles

Alastair Oswald, Carolyn Dyer and Martyn Barber

ENGLISH HERITAGE

Published by English Heritage at the National Monuments Record Centre,
Great Western Village, Kemble Drive, Swindon SN2 2GZ

© English Heritage 2001
Images (except as otherwise shown) © Crown copyright. NMR
Applications for the reproduction of images should be made to the
National Monuments Record

First published 2001

ISBN 1 873592 42 6

Product Code XA20011

*British Library Cataloguing in Publication Data*
A CIP catalogue record for this book is available from the British Library

Edited by Mike Ponsford
Cover design by Mark Simmons
Designed by Chuck Goodwin
Edited and brought to press by English Heritage Publications Department
Printed by Latimer Trend

# Contents

# Illustrations

# Acknowledgements

This publication is the outcome of a three-year-long multi-disciplinary project carried out on a national scale by the Royal Commission on the Historical Monuments of England (RCHME), which merged with English Heritage on 1 April 1999. As a result, the list of those involved, both within the organisation and outside it, is lengthy. The project was planned and initially coordinated by Peter Topping. The preparation of this book was overseen by Paul Everson, while Humphrey Welfare offered advice and constructive criticism.

Perhaps the most important contribution is the work of those of who have been involved in recording the sites and monuments. Martyn Barber was responsible, with assistance from Kate Fernie, for much of the documentary research which accompanied most surveys. Carolyn Dyer was responsible for coordinating the air photographic transcriptions and analysis. She was assisted by Antonia Kershaw and Fiona Small, with contributions by Bob Bewley, Yvonne Boutwood, Anne Carter, Jonathon Chandler, Henrietta Clare, Simon Crutchley, Victoria Fenner, Peter Horne, David MacLeod, Julia Millard and Helen Winton. Every member of the Field Archaeology Section contributed to the fieldwork: Chris Dunn, Martin Fletcher, Hazel Riley and Simon Probert participated in much of the recording in the South-West; Mark Bowden, Keith Blood, Amy Lax and Colin Lofthouse were involved in the North of England; sites in the remainder of the country were investigated by Stewart Ainsworth, Graham Brown, Moraig Brown, Wayne Cocroft, Mark Corney, Dave Field, Marcus Jecock, Dave McOmish, Alastair Oswald, Paul Pattison, Trevor Pearson, Nicky Smith, Peter Topping and Rob Wilson-North, with assistance on some sites from Martyn Barber and Carolyn Dyer.

Alun Bull carried out most of the photographic recording for the project on the ground. Computer aided design (CAD) software has been used in this book to generate all the published illustrations directly from the archive plans produced by the fieldworkers. This advance owes much to Trevor Pearson, who was responsible for the main body of illustrations. Philip Sinton completed a number of the figures. Robin Taylor, initially as head of RCHME's Publications Section and subsequently as Manager of English Heritage's Academic and Specialist Publications Team, was a member of the project team from the outset; his experience in archaeological research and book production have been equally valuable. In the editing stages, he was assisted by Diane Williams and Tertia Barnett. The text was edited and indexed by Mike Ponsford and the summary was translated into French and German by SR Translations.

Within the RCHME, the draft text was read and commented on by Stewart Ainsworth, Bob Bewley, Dave Field, Paul Everson, Dave McOmish, Robin Taylor, Pete Topping and Humphrey Welfare. Outside the RCHME, Mike Allen, Alistair Barclay, Richard Bradley, Ros Cleal, Tim Darvill, Philip Dixon, Peter Drewett, Mark Edmonds, Chris Evans, Frances Healy, John Schofield, Ian Kinnes, Roger Mercer, Rog Palmer, Francis Pryor, Julian Thomas and Alasdair Whittle all commented on an early draft of the text. The authors are particularly grateful to Richard Bradley and especially Frances Healy for agreeing to re-read the amended text.

# Illustration acknowledgements

Unless otherwise stated, all illustrations are © Crown copyright. NMR. The negative numbers of ground and aerial photographs are given in brackets with the captions. Aerial photographs are also referenced by their source and date. English Heritage is grateful to the various institutions and individuals who permitted the photographing of material in their care and the reproduction of copyright material. In particular, English Heritage is grateful to the following institutions: The British Library (Figs 2.3, 5.30), The Bodleian Library (Fig 2.2), The Courtney Library, Royal Institution of Cornwall (Fig 2.5), Cambridge University Committee for Aerial Photography (Figs 2.24, 2.26, 4.10), Cambridge University Press (Figs 2.14 and 2.27), Canterbury Archaeological Trust (information for Fig 4.2), Essex County Council (Fig 1.5), Museum of London (Figs 5.32, 7.5), RCAHMS (Figs 3.7, 5.4), RCAHMW (Fig 3.19), The Society of Antiquaries (Figs 2.2, 2.21), Sussex Archaeological Society (Figs 2.12, 2.15, 8.4) and the following individuals: Niels Anderson and Louise Hilman (Fig 3.13), Desmond Bonney (Fig 3.12), Barry Cunliffe (Fig 2.28), Roger Mercer (Fig 7.4), Rog Palmer (Fig 6.1), and Alasdair Whittle and Joshua Pollard (Fig 7.1).

Figures 1.3, 1.4, 2.7, 2.8, 2.16, 2.20, 3.2, 3.3, 3.4, 3.6, 3.7, 3.11, 3.14, 3.17, 3.18, 3.19, 3.20, 4.2, 4.4, 4.5, 4.6, 4.8, 4.9, 4.11, 4.14, 4.15, 4.16, 4.17, 4.18, 4.21, 4.22, 4.25, 5.2, 5.3, 5.5, 5.7, 5.10, 5.11, 5.16, 5.17, 5.18, 5.20, 5.21, 5.23, 5.24, 5.25, 5.31, 6.6, 6.7, 7.2, 7.3, 8.1, 8.3, 8.5, 8.6, 8.7, 8.9, 8.10, 8.11 and 8.13 are based on the Ordnance Survey map with the permission of Ordnance Survey on behalf of The Controller of Her Majesty's Stationary Office, © Crown copyright. All rights reserved. Unauthorised reproduction infringes Crown copyright and may lead to prosecution or civil proceedings. Licence Number GD030859G.

Every effort has been made to trace copyright holders and English Heritage wishes to apologise to any who may have been inadvertently omitted from the above list.

# Notes on the site plans

Plans of sites surviving wholly or partially as earthworks were surveyed on the ground at a scale of 1:1 000 and are reproduced here at 1:2 500. Plans of sites levelled by ploughing, now detectable only as cropmarks on aerial photographs, were transcribed at 1:2 500 and are reproduced at the same scale, the sole exception being the unusually large enclosure at Crofton in Wiltshire, which is reproduced at 1:5 000 (see Fig 4.21). Schematic plans are reproduced at a scale of 1:10 000. The choice of similar scales of reproduction is intended to allow direct comparison between all the plans and correspondence with Ordnance Survey basic scale maps. It should be noted, however, that the earthwork surveys offer a much higher degree of metrical precision than the transcriptions of aerial photographs. The latter generally provide accuracy in the region of ±2m and sometimes slightly poorer, depending on the quality of the photography, the variation in the local topography and the availability of reliable control in the vicinity.

On the site plans, the archaeological information is depicted in black. On those produced by earthwork survey, hachures ('tadpoles') are used to represent slopes: the broader ends indicate the top of slope and the density of the hachures the steepness of the slope. Since the interpretation of earthworks is not an objective science, hachures allow surveyors to use their skill and judgement more effectively than close contouring. On plans produced by aerial survey, solid black represents ditches and other features cut into the ground; stipple has been used where the interpretation of the surviving traces is more open to doubt. Grey tone is used to represent traces of banks that no longer survive as earthworks to any appreciable degree. Contours at 5m intervals are also depicted in black. These have in most cases been derived from Ordnance Survey 1:10 000 maps, and are reproduced with the permission of Ordnance Survey as detailed in the Illustrations acknowledgements. Having been enlarged by a factor of four to match the scale of the archaeological plans, these contours offer only approximate accuracy, but are nevertheless considered to give a sufficiently accurate impression of the general lie of the land. Contours at 0.5m intervals have been used in some instances to depict slighter topographic changes; these have been obtained through new ground surveys. Ordnance Survey map detail is reproduced, screened grey, as detailed in the Illustration acknowledgements. The depiction of this modern information serves in some instances to explain why certain parts of the archaeological plan appear incomplete and is intended in all cases to allow the sites to be located more easily. National Grid coordinates, set at 100m intervals, are shown along the margins of the plans. Unless otherwise indicated, grid north is to the top of the page.

# Summary

Neolithic causewayed enclosures are amongst the oldest, rarest and most enigmatic of the ancient monuments found in Europe. First recognised as a distinct type in the 1920s, sixty-nine certain or probable examples have now been identified in the British Isles. As a class, they are second to none in importance, for while their precise functions remain unclear, they represent the first non-funerary monuments and the earliest instances of the enclosure of open space. They rightly stand at the forefront of academic debate, but as yet are barely known to the general public.

This book presents an overview of the findings of a systematic national programme of research into the entire class of monument, carried out over a three-year period. Every certain, probable and suggested causewayed enclosure in England has been investigated through integrated aerial and field survey (Fig 1.1). Specialist reconnaissance flying has been undertaken, along with the systematic analysis of aerial photographs taken from the 1920s onwards. This has greatly increased the number of sites known, turning the spotlight onto many that have received little or no attention from archaeologists in the past. As the plans of most causewayed enclosures identified from the air have only been plotted sketchily or incompletely up to the present, the aerial surveys now available offer a new basis for improved understanding. Analytical field investigations of the few that are well preserved as earthworks have also squeezed fresh information out of monuments long familiar to archaeologists. Far from merely confirming the efforts of past fieldworkers, these detailed surveys have led to the rejection of some long-held theories. New interpretations can now be proposed as to how the monuments might have been constructed and modified over the course of time. Recording of the topographic settings of all the sites has firmly anchored the new plans within the contexts of their landscapes.

The new surveys have been supported by a re-examination of the findings of earlier archaeological researchers, although in only a few instances have attempts been made to track down or re-evaluate in detail the finds or paper records from excavations. Information has been gathered from numerous other sources, both published and unpublished. The latter includes material held in English Heritage's unique public archive, the National Monuments Record.

This book significantly advances the understanding of causewayed enclosures both as individual monuments and as a class. It is a major contribution to the understanding of the British Neolithic and, more generally, to 'landscape archaeology'. Above all, it aims to make available an accurate statement of the forms and landscape settings of causewayed enclosures – essentially raw data – which will provide a foundation for future research, management and understanding. This volume represents the tip of an iceberg: plans, photographs and written reports comprising detailed descriptions and interpretations of individual sites are available, and may be consulted at the public archive of English Heritage: the National Monuments Record.

# Résumé

Les enclos à enceintes interrompues du néolithique font partie des monuments archéologiques les plus anciens, les plus rares et les plus énigmatiques jamais trouvés dans l'Europe. Reconnus pour la première fois dans les années 1920 comme appartenant à un type distinct, soixante-neuf exemples certains ou probables ont désormais été identifiés sur les îles britanniques. En tant que catégorie, ils sont d'une importance inégalable car, bien que leurs fonctions précises restent floues, ils ne représentent pas moins les tous premiers monuments non funéraires et les premiers exemples d'enceintes de l'espace ouvert. Ils figurent à juste titre en toute première ligne des débats académiques et restent cependant pratiquement inconnus du grand public.

Ce livre présente une vue d'ensemble des découvertes réalisées suite à un programme national d'étude systématique entrepris au niveau de l'ensemble de cette catégorie de monument, effectué sur une période de trois ans. Chaque enclos à enceintes interrompues certain, probable et suggéré situé en Angleterre a été examiné au moyen d'une étude intégrée des relevés aériens et sur le terrain. Des vols de reconnaissance spécialisée furent entrepris, ainsi qu'une analyse systématique des photos aériennes prises depuis les années 1920. Cela a permis d'élargir grandement le nombre de sites connus, en mettant en évidence de nombreux sites qui, par le passé, n'avaient reçu que peu voire aucune attention de la part des archéologues. Les plans de la plupart des enclos à enceintes interrompues identifiés par avion n'avaient donné lieu qu'à des relevés superficiels ou incomplets, et les études aériennes désormais disponibles offrent une nouvelle base pour mieux les comprendre. Les études analytiques sur le terrain des rares enceintes bien préservées sous forme d'ouvrages de terre ont apporté de nouvelles informations, même à partir des monuments connus depuis longue date par les archéologues. Bien plus que de se contenter de reprendre les travaux de chercheurs passés, ces études détaillées ont abouti au rejet de certaines théories défendues depuis longtemps. Il est désormais possible d'avancer de nouvelles interprétations quant à la raison éventuelle de la construction de ces monuments et de leur modification au fil du temps. Le fait d'enregistrer les lieux topographiques de tous les sites a fermement relié les nouveaux plans au contexte de leur paysage.

Les nouvelles études ont été étayées par un réexamen des découvertes faites par les chercheurs archéologiques passés, bien que dans de rares cas seulement des tentatives furent faites pour retrouver ou réévaluer dans le détail les trouvailles ou les enregistrements écrits émanant de fouilles. Des informations ont été recueillies auprès de nombreuses autres sources, à la fois publiées et non publiées, ces dernières comprenant les archives

publiques uniques d'English Heritage: le *National Monuments Record* (Registre national des monuments).

Ce livre fait avancer de manière significative notre compréhension des ouvrages de terre néolithiques, aussi bien en tant que monuments pris individuellement qu'en tant que catégorie. Il représente une contribution de premier ordre à la compréhension du monde de l'époque néolithique en Grande-Bretagne, et de «l'archéologie du paysage» d'un point de vue plus général. Par-dessus tout, il vise à donner un compte-rendu précis des formes et des emplacements au sein du paysage des ouvrages de terre néolithiques, principalement sous forme de données brutes, compte-rendu qui apportera les fondements aux travaux de recherche futurs, à leur gestion et aux connaissances qu'ils apporteront. Ce volume ne constitue que la partie émergée de l'iceberg : les plans, photos et rapports écrits comprenant des descriptions et des interprétations détaillées de sites individuels sont disponibles et peuvent être consultés aux archives publiques du English Heritage: le *National Monuments Record.*

# Zusammenfassung

Jungsteinzeitliche Grabenwerke gehören zu den ältesten, seltensten und rätselhaftesten, vorgeschichtlichen Denkmälern. Erstmals in den zwanziger Jahren des vorigen Jahrhunderts als besonderer Typus beschrieben, wurden bis heute 69 als sichere oder vermutete Beispiele erkannt auf den britischen Inseln. Obwohl die genaue Funktion dieser Grabenwerke unklar bleibt, sind sie doch von überragender Bedeutung. Sie stellen die ersten Monumentalbauten dar, die offenen Raum umschlossen und die nicht Bestattungszwecken dienten. Zu Recht im Vordergrund der wissen-schaftlichen Debatte stehend, sind sie der breiten Öffentlichkeit jedoch nur wenig bekannt. Das Buch vermittelt einen Überblick über die Ergebnisse eines systematischen nationalen Forschungsprojektes, das für drei Jahre der Gesamtheit dieser Monumente galt. Jedes sichere, mögliche und vermutete Grabenwerke in England wurde durch integrierte Flugprospektion und Geländearbeit untersucht. Begleitend zur systematischen Auswertung seit 1920 entstandener Luftbilder wurden erneut gezielte Prospektionsflüge durchgeführt. Auf diese Weise hat sich die Zahl der bekannten Fundstellen erheblich vergrößert und in das Rampenlicht gerieten viele Anlagen, die in der Vergangenheit wenig oder keine Interesse der Archäologen fanden. Weil Pläne der meisten aus der Luft entdeckten Grabenwerke bis heute nur unvollständig oder skizzenhaft vorliegen, erlauben die Ergebnisse der jüngsten Flüge ein besseres Verständnis der Anlagen. Gründliche Feldforschung an den wenigen Objekten, die obertägig gut als Erdwerke

mit Wall und Graben erhalten sind, hat den Archäologen, denen sie schon lange bekannt sind, noch neue Erkenntnisse über die Bauwerke beschert. Die jüngsten Prospektionen wurden durch die Neubewertung von Ergebnissen früherer archäologischer Forscher unterstützt, ohne dass deren Unterlagen nur bloßer Bestätigung dienten. Allerdings wurde dabei nur in wenigen Fällen versucht, deren Funde und Aufzeichnungen von Ausgrabungen aufzuspüren und im Detail zu untersuchen. Ergänzend wurden publizierte und unpublizierte Informationen aus zahlreichen sonstigen Quellen zusammengetragen. Zu letzteren zählt Material aus dem *National Monuments Record*, dem einzigartigen öffentlichen Archiv von English Heritage.

Dieser Band trägt erheblich zum Verständnis einzelner neolithischer Grabenwerke sowie auch des Denkmaltyps bei. Es liefert damit einen wichtigen Beitrag zum Verständnis des britischen Neolithikums und der allgemeinen "Landschaftsarchäologie". Sein Ziel ist es, Form und Lage der neolitischen Grabenwerke in der Landschaft treffend zu beschreiben und damit Basisinformationen für deren weitere Erforschung, sowie für das Verständnis und den Schutz dieser Denkmäler zu liefern. Wie die Spitze eines Eisbergs verrät die Publikation, was bei English Heritage im öffentlichen Archiv, dem *National Monuments Record*, als sein riesiger unbekannter "Unterwassersockel" für die Forschung bereitliegt: Pläne, Fotografien sowie detaillierte Beschreibungen und Erklärungen einzelner Denkmäler.

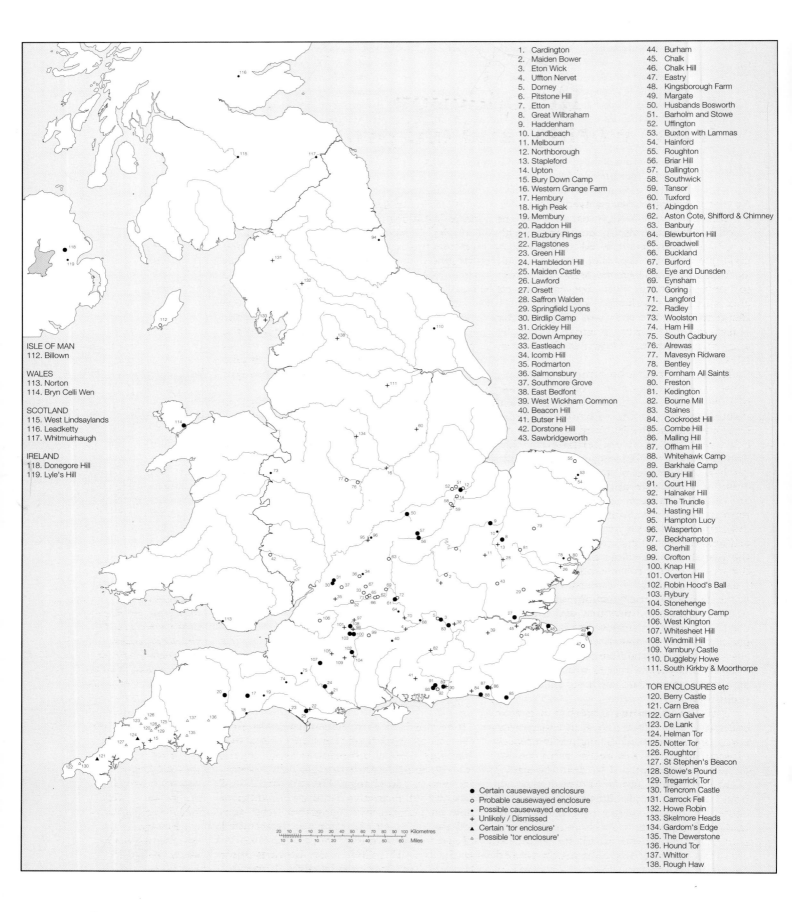

1. Cardington
2. Maiden Bower
3. Eton Wick
4. Uffton Nervet
5. Dorney
6. Pitstone Hill
7. Etton
8. Great Wilbraham
9. Haddenham
10. Landbeach
11. Melbourn
12. Northborough
13. Stapleford
14. Upton
15. Bury Down Camp
16. Western Grange Farm
17. Hembury
18. High Peak
19. Membury
20. Raddon Hill
21. Buzbury Rings
22. Flagstones
23. Green Hill
24. Hambledon Hill
25. Maiden Castle
26. Lawford
27. Orsett
28. Saffron Walden
29. Springfield Lyons
30. Birdlip Camp
31. Crickley Hill
32. Down Ampney
33. Eastleach
34. Icomb Hill
35. Rodmarton
36. Salmonsbury
37. Southmore Grove
38. East Bedfont
39. West Wickham Common
40. Beacon Hill
41. Butser Hill
42. Dorstone Hill
43. Sawbridgeworth
44. Burham
45. Chalk
46. Chalk Hill
47. Eastry
48. Kingsborough Farm
49. Margate
50. Husbands Bosworth
51. Barholm and Stowe
52. Uffington
53. Buxton with Lammas
54. Hainford
55. Roughton
56. Briar Hill
57. Dallington
58. Southwick
59. Tansor
60. Tuxford
61. Abingdon
62. Aston Cote, Shifford & Chimney
63. Banbury
64. Blewburton Hill
65. Broadwell
66. Buckland
67. Burford
68. Eye and Dunsden
69. Eynsham
70. Goring
71. Langford
72. Radley
73. Woolston
74. Ham Hill
75. South Cadbury
76. Alrewas
77. Mavesyn Ridware
78. Bentley
79. Fornham All Saints
80. Freston
81. Kedington
82. Bourne Mill
83. Staines
84. Cockroost Hill
85. Combe Hill
86. Malling Hill
87. Offham Hill
88. Whitehawk Camp
89. Barkhale Camp
90. Bury Hill
91. Court Hill
92. Halnaker Hill
93. The Trundle
94. Hasting Hill
95. Hampton Lucy
96. Wasperton
97. Beckhampton
98. Cherhill
99. Crofton
100. Knap Hill
101. Overton Hill
102. Robin Hood's Ball
103. Rybury
104. Stonehenge
105. Scratchbury Camp
106. West Kington
107. Whitesheet Hill
108. Windmill Hill
109. Yarnbury Castle
110. Duggleby Howe
111. South Kirkby & Moorthorpe

**ISLE OF MAN**
112. Billown

**WALES**
113. Norton
114. Bryn Celli Wen

**SCOTLAND**
115. West Lindsaylands
116. Leadketty
117. Whitmuirhaugh

**IRELAND**
118. Donegore Hill
119. Lyle's Hill

**TOR ENCLOSURES etc**
120. Berry Castle
121. Carn Brea
122. Carn Galver
123. De Lank
124. Helman Tor
125. Notter Tor
126. Roughtor
127. St Stephen's Beacon
128. Stowe's Pound
129. Tregarrick Tor
130. Trencrom Castle
131. Carrock Fell
132. Howe Robin
133. Skelmore Heads
134. Gardom's Edge
135. The Dewerstone
136. Hound Tor
137. Whittor
138. Rough Haw

● Certain causewayed enclosure
○ Probable causewayed enclosure
• Possible causewayed enclosure
+ Unlikely / Dismissed
▲ Certain 'tor enclosure'
△ Possible 'tor enclosure'

20 10 0 10 20 30 40 50 60 70 80 90 100 Kilometres
10 5 0 10 20 30 40 50 60 Miles

# 1
# Introduction
## 'New worlds' and old problems

At first encounter, causewayed enclosures are unlikely to seem the most evocative of Neolithic monuments. By comparison with long barrows and chambered tombs, whose mystique is almost tangible, or henges such as Avebury, whose earthworks cannot fail to impress by their sheer size, causewayed enclosures may even seem disappointingly insignificant. Yet they are amongst the oldest, rarest and most enigmatic of all the ancient monuments known in the British Isles.

In form, described simply, a typical causewayed enclosure is a roughly circular or oval area surrounded by one or more discontinuous circuits of bank and ditch. In many cases, the bank may once have been reinforced or embellished with a timber structure. To date, no such simple catch-all description of the purpose of these enclosures has been agreed. Certainly, they are of extraordinary importance, for they represent the earliest form of non-funerary monument and the first instance of the artificial enclosure of open space known in the British Isles. Despite their importance, the activities that went on within the enclosed areas remain only dimly understood. A better understanding of the function, or functions, of causewayed enclosures may well shed light on many of the important social and economic changes that occurred during the first half of the 4th millennium BC. For this reason, these monuments must claim the attention of anyone with an interest in prehistory.

This book brings together a major collection of large-scale plans of causewayed enclosures, generated through new archaeological field surveys and the analysis of aerial photographs. The translation of slight earthworks and faint cropmarks into bold black and white plans may sometimes cause complex monuments to appear misleadingly simple, static and two-dimensional. Excavated evidence, in all its different aspects, can obviously do much to add colour and depth to the picture provided by surface survey. Yet ever since the monuments were first recognised as a distinct class in the late 1920s, the discontinuous form of the circuits has repeatedly been the foundation for arguments as to what the enclosures may have looked like and how they might have been used by people almost six thousand years ago. Even at the few sites where extensive excavations have taken place, the information contained in the form of the plans has always been treated as an important clue as to how the monuments were built and what purposes they might have served.

It is, therefore, perhaps surprising that very few compilations of accurate plans of the earthworks and cropmarks in question have been produced. This publication provides the first major corpus of large-scale plans since the publication in 1930 of a pioneering account of 'Neolithic Camps' by Cecil Curwen (1930), the active prehistorian who lived and worked in Sussex. Needless to say, there have been numerous subsequent discoveries and advances in understanding. Yet a collection of plans at a relatively small scale, published by aerial photographer Rog Palmer (1976), has been the only major update of Curwen's work. Based on systematic survey from the air and on the ground, this book aims to provide the broad foundation now necessary for improved understanding and management of the class as a whole.

## The Neolithic background

Since the idea of the Neolithic was first conceived, this final period of the Stone Age has been synonomous with rapid, widespread technological and social innovation and change. The introduction of causewayed enclosures is one of a number of new phenomena which together have often led the period to be seen as a watershed of great cultural importance – a new world. In the earlier Neolithic, there is evidence for the first time for arable agriculture and

*Figure 1.1 (facing page) Distribution of sites investigated, including the sixty-nine certain and probable causewayed enclosures that form the core of this book. Since the evidence which led certain sites to be put forward as potential causewayed enclosures has never been improved upon, these are still treated as possible examples. In other instances, where the evidence now available suggests or proves that the original suggestion was incorrect, these sites are listed for the sake of completeness.*

pastoralism, for so-called 'industry' – the mining of flint and the quarrying of other types of stone, for the adoption of new forms of domestic and monumental architecture and for major changes in other aspects of material culture, including the first use of pottery and of new varieties of stone tools. It has often been argued that these developments must have been accompanied by a sudden switch from the relatively mobile lifestyle of Mesolithic 'hunter-gatherers' to a sedentary settlement pattern. Current theories stress, however, that the innovations of the earlier Neolithic were spread over the course of several centuries and that the accompanying social changes would have been an equally gradual transformation (*see* eg Thomas 1991).

Causewayed enclosures represent the first forms of monumental enclosure to be built in England, but not the first monuments, appearing several hundred years after the earliest long barrows. Burial monuments, which in one form or another continued to be built throughout the Neolithic and into the earlier Bronze Age, are sometimes found in close association with causewayed enclosures. Both long barrows and cause-wayed enclosures can be seen as expressions of social unity. Both types of monument were products of communal labour and both seem to have been places where people came together on particular occasions, thus re-affirming their links with each other, with the area they inhabited and with the past. Both can also be seen as expressions of increasing dominance over the natural world, at a time when the creeping adoption of agriculture was beginning to alter the balance between humans and the land they lived in and exploited.

Due to the relatively large number of excavations that have taken place on causewayed enclosures and long barrows, much of what little is known of earlier Neolithic society has been revealed through its monuments. In many areas, evidence for settlement is in one sense plentiful, in terms of scatters of artefacts that can be recovered from ploughed fields, and pits occasionally chanced upon by excavations. Yet in the British Isles as a whole, the plans of fewer than forty Neolithic houses are known. These long houses are usually found singly rather than in groups and seldom at causewayed enclosures (Thomas 1996b). It remains difficult, therefore, to reach a satisfactory interpretation of the evidence, so much so that it is still openly debated to what extent people were settled at all. The general picture of earlier Neolithic settlement in England (if there truly was any in a sedentary sense) is one of small communities, isolated and fairly widely scattered (*see* eg Topping 1997b; Edmonds 1999).

The environment in which these communities existed is also primarily known through studies carried out in the course of excavations of monuments (eg Thomas 1982). The evidence comes in three main forms: the snails and other mollusca sensitive to environmental change, the well-preserved plant and seed remains that sometimes survive in water-logged conditions, and the carbonised grains of seed and pollen that may survive in some soil conditions. The study of soil micromorphology is another branch of archaeological science with great potential for the understanding of the Neolithic environment that is just beginning to make an impact (eg French 1990). Apart from the monuments themselves, peat bogs provide another important source of evidence for the environment (eg Parker 1997). Peat bogs sometimes preserve pollen, which can reveal how environmental conditions developed over much longer periods. During the earlier Neolithic, much of the landscape was still covered with deciduous woodland, comprising oak, elm, ash and lime, among other species. In some areas, however, there may have been patchworks of clearings, some fairly extensive, but others perhaps no larger than a small field. At any one time, a number of these clearings might have been under cultivation with cereal crops or rough pasture, while in others the woodland may have begun to regenerate, with hazel, hawthorn and birch.

## Chronology

The types of artefact produced in the earlier Neolithic (principally pottery and stone tools) do not permit the kind of reasonably precise dating frameworks based on stylistic changes that have been worked out for later prehistory and the historic period. Radiocarbon dating of excavated organic material such as bone and charcoal (and more rarely dendrochronlogical dating of well preserved samples of timber) offer infrequent but relatively accurate insights into the dating of monuments and other archaeological features. Throughout this book, calibrated calendrical dates are given (eg 3,700 BC), rather than uncalibrated radiocarbon dates.

The precise dating of most individual causewayed enclosures remains a very grey area. Nevertheless, the monuments are now established as a phenomenon of the 4th millennium BC in the British Isles, with the available radiocarbon dates suggesting a *floruit* of around 3,700 to 3,300 BC (Fig 1.2). They belong to the earlier Neolithic, therefore, but not to its very earliest stages. The construction of long barrows, the mining of flint, the use of pottery, the adoption of domesticated plants and animals are all attested in the archaeological record at various stages in the four or five centuries prior to the construction of the earliest enclosures. What was once regarded as the Neolithic 'revolution' now seems to have been a gradual appearance of a range of phenomena. This has led archaeologists to question whether there was necessarily any direct link between the change from hunter-gatherer to sedentary farmer and also the wider social and cultural changes seen in the earlier Neolithic.

## Causewayed enclosures as a class of monument

In England, only sixty-six causewayed enclosures are currently known or reliably supposed to have existed. This total remains remarkably small compared to, for example, the 1,500 Iron Age hillforts in the country, or indeed the 600 Neolithic long barrows currently known to have existed. Of this small number of causewayed enclosures, only fifteen survive to any extent as upstanding earthworks, and only ten of these could be described as well preserved. Causewayed enclosures have conventionally been identified and classified on the basis of their most obvious shared characteristic – the form of their plans. They are distinguished above all by the immediately striking aspect of their forms: the frequent but irregularly-spaced causeways, or short stretches of undug ground, which occur along the length of the ditches. In the past, much discussion has centred on the question of why the perimeters should have enclosed a space, but apparently in such a way as to deliberately create many points of access.

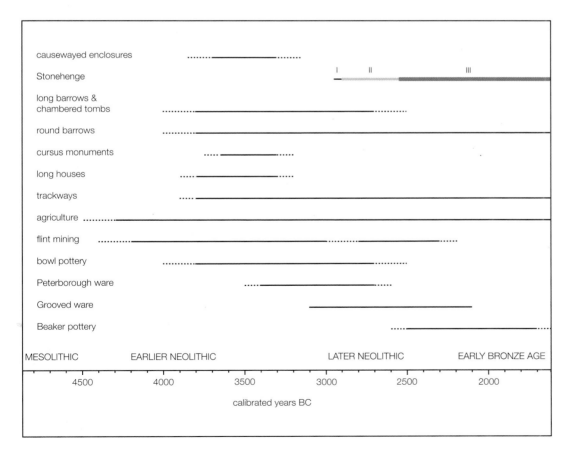

Figure 1.2
Time chart, illustrating the appearance of causewayed enclosures and other phenomena associated with the Neolithic. The period was long regarded as one of rapid – almost revolutionary – change, but it now seems more likely that innovations were introduced in a piecemeal fashion over the course of several centuries.

As with any other type of monument grouped together as a class, there is little uniformity in the precise appearances of causewayed enclosures. For example, a simple one like that at Burford in Oxfordshire may comprise a single oval circuit of causewayed ditch (Fig 1.3). At Burford, all trace of any bank that may have accompanied the ditch has been erased by ploughing, as has any evidence that might otherwise have survived for timber structures in the central space. The site has never been excavated, but at some point in the future, excavation may well reveal the existence of structures and deposits unrecognisable on aerial photographs. Until that time, interpretations must continue to rely on surface evidence alone.

A more complex causewayed enclosure may comprise several circuits of causewayed ditch. Sometimes the circuits were built tens of metres apart, as at Robin Hood's Ball in Wiltshire (Fig 1.4), but sometimes they were much more closely spaced. At Robin Hood's Ball, where the monument has not been affected by ploughing, each ditch circuit is still accompanied by an internal bank. In terms of what can be seen on the ground today, even well preserved examples like this are admittedly 'feeble works' (to borrow a frank phrase from Hadrian Allcroft's description (1916) of the causewayed enclosure on Combe Hill in East Sussex). Small-scale excavations have taken place on the site (Thomas 1964; Richards 1990, 61–5), yet the plan of the earthworks still offers much information about what the monument could have looked like in the Neolithic and how it may have changed over the course of time.

Why were causewayed enclosures built, for what purpose and what did they signify? These questions are old problems which have tantalised archaeologists since the monuments were first identified. A precise definition of their function is still beyond reach: the answer must be offered with caution and qualification. The class has been given a name – causewayed enclosures – that merely describes the way in which the monuments were constructed, in part because the purposes they served are not fully understood. Past and current ideas on the subject will be reviewed in this book.

*Figure 1.3*
*The cropmark recorded through aerial survey at Burford in Oxfordshire represents a causewayed enclosure in its simplest form. The roughly circular circuit of ditch comprises at least twenty segments. Although there seem to be numerous ways through the circuit into the central space of the enclosure, the in-turned ditch terminals on either side of one of the causeways probably mark the position of a more important entrance, or perhaps the only one. Ploughing, which may have begun in the Iron Age or even earlier, has obliterated any trace of bank that may have accompanied the ditch. A bank or a timber palisade, which might not be detectable from the air, may have limited access more than the form of the ditch would suggest.*

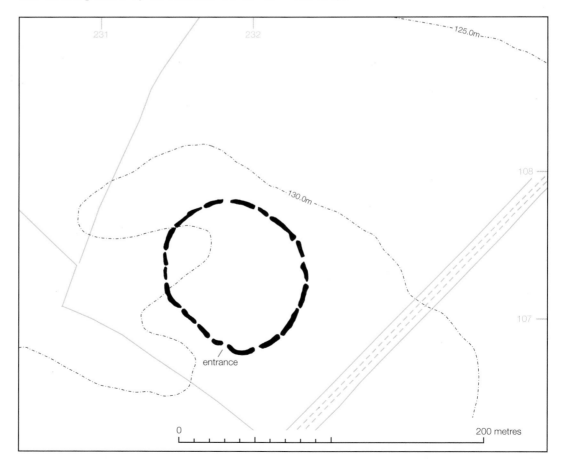

# The background and aims of this book

This book is the outcome of a national programme of research carried out over a period of three years. The unprecedented breadth of coverage has been matched by an acknowledged expertise in archaeological survey, both from the air and on the ground. The wealth of aerial photographs and other archival material held in the National Monuments Record, as well as other collections, has been exploited. Where appropriate, the findings of past and current excavations and geophysical surveys have been integrated into this research.

Archaeological survey is concerned above all with the analysis of the plans of monuments and the form of upstanding earthworks, where these survive. New surveys have therefore been undertaken of all certain, probable and suggested causewayed enclosures, except in the few cases where the enclosure in question has been rejected outright as being of Neolithic date, or where there has already been extensive excavation or very detailed survey by others. The majority of causewayed enclosures no longer survive as earthworks, but cropmarks recorded through aerial photography have been transcribed to produce plans generally accurate to ±2m at a scale of 1:2 500. Where earthworks survive, it has been possible to analyse their form through detailed fieldwork on the ground and plans with greater metrical accuracy have been produced at a scale of 1:1 000.

Although the research was national in scope, there is a bias towards central and southern England inherent in concentrating on causewayed enclosures alone. Taking into account the variable form of Neolithic monuments, however, the project was deliberately inclusive in considering

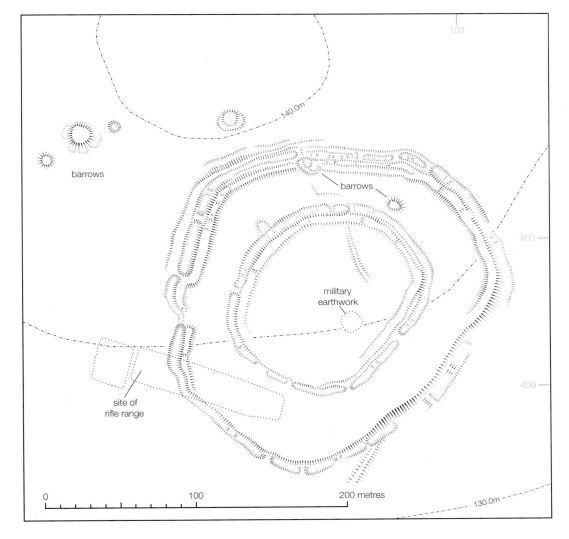

*Figure 1.4*
*The causewayed enclosure at Robin Hood's Ball in Wiltshire (the name belongs to a nearby plantation, rather than to the enclosure itself). Although relatively recent military activity has damaged the monument, the area has never been ploughed. Detailed survey of the upstanding earthworks can therefore begin to reveal the variable size and shape of both the ditch segments and the adjacent bank. On the northern side of the enclosure in particular, the complexity of the earthworks suggests episodes of rebuilding. Note the close association of the causewayed enclosure with several round barrows, which may be later Neolithic, Bronze Age or later still in date. Such a relationship is unlikely to be accidental, suggesting that people continued to venerate the earlier monument long after it had ceased to be used in its original form.*

Figure 1.5
*Few prehistoric monuments present greater problems than causewayed enclosures when an attempt is made to reconstruct their appearance. This painting by Frank Gardiner is based on the evidence from the partly excavated causewayed enclosure at Orsett in Essex (see Figs 2.26 and 3.11), but reflects current theories about the nature of such sites more generally. It is impossible to be certain on the basis of the excavated evidence whether all the banks and ditches were in use at the same time. The bank between the two closely spaced ditches has been portrayed as an almost continuous barrier, but the earthwork had been entirely ploughed away and other interpretations of the evidence are possible. (Essex County Council)*

Figure 1.6
*The causewayed enclosure on Windmill Hill in Wiltshire, long regarded as the classic 'type-site', is among the best preserved in England. In the foreground, cultivation terraces, probably of Bronze Age or Iron Age date, seem to have left the enclosure largely untouched (see Fig 2.8). In more recent times, the survival of the monument has been directly threatened: much of the far side of the middle and outer circuits have been degraded by ploughing and in the 1920s the construction of a radio mast was averted, in part due to protests by concerned archaeologists. The land is now protected under the ownership of the National Trust; the unploughed downland pasture is also highly valued for its ecological resources. (NMR 15403/21)*

Figure 1.7
The causewayed enclosure in the parish of Eastleach in Gloucestershire is one of a few sites in riverine locations to show significant variation in the width (and therefore perhaps depth) of the ditches. A number of upland enclosures, including that on Windmill Hill, are comparable in having more massive outer circuits. The plan suggests two or three main phases of construction (see Fig 3.17). The kidney-shaped plan of the three inner circuits appears to have been intended to emphasise the position of principal entrances. (NMR 4611/30)

Figure 1.8
The causewayed enclosure in the parish of Aston Cote, Shifford and Chimney in Oxfordshire. The site was one of many recorded for the first time through aerial reconnaissance in the late 1960s and early 1970s. This enabled Rog Palmer (1976) to compile a corpus of forty-three possible examples. On this photograph, parts of three ditch circuits are visible, but there are slight indications that there may be a fourth. The more yellow crop growth indicates that this enclosure, like many others, was sited on a low gravel rise, which would have been slightly more prominent prior to the deposition of layers of alluvial silt. (NMR 4671/18)

enclosures that may have been similar to causewayed enclosures, or contemporary with them. As a result, monuments as far afield as Cumbria, Northumberland and Cornwall were investigated. Through cooperation with the Royal Commission on the Ancient and Historical Monuments of Wales (RCAHMW), the Royal Commission on the Ancient and Historical Monuments of Scotland (RCAHMS) and other organisations, the project was expanded to encompass the whole of the British Isles (Fig 1.1). Some of the enclosures recorded may not in fact be conventional causewayed enclosures, and some as yet have little or no firm evidence for an earlier Neolithic date.

This book is not intended to be a detailed inventory of all the monuments investigated in the course of the three-year project, for that is the function of the National Monuments Records. The book has, however, three central aims that arise naturally from the broad and systematic coverage provided by the project. Above all, it attempts to illustrate the similarities and differences that exist in the form of causewayed enclosures and to advance understanding of why this variation occurs. To set the scene for this study, Chapter 2 reviews the history of previous archaeological research, showing how knowledge and understanding of the form of causewayed enclosures has developed to date, and shapes our understanding at present. Chapter 3 describes the basic constructional elements common to all causewayed enclosures, as they are currently known through survey and excavation. Chapter 4 considers the more complex matters of how these elements were combined to produce the many different variations in overall form. Written descriptions of individual sites are kept to a minimum.

Secondly, the book aims to set the monuments in the contexts of their surrounding landscapes. Field and aerial survey together are well placed to study the wider physical setting of each monument. In addition to the major field surveys, field observations of every certain, probable and suggested causewayed enclosure in the British Isles have been carried out, including those where earthworks no longer survive, in order to assess their topographic settings. To convey an impression of the plan of a site as it would have appeared on the ground in three dimensions is a challenge for any printed account and one that few studies have attempted to meet. Chapter 5 emphasises the setting of enclosures in their physical landscapes through the use of photography, three-dimensional ground modelling and the depiction of topographic information. Chapter 6 looks at the relationship of causewayed enclosures to other monuments, settlements and territories in the light of survey evidence. Chapter 7 reviews the excavated evidence and so examines the same issues from a different perspective.

The third major aim of this book is to trace the later treatment of causewayed enclosures. Chapter 8 shows how, after their disuse, some of the monuments seem to have continued to influence the pattern of later activity on the sites. At the same time, it demonstrates how later land-use and deliberate reuse transformed the appearance of the original monuments. This underlines how fragile the traces that survive at present are, and why it is now so important to actively conserve the remaining few.

Most importantly, this book aims throughout to create a platform for future fieldwork, research and management, by bringing together a large sample of the survey plans. Work of this kind, whether by students, local societies or professional bodies, is likely to be concentrated on specific causewayed enclosures or regions. It is intended, therefore, to offer a broader foundation on which research strategies may be based and against which sites may be compared: here a balance is sought between the need to treat each causewayed enclosure as a unique individual in its own context and the opportunity to offer an overview of the class of monument as a whole.

# 2
# Previous research

## The idea of Stone Age 'camps'

The acceptance of causewayed 'camps', as they were initially called, as a class of monument characteristic of the Neolithic period emerged from a series of excavations undertaken in the 1920s, most notably at the causewayed enclosure on Windmill Hill near Avebury in Wiltshire. Several important publications appeared in the wake of these investigations, in particular Cecil Curwen's synthesis of the newly available evidence, entitled simply 'Neolithic Camps' (Curwen 1930). At the time when the first trench was being excavated at Windmill Hill in August 1922, the Neolithic as a concept had existed for nearly sixty years. It had been the focus of considerable debate, even if there was little other than long barrows and polished stone axes that could be confidently linked with it. The notion that some of the earthwork 'camps' scattered

about the British countryside might have been constructed in the Neolithic was not new, but by the 1920s it was no longer a belief that commanded academic respectability. In his opening paragraph, Curwen made reference to 'erroneous popular beliefs', including ' . . . the tendency hastily to attribute prehistoric hillforts either to the Stone Age or to the Romans, most of such forts having in all probability been reared by the people of the Early Iron Age' (Curwen 1930, 22).

With the fresh information at his disposal, Curwen demonstrated that while Neolithic 'camps' were a reality, they were rather different in form and character from what popular belief had previously envisaged.

Until the later 19th century, theories concerning the origin of 'camps' had stemmed from ideas rooted in classical or historical sources, or in local tradition.

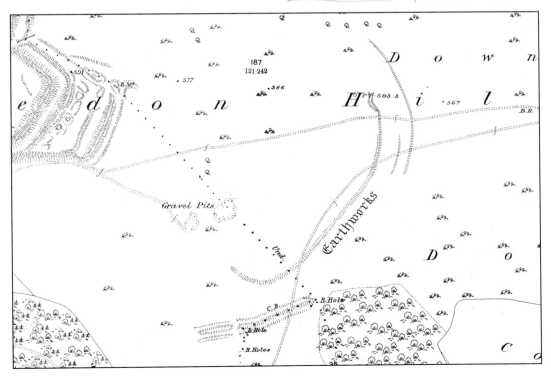

*Figure 2.1*
*Hambledon Hill in Dorset, as portrayed on the Ordnance Survey's First Edition 25-inch map (Dorset, sheets XV.5 and 6, 9 and 10). The plan, surveyed c 1886, is among the earliest large-scale depictions of part of a causewayed enclosure. Hambledon Hill lies on the western fringe of the vast estate of Lt-Gen Pitt Rivers, Cranborne Chase, and the complex of well-preserved prehistoric monuments, including the 'old camp' adjacent to the Iron Age hillfort, apparently attracted his interest (Dorset CRO D/PIT: P24). It is possible that its inclusion by the Ordnance Survey, which was still a military organisation at that time, was due partly to prompting by the General. For the new plan, see Figure 4.16.*

9

Occasionally, the slight and irregular nature of the earthworks prompted suggestions that a pre-Roman ('Ancient British' or 'Celtic') date might be appropriate. In some instances, these speculations could be supported by the presence of more substantial earthwork 'forts', which were at that time assumed incorrectly to be of Roman or later date and which overlay or were adjacent to those in question, as at Whitesheet Hill in Wiltshire (Colt Hoare 1812, 43) or Hambledon Hill in Dorset, for example (Warne 1872, 65–9; Fig 2.1).

From the later 19th century, attempts to classify and explain all such monuments worked within an intellectual framework which conceived of the 'Three Ages' of the pre-Roman past – Stone Age, Bronze Age and Iron Age – as representing universally applicable stages of social and technological evolution (Trigger 1989, 60–1, 114–18). Each age was characterised both by certain kinds of archaeological remains and also by inferences about ancient society drawn largely from research carried out by anthropologists. The idea of the Neolithic was first introduced by Sir John Lubbock in 1865. His division of the Stone Age into Palaeolithic and Neolithic allowed the idea of a separation in terms of both chronology and social evolution between mobile hunter-gatherer and sedentary farmer. For example, William Boyd Dawkins described how

the palaeolithic man lived by hunting the wild animals . . . , armed with rude implements of stone and bone, and ignorant of all the domestic animals including the hunting dog. He was a fire-using nomad, without fixed habitation. On the other hand the Neolithic man appears before us a herdsman and tiller of the ground, depending upon his domestic animals and the cultivated fruits and seeds rather than on hunting; master of the potter's art, and of the mysteries of spinning and weaving, and seeking the materials for his tools by mining. He lived in fixed habitations, and buried his dead in tombs (Boyd Dawkins 1894, 288).

The interval between the two stages came to be viewed, in the British archaeological record at least, as a hiatus of unknown duration (eg Boyd Dawkins 1894; Munro 1908; see also Sturge 1909). Belief in the existence of such a gap gradually declined, however, and by the 1930s the idea of an intervening 'Mesolithic' period was firmly established (Clark 1936; Rowley-Conwy 1996; Pluciennik 1998). It was considered that the changed social and economic circumstances envisaged for the Neolithic, particularly the introduction of agriculture (whether arable, pastoral or mixed), would have promoted a more settled existence with a greater attachment to the land and to particular places. Consequently, the construction of defences for the protection of both people and animals was regarded as an essential requirement (eg Lane Fox 1869a; Clark 1880; King 1880; Gould 1901; Clift 1907; Allcroft 1908). Classification schemes for 'camps' tended to follow a straightforward path. The simplest forms of enclosure, such as forts built so as to enclose the tips of promontories and those with the slightest earthworks, were assumed to belong at the start of the sequence. 'The oldest camps should be simplest in trace, with the weakest rampart and the smallest command, because the tools were in stone' (King 1880, 338). The general adoption of the word 'camp' by the Ordnance Survey to denote a wide variety of enclosures surviving as earthworks (but initially in reference to Roman temporary camps) reinforced this idea of a defensive purpose, while the term also lent itself later to more pastoral or seasonal interpretations (Evans 1988a, 49).

Inferences drawn from casual finds collected from the surface as well as from excavations, which still employed rather crude methods, were highly influential in supporting the idea of Neolithic 'camps'. The presence of quantities of worked flints lying on the ground within or adjacent to such monuments was often regarded as reasonable evidence for the likely date of the earliest construction and occupation. This was the approach followed by Col Augustus Lane Fox (later to become Lt-Gen Pitt Rivers) in his assessment of the hillforts of the Sussex Downs (Lane Fox 1869a and b). His investigations were largely stimulated by a desire to use excavation to support the evidence from surface finds that some of the hillforts in question might have originated in the Stone Age. At Cissbury Ring in West Sussex, for example, it was only when excavation showed the flint mines there to be earlier than the ramparts that a date later than the Neolithic was seriously considered for the hillfort (Lane Fox 1876; Barber et al 1999). Although the flint mines are indeed of earlier Neolithic date, the hillfort is now known to have originated in the Iron Age. Similarly, Clift (1907, 61) suggested a Neolithic origin for Maiden Castle in Dorset on the basis of the slight and simple form of the earliest recognised ramparts and the quantity of Neolithic material that had been recovered from the immediate vicinity. Excavation has since shown that the rampart in question is an early phase of the Iron Age hillfort, although in fact it directly overlies the earthworks of a Neolithic causewayed enclosure (Wheeler 1943; Sharples 1991a).

As late as 1914, John Williams-Freeman, discussing the presence of worked flints at Danebury hillfort in Hampshire, could still state that 'General Pitt Rivers and others have made excavations into several, perhaps half a dozen, of these hillforts without finding anything which could ascribe them to a later period than the Neolithic' (Williams-Freeman 1915, 155). He himself, however, was of the opinion that many were likely to be of later origin.

The situation was dramatically altered in the years following the First World War, a period which saw a significant increase in the number of excavations of hillfort ramparts. By 1932, Christopher Hawkes could refer to no fewer than seventy-two hillforts '. . . from which evidence of Pre-Roman Iron Age date has been obtained, and while others in Wales and perhaps in the north belong to the Roman period, no examples earlier than the Iron Age are known . . . '(Kendrick and Hawkes 1932, 161). Following Curwen's article (1930), the newly recognised class of 'causewayed camps' (a term which appeared in print for the first time within the same volume) was excluded from this statement.

## A problem of recognition

While many of the earthworks previously thought to be Neolithic could by the 1930s be shown to be of later origin, some of the enclosures which are today accepted as, or suspected to be, Neolithic causewayed

*Figure 2.2*
*Sir Richard Colt Hoare (1812, 176) commented that the causewayed enclosure at Robin Hood Ball (as it was then known) had an entrance towards the north. The earliest known depiction of the enclosure, this plan by Flinders Petrie drawn in 1877 provides no supporting evidence for this suggestion and nor does the new survey (see Fig 1.4). Colt Hoare also stated that the enclosure had been damaged by ploughing, but this was presumably specu-lation based on the slightness of the earthworks. (Reproduced from the Petrie Collection by kind permission of the Society of Antiquaries of London)*

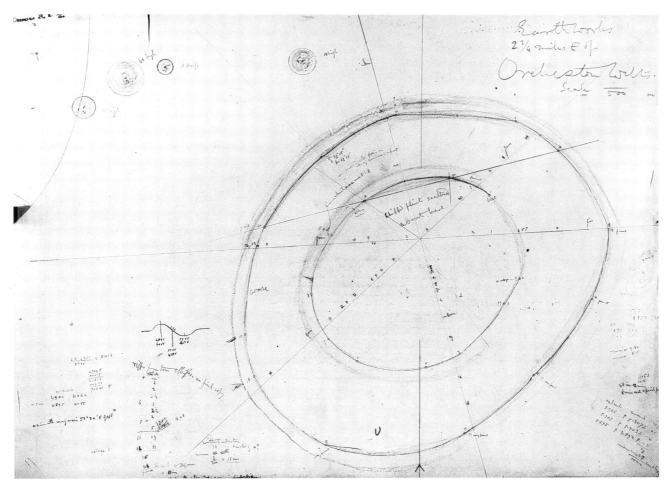

enclosures had received earlier attention. In the 18th century, William Stukeley briefly described the causewayed enclosure on Windmill Hill (Stukeley 1743). In the later 19th century, part of the main causewayed enclosure on Hambledon Hill in Dorset (Fig 2.1) and the enclosure at Robin Hood's Ball in Wiltshire had been surveyed (Colt Hoare 1812, 176 and Fig 2.2). Whitehawk Camp (Fig 2.3) and the enclosure at Combe Hill, both in East Sussex, had also been surveyed and their likely

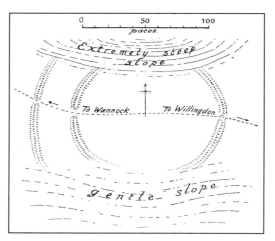

*Figure 2.3*
*The causewayed enclosure known as Whitehawk Camp in East Sussex (compare with the new survey: Fig 5.31). Skinner appears to have recognised the presence of several gaps in the banks, but does not seem to have regarded these as original features. The symmetry of his sketch is emphasised by his depiction of the ditches, which join the enclosure tangentially. Their date is still uncertain, though they may represent boundary earthworks added in the Bronze Age. (The Revd J Skinner's 1821 sketch is reproduced from the Revd J Skinner Collection, MS 33, 658, 40;41, by kind permission of the British Library)*

*Figure 2.4*
*The causewayed enclosure on Combe Hill in East Sussex, as surveyed by Hadrian Allcroft (1908, fig 222). He later described it as a 'feeble work' (1916, 83). He argued that Whitehawk Camp and the enclosure on Combe Hill 'are almost beyond doubt of British construction, and very early construction to boot' (1908, 312). In common with most early archaeologists, however, he assumed that the gaps in the earthworks (see Fig 8.5) showed that the enclosure was unfinished or had been damaged by more recent activity. His depiction deliberately compensates so as to show the monument in what he considered would have been its intended or original form.*

origins speculated upon (Allcroft 1908, 675; 1916, 83–4 and Fig 2.4). Meanwhile, in Cornwall, Charles Henderson surveyed two stone-built enclosures at Trencrom Hill and Carn Brea during the years 1914–17, describing both as 'Neolithic cities'. His dating of the enclosure on Carn Brea appears to have been influenced by the discovery some years previously of material identified as being of Neolithic date, while his attribution of the enclosure on Trencrom Hill to the same period was based on the similarity of the stony banks to those at Carn Brea (Henderson MSS 'Antiquities of Cornwall', Courtney Library, Royal Institution of Cornwall, Truro, and Fig 2.5). Modern excavation has shown Henderson's inference about the date of the earlier enclosure on Carn Brea to be correct, while it has again been suggested that the enclosure on Trencrom Hill is of Neolithic origin, although firm evidence is still lacking (Mercer 1981, 191). It remains uncertain, however, whether these so-called 'tor enclosures' are directly comparable to the causewayed enclosures found further to the east (*see* Chapter 5: 'Tor enclosures': causewayed enclosures built in stone?).

Prior to the work at Windmill Hill, only two causewayed enclosures are known to have seen episodes of excavation. During the 1890s, quarrying adjacent to the Iron Age hillfort known as Maiden Bower in Bedfordshire had uncovered Neolithic features, including possible segments of a causewayed ditch (Smith 1894; 1915). The correct date of the pottery and other artefacts salvaged from them was not, however, realised until around forty years later (Piggott 1931). More important were the excavations undertaken in 1908–9 by Maud and Benjamin Cunnington at Knap Hill in Wiltshire (Cunnington 1909; 1911–12; *see also* Figs 2.6 and 2.7). There, where the main causeways are broad and spaced at fairly regular intervals, the excavators recognised the discontinuous form of the earthwork as a deliberate and original feature apparently representing ' . . . a method of defence hitherto unobserved in prehistoric fortifications in Britain' (Cunnington 1909, 49). The excavation was originally undertaken with the aim of discovering the date of the earthworks. For this, the Cunningtons were reliant on the artefacts recovered. In the absence of a reference collection of well dated material, they speculated that the pottery they had recovered, and by inference the 'camp' itself, might predate the introduction of Beaker pottery; in other words, it might be Neolithic in origin. They were forced to conclude, however, that 'Until some distinguishing characteristic is recognized between undecorated pottery of the Bronze Age and Neolithic periods in Britain, if indeed there be any such characteristic, it is impossible to form an opinion as to which period the pottery belongs' (Cunnington 1911–12, 57).

Subsequently, little note appears to have been taken of the site until two decades later, when the Cunningtons' speculations were corroborated by the discoveries of the Revd H G O Kendall and Alexander Keiller at Windmill Hill.

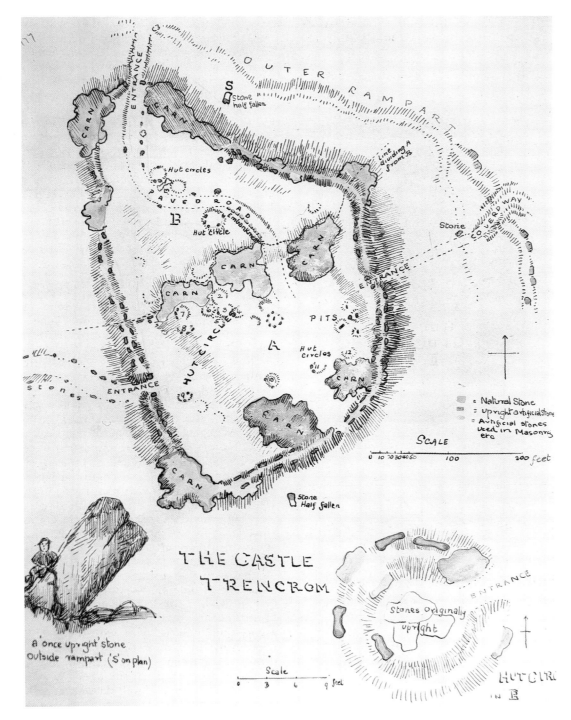

Figure 2.5
Charles Henderson's survey of the stone-built enclosure on Trencrom Hill in Cornwall, undertaken between 1914 and 1917. In addition to his site plan, drawn to a scale of 100ft to 1in, Henderson also produced larger scale plans and sketches of some of the hut circles, which are likely to be of Iron Age date, and other more fanciful features. In his written description of the site, he commented that '. . . though usually called a hill castle . . . in fact the whole of the hill was one large Neolithic city like Carn Brea'. Shortly after the new survey, an investigation by the Cornwall Archaeological Unit (Herring 1999) rediscovered an assemblage of earlier Neolithic flints excavated on Trencrom Hill in 1911. The fine quality of the flints suggests that they represent a small selection from a much richer deposit. This adds even more weight to the probability that the enclosure is of Neolithic origin. (From Antiquities of Cornwall Volume II, 177, reproduced by kind permission of the Courtney Library, Royal Institution of Cornwall)

*Figure 2.6*
*Lithograph of the causewayed enclosure on Knap Hill in Wiltshire. Seen from the north, the enclosure presents visually impressive earthworks (see Fig 2.7). Consequently, the monument was the earliest to be remarked upon: in the 1680s, John Aubrey mentioned 'a small Roman Camp above Alton'. In 1814, Sir Richard Colt Hoare remarked that 'from the worn state of its ramparts, I should conclude [it] to be of very high antiquity' (Colt Hoare 1812, 11).*

*Figure 2.7*
*Investigations by the Cunningtons at the causewayed enclosure on Knap Hill in Wiltshire in 1908–9 were the first excavations at the site, and it was here that the causewayed form of the earthworks was first recognised as an original feature. 'It was thought at first that, as often happens on ancient banks, some of these gaps were due to cattle tracks, or possibly had been made for agricultural purposes. There was, however, a certain regularity about them, and it was difficult to see why on such an isolated spot so many tracks should have been made. . . . Excavations clearly showed that none of these gaps in the rampart are the result of wear or of any accidental circumstance, but they are actually part of the original construction of the camp' (Cunnington 1909, 50).*

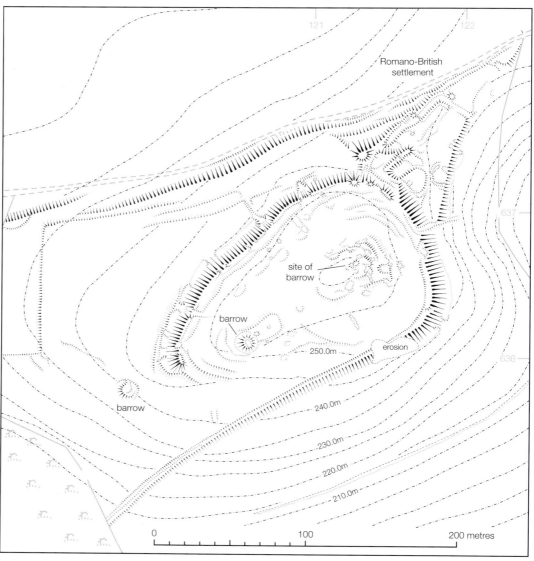

## The impact of Windmill Hill

It is difficult to overestimate the impact that the recognition and excavation of the causewayed enclosure on Windmill Hill in Wiltshire had on the understanding of the British Neolithic (Fig 2.8). Prior to excavations there, the idea of Neolithic 'camps' had largely been a matter of supposition drawn from particular ideas about social evolution, coupled with the coincidental presence on the surface, and in some cases from excavations, of pottery and stone artefacts. By the early 1920s, the growing number of excavated Iron Age hillforts, along with continuing uncertainties over typological sequences for pottery styles and stone tools, had left the Neolithic as a pre-Bronze Age period of uncertain duration. Some had even argued that it should be measured in hundreds of thousands of years (eg Sturge 1909, 104). The period had few widely agreed diagnostic characteristics apart from the polished axe and the long barrow, a state of affairs which had, for example, contributed to the long-running debate over the true chronology of flint mining (*see* Smith 1912; Clark and Piggott 1933; Barber *et al* 1999). The excavations on Windmill Hill were to provide a large assemblage of artefacts which demonstrably predated Beaker pottery, at a time when that style and the other types of objects associated with it were widely accepted as heralding the beginning of the Bronze Age (Abercromby 1912, 9–16). As a result the excavations offered a springboard for a fundamental re-evaluation – in fact a revolution – of ideas about the British Neolithic.

Despite the pre-eminent position of Windmill Hill in the study of British prehistory, the excavations undertaken there in the 1920s did not run according to plan and have never been fully published. A monograph prepared by Isobel Smith was published (1965), but this represented an extended summary of an incomplete archive, supplemented by the results of her own smaller-scale excavations. The story of the excavations at Windmill Hill needs to be understood if their results are to be fully appreciated. Contemporary ideas about the Neolithic, the chosen methods of excavation and recording and the personal relationships between those involved all played a part in shaping the subsequent course of the study of causewayed enclosures.

## Windmill Hill: discovery and excavation

By the 1920s, Windmill Hill and its immediate surroundings had been 'famous for decades . . . as a paradise of the surface flint hunters' (Keiller 1934, 188), among whose number was the Revd H G O Kendall, rector of Winterbourne Bassett, which lies only 4km (2.5 miles) to the north of the site. A keen and active collector of prehistoric flints, he published several papers on his discoveries and on issues related to flintworking (eg Kendall 1914; 1919a; 1919b; 1922). He also undertook a series of small-scale excavations at the Neolithic flint mines at Grime's Graves in Norfolk between 1919 and 1924 (MS notes and diary, Alexander Keiller Museum, Avebury) and at the stone axe 'factory' site of Graig Lwyd in North Wales (Kendall 1927).

Kendall's interest in the 'camp' on the hill eventually led him to begin intermittent excavation in August 1922 (Kendall 1923). Over the following six months, he gradually explored an area of the north-eastern sector of the outermost ditch of the outermost circuit (Fig 2.9), although when he began digging, neither the middle nor the inner circuit had been identified. Among his finds were potsherds which he suspected might be Neolithic, a theory confirmed for him by both E T Leeds and O G S Crawford. At the time, Leeds was Assistant Keeper of the Department of Antiquities at the Ashmolean Museum in Oxford. In 1926–7 he was to excavate at the first causewayed enclosure to be discovered in a riverine location, at Abingdon in Oxfordshire. Crawford, the Ordnance Survey's first Archaeological Officer, subsequently became an occasional visitor to the excavations on Windmill Hill and was present on the occasion of a significant discovery. Kendall's notebook (in the Alexander Keiller Museum, Avebury) states that on 13 January 1923 'O G S Crawford accompanied us. I showed him a curving hollow on top of W. H. Together we discovered this and another to be concentric ditches, within the outer rampart and ditch'. Crawford's own account (1953, 133) implies that by this point, the causewayed nature of the main circuit had been recognised, while inspection of the two newly discovered circuits confirmed that these too were interrupted by causeways. This is not mentioned by Kendall, however, and it may be that thirty years on, Crawford's recollections were a little out of sequence.

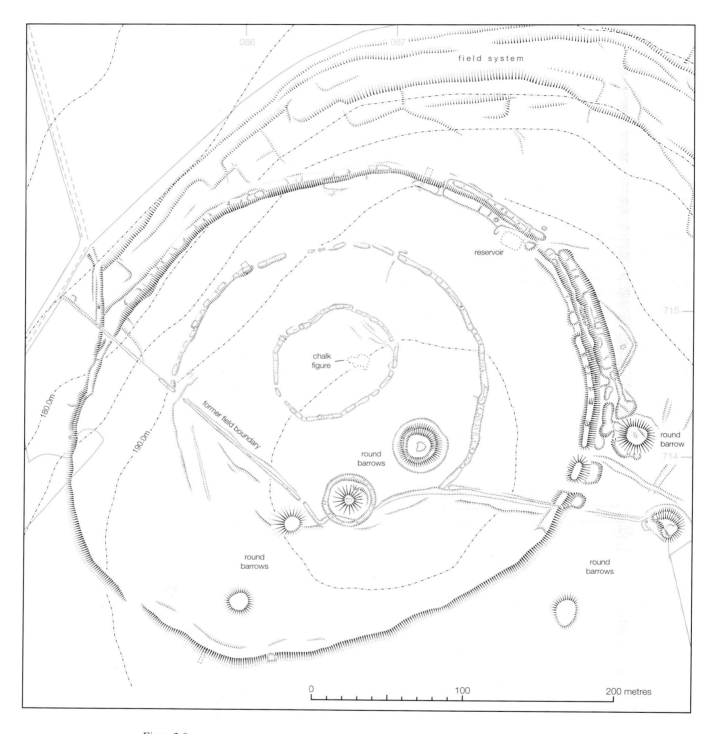

*Figure 2.8*
*The causewayed enclosure on Windmill Hill near Avebury in Wiltshire. The outer circuit comprises some of the most massive earthworks of any causewayed enclosure in England; the bank is up to 1m high and the ditch of corresponding depth. Consequently, this circuit was recognised first (see Fig 1.6) and was the object of the earliest excavations, started in 1922. The inner and middle circuits, which are very much slighter earthworks, were correctly interpreted in 1923 through the expertise in field survey brought to bear by the Ordnance Survey's Archaeological Officer, O G S Crawford. It should be noted that the size and form of the earthworks on the north and east results directly from Alexander Keiller's efforts at reconstruction in the wake of his excavations.*

*Figure 2.9*
*The Revd H G O Kendall, standing in front of the first section through the ditch of the outer circuit of the causewayed enclosure on Windmill Hill, August 1922. Kendall began his excavations in August 1922. His notebooks, held in the Alexander Keiller Museum at Avebury, record the work in some detail. Kendall, who died in April 1928, never published a full account of his work at Windmill Hill, although a summary appeared in 1923. That account suggests that the causewayed nature of the earthwork was not apparent to him at the time of writing, though he noted that 'a trench dug some years ago a few yards [from his excavation] to carry a water-pipe showed that at that point there was no fosse and no trace of a bank. Possibly this marks an original entrance with a causeway over the ditch . . .'. (NMR AA76/910)*

*Figure 2.10*
*Keiller's 'Cutting I' through the middle circuit of the causewayed enclosure on Windmill Hill, 22 April 1925. He originally intended to excavate the entire site in a series of three-year campaigns, each followed by a year devoted to publishing the results, '. . . but a certain portion of each distinctive part of the site will be left unexcavated and provisions will be made for leaving these portions unexcavated for at least one century' (Crawford 1927). This plan was thwarted by the need to re-excavate the trenches supervised by Gray in the first year. (NMR BB81/2951)*

*Figure 2.11*
*Harold St George Gray*
*and others, examining one*
*segment of the ditch of the*
*outermost circuit of the*
*causewayed enclosure on*
*Windmill Hill, 24 May*
*1926. Although the bank*
*associated with the ditch*
*survives relatively well,*
*excavation of the ditch*
*proved more rewarding*
*due to the greater*
*quantity of artefacts that*
*could be found. Despite*
*improvements in*
*excavation techniques,*
*interpretations of the*
*functions of causewayed*
*enclosures are still*
*constrained by the fact that*
*deposits are only well*
*preserved in the ditches.*
*(NMR BB81/2959)*

Crawford was also responsible for bringing Windmill Hill to the attention of Alexander Keiller, heir to the famous Dundee-based marmalade firm and a keen amateur archaeologist. Keiller was one of many individuals contacted by Crawford in the face of an ultimately unsuccessful attempt by the Marconi Wireless Company to establish a radio station in the area (Crawford 1953, 133–4). From 1924 onwards, Keiller set about the tasks of purchasing, surveying and excavating the site (Fig 2.10). Meanwhile, the unusual interrupted nature of the enclosure earthworks at both Windmill Hill and at Knap Hill, along with evidence for their Neolithic date, led Keiller and Crawford to search for similarly-constructed 'camps' in an attempt to confirm the existence of a uniquely Neolithic form of enclosure. Their research, and the ensuing excavations by Keiller, Curwen and others, resulted a few years later in the publication of Curwen's (1930) paper 'Neolithic Camps' in the archaeological journal *Antiquity*, itself founded and edited by Crawford. The paper was originally to have been written by Keiller, based on the information he and Crawford had been compiling since 1924, but when illness prevented him from doing so, Crawford invited Curwen to take over.

As already noted, the preparation, execution and publication of Keiller's 1925–9 excavation campaign did not run smoothly. Initially, Keiller was obliged to employ Harold St George Gray to oversee the digging (Figs 2.11 and 2.12). Gray had formerly been an assistant to Pitt Rivers during the General's famous series of excavations on his Cranborne Chase estate during the late 19th century. He had himself subsequently directed excavations at Avebury, as well as at the late Iron Age 'lake villages' at Glastonbury and Meare in Somerset, among other sites (Bulleid and Gray 1911; 1917; 1948; Gray 1935; Gray and Bulleid 1953; Gray and Cotton 1966; Coles 1987; Coles and Minnitt 1995). The reason for Gray's employment seems to have lain in concerns among members of the Wiltshire Archaeological Society, in particular the Cunningtons, about Keiller's lack of archaeological experience and his status as an 'outsider'. Keiller reluctantly agreed, but his correspondence with Crawford (held by the Alexander Keiller Museum, Avebury) makes clear his dissatisfaction with the arrangement and his increasing frustration with Gray's techniques and standards of excavation. The letters, diaries and notebooks in the

*Figure 2.12*
*The contrast between the approaches of Keiller (kneeling) and Gray (seated) is abundantly clear from this photograph. (Alexander Keiller Museum, Avebury)*

Keiller Museum indicate a less than harmonious relationship between Keiller and Gray from an early stage. For example, as early as 9 August 1925, Keiller informed Crawford that 'If there is one thing that tends to give vindictiveness towards you from me the precedence over gratitude it is your introduction of us to Gray: he is the one arch[aeologist] that I have met that I wholeheartedly despise (Cunningtons excluded) . . . oh, yes, yes, yes!' (letter in Alexander Keiller Museum).

Gray's participation in the excavations at Windmill Hill ended in 1927 during the third season, when he was dismissed by Keiller (letter from Keiller to Crawford dated 31 May 1927, Alexander Keiller Museum). The large quantity of finds recovered from some of the trenches overseen by Gray in 1925 when they were re-opened at the start of the 1927 season was a major factor in Keiller's decision, although he considered it long overdue. From the outset, animal remains had literally been a bone of contention, much having been discarded by Gray without proper recording. His dismissal was followed by the re-excavation of all the trenches dug in the first two years. Since animal bone was seldom accorded the attention given to

pottery at that date, Keiller's concerns now seem far-sighted. The presence of animal bone and the manner of its deposition are now recognised as crucial evidence for the ways in which causewayed enclosures were used.

Keiller himself could clearly be difficult to work with. Stuart Piggott, who first encountered him in 1928 while studying the pottery from Windmill Hill, was employed by Keiller as a research assistant for five years from 1933. He referred to Keiller's 'fantastic perfectionism and an absorption in detail as meticulous as it seemed pointless to others' (in Smith 1965), while Crawford (quoted in Piggott 1983) described him as 'erratic and infuriating'. Keiller seemed to agree with such opinions, writing on one occasion that ' . . . I am a machine draughtsman at heart and, since machine draughtsmen are notoriously pig-headed, stubborn and conservative folk as regards their job, I am likely to remain so . . . ' (letter, Keiller to Gray, 4 May 1928, in the Keiller Museum, Avebury).

Whatever the case, while Keiller may have felt a need to demonstrate his superior ability as an excavator, similar criticisms of Gray have been made by others (*see* eg Bradley 1989; Bowden 1991, 163–4).

A further insight into the relationship between Gray and Keiller is offered by a series of limericks composed by Keiller (in a notebook held in the National Monuments Record). This book had been used first during fieldwork for Crawford and Keiller's (1928) *Wessex From The Air*, a pioneering work on the recording and interpretation of earthworks through aerial photography (*see* Fig 2.19). The limericks, collected under the heading 'Annals of an Old Fool', suggest that Gray's methods were ill-suited to the complex nature of the deposits and features. One example goes

There was an old fool with a fork
Who attacked a sheer wall of the chalk
Shouting 'Widen it, man
Till it equals the plan
After all, it's my drawings that talk'.

Taken together, the unpublished evidence implies that Keiller recognised the importance of recording all finds and of noting the minor differences and irregularities in archaeological deposits that are now recognised as essential in understanding processes of construction and deposition in the ditches of causewayed

*Figure 2.13*
*E C Curwen's workmen, excavating Cutting 6 through the fourth circuit at Whitehawk Camp in East sussex in 1932–3, with Cutting 2 in the foreground. Curwen's earlier trenches at The Trundle had attracted comment for their neatness (see Fig 2.15). Photographs of the 1932–3 excavations suggest, however, that techniques were perhaps dictated by the 'rescue' conditions under which Curwen was working, in advance of the extension of Brighton racecourse across the centre of the causewayed enclosure (Curwen 1934). The photographs show that once the topsoil had been stripped off to the level of the natural chalk, spoil from the ditch was dumped within the trenches. The two baulks between the three excavated cuttings were then removed (Cuttings 3 and 5). As this method of excavation, together with the type of digging tools in evidence, cannot have been at all conducive to neatness it is possible that details may have been overlooked. There are also notable differences between the ditch as shown in this photograph and as portrayed in the published plan and section. As a result, though some of the finds from the excavations have been retained, the value of any detailed re-analysis may be diminished. (Sussex Archaeological Society)*

enclosures. On the other hand, Gray seems to have been altogether less meticulous, his techniques unchanged since the 1890s and based on his understanding of the relatively simple ways in which Bronze Age and Iron Age sites were constructed. He also seems to have made inappropriately straightforward assumptions about how artefacts came to be deposited and, by extension, their relative worth for understanding the ways in which the site was used. That Gray's techniques were rather closer to the norm than Keiller's at that time is implied by an anecdote recalled many years later by Stuart Piggott, concerning his participation in Curwen's excavations at The Trundle in West Sussex

> I visited the last season's excavation [at Windmill Hill] in 1929, and was impressed by the orderly lay-out of the cuttings. Technique at The Trundle in 1928 was rather primitive, with the turf roughly hacked off the approximate area of excavation, but in 1930 I laid out a formal rectilinear cutting in the Windmill Hill manner. Reginald Smith emerged from the British Museum to visit us – bowler hat, pince-nez glasses, dark suit with rose in button-hole – and sizing up the situation, commented briefly 'Very marmaladish' (Piggott 1983, 30).

Photographs of the 1928 excavation trenches at The Trundle, and indeed Curwen's 1932–3 excavations at Whitehawk Camp in East Sussex (Fig 2.13), confirm that Keiller's insistence on precision in both excavation and field recording were exceptional.

## Understanding Windmill Hill

In the five seasons that the excavations at Windmill Hill lasted, Keiller investigated substantial portions of the ditches of the inner and middle ditch circuits, as well as a shorter stretch of the outer circuit and a considerable area within the inner circuit. In the process, a large quantity of Neolithic and Early Bronze Age material was recovered, representing an assemblage then unparalleled in Britain in terms of both quantity and quality. Despite his own stated intentions, however, the results of Keiller's work at Windmill Hill (and at Avebury) were not fully published during his own lifetime. That he made a start on writing up the results is demonstrated by

proofs (from the Clarendon Press, Oxford, in the Alexander Keiller Museum, Avebury) containing detailed descriptions of the 1925 excavations. The content of these, however, and of the few notes that were published by Keiller (eg 1932; 1934; 1939) appear to accord fully with Keiller's statement to Gray (in a letter dated 5 May 1925, held in the Alexander Keiller Museum, Avebury) that ' . . . theory is not within our province, since our task is primarily that of those in the field, viz. to record facts for the arm-chair theorists of this and future generations . . . '. This does not mean, however, that Keiller steered clear of speculation on the nature of the site. In the same letter to Gray, referring to the ditch segments of the causewayed enclosure, he argued that

> . . . these pits are not 'fire-pits', as the Cunningtons claim, nor dwelling pits, but as Hawley suggests, stone holes for flat bottomed stones. Might it not be that Windmill Hill was originally a monstrous stone circle; that the stones were removed, presumably to Avebury, and that there-upon the area within the ditch surrounding the outer circle of stones was utilised as a habitation site, and one or two other ditches added.

The possibility that megaliths had once stood on Windmill Hill was inferred by Keiller from the large quantities of chips

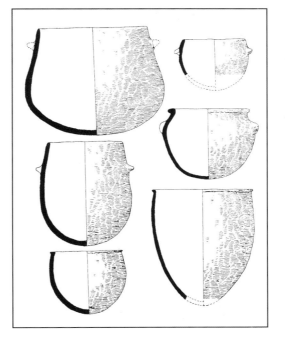

Figure 2.14
Plain and decorated earlier Neolithic bowls from The Trundle. This type of bowl pottery, which was first encountered at Windmill Hill, proved particularly important: it was present on all of the excavated causewayed enclosures, it could be classified into identifiable styles and it was also perceived as an important indicator of different cultural groupings and the relationships between them.
(Reproduced from Piggott 1954, fig 10; Cambridge University Press)

and fragments of sarsen stone – the same kind of stone used at nearby Avebury – found during his excavations. Subsequently, the idea of the stone circle on Windmill Hill was abandoned, although, along with many contemporaries, he continued to believe that the enclosed area represented a place of settlement.

A detailed summary of Keiller's work eventually appeared in a monograph prepared and published by Isobel Smith in 1965, a volume that is now considered a milestone in the study of causewayed enclosures. Smith, who had recently completed a doctoral thesis on Neolithic pottery (Smith 1956), was employed by Keiller's fourth wife to prepare an account of her late husband's work at Windmill Hill and Avebury. The lengthy delay in publication might seem at odds with the influence exerted by the site; by 1965 Windmill Hill had long been central to any discussion of southern Britain in the Neolithic. Keiller's willingness to allow interested researchers access to his finds was important in this respect. As early as 1927, E T Leeds coined the term 'Windmill Hill Ware' to denote the particular style of pottery identified at the site. Far more significant was Stuart Piggott, who took the opportunity to study the finds made at Windmill Hill in the 1928 season, while based in London as an employee of the Royal Commission on the Ancient and Historical Monuments of Wales. Piggott made extensive use of the unrivalled pottery assemblage from Windmill Hill in preparing his 1931 paper on British Neolithic pottery (Fig 2.14). It was largely through his publications that Windmill Hill rapidly became established as the type-site for the Neolithic in southern Britain.

The shortcomings of Keiller and Gray's excavations gradually became apparent, particularly regarding the surviving finds and the paper records. In 1957, while preparing her publication of Keiller's work, Isobel Smith (1959) undertook her own small-scale excavations at the site in order to clarify certain matters. One particular difficulty, the full significance of which has only been recognised in more recent years, concerns Keiller's technique of excavating the ditch deposits. Although his own excavations were conducted to a high standard, he used the then common technique of digging in a series of shallow spits rather than by stratigraphic layers or contexts and only recorded the depositional sequence from the sections. Such techniques had been used by Pitt Rivers, with Gray in attendance, during the late 19th century (Bowden 1991). As a result, while the precise position of important artefacts may have been carefully recorded, their actual depositional context often remains uncertain. Depth was regarded as a straightforward indicator of relative age, an assumption that would not always have been correct, given the complex formation of the layers. There are clear implications for any typological sequences for artefacts derived from such records of the ditch deposits.

It is important to realise the consequences of the improved understanding of the processes by which deposits formed in ditches and improvements in excavation methods for the interpretation of the kinds of activities represented at causewayed enclosures. During the excavations at Windmill Hill and throughout the 1930s, artefacts and layers in ditches were generally explained in one of two ways. Either they were the result of an entirely natural silting process, in which some residue of adjacent human activity or occupation inevitably became incorporated, or they were the products of activities carried out within the ditch itself. A consequence of the latter theory was that for more than fifty years, the pits and ditches encountered in excavations were often believed to be the actual dwellings of prehistoric people, particularly if they contained quantities of pottery, animal bones and other apparently domestic rubbish (Evans 1988a). Belief in these 'pit-dwellings', as they were generally known, was in decline by the 1930s, and was effectively ended in Britain by the results of Gerhard Bersu's excavations at the Iron Age settlement of Little Woodbury, Wiltshire in 1938–9, which proved that postholes represented the remains of sophisticated timber buildings (Bersu 1940). Just a few years previously, however, E T Leeds, Cecil Curwen and others envisaged that people had actually lived in the ditches of the causewayed enclosures at Abingdon and The Trundle (Curwen 1931,109–11 and Fig 2.15). Abbé Breuil, the French prehistorian, offered the same explanation for the quantity of material in the ditches at Windmill Hill (Crawford 1937; Evans 1988a). To a considerable extent such ideas stemmed from the apparent absence of evidence for any standing structures at the few known Neolithic sites: people simply had to have lived somewhere. In discussion following a presentation by

*Figure 2.15
Stuart Piggott, examining
Curwen's excavations of
the causewayed enclosure
at The Trundle in West
Sussex, 1930: a ditch
segment in the 'second
ditch', cuttings III and IV.
The holes in the base of the
ditch were regarded by
Curwen as pick-holes,
representing attempts to
break up the chalk
forming the floor of the
ditch. Five shallow
postholes were found
around the sides of the
ditch segment. Only
one produced any
artefacts – a single serrated
flint flake. They were
therefore undated and
there appears to be no clear
stratigraphical proof that
they were contemporary
with the ditch segment.
The segments on either
side were also accompanied
by a few postholes.
Curwen interpreted these
postholes as the remains of
some form of roof. He
consequently suggested that
the entire circuit had been
a row of roofed Neolithic
pit-dwellings (Curwen
1931). The presence of
human remains in such
pit-dwellings at several
sites inevitably aroused
curiosity. At Whitehawk
Camp, the presence of
burnt skull fragments in
one ditch segment led
Curwen to suggest that
'It is difficult to avoid the
view that these may be
relics of cannibalism'
(Curwen 1934, 112).*

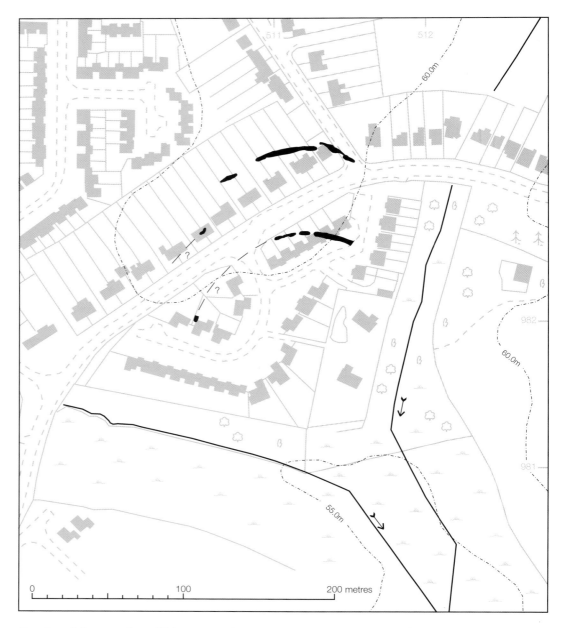

*Figure 2.16*
*The causewayed*
*enclosure at Abingdon in*
*Oxfordshire. Until the*
*discoveries made at*
*Staines in 1961–3, the*
*enclosure at Abingdon*
*remained the sole example*
*of a causewayed enclosure*
*in a lowland, riverine*
*location. Given that the*
*valley bottoms were*
*thought to have been*
*densely forested and*
*possibly swampy, the*
*apparent occupation at*
*Abingdon, which lies*
*at the tip of a low*
*promontory just above*
*the valley floor, was*
*consequently treated as*
*an anomaly. Note that the*
*excavators' plan slightly*
*mislocated the position of*
*the causewayed enclosure.*
*(Based on Case 1956,*
*fig 3)*

Leeds of the results of his excavations at Abingdon to the Society of Antiquaries of London, Reginald Smith of the British Museum noted that 'people living in such a trench could not have been far above the level of savages' (Fig 2.16; reported in Leeds 1927, 463–4; 1928, 477). The Society's president expressed surprise that 'any one chose to live in such trenches and thought holes would have been preferable'. His suggestion that a flooring of bone fragments and antler combs would have offered some discomfort was countered by Leeds' claim that 'primitive man was proof against such inconveniences'. More than a generation later, Isobel Smith's (1965)

re-assessment of the Windmill Hill evidence represented an important development in the understanding of the ways in which the people who used Neolithic monuments (and prehistoric sites in general), could have carefully selected material and deliberately organised its deposition. Coupled with a growing emphasis on the recording of excavated finds according to the context of their deposition, her recognition of the character of these deposits established the idea of intermittent episodes of deliberate deposition and selective recutting in the ditches of causewayed enclosures, an idea which is now fully accepted.

# Research and discovery after Windmill Hill

In 1930 Curwen discussed sixteen British enclosures in Britain which could, with varying degrees of confidence, be considered candidates for a Neolithic origin (Fig 2.17). By that date, five of these had been confirmed as Neolithic by excavation: the causewayed enclosures at Knap Hill and Windmill Hill in Wiltshire, Abingdon in Berkshire, The Trundle in West Sussex (Curwen 1929b; 1931) and Whitehawk Camp in East Sussex (Williamson 1930; *see also* Curwen 1934; 1936). Another five were considered as strong possibilities on the basis of the form of their earthworks, although only three of these, the causewayed enclosures at Combe Hill in East Sussex (Musson 1950), Robin Hood's Ball (Thomas 1964) and Rybury in Wiltshire (Bonney 1964), were subsequently proved to have been correctly identified. Of the remaining six 'possible or doubtful sites', only that at Barkhale Camp in West Sussex has subsequently been confirmed beyond doubt by excavation (Leach 1983). The ditch segments underlying the Iron Age hillfort known as Maiden Bower in Bedfordshire, however, also seem very likely to be part of a causewayed enclosure (Matthews 1976). The site was originally included in Curwen's list for the wrong reasons, for he emphasised the 'suggestive' plan of the rampart of the overlying Iron Age hillfort, which is interrupted by a number of relatively recent breaches around its circuit. Although subsequent salvage work in the adjacent quarry has confirmed the presence of a ditch of Neolithic date beneath the later earthwork (Matthews 1976), its identification as a causewayed enclosure remains probable rather than definite (Fig 2.18).

The remainder of Curwen's sixteen sites highlight a willingness at this early stage of research to treat any enclosure with interruptions or causeways as a potential Neolithic causewayed enclosure. The sole example identified on the basis of cropmarks photographed from the air was at Overton Hill, near Avebury in Wiltshire. This interpretation has subsequently been shown to be incorrect. The enclosure known as Buzbury Rings in Dorset and the ditch within Yarnbury Castle in Wiltshire, both of which are certainly of Iron Age date, were also incorrectly identified as causewayed enclosures. The slight earthwork

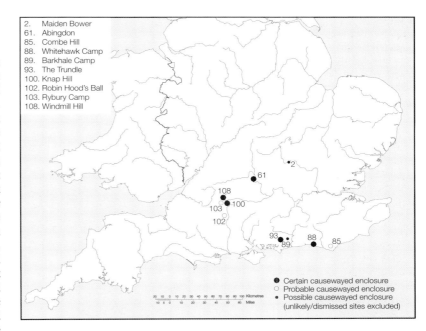

2. Maiden Bower
61. Abingdon
85. Combe Hill
88. Whitehawk Camp
89. Barkhale Camp
93. The Trundle
100. Knap Hill
102. Robin Hood's Ball
103. Rybury Camp
108. Windmill Hill

● Certain causewayed enclosure
○ Probable causewayed enclosure
• Possible causewayed enclosure (unlikely/dismissed sites excluded)

*Figure 2.17*
*The distribution of causewayed enclosures in 1930, as identified by Cecil Curwen. All but one of the enclosures, that at Abingdon, were located on chalk uplands.*

within the Iron Age hillfort known as Scratchbury Camp in Wiltshire has not been seriously regarded as being of Neolithic date since Curwen's time. In a small-scale excavation undertaken on the earthwork only Iron Age artefacts, were found, but as the bottom of the ditch was not reached, Curwen's interpretation could not be ruled out (Annable 1958, 17). Surface survey suggests that the interrupted appearance results from the damage caused by relatively recent cultivation (Lewis forthcoming). A few years after the publication of Curwen's article, an enclosure at West Wickham Common in Greater London was identified as a causewayed enclosure (Hogg and O'Neil 1937; 1941; Hogg 1981), but the earthworks seem more likely to be an unfinished Iron Age hillfort. At about the same date, quarrying near Badshot in Surrey appeared to have unearthed evidence for a causewayed enclosure with at least two concentric circuits (Lowther 1936). Alexander Keiller and Stuart Piggott were invited to direct excavations, but eventually concluded that the alleged circuits could only be interpreted as ditches flanking a long barrow completely levelled by ploughing (Keiller and Piggott 1939, 135; *see* Fig 4.27).

One curious omission from Curwen's paper is the main causewayed enclosure on Hambledon Hill in Dorset, best known from the campaign of excavations undertaken between 1974 and 1986 by Roger Mercer (Mercer 1980a and b; 1988; Mercer and

*Figure 2.18*
*Section through the ditch*
*of the probable causewayed*
*enclosure at Maiden*
*Bower in Bedfordshire,*
*exposed in a 19th-century*
*quarry face. Finds of*
*Neolithic flints were made*
*in the vicinity of Maiden*
*Bower in the mid-19th*
*century. In 1878,*
*Worthington Smith first*
*surveyed the earthworks of*
*the enclosure now known*
*to be a hillfort of early Iron*
*Age date. Later, he wrote*
*that 'the surface of the*
*land is . . . strewn,*
*especially within the camp,*
*with worked flakes of*
*white flint' (Smith 1915).*
*Interestingly, this*
*concentration may actually*
*lie outside the Neolithic*
*circuit. Subsequently,*
*attention turned to*
*sub-surface features*
*revealed by chalk*
*quarrying on the*
*north-west side of the*
*hillfort. In 1897–9, Smith*
*(1904) referred to five*
*'ancient excavations'*
*which were later*
*interpreted as five*
*segments of the ditch of a*
*causewayed enclosure.*
*Though the full plan of the*
*monument remains*
*uncertain, the U-shaped*
*form of the ditch and the*
*character of the deposits*
*lend support to this*
*interpretation.*

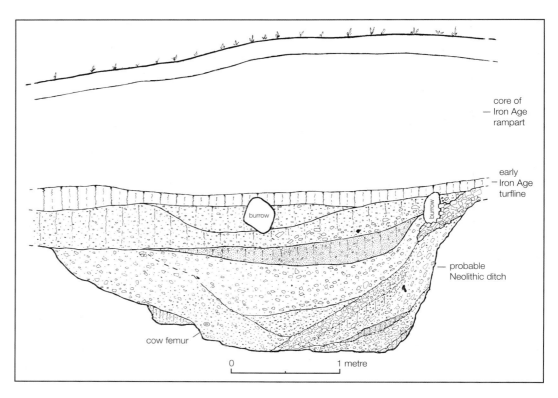

Healy in preparation). The slighter earth-works of the 'old camp' adjacent to the more massive ramparts of the Iron Age hillfort had been attracting comment since the later 19th century, while the causewayed form of the earthworks was clearly visible on a photo-graph published in Crawford and Keiller's *Wessex from the Air* (1928 and Fig 2.19).

Perhaps the two most notable discoveries of the following years, both of which occurred during the 1930s, were the most unexpected. At both Hembury in Devon and Maiden Castle in Dorset, it was the massive hillfort ramparts and the assumed Iron Age occupation which were the intended object of the campaign of excavations undertaken by Dorothy Liddell (Alexander Keiller's sister-in-law) and by Mortimer Wheeler respectively. In her excavations, Liddell recovered large quantities of worked flint during the first season in 1930, but uncovered no features which could be dated earlier than the Iron Age. This prompted initial speculation that flint might also have been used in the Iron Age. From the following season onwards, however, Neolithic features were discovered in the form of the now familiar ditch segments (Fig 2.20), as well as pits, post-holes and a possible 'house', demonstrating clearly that a causewayed enclosure no longer visible on the surface had preceded

the substantial Iron Age ramparts (Liddell 1930; 1931; 1932; 1935). At Maiden Castle, notwithstanding earlier speculation (*see* above, this chapter: The idea of Stone Age camps), the discovery of the Neolithic remains apparently came as a complete surprise to Wheeler (Hawkes 1982, 168–9; Sharples 1991a, 1). This probably under-lines the extent to which he had focussed his attention on the Iron Age occupation (Wheeler 1943 and Fig 2.21).

## Aerial survey and excavation: an abundance of data

After the Second World War, discovery and excavation tended for some time to be rather piecemeal, generally concentrating on enclosures surviving as earthworks that were already known or suspected to be of Neolithic origin, including those on Combe Hill (Drewett 1994), Whitesheet Hill (Piggott 1952), Hambledon Hill (Farrar 1951, 105–6; RCHME 1970), Knap Hill (Connah 1965; 1969), Rybury (Bonney 1964), Robin Hood's Ball (Thomas 1964; Richards 1990, 61–5) and Maiden Bower (Matthews 1976). The presence of cause-ways in the ditches was by then established as the principal means of recognising enclosures of possible Neolithic date.

*Figure 2.19*
*The main causewayed enclosure and Iron Age hillfort on Hambledon Hill: aerial photograph taken in 1924 by Alexander Keiller before the destruction of many of the Neolithic earthworks by ploughing (see also Fig 4.16). The first detailed analysis of the earthworks on Hambledon Hill was made by Eric Gardiner in the light of Keiller and Crawford's photographs, which still remain among the most dramatic and informative images of the complex of monuments (Gardiner 1925; Gardiner in Crawford and Keiller 1928, 44–55). Gardner's suggestion of a Neolithic date for the main causewayed enclosure was based primarily on the proximity of the two long barrows and the recovery of a few flint flakes and a flint scraper from flint diggings within the circuit. Gardiner was well aware that a causewayed construction technique was beginning to be viewed as a diagnostic feature of Neolithic enclosures, but in the case of Hambledon, he attributed the causewayed appearance of the main enclosure to damage by later cart-tracks. This misinterpretation probably explains the otherwise surprising omission of the site from Curwen's (1930) discussion of 'Neolithic camps'. (ALK 7442/245)*

Figure 2.20
The causewayed enclosure
at Hembury in Devon. As
at Maiden Castle, the plan
of the ramparts of the Iron
Age hillfort hint at the
presence of the underlying
causewayed enclosure, but
the precise arrangement
was only revealed by
Liddell's excavations. The
coincidence in the locations
of hillfort and causewayed
enclosure at these and other
sites doubtless reinforced the
early view that the two
types of enclosure were
directly analogous to each
other in terms of function.
(Based on Liddell 1935,
plate 21).

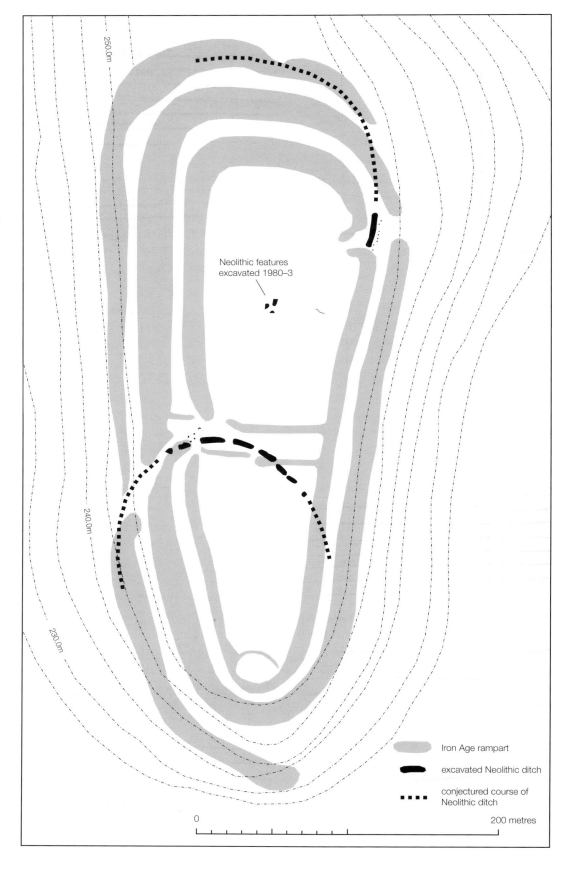

Neolithic features
excavated 1980–3

Iron Age rampart

excavated Neolithic ditch

conjectured course of
Neolithic ditch

0                    200 metres

*Figure 2.21*
*Mortimer Wheeler's excavation in 1937 of the ditch of the earliest Iron Age hillfort at Maiden Castle in Dorset, with the terminal of one of the Neolithic ditch segments revealed beneath it (Site R, looking south). Since Wheeler's overriding concern was with the development of the Iron Age defences, the recording of the Neolithic features was not carried out to the same standard. The famous 'box trenches', were not well suited to the complex nature of the Neolithic deposits. One ditch was not identified as part of the causewayed enclosure until fifty years later (Sharples 1991). (NMR CC83/1349; Society of Antiquaries of London)*

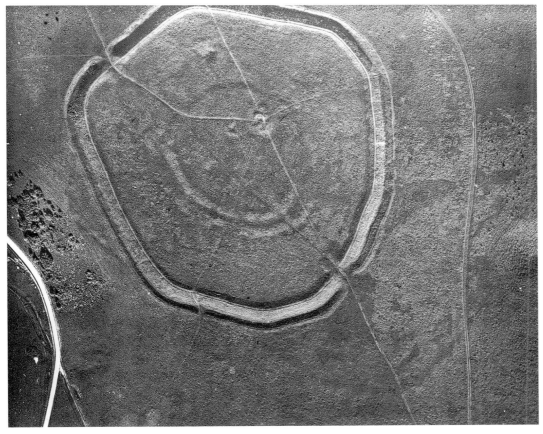

*Figure 2.22*
*An aerial photograph of The Trundle in West Sussex, taken in 1925 at the instigation of O G S Crawford. Within the area of the Iron Age hillfort are much slighter earthworks which Crawford suggested were the remains of a Neolithic causewayed enclosure. 'It was in order to put this to the test that the writer carried out excavations in the camp . . .' (Curwen 1929, 33–4). Reappraisal of this excellent photograph by Richard Bradley (1969) led to the identification of a possible continuation of the outer circuit, to the west of the hillfort, depicted in Fig 8.6. (NMR (English Heritage). Crawford Collection)*

Figure 2.23
The plan of the causewayed enclosure underlying The Trundle hillfort made by Curwen in 1928 remained the most detailed analysis of the earthworks until the survey carried out in 1995 (Fig 8.6). Curwen claimed that some ditch segments were only identified using a technique called 'bowsing', which involved beating the ground with an 8lb hammer to detect the changes in resonance caused by sub-surface features. In fact all the segments he detected by this technique are actually visible as very slight earthworks, suggesting that he may have used bowsing partly to lend credence to his visual observations, at a time when there would have been scepticism that such subtle variations were meaningful.

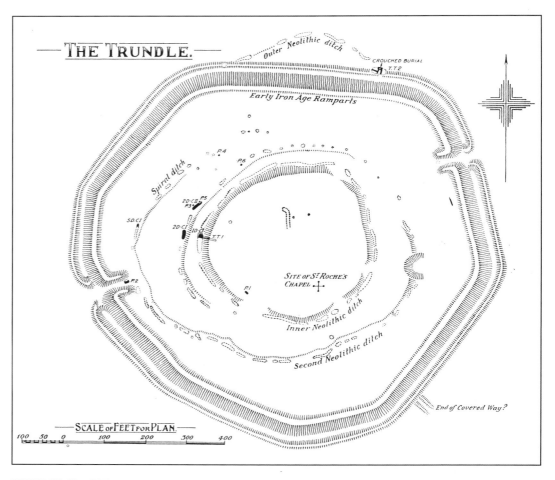

THE TRUNDLE.

Outer Neolithic ditch

CROUCHED BURIAL
T.T.2

Early Iron Age Ramparts

Spiral ditch

SITE OF ST ROCHE'S CHAPEL

Inner Neolithic ditch

Second Neolithic ditch

End of Covered Way?

SCALE OF FEET FOR PLAN.
100 50 0 100 200 300 400

Figure 2.24
The plough-levelled causewayed enclosure at Sawbridgeworth in Hertfordshire, photographed in July 1962. An appreciation of the topographic setting of the enclosure makes its plan easier to understand (see Fig 5.18). Comparable cropmarks were recorded for the Cambridge University collection at Fornham All Saints in Suffolk, Barholm in Lincolnshire, and Orsett in Essex (St Joseph 1964; 1970; 1973), though there was initially some doubt as to whether these low-lying sites represented a separate class of monument. (Cambridge University Collection of Air Photographs; copyright reserved: AGA 75)

Although the value of aerial survey had been realised for some time, its potential for the identification and interpretation of sites from the prehistoric periods and the Neolithic in particular was for long held in check by a belief among archaeologists that the technique would be most effective in upland areas. This rested upon the assumption, itself derived from the distribution of surviving earthworks, that human activity in prehistory would have been largely confined to the higher ground and that the lower-lying valleys and river terraces were densely forested and largely devoid of occupation until much later (eg Curwen 1929b, 6; see also RCHME 1960; Cunliffe 1992; Bradley 1992). Yet the possibility that causewayed enclosures might exist in valley locations had been demonstrated as early as 1926 by Leeds' discoveries at Abingdon (Leeds 1927; 1928), where the site had been discovered as a result of gravel extraction. Further confirmation came in 1961 with the start of excavations at another causewayed enclosure in the Thames Valley, at Staines in Surrey (Robertson-Mackay 1987). That site was also excavated in advance of gravel extraction, having been first recognised as a cropmark as late as 1959.

From the mid-1960s onwards, it gradually became clearer that the apparent absence of prehistoric monuments from lower-lying locations, including the river gravels, was not so much due to the avoidance of valley bottoms in prehistory as to the intensity of subsequent agriculture on the fertile alluvial soils. This realisation owes much to the increase in aerial photography as a method of survey, which concentrated on those parts of the modern landscape under arable cultivation that had previously been overlooked by archaeologists. Ironically, the earthworks of many of the causewayed enclosures noted by Curwen in 1930 had actually been identified from the air by Crawford and Keiller. In fact, Curwen's own excavations at The Trundle had followed from Crawford's recognition of causewayed earthworks on an aerial photograph (Figs 2.22 and 2.23). By the end of the 1960s, a number of enclosures with interrupted ditches had been recognised as cropmarks, notably through work in East Anglia by J K St Joseph (1964; 1966; 1970; 1973; Fig 2.24). Rog Palmer's analysis, written originally as an undergraduate dissertation and then published (1976), listed twenty-eight sites recorded as cropmarks within a total of forty-three causewayed enclosures, although not all have withstood subsequent scrutiny.

Earlier studies of the causewayed enclosures surviving as earthworks on the chalk uplands continued to exert a strong influence on interpretations of the nature and purpose of causewayed enclosures. For a while, there was some uncertainty as to whether the increasingly large number of low-lying 'interrupted ditch enclosures', as they were briefly known, could be directly compared with the upland causewayed enclosures identified on the basis of the form of their earthworks and in some cases excavated evidence (eg Wilson 1975; Palmer 1976). By 1970, St Joseph had photographed twenty-one such enclosures visible from the air as cropmarks, yet in 1971 Isobel Smith listed only those sites proven by excavation, even though she was aware that many potential new discoveries were being made. On the basis of the excavation of several low-lying sites initially detected as cropmarks, it is now generally accepted that interrupted ditch enclosures

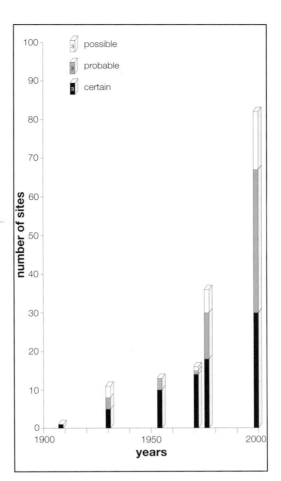

Figure 2.25
Discovery and confirmation of causewayed enclosures in England over the course of the 20th century: the excavations by the Cunningtons at Knap Hill in 1908; Curwen's tally in 1930; Piggott's in 1955; Smith's in 1971; Palmer's in 1976 and RCHME's in 1999. The graph excludes identifications that have subsequently proved false. Note the sudden leap in numbers in the early 1970s, brought about almost entirely by aerial photographic reconnaissance of low-lying areas over the previous fifteen years.

Figure 2.26
The cropmark of the causewayed enclosure at Orsett in Essex was first recorded during aerial reconnaissance by the Cambridge University Committee for Aerial Photography in 1961. The enclosure, depicted in Figs 1.5 and 3.11, lies at the end of a spur, overlooking a minor tributary of the Thames. Excavations in 1975 (Hedges and Buckley 1978) confirmed the link between 'interrupted ditch enclosures' and the causewayed enclosures surviving as earthworks. (Cambridge University Collection of Air Photographs; copyright reserved: K17-U 117)

and causewayed enclosures represent a single class of monument. It is primarily through aerial survey that the number of causewayed enclosures has continued to grow (Fig 2.25).

The full impact of aerial survey in the 1970s also coincided broadly with more intensive, large-scale excavations of individual sites and complexes of monuments, in contrast to the small-scale trenching that had been the norm since the Second World War. At Crickley Hill in Gloucestershire (Dixon 1988), another causewayed enclosure was unexpectedly discovered during the excavation of an Iron Age hillfort. Excavation of the causewayed enclosure recorded as a cropmark at Orsett in Essex (Fig 2.26) finally confirmed the link with 'interrupted ditch enclosures' (Hedges and Buckley 1978). At Offham Hill in East Sussex, rescue excavation highlighted the damage being done to such monuments by modern agriculture (Drewett 1977). Excavation and fieldwork on the complex of causewayed enclosures and long barrows on Hambledon Hill in Dorset (Mercer 1980a and b; 1988; Mercer and Healy in preparation) perhaps did more than any other project to transform understanding not only of an individual site, but also of the class of monument and of the earlier Neolithic in general. Subsequently, there have also been substantial excavations at the causewayed enclosures on Briar Hill in Northamptonshire (Bamford 1985), at Etton in Cambridgeshire (Pryor 1987; 1988a; 1988b; 1998b; Pryor and Kinnes 1982; Pryor et al 1985) and at Haddenham in Cambridgeshire (Evans 1988b; Hodder 1992; Evans and Hodder forthcoming).

Work has been renewed on some sites excavated previously: Maiden Castle in Dorset (Sharples 1991a), Hembury in Devon (Todd 1984) and Windmill Hill in Wiltshire (Evans 1966; 1972; Whittle 1990; 1993; Whittle et al 1999). The principal publications resulting from all excavations of causewayed enclosures are listed in the gazetteer (Appendix).

This enormous expansion in the quantity of raw data available from causewayed enclosures has not, however, made their interpretation any easier. Shifts in interpretation were, initially, fairly straightforward consequences of the results of the latest excavations and contemporary perceptions of the Neolithic as a whole. The present variety of evidence available from different sites underlines how unlikely it is that a single all-embracing interpretation for these monuments will be found (see Chapter 8).

## Changing perceptions since 1930: causewayed enclosures and the Neolithic

The impact of the discovery and excavation of causewayed enclosures on contemporary perceptions of the British Neolithic was far-reaching. The recognition of a class of monument that was not primarily funerary in function had immediate and fundamental implications for interpretations of society and economy during the period. The excavated assemblages of pottery, worked flint and stone and animal bone both confirmed certain criteria already deemed characteristic of the Neolithic and permitted links to be made with other monuments, most notably the long barrows and the flint mines (Clark and Piggott 1933). In addition, the study of pottery styles and stone tool types provided the basis of a new relative chronological sequence (eg Piggott 1931) and allowed attempts to establish links with material from sites on the European mainland (eg Childe 1931).

The best known treatment of the evidence is Stuart Piggott's synthesis, entitled *Neolithic Cultures of the British Isles* (1954), which represented the culmination of research and debate on the Neolithic since the Windmill Hill excavations. Piggott, by then Professor of Prehistoric Archaeology at the University of Edinburgh, bound together what was essentially a disparate collection of

*Figure 2.27
The 'Windmill Hill
Culture'. Having defined
the limits of the culture,
Piggott traced its
expansion northwards.
The belief that innovation
and change in Neolithic,
Bronze Age and Iron
Age societies must have
originated in Wessex has
been slow to fade.
(Redrawn from Piggott
1954, fig 1; Cambridge
University Press)*

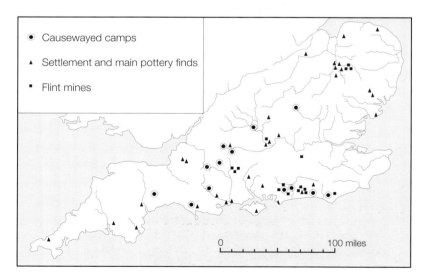

- ● Causewayed camps
- ▲ Settlement and main pottery finds
- ■ Flint mines

0       100 miles

types of monument and artefact to create a descriptive account of the British Neolithic. His approach was 'culture-historic', aiming to identify geographically and chronologically restricted groups of people or 'cultures' through the recognition of recurring associations of types of site and artefact. The causewayed enclosure on Windmill Hill was treated as a 'type-site' and used as a link for the whole study (Fig 2.27). At the time of Piggott's analysis, the 'Windmill Hill Culture' was thought to have been restricted in geographical terms to the Lowland Zone as defined by Cyril Fox (1932): principally Britain to the south of the Humber, but excluding much of Wales and the uplands of the South-West. In terms of chronology, it was held to represent an earlier phase of the Neolithic. The later phase was thought to be represented primarily by the appearance and spread of Peterborough Ware pottery and its users, during the currency of which the 'Beaker Folk' and the Bronze Age arrived. Underpinning Piggott's approach (and indeed much discussion of the Neolithic since the 1920s) was the assumption that change in the British archaeological record tended to have been imported from the European mainland, usually through the migration of groups of people. The excavations at Windmill Hill in particular had allowed the period to be placed securely for the first time within a broader European context. Curwen's (1930) article had included a brief discussion of Neolithic 'camps' in France and Germany. The stylistic affinities of the pottery assemblages had stimulated attempts to discover whence the Neolithic lifestyle and its material culture had come (eg Hawkes 1935; Piggott 1955; Case 1969; *see also* Bradley 1998a, 189).

Little of Piggott's explanatory framework for the British Neolithic remains intact today, however. An early blow came from the dating of Neolithic deposits by radiocarbon determination, a technique which in 1954 was still in its infancy. The more accurate dating evidence not only dramatically stretched the period in chronological terms, but also required a review of the sequence in which types of monuments and artefacts came to prominence and, therefore, the relationships between them. Piggott had assigned a span of just 500 years to his Neolithic (2,000 BC to 1,500 BC), the components of which are now spread more comfortably across the 4th and 3rd millennia BC. Equally significant has been the decline of the

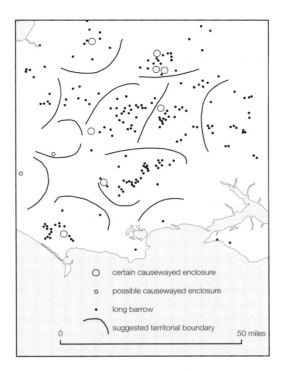

Figure 2.28
Hypothetical territories in Wessex. Barry Cunliffe's analysis was based on the earlier work of Colin Renfrew (1973), which had essentially applied mathematical Thiessen polygons to the distribution of long barrows and causewayed enclosures. In the absence of more reliable evidence for Neolithic settlement, the correlation between the two types of monument remains a key argument for the existence of territories. (Redrawn from Cunliffe 1993, fig 2.6)

culture-historical outlook of the sort typified by Piggott's account. The belief that the inception of the Neolithic in Britain was primarily an introduction from the European mainland, however, involving considerable cross-Channel movement of people, proved resilient to criticism until the mid-1980s. Current approaches tend to emphasise greater continuity with the preceding Mesolithic and succeeding Bronze Age (eg Kinnes 1988; Pryor 1988b; Barrett 1994). Indigenous hunter-gatherer groups are credited with a more active role in bringing about social and economic changes that are regarded as developments of the Neolithic. The origins of new ideas, rather than people, are traced back to the European mainland. It is no longer thought, however, that there was a clear, sudden and fundamental break with the past, nor is the Neolithic still viewed as a uniform phenomenon across large spans of space and time (Thomas 1991; 1993).

Some elements of current theories concerning the Neolithic mirror earlier ideas derived from the first excavations of causewayed enclosures. For example, many interpretations of the 1990s emphasise the probable mobility of the Neolithic population and consequently play down the importance of arable agriculture (eg Thomas 1991, 28; Whittle 1997). As described above, the belief that the arrival of agriculture could be equated with a more sedentary lifestyle was born almost with the concept of the Neolithic itself. The recognition of causewayed enclosures as a class of Neolithic monument initially strengthened this belief, for they were generally believed to be analogous to Iron Age hillforts, which were usually interpreted as defended settlements. To an extent, this assumption was a continuation of earlier ideas about the need for defence in prehistoric society, but it was certainly supported by coincidences in the location of hillforts and causewayed enclosure at places such as Maiden Castle and Hembury. There was little direct evidence for arable agriculture or for domestic structures from excavations on most causewayed enclosures, however, in contrast to the sizeable assemblages of animal bones. This gradually led to a shift in opinion and an acceptance that from the inception of the Neolithic pastoralism may have been the dominant way of life and mode of subsistence. It was thought that arable agriculture would have fulfilled a secondary role in food production until well into the Bronze Age. This line of thought was probably encouraged by the concentration of archaeological research on the southern chalk downlands and other upland areas, large parts of which were used for rough grazing at that time (*see* eg Curwen 1938; 1946). Curwen (1938, 37) argued that at Whitehawk Camp

. . . the vast quantities of bones of ox, pig and sheep found...indicates the relatively large part played by stock-raising. This high ratio of cattle to corn implies nomadic conditions. Moreover, the slight degree of terracing of the plots, contrasted with the enormous lynchets on the sites of the settled villages of the later prehistoric periods, shows that no single site was occupied, or at least cultivated for very long . . . On the other hand the Neolithic A folk [ie the earliest of the Neolithic 'cultures'] can scarcely have been entirely nomadic in their habits, for it seems likely that there may have been some sort of tribal organization centred on the causewayed camps as permanent nuclei.

The increase in the quantity and quality of excavations and in particular the crucial impact of aerial survey from the 1960s onwards contributed greatly to changing perspectives. The theoretical outlooks that were emerging around the same time encouraged new perspectives on the role of causewayed enclosures and other monuments within prehistoric society. Studies such as those of Humphrey Case (1969) and Colin Renfrew (1973) put forward the idea of treating monuments as indicators of both social complexity and territoriality, within an explanatory framework derived from anthropological models (Fig 2.28). The causewayed enclosures were thought to have been located at the centres of social territories (eg Barker and Webley 1978; Drewett 1977, 226–8; Case 1982, 2–5): the very fact of their existence was considered to be proof of a process of increasing social complexity. The presence of exotic artefacts prompted suggestions that trade and exchange were in some way controlled from these centres. Calculations of the labour input required for the construction of the enclosures suggested the emergence of powerful leaders in a society that was seen as becoming increasingly hierarchical over time (Renfrew 1973; Startin and Bradley 1981; Bradley 1984a). Attempts were made to discern regions and territories through the distribution of different types of enclosure (Palmer 1976). Sometimes these regions appeared to be loosely associated with pottery 'style-zones' defined on the basis of particular formal and stylistic characteristics of pottery (Bradley 1984a, 34; but *see* Cleal 1992), echoing earlier culture-historical approaches to the interpretation of pottery distributions.

Yet these studies continued to adhere to the idea that social change would have followed an evolutionary path, and to rely on a generalised view of the monuments and other archaeological data (*see also* Harding 1995). From the 1980s onwards, it was increasingly accepted that such assumptions are far from safe, given the long histories of construction and reconstruction evident at some causewayed enclosures (Evans 1988c). It appears that the enclosures did not lie at the heart of territories, but on their peripheries (Thomas 1982; Gardiner 1984; Evans *et al* 1988). The presence of artefacts of non-local origin in the ditches is thought more likely to indicate the long-distance ties of particular communities and the importance of particular places, than to be evidence for trade or exchange (Thomas 1991, 35–6; Bradley and Edmonds 1993; Edmonds 1993; 1995, 68–73). In the late 1990s, the tendency is to consider individual monuments as expressions of social unity, but in a Neolithic landscape that is seen to be more fragmented and diverse, both in terms of land use and social relations (papers in Topping 1997b).

# 3
# The constructional elements

The perimeters of causewayed enclosures, like those of many other prehistoric enclosures, made use of a limited range of constructional elements: ditches, banks and timber structures (Fig 3.1). As important as the enclosing boundaries themselves were the entrances, which marked the threshold between the outside world and the reserved space of the interior (Hodder 1990, 127–8; Edmonds 1993, 111). This chapter illustrates the basic features that were combined to produce the wide range of forms discussed in Chapter 4.

## Ditches and recutting

Chapter 2 traced the process by which the segmented ditches of causewayed enclosures have come to be gradually recognised as the most important defining characteristic of this class of monument. Even where the ditch appears continuous as an earthwork or cropmark, excavation has usually shown that a similar digging technique was used. The segments were not necessarily all dug at the same time: new ones may have been added and existing ones may have been lengthened or amalgamated, producing a range of plan forms (Bedwin 1984, 18). It has been suggested that this apparently piecemeal construction technique results from small gangs having responsibility for digging out separate segments (Startin and Bradley 1981, 291). This theory is open to question, but is amongst the most convincing put forward to date (see Chapter 7).

The ditches of more than half of all causewayed enclosures comprise segments less than 20m long on average. In some cases, for example at the enclosures recorded as cropmarks at Burford in Oxfordshire and at Freston in Suffolk (Figs 1.3 and 3.14), the segments are of fairly even length, perhaps indicating that the technique was not quite as disorderly as it first appears. There is considerable variation in length between different causewayed enclosures, however. A small number, including those recorded by aerial survey at Upton in Cambridgeshire

(Fig 3.2) and at both Radley (see Fig 4.22) and Eynsham in Oxfordsire have ditch segments only a few metres long – so short that they could be described as elongated pits. At the other extreme, the enclosure on Court Hill in West Sussex was initially thought to be continuously ditched. A small-scale trial excavation discovered one causeway, however (Bedwin 1984), and subsequent survey from the air and on the ground has revealed the existence of a few more possible causeways (Fig 3.3). This

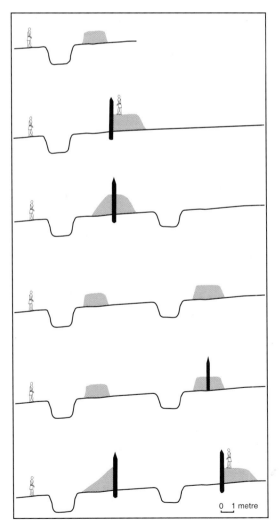

*Figure 3.1*
*Many possible combinations of bank, ditch and palisade may have been used to form the perimeters of causewayed enclosures. Since most evidence survives for the ditches, greater emphasis has been placed upon them. In many cases ploughing has destroyed the banks and the postholes for timber superstructures, especially where these were shallow or supported entirely by the bank. The existence of any bank must then be deduced from the nature of deposits excavated in the ditch.*

*Figure 3.2*
*The ditch of the*
*causewayed enclosure at*
*Upton in Cambridgeshire*
*appears to have been dug*
*as a series of short pit-like*
*segments, particularly*
*along its southern side.*
*What appears to be a*
*fenceline or pit alignment*
*across the site is very*
*probably prehistoric,*
*but is unlikely to be*
*contemporary with the*
*enclosure.*

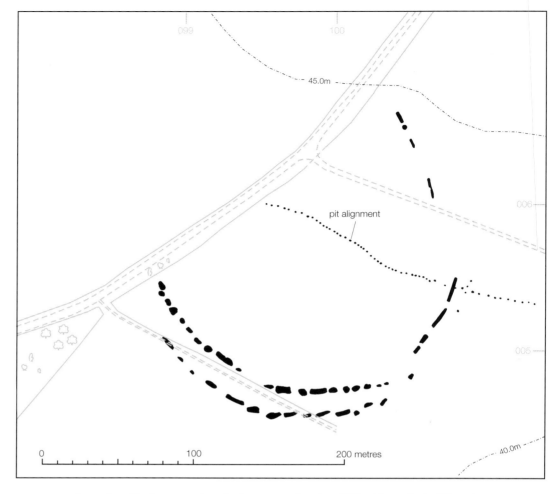

suggests that the ditch may simply have comprised longer segments or, as suggested by the excavator, that it may have been dug as a series of interlinked segments. In either case, the technique is similar in essence to that evident at other causewayed enclosures.

There can be variation in the length of the ditch segments between different circuits of the same enclosure. For example, three of the four segments which comprise the outer circuit of the enclosure recorded as a cropmark at Broadwell in Oxfordshire seem to be almost twice as long as most of the segments that form the inner two circuits (*see* Fig 5.17). The length may also differ greatly around even a single circuit, so that their average length may give a rather imprecise measure of the degree of variation. For instance, the ditch of the outer circuit of the causewayed enclosure recorded as a cropmark at Dallington in Northamptonshire seems to have segments between approximately 5m and 40m long (Fig 3.4). Similarly, the segments that can be recognised as earthworks along the inner

circuit of The Trundle in West Sussex range from 3m to 28m in length (*see* Fig 8.6). Alasdair Whittle (1993, 44) has suggested that the middle circuit of the causewayed enclosure on Windmill Hill may have comprised alternating long and short segments, but this does not appear to have been the case elsewhere. Excavated evidence from other enclosures suggests that the degree of variation suggested by survey (Fig 3.5) may be fairly representative (eg Smith 1965, fig 3; Mercer 1988, fig 5.3; Pryor 1988a, fig 6.3).

As described in Chapter 2, Isobel Smith first pointed out that the ditch segments excavated at Windmill Hill in Wiltshire appeared to have been cleaned out and recut at intervals (Smith 1965, 15–17; 1966; 1971, 96–8). Recutting was often associated with the placement of ritual deposits, comprising everything from polished stone axes and human skulls to joints of meat and broken pottery. It is as though the monuments were never regarded as finished entities, but rather as projects requiring continual endeavour (Evans 1988c, 85–8). This episodic reconstruction process is central to the current understanding of how most causewayed enclosures were used and reached their eventual forms (Thomas 1991; Edmonds 1993; Bradley 1998b, 68–82).

The recuts were sometimes carefully dug so as to preserve the positions of the original causeways and as if to show respect for the original form of the monument. At Briar Hill in Northamptonshire, 80 per cent of the excavated ditch segments showed evidence of at least one recut, and some as many as five (Bamford 1985, 32). At Etton in Cambridgeshire up to eight episodes of recutting were evident in some segments (Pryor et al 1985, 288; Pryor 1988b, 352).

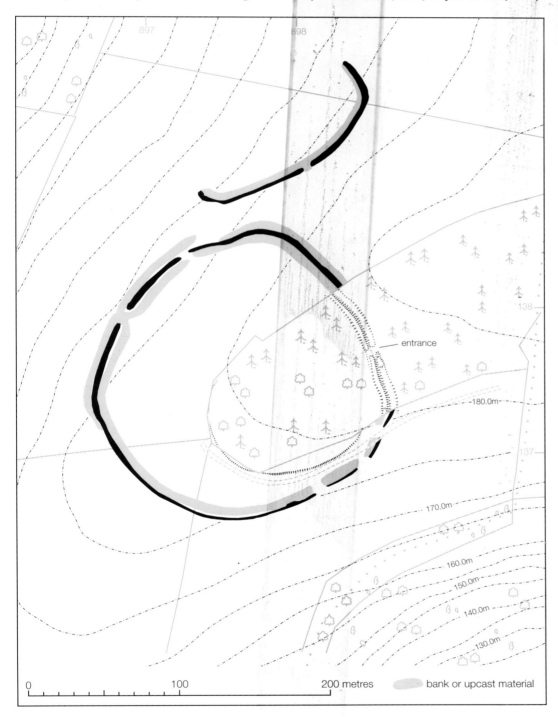

entrance

| | | |
|---|---|---|
| 0 | 100 | 200 metres |

bank or upcast material

Figure 3.3
The causewayed enclosure on Court Hill in West Sussex was initially thought to be unusual in having a continuous ditch (Bedwin 1984). Ploughing has reduced much of the circuit to a low scarp, but the woodland on the summit of the spur has preserved a short stretch, including a central in-turned entrance causeway. From the air, two or three more possible causeways can be identified in the plough-damaged section. More importantly, trial excavation in 1982 revealed a 'semi-causeway', suggesting that the construction technique may have been the same as that used at enclosures with more obvious causewayed ditches.

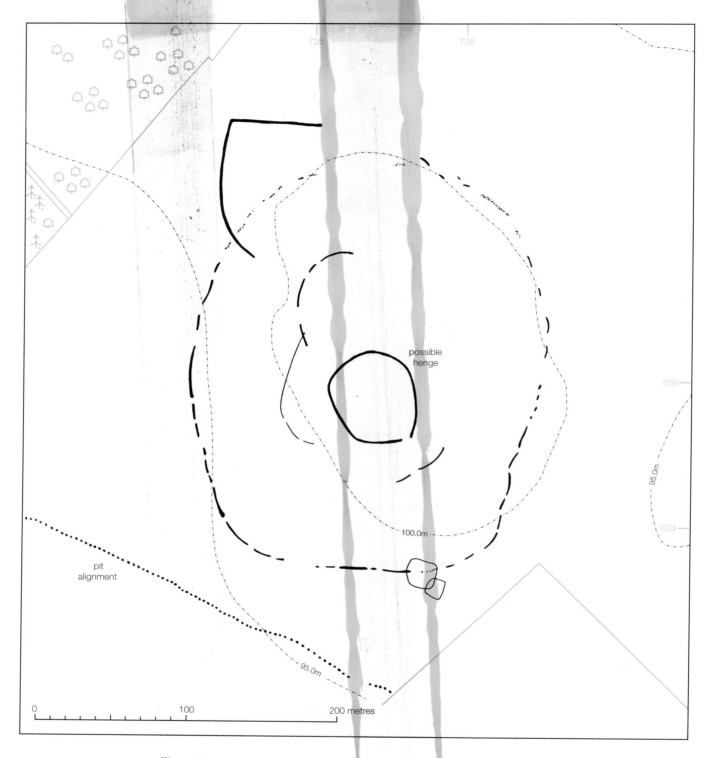

*Figure 3.4*
*The cropmarks at Dallington in Northamptonshire were first recorded by the Cambridge*
*University Committee for Aerial Photography in July 1962. Since then, the site has been*
*investigated by fieldwalking, geophysical survey and was finally confirmed as a causewayed*
*enclosure through trial excavation by the Oxford Archaeological Unit in 1992. The more*
*continuous ditch circuit with a single entrance has been interpreted as a possible henge*
*(Bamford 1985, 136).*

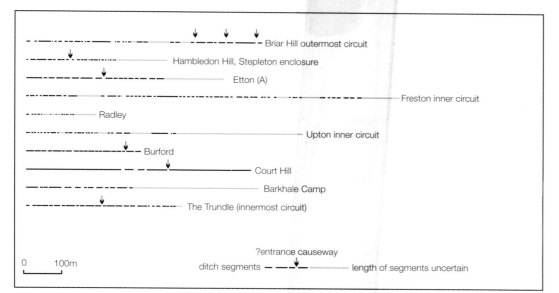

*Figure 3.5*
*Following his excavations at the causewayed enclosure at Haddenham in Cambridgeshire, Chris Evans proposed a method of depicting the variation in the lengths of different segments graphically, so that the plans of different enclosures can be directly compared. This technique has not been widely adopted, mainly because the quality of data varies between sites recorded by excavation, earthwork survey and aerial photographic analysis.*

The causeways were not always maintained intact, however. Where they were dug away at a later date, this often seems to have resulted in low ridges or 'semi-causeways' in the base of the ditch. These were noted, for example, during the excavations at Windmill Hill, at Orsett in Essex and at Briar Hill (Smith 1965, 7; Hedges and Buckley 1978, 228; Bamford 1979, 4). At Birdlip Camp in Gloucestershire, the line of the ditch was moved slightly eastward with each successive recut. The position of the one causeway encountered in the small-scale excavation was approximately maintained, but was displaced a little to one side or the other (Darvill 1982, 23; *see also* Dixon 1988, 81).

While full causeways are often clearly evident on aerial photographs, the slight variations in depth and semi-causeways created by recutting can seldom be identified with confidence (Hedges and Buckley 1978, 228). The minor irregularities in plan that are, however, frequently evident probably result from the same process. Where segments of ditch have a 'chain-link' or 'string of sausages' appearance, as do parts of the cropmarks at Barholm in Lincolnshire, Southmore Grove in Gloucestershire and Southwick in Northamptonshire (Fig 3.6; *see* Figs 5.23 and 8.10), this is likely to be because longer stretches were formed through the amalgamation of several shorter segments. The possible causewayed enclosures identified in Scotland, such as that at Leadketty in Perthshire (Fig 3.7), generally have fewer complete causeways than the enclosures in the south of England, but are characterised by ditches whose courses waver slightly from side to side. This may indicate that these apparently more continuous ditches were also dug as interlinked segments. In southern England, several causewayed enclosures preserved as earthworks offer clearer evidence for recutting. This usually takes the form of slightly deeper hollows along the course of longer ditch segments, as found, for example, on the northern side of the enclosure at Robin Hood's Ball in Wiltshire and at The Trundle (Fig 1.4; *see* Fig 8.6). While survey techniques can point to the presence of recuts, however, they can seldom discern the same subtleties as those revealed by excavation.

Both aerial and earthwork survey suggest that the majority of the ditch segments are between 2m and 5m wide, and most excavated examples correspond to this (Fig 3.8). Their depth is impossible to gauge accurately from the air, and the shallowest sections may not be visible at all, as excavations at Ramsgate in Kent have shown (Shand 1998; *see* Fig 4.2). The ditches best preserved as earthworks are at least 0.6m deep on the surface, but most are slighter. Some are identifiable only as patches of more verdant vegetation (cropmarks in effect). These differences probably do not in most cases reflect the original depths of the ditches, but rather the state of preservation of the earthworks. The apparent absence of parts of the outer ditch at Combe Hill in East Sussex, however, where most of the earthworks are well preserved, may be because certain sections were deliberately levelled during the earlier Neolithic (*see* Fig 8.5). On excavation,

Figure 3.6
The causewayed enclosure
at Barholm in
Lincolnshire. The clarity
of the cropmark allows the
recognition of minor
irregularities in the
individual ditch segments.
This suggests that they
were dug as shorter
sections that were
eventually amalgamated.
The pair of ditches bending
to the east of the enclosure
probably represents an
earlier route of the present
road. The former course of
a minor stream, now
canalised into a field
boundary ditch, is also
visible as a cropmark.

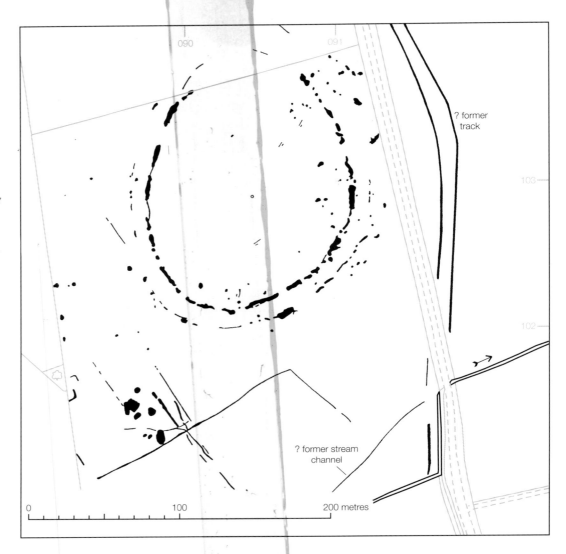

Figure 3.6
The causewayed enclosure at Barholm in Lincolnshire. The clarity of the cropmark allows the recognition of minor irregularities in the individual ditch segments. This suggests that they were dug as shorter sections that were eventually amalgamated. The pair of ditches bending to the east of the enclosure probably represents an earlier route of the present road. The former course of a minor stream, now canalised into a field boundary ditch, is also visible as a cropmark.

the majority of ditch segments have proved to be between 1m and 2m deep. The original depth cannot always be determined accurately, due to the removal of up to 1m by later ploughing, erosion and in some cases the natural chemical dissolution of chalk (Drewett 1977, 205; 1980; Mercer 1980c; 1988, 93).

Almost all the ditches that have been excavated appear originally to have had a U-shaped profile, with a flat base and nearly vertical sides (Fig 3.8). In some cases, particularly where the ditches were dug into softer sands and gravels, the sides have eroded to much gentler slopes (eg *see* Fig 3.8). The ditches of many long barrows and cursus monuments are of similar size and shape. Several explanations have been put forward as to why this distinctive profile may have been preferred over the V-shape used so wisely from the later Bronze Age

onwards. There are several possible practical considerations, and the available tools and digging methods may have been relevant. For instance, certain sedimentary rocks such as sandstone and chalk tend to fracture in horizontal planes; this could have made a level base easier to cut, especially if picks made of red deer antler were used to lever up blocks (Curwen 1931, 106; *see also* Lane Fox 1876, 382–3). Yet this does not wholly account for the fact that many ditches cut into gravel subsoils also have a flat base and steep sides. It has been suggested that the U-shape may have eroded less quickly and would therefore have been relatively easy to maintain (Whittle 1977, 227). Observation of the experimental earthwork on Overton Down in Wiltshire, however, indicates that a ditch cut with a U-shaped profile eroded into a shallower V-shape within sixteen years of its creation (Bell *et al* 1996, fig 14.2).

This may have been a factor in the frequency with which the ditches of many causewayed enclosures were recut, but it does not explain why the U-shape was favoured in the first place. In addition, there is evidence from a number of excavated sites that ditches were deliberately filled in soon after being dug, possibly to cover the mass of animal and human bones that had been ritually deposited there (Smith 1965, 15–17; 1966; 1971, 96–8; Leach 1983, 22; Bedwin 1992, 5). Given this behaviour, it seems doubtful whether the long-term stability of the profile when exposed would have been an important concern. The carefully placed ritual deposits suggest that the ditches were more than mere quarries for the bank material and that there may have been less practical reasons behind the U-shaped profile (Evans 1988c, 89; contra Piggott 1954, 24; Copley 1958, 46; Mercer 1988, 89). A level base may have been necessary to display these special deposits, or to allow

the performance of whatever rituals accompanied the acts of deposition (*see* Chapter 7).

The apparent contradiction of an earthwork designed to enclose whilst retaining numerous entrances has given rise to puzzlement and debate since the characteristic was first remarked upon (eg Curwen 1929b, 73–5; 1930, 49–50). Francis Pryor, the excavator of the enclosure at Etton has expressed the paradox in a nutshell, remarking that the causewayed ditches 'enclose, yet at the same time do so both with manifest and with calculated inefficiency' (Pryor 1988a, 125). This impression has been reinforced since the 1970s by the shift in attention away from the causewayed enclosures preserved as earthworks towards those identified as cropmarks. At these sites the perimeters appear especially discontinuous, because very little evidence survives for whatever earthen banks and timber barriers may have accompanied the ditches.

*Figure 3.7*
*The enclosure at Leadketty in Perthshire has few complete causeways but ditches whose courses waver, suggesting that the construction technique may have been similar to that used at more typical causewayed enclosures. Although fieldwalking has recovered a concentration of Neolithic flintwork from the location, making the site the most likely of the possible causewayed enclosures identified in Scotland, a later date cannot yet be ruled out. (Crown copyright: RCAHMS)*

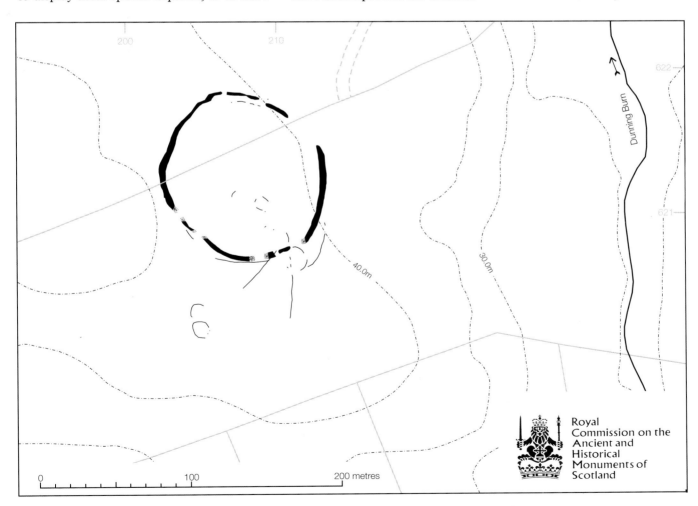

Royal Commission on the Ancient and Historical Monuments of Scotland

*Figure 3.8*
*Excavated sections through the ditches of causewayed enclosures, showing the similarity in their distinctive U-shaped profiles. The interior of the enclosure (that is, the probable position of the bank) is to the left in each case: 1 based on Drewett 1977, fig 3; 2 based on fig 2.18; 3 based on Ford 1991–3, fig 5; 4 based on Sharples 1991, fig 50; 5 based on an unpublished drawing by Desmond Bonney, held in Dorset County Museum; 6 based on Curwen 1929b, plate III; 7 based on Pryor 1988, fig 6.5; 8 based on Smith 1965, fig 6; 9 based on Robertson-Mackay 1987, fig 7; 10 based on Hedges and Buckley 1978, fig 13; 11 based on Case 1956, fig 2; 12 based on Bamford 1985, fig 7.2; 13 based on Connah 1965, fig 2; 14 based on Liddell 1931, fig 4; 15 based on Evans 1988b, fig 7.4; 16 based on an unpublished drawing by V Seton-Williams (note that the two basal layers of 'chalk rubble' are not depicted on the version published by Leach 1983, fig 3).*

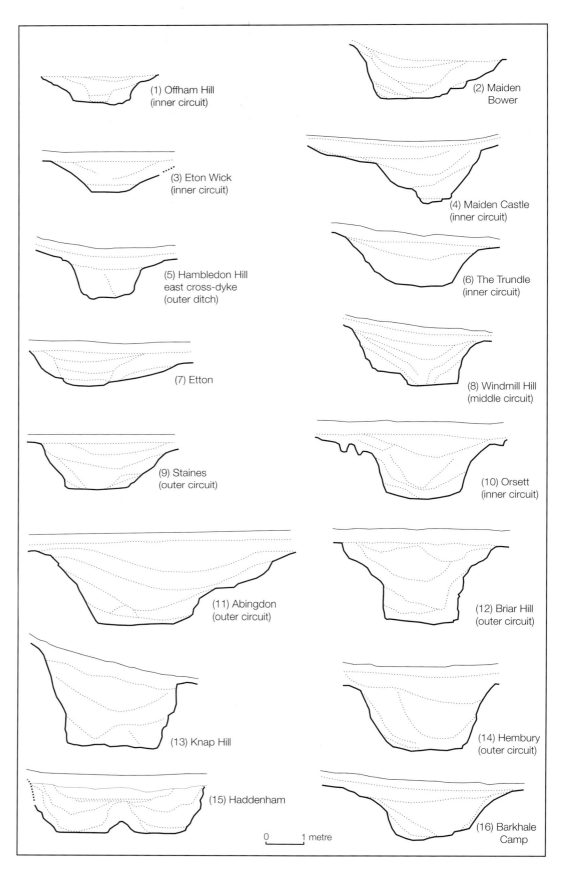

(1) Offham Hill (inner circuit)

(2) Maiden Bower

(3) Eton Wick (inner circuit)

(4) Maiden Castle (inner circuit)

(5) Hambledon Hill east cross-dyke (outer ditch)

(6) The Trundle (inner circuit)

(7) Etton

(8) Windmill Hill (middle circuit)

(9) Staines (outer circuit)

(10) Orsett (inner circuit)

(11) Abingdon (outer circuit)

(12) Briar Hill (outer circuit)

(13) Knap Hill

(14) Hembury (outer circuit)

(15) Haddenham

(16) Barkhale Camp

0    1 metre

# Banks

The banks of causewayed enclosures have attracted far less attention than the ditches, as a result of the rarity of their survival and the scarcity of artefacts contained within them. At most causewayed enclosures recorded as cropmarks, no evidence for banks can be discerned through survey. Excavation of the well preserved enclosure at Etton discovered only a single short section of bank (Pryor 1988a, 110) and their existence on other sites recorded as cropmarks has been doubted (Evans 1988b, 133–4). Intermittent traces are visible at a small number of sites, however, including Sawbridgeworth in Hertfordshire (*see* Fig 5.18). At certain enclosures, such as those at Orsett and Briar Hill, although no banks can be detected on aerial photographs, excavation has suggested that they formerly existed (Hedges and Buckley 1978, 234; Bamford 1985, 37–9). The layers in the ditch were found to have built up asymmetrically, from which it was inferred either that a bank had been deliberately pushed back into it, or that material had eroded more quickly from a newly built earthwork along one edge. The precise form of the destroyed banks was, however, impossible to deduce.

In England, only fourteen causewayed enclosures survive to any extent as earthworks (Fig 3.9). Including the causewayed enclosure on Donegore Hill in County Antrim (*see* Fig 5.3), parts of between twenty-five and thirty circuits of ditch are represented. Field survey suggests that all but one of these probably had a bank running along the inner edge of the ditch. The sole exception is the inner circuit of the causewayed enclosure on Windmill Hill (Fig 2.8). There too, excavation indicates that a bank was originally present and that it was deliberately levelled into the ditch (Smith 1965, 15–17; 1966). It seems highly probable, therefore, that banks would have accompanied the ditches of most of those enclosures recorded as cropmarks, even where no evidence for their existence can be detected.

In some cases, the banks were separated from the ditch by level berms up to 3m wide, which are still evident even from the eroded earthwork remains. The banks are also perforated by causeways of level ground, but very seldom at such frequent intervals as the ditches. As Curwen (1930, 49) first pointed out, partial interruptions

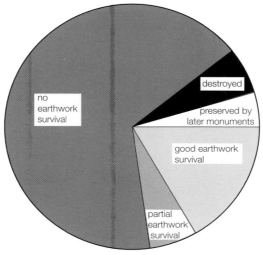

*Figure 3.9*
*The condition of*
*causewayed enclosures*
*in the British Isles.*

are more common than complete causeways, recalling the greater frequency of the 'semi-causeways' in the ditch. The exceptional examples in this respect are the enclosure on Knap Hill in Wiltshire and Barkhale Camp in West Sussex, where detailed survey shows that the bank segments are precisely the same length as the adjacent ditch segments (Figs 2.7 and 3.10). Typically, the causeways in the ditch outnumber those in the bank by between three and six to one. At Hambledon Hill, some of the causeways in the bank of the main causewayed enclosure do not correspond to causeways in the ditch, but are slightly offset (*see* Fig 4.16). Some banks, such as that of the inner circuit at The Trundle and both circuits at Robin Hood's Ball, Birdlip Camp and Dorstone Hill in Hereford and Worcester, appear to have been very nearly continuous (Fig 1.4; *see* Figs 8.6 and 4.14). The correspondence evident in the cropmarks of the two closely spaced ditch circuits at Orsett suggested that they may have been dug on either side of a single almost continuous bank (St Joseph 1973, 236; Fig 3.11). Although the correspondence is arguably much less close than was initially suggested, this interpretation was subsequently supported by the excavated evidence, as described above and reconstructed in Figure 1.5 (Hedges and Buckley 1978, 236). The evidence for a bank behind the inner of the two ditches was inconclusive. There may have been a similar arrangement at several causewayed enclosures recorded only as cropmarks, such as those at Sawbridgeworth in Hertfordshire, Freston in Suffolk, Northborough in Cambridgeshire, Mavesyn Ridware in Staffordshire and Eastry in Kent (*see* Figs 5.18, 3.14, 5.16 and 4.18).

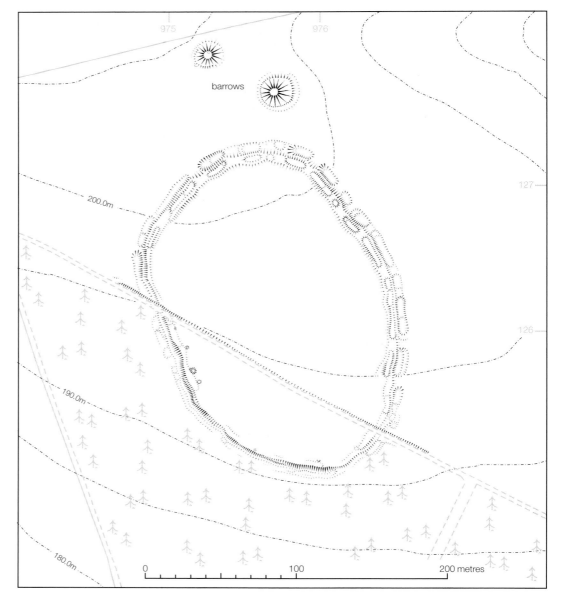

*Figure 3.10*
*Barkhale Camp in West Sussex is one of the few enclosures preserved as earthworks where the bank segments are precisely the same length as the ditch segments. Although some stretches of the ditch show signs of recutting, the original length of the bank segments appears to have been deliberately maintained. The part of the enclosure to the south of the track lay in woodland until 1978 and is consequently less well preserved.*

At the majority of these sites, relatively few of the causeways in the ditches would have allowed direct access into the interior of the enclosure. If the small proportion of causewayed enclosures preserved as earthworks is truly equivalent to those recorded as cropmarks, then it may be that too much emphasis has been placed on the 'permeable' design of the boundary ditches and the supposed multiple points of entry. Banks may have played a role of equal or greater importance than the ditches in defining the perimeters of causewayed enclosures: access may have been much more restricted than the frequent causeways in the ditches would suggest. The number of entrances is an issue that will be revisited below.

On the basis of the volume of material available from the ditches, it has been calculated that if the banks at Briar Hill were more or less continuous, they could originally have been approximately 1m high and 2m wide (Bamford 1985, 39). The largest banks in England now survive to only 0.5m high, although the outer downs-lope faces are sometimes considerably more pronounced (Fig 3.12). In most cases, erosion has caused them to spread to widths of up to 6m. Some banks that have been excavated have proved to survive as little more than rises in the natural bedrock and overlying ploughsoil, since the bedrock had been protected from erosion and ploughing by the overlying mass of the bank (*see* eg Drewett 1977, 205; Mercer 1980a, 46; Bedwin 1984, 14).

In some cases where a bank that survives well has been excavated, for example at Windmill Hill and Robin Hood's Ball, it seems to have been constructed simply as a dump of the material excavated from the ditch (Smith 1959, 154; 1965, 5–6; Thomas 1964, 10). Early excavators suggested that the dumps of chalk rubble may have been deliberately grouted with chalk mud to create a more stable mass (eg Curwen 1936, 66). Observations of the experimental earthwork on Overton Down, however, indicate that a process of concretion occurs naturally after about thirty years, both in the bank and in the ditch deposits (Jewell and Dimbleby 1966, 319; Bell *et al* 1996, 74).

From certain enclosures, including those at Windmill Hill and Orsett, there is evidence that the turf was stripped from the

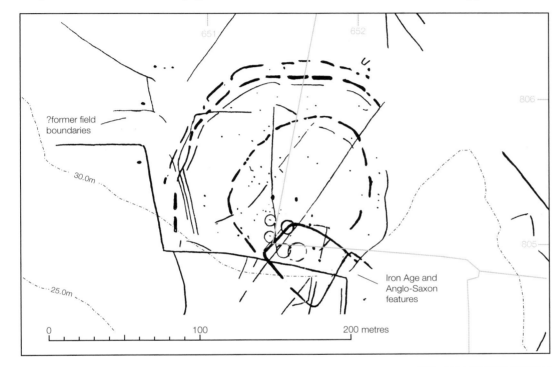

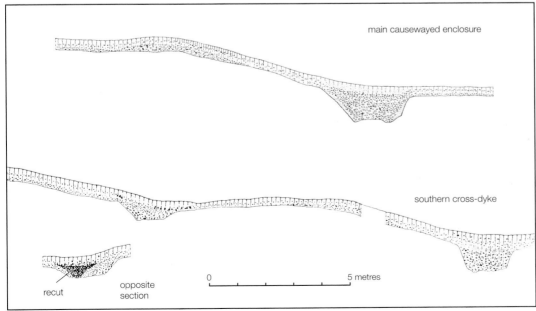

*Figure 3.11*
*The outer circuits of the causewayed enclosure at Orsett in Essex were initially described as corresponding closely to each other, both in general layout and in their minor irregularities (St Joseph 1973). This prompted the suggestion, supported by subsequent excavation, that they had been built on either side of a single central bank (see Fig 1.5; Hedges and Buckley 1978). Yet the ditches correspond no more closely than those where there were certainly two banks, even when the circuits were dug at different dates. Other interpretations of the form of the perimeter at Orsett are therefore possible.*

*Figure 3.12*
*Sections through the perimeter of the main causewayed enclosure on Hambledon Hill and the adjacent 'southern cross-dyke', from drawings by Desmond Bonney held in Dorset County Museum. Note the negligible height of the banks — some of the best preserved in England! The RCHME survey of 1959 and Bonney's excavated sections are important because they record the condition of the earthworks immediately prior to modern ploughing in 1964, when two-thirds of the main causewayed enclosure was levelled.*

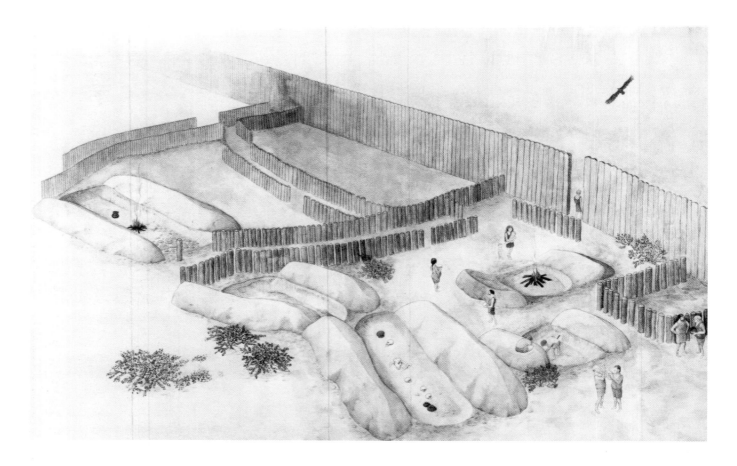

*Figure 3.13*
*Reconstruction of one of*
*the palisaded enclosures*
*adjoining the causewayed*
*enclosure at Sarup in*
*Denmark. Although there*
*are no direct parallels in*
*England for the elaborate*
*timber structures found at*
*Sarup, there are*
*indications that similar*
*principles may have lain*
*behind timber screens such*
*as that found behind one of*
*the entrances into the*
*enclosure at Orsett (Hedges*
*and Buckley 1978, fig 14),*
*and the so-called 'barbican'*
*outside the entrance into the*
*Stepleton enclosure on*
*Hambledon Hill. (Niels*
*Andersen and Louis*
*Hilmar)*

intended course of the bank immediately prior to its construction, perhaps to construct a wall of stacked turves to stabilise the loose material (Smith 1959, 154; Hedges and Buckley 1978, 234). A late phase of the bank at Crickley Hill in Gloucestershire was reinforced by a series of interlocking cells built of stone, a technique reminiscent of the Neolithic chambered tombs found in the Cotswold-Severn region (Dixon 1988, 82 and fig 4.4). At a number of other causewayed enclosures, excavation has revealed evidence for timber structures. These may have served as simple revetments for the banks, but they may have projected well above the banks to form palisades, as discussed below.

## Timber structures

Most evidence for the various forms of timber structure that may have accompanied the banks and ditches has been revealed by excavation. It has been suggested that some palisades show typological links with

causewayed enclosures on the European mainland (Hedges and Buckley 1978, 250–2), but the arrangement in England is generally less complex. At Sarup in Denmark and Calden in Germany, for example, the palisades accompanying the banks and ditches formed a maze-like series of outworks and small annexes (Fig 3.13; Andersen 1997, figs 16, 17 and 29; Raetzel-Fabian and Kappel 1991, 3). Such elaborate structures cannot be identified with certainty elsewhere in England, but it has been suggested that the undated postholes surrounding a segment of ditch at The Trundle may have supported a similar structure (Bradley 1993, 87). A concentration of postholes next to the perimeter of the Stepleton enclosure on Hambledon Hill was interpreted by the excavator of the site as a 'barbican' flanking the entrance, but may alternatively represent a palisaded annexe or even a later structure (*see* Fig 3.20; Mercer 1988, 100 and fig 5.3). In general, it would appear that the use of timber was simply one of the basic constructional elements used at

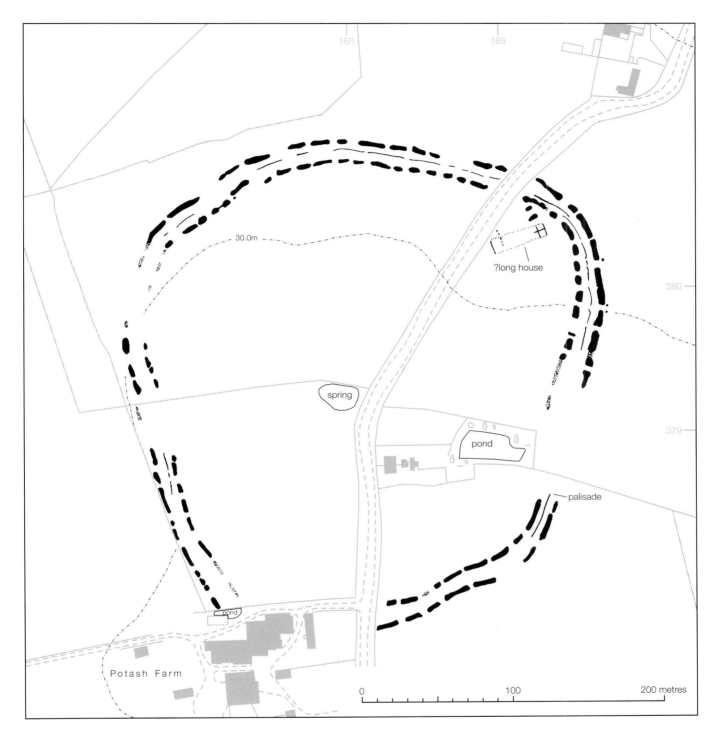

*Figure 3.14*
*The palisade trench between the circuits of the causewayed enclosure at Freston in Suffolk appears to be more continuous than the ditches, suggesting that there can have been relatively few genuine entrances. It is possible that there may either have been a single bank between the ditches, as suggested by the excavators of the enclosure at Orsett, or two banks, of which only the outer had a timber reinforcement. What appears to be a Neolithic long house in the north-eastern quadrant of the interior may be contemporary with the enclosure, but Anglo-Saxon halls are similar in form.*

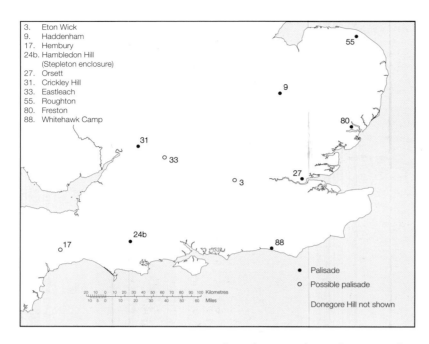

3.   Eton Wick
9.   Haddenham
17.  Hembury
24b. Hambledon Hill
     (Stepleton enclosure)
27.  Orsett
31.  Crickley Hill
33.  Eastleach
55.  Roughton
80.  Freston
88.  Whitehawk Camp

●  Palisade
○  Possible palisade

Donegore Hill not shown

*Figure 3.15*
*Distribution of*
*causewayed enclosures*
*with timber palisades and*
*other timber structures.*

causewayed enclosures throughout north-western Europe.

At Hambledon Hill, a section of the innermost bank and ditch of the triple causewayed linear earthwork that joined and in part replaced the circuit of the Stepleton enclosure was found to have been deliberately set on fire, apparently in an attack. The carbonised wood preserved good evidence for the way in which the timber revetment had been constructed (Mercer 1980a, 51; 1980b; 1985; 1988, 101–5). The structure comprised a frame of oak posts supporting panels of hazel wattle, perhaps standing as much as 3m high (*see* Fig 7.4). A similar structure may have been added to the outer circuit of the causewayed enclosure on Raddon Hill in Devon, although this may prove to be of Iron Age date (*see* Fig 5.2; Gent and Knight 1995). It has been calculated that the construction of the causewayed linear earthwork on Hambledon Hill might have required around 10,000 large timbers (Mercer 1988, 101). As Roger Mercer pointed out, this estimate clearly has significant implications for the understanding of the organisation of labour and the effects of the construction of the complex on its environs. Excavations of the bank at Donegore Hill in County Antrim indicate that some sections were accompanied by a continuous palisade (*see* Fig 5.3; Mallory 1993). At Whitehawk Camp in East Sussex and at the enclosures at Dorstone Hill and at Crickley Hill, isolated

pits and discontinuous lines of postholes discovered through excavation have been interpreted as evidence for timber palisades (Curwen 1954, 77; Pye 1967–9; Dixon 1988, fig 4.4). Alternatively, in some cases they may represent timber-built circuits pre-dating the construction of the earthworks (Thomas 1964, 12; Smith 1965, 28; contra Malone 1989, 54). This raises the possibility that some enclosures may never have acquired earthworks at all. Indeed, an earlier Neolithic enclosure at Lyles Hill, near Donegore Hill in County Antrim, seems to have been defined solely by a timber palisade, although it has been suggested that a levelled bank and ditch may yet await discovery (Simpson and Gibson 1989). At Hembury, a line of postholes runs along the outer edge of the ditch of the outer circuit (Fig 2.20; Liddell 1935, plate 25), perhaps indicating that there was a timber barrier not precisely contemporary with the earthworks.

It is possible that the banks of many other enclosures were reinforced or embellished by timber structures. If the timbers rested in very shallow postholes, however, or were held in place entirely by the bank so that they did not penetrate the original ground surface at all, little or no trace of them could be detected. Even at those causewayed enclosures best preserved as earthworks, no evidence for timber structures can be identified through surface survey. At certain sites, aerial survey has identified narrow, nearly continuous ditches, which may have been foundation trenches for timber palisades. At Freston in Suffolk, traces of a palisade trench lie midway between a closely spaced pair of ditches, perhaps on the line of a central earthen bank (Fig 3.14). At Roughton in Norfolk and Haddenham in Cambridgeshire, palisade slots lie around 6m behind the edge of the ditch, perhaps reinforcing the rear of an earthen bank (*see* Fig 6.7). There are hints that the palisade trench, like the banks of many of those enclosures preserved as earthworks, was discontinuous, but with less frequent interruptions than existed in the ditch (*see also* Evans 1988b, 133; Mordant and Mordant 1988, fig 13.3).

In a few instances, palisades may have been free-standing, unaccompanied by any bank. At Orsett, for example, the absence of assymetrical silting in the inner of the outer two ditch circuits suggested that there had been not been a bank along the line of the palisade, which lies about 3m back from the edge of the ditch (Hedges and Buckley 1978, 236). At Haddenham, the variation in the distance between the edge of the ditch and the palisade trench (between 2m and 11m) initially suggested to the excavator that a bank could not have followed the same course and, therefore, that there was perhaps no bank at all (*see* Fig 4.11; Evans 1988b, 130–5). Excavations showed that the timbers were up to 0.3m in diameter and therefore possibly up to 3m in height. Other interpretations of the evidence are possible in both cases, however. At Orsett, the palisade may have fronted a bank, thus reducing the silting which was recorded from the turf-revetted bank between the ditch circuits. The west side of the enclosure at Haddenham was interpreted by the excavator as its front (Fig 4.11), and on that side there may simply have been a broader level berm between the ditch and a bank fronted by the palisade.

It has been suggested that the majority of these continuous internal palisades lie in the east of England (Evans 1988b, 140 and Fig 3.15). Among the low-lying enclosures in the Upper Thames Valley, however, the innermost circuit at Eastleach may represent a massive continuous palisade (*see* Figs 1.7 and 3.18). What appears to be an almost continuous palisade trench has also been recorded as a cropmark outside the outer ditch at Eton Wick in Berkshire, but a small-scale excavation was unable to confirm its purpose or its relationship to the main earthworks (Ford 1991–3, 30). There are also a few possible examples further west, at the sites recorded as cropmarks at Norton in Glamorganshire and at Icomb Hill in Gloucestershire. Excavation of the causewayed enclosure on Donegore Hill suggests that the palisade may have accompanied the bank on the west side of the circuit, but lain several metres behind it on the east – if the palisade was contemporary with the earthworks at all (*see* Fig 5.3; Mallory 1993). More importantly, it is possible that the discontinuous lines of postholes recorded along the lines of banks elsewhere in England, such as those at Crickley Hill and Robin Hood's Ball, may have provided support for essentially very similar timber structures. If the evidence for the banks was not so clear, the lines of postholes might be more readily comparable with the continuous palisades in eastern England.

# Entrances

As noted above, the banks of those causewayed enclosures preserved as earthworks are generally more continuous than the adjacent ditches. This implies that there were probably far fewer entrances into the interior than the numerous causeways in the ditches might suggest. Even at the few sites where earthworks are well preserved, however, it is usually difficult to identify definite entrances with confidence. Any or all of those causeways whose positions coincide in both the ditches and the banks may have allowed people to pass directly into the interior.

At most causewayed enclosures where formal entrances can be identified, there generally seem to have been less than five and most often only one (Fig 3.16). Inward or outward deflections in the course of a circuit often seem to have been intended to emphasise their positions (Evans 1988b, 139; 1988c, 90 and fig 8.2). For example, despite the rather irregular overall plan of the enclosure at Haddenham, the western side is much straighter, with a slight in-turn in the ditch segments and palisade on either side of a broad central causeway (*see* Fig 4.11). Another possible in-turned entrance lies at the apex of the south-western corner and an out-turned one at the south-eastern corner. The plan of the straighter western side suggested, however, that it may have been designed as a frontal 'façade' flanking the most important entrance (Evans 1988b, 139). There are several other sites that may have been comparable in this respect. The causewayed enclosure on Court Hill and the inner circuit at Staines in Surrey (Figs 3.3 and 3.17) are both almost D-shaped in plan, apparently with single in-turned entrances midway along the straighter sides. The inner circuit at Windmill Hill and the inner two circuits at Eastleach in Gloucestershire (Fig 3.18) are kidney shaped in their overall plans, apparently so that the overall design should emphasise the positions of single entrances at the apex of the concave sides. In some cases, in-turned ditch terminals along the length of otherwise smoothly curving circuits suggest that certain causeways were more important than others. Single in-turned entrances can be distinguished at the enclosures recorded by aerial survey at Burford and Eynsham and by earthwork survey at Halnaker Hill in West Sussex (Fig 1.3 and *see* Fig 8.12).

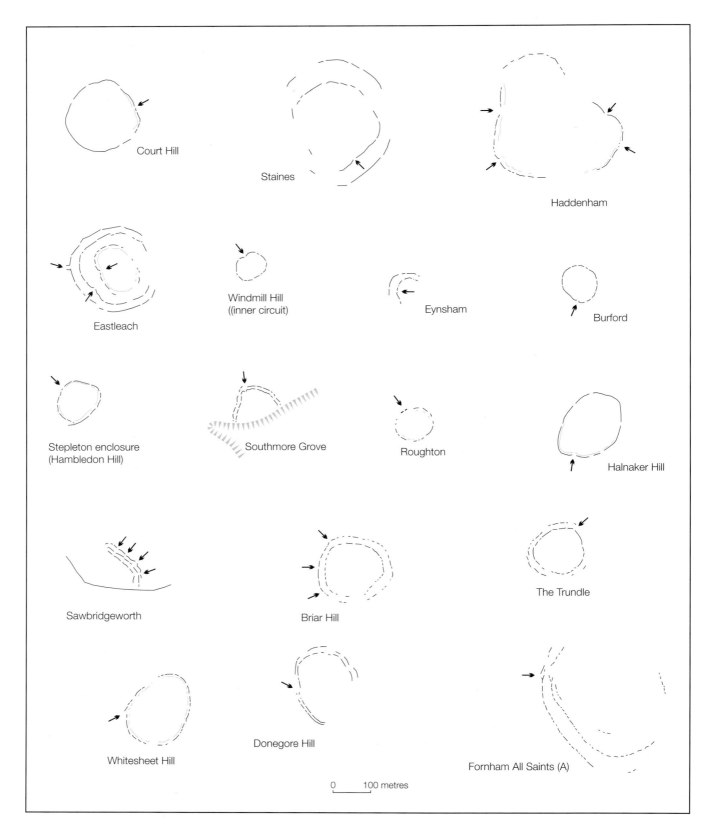

*Figure 3.16*
*Principal entrance causeways, as suggested by the plans of the enclosures.*

Three of the four probable entrances in the outermost of the three ditch circuits recorded as cropmarks at Sawbridgeworth appear to be emphasised in this way, while the fourth is out-turned (*see* Fig 5.18). Among the other probable entrances flanked by slightly out-turned ditch segments are one excavated on the north-west of the outer circuit at Briar Hill and one suggested by earthwork survey on the north-eastern side of the inner circuit of The Trundle (*see* Figs 4.4 and 8.6).

There are several more unusual entrances. On the northern side of the enclosure at Southmore Grove, the inner circuit of ditch recorded as a cropmark has an entrance flanked by typical in-turned terminals (*see* Fig 5.23). This coincides with a chicane-like offset between the terminals of the outer circuit, which perhaps corresponded to a bank intended to screen the interior of the enclosure from view, or to funnel the approach. A similar design may be evident in the plans of the western sides of the enclosures on Donegore Hill and Whitesheet Hill (*see* Figs 5.3 and 8.3) and

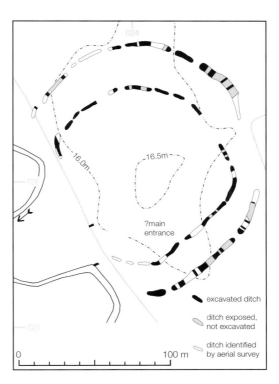

*Figure 3.17*
*Following extensive excavation of the causewayed enclosure at Staines in Surrey, where no earthworks survived, it was suggested that there may have been at least seven points of entry through the inner circuit (see also Fig 7.5). The plan would suggest that there may have been a single principal entrance midway along the straighter south-east side, flanked by in-turned ditch terminals as at many other sites. (Based on Robertson-Mackay 1987, fig 11)*

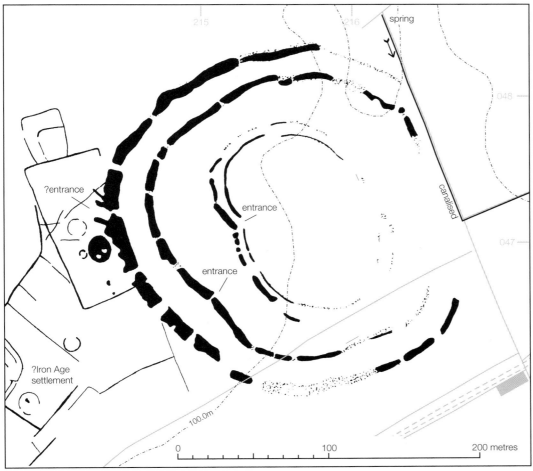

*Figure 3.18*
*The causewayed enclosure at Eastleach in Gloucestershire. The entrance through the two inner circuits (the inner is possibly a massive palisade trench) is relatively simple to identify on the basis of the plan: the kidney-shaped design is very similar to that of the inner circuit at Windmill Hill. The third circuit seems to have a similar plan, if less pronounced, but the probable entrance is slightly offset from that of the inner circuits. The entrance through the outermost circuit may be the causeway flanked by the broadest segments of the ditch. Note the two narrower out-turned ditches on either side of the causeway, perhaps indicating that there were timber palisades extending outwards like antennae.*

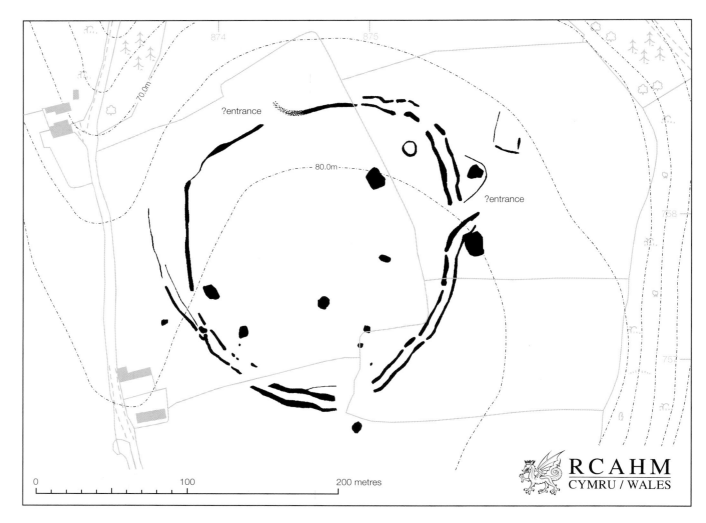

?entrance

80.0m

?entrance

RCAHM
CYMRU / WALES

0    100    200 metres

*Figure 3.19*
*The possible causewayed*
*enclosure at Norton in*
*Glamorganshire, recognised*
*in 1996, is only the second*
*such monument to be*
*identified in Wales (Driver*
*1997). The siting of the*
*enclosure and the form of*
*parts of the ditches are*
*convincing and a small*
*quantity of worked flint has*
*been noted on the surface.*
*The long out-turned ditches*
*on the east, north and*
*perhaps west are, however,*
*difficult to parallel at other*
*causewayed enclosures; a*
*later date cannot yet be*
*ruled out. (Crown*
*copyright: RCAHMW)*

at two or three points in the circuits of the possible causewayed enclosure at Norton (Fig 3.19; Driver 1997). On the north-west side of the earlier part of the enclosure at Fornham All Saints in Suffolk, sharply out-turned lengths of ditch in both the widely spaced circuits may have formed outworks (*see* Fig 4.25). These are reminiscent of the outworks known as 'crabs claws' found at certain causewayed enclosures on the European mainland, particularly in western France (*see* eg Andersen 1997, fig 271).

In other cases, the earthworks flanking an entrance may have been enlarged in order to emphasise its position (Mercer 1980a, 49–51; 1980b; Bamford 1985, 39). For example, both the bank and the ditch of the innermost circuit at The Trundle increase in size on either side of the out-turned entrance. The present condition of the earthworks in this instance apparently reflects a genuine difference in their original size. At Eastleach, the outermost ditch broadens gradually

towards the probable entrance (Fig 3.18). At Roughton, a pair of much broader segments of ditch recorded through aerial survey on the north-western side of the enclosure may indicate the position of an entrance, although there are a number of other possibilities (*see* Fig 6.7). In the absence of clearer evidence from the plan, causeways that are simply broader than the others may be interpreted as entrances.

At a small number of sites, evidence for timber entrance structures has been discovered through excavation. The entrance excavated at Orsett (Figs 1.5 and 3.11; Hedges and Buckley 1978, fig 14) and the south-western entrance recorded by aerial survey at Haddenham (*see* Fig 4.11) seem to have been screened by in-turned lengths of palisade immediately behind the openings in the main circuit. A similar arrangement might account for the offset earthworks on either side of the suggested entrances at Donegore Hill, Southmore Grove and

Whitesheet Hill (*see* Figs 5.3, 5.23 and 8.3). At Crickley Hill and Whitehawk Camp, rows of postholes extending inwards from certain causeways were interpreted as entrance passages (*see* Figs 4.15 and 5.31; Curwen 1934, 105; Dixon 1988, fig 4.1). At the Stepleton enclosure on Hambledon Hill, a concentration of postholes was found outside the perimeter, adjacent to a broad causeway thought to be an entrance (Fig 3.20; Mercer 1988, 100 and fig 5.3). The structure was consequently interpreted as a 'barbican', but the plan of the earthworks suggests that another broad causeway, lying midway along the same side of the enclosure between slightly in-turned ditch terminals, may have been the actual entrance. The nature of the timber structure is therefore open to other interpretations (*see* above, this chapter: Timber structures).

Elsewhere, there may have been gateways of a more simple form. Two large pits recorded as cropmarks on either side of the south-eastern entrance at Haddenham are suggestive of a pair of postholes for a possible gate (*see* Fig 4.11), and excavation at Etton revealed a similar structure (Pryor 1998a, 57; 1998b). At Briar Hill and Hembury in Devon groups of pits have also been interpreted as evidence for gateways (Bamford 1985, 37; Liddell 1935, plate 21). At Billown on the Isle of Man, the approach to a probable gateway was found to have become worn and a cobbled surface had been laid across the causeway (Darvill 1998, fig 4). Where no entrance can be singled out on the basis of the plans, concentrations of artefacts in certain ditch terminals may denote the entrances, as has been suggested at Staines (Robertson-MacKay 1987, 38 and fig 11). It is arguably very difficult, however, to differentiate between these and other special deposits found elsewhere around the circuit.

It is also difficult to discern any pattern of orientation among the probable entrances. Francis Pryor, excavator of the causewayed enclosure at Etton, has noted

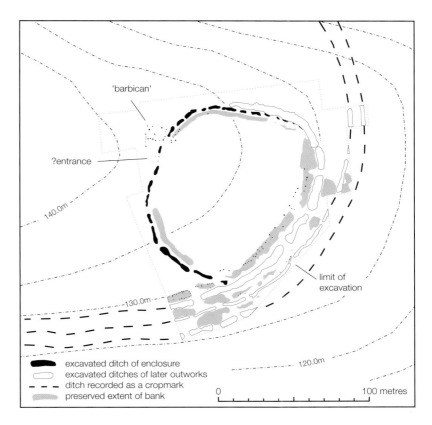

that the entrances face approximately west, east and north. The southern side of the circuit has been destroyed, but there are indications that there may have been a fourth entrance on that side (Pryor 1998a, 57; 1998b, 356). Generally, however, there is no trend towards any particular cosmological direction amongst cause-wayed enclosures, as has been suggested for long barrows and long houses (Ashbee 1984, fig 20; Hodder 1984, 63; 1990, 169–74). In some instances, discussed further below, the natural topography restricts the approach and the location of the entrances reflects this. There is little consistency in the orientation in relation to the topography amongst those enclosures where there is no obvious restriction to the choice of direction.

*Figure 3.20*
*The Stepleton enclosure on Hambledon Hill in Dorset, together with parts of the later outwork and the causewayed double bank and ditch known as the 'Hanford-Stepleton outwork'. Numerous pits and postholes were discovered in the interior, but only those thought relevant to the perimeter and entrance are shown here. Note the discrepancy between the position of the postholes interpreted as a 'barbican' and the central causeway between in-turned ditch segment. (Based on Mercer 1988, fig 5.3)*

# 4
# The forms of causewayed enclosures

## Classification: discerning order in diversity

The work of E C Curwen, Alexander Keiller and others in the 1920s and 1930s established a broad consensus with regard to the typical form of causewayed enclosures. Yet if causewayed enclosures at first appear straightforward to characterise, on closer consideration they prove just as difficult as any other type of prehistoric monument (Evans 1988a, 47–9). As described in Chapter 2, not everything with causewayed earthworks has turned out to be a causewayed enclosure; there are many enclosures included in the class that do not conform very closely to the stereotype. The simple constructional elements described in Chapter 3 were combined in various ways to produce a wide diversity of plan forms. Ironically, it cannot even be taken for granted that the earthworks were in all cases causewayed, or that they were always fully enclosed.

The aim of classification is to identify characteristics typical of the class and to highlight the differences exhibited by individual monuments, in order to understand better the ideas that are embodied both in the class and the individual. Inevitably, schemes of classification have generally been based upon those features that survive and stand out at present. There is an implicit assumption in the archaeological literature written when these monuments were first being recognized and defined, (which has continued up to the present) that characteristics that can be detected today were the most important elements to Neolithic people as well. It is important not to lose sight of the fact that those who built and used them may have distinguished between causewayed enclosures with similar forms according to physical characteristics that can no longer be detected, or according to different functions – for example, sites for feasting or trading, for use in spring or autumn, for the living or the dead. Their forms were not dictated by blueprints and any attempt to impose order on such diversity risks painting a misleading picture of homogeneity (Bradley 1993, 71–2; Bestley 1993, 91–2). Nor did they remain static, but changed in form, function and meaning over the course of time (Thomas 1991, 32–41; Bradley 1998b, 68–82).

Most prehistoric monuments are initially identified and classified on the basis of their form as recorded by aerial or surface survey. Occasionally, this evidence can be misleading. For example, a cropmark at Eye and Dunsden in Oxfordshire is quite convincing as a causewayed enclosure (Fig 4.1), yet excavations carried out in 1974 on the site could find no evidence for the existence of the monument (Oxford Archaeological Unit 1974). On the other hand, excavations undertaken at Ramsgate in Kent in 1997–8 of part of an enclosure first detected as a cropmark (Fig 4.2) not only proved it to be a causewayed enclosure, but also showed it to have more circuits than suspected from the air (Shand 1998).

With these potential problems in mind, classification of the monuments according to their form, especially as recorded by

*Figure 4.1*
*Cropmarks in the parish of Eye and Dunsden in Oxfordshire appear to represent part of a causewayed enclosure with two widely spaced circuits. A trial trench dug by the Oxford Archaeological Unit failed to find any evidence to support the existence of the monument, but the location of the trench was imprecisely recorded. (NMR 211/357)*

survey, may seem an insecure foundation for understanding. Of the sixty-six sites in England accepted as certain or probable causewayed enclosures, thirty-six – just over half of the total – have been excavated to some degree. Many of these excavations were small trial trenches, however, some were carried out prior to the recognition of recutting at Windmill Hill (Smith 1959; 1965), several have not been fully published and six were unable to advance the interpretation reached from the survey evidence in any significant respect. Only eleven sites (around 15 per cent of the total) have seen modern excavation of reasonably large areas. Until such time as excavation provides more complete information about a larger number of causewayed enclosures, survey offers the only form of readily comparable evidence. Attributes of the plans, such as the nature of the constructional elements, the size and shape of the area enclosed and the number of circuits are amongst the few characteristics where links can be made between excavated and unexcavated monuments.

David Wilson suggested that there may have been at least four different types of causewayed enclosure, based on their locations, the numbers of circuits and the presence of outworks (Wilson 1975). Since the publication of Rog Palmer's work in 1976, his typology, which is based on the number and spacing of the circuits, has provided the most commonly used benchmark (Palmer 1976 and Fig 4.3). This chapter presents an overview of the forms of causewayed enclosures and discusses the principal issues relating to the classification of sites according to their physical attributes.

## Plan forms

The nature of the planning of prehistoric monuments is central to a dispute over the form of the enclosure on Briar Hill in Northamptonshire (Fig 4.4). The excavators of the site suggested that the circular inner circuit and the outer pair of circuits, which are approximately circular, were deliberately laid out eccentrically in relation to each other, following a design based upon principles of symmetry, proportion and geometry (Chapman 1985, 57; Bamford 1985, 132–3). This proposal was rejected out of hand by the excavator of the causewayed enclosure at Haddenham in Cambridgeshire, who concluded that the

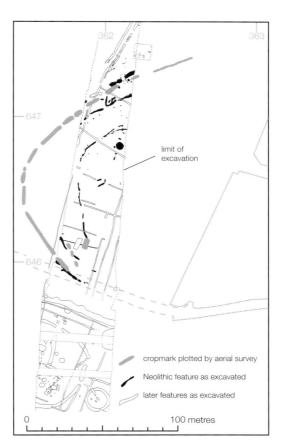

limit of excavation

cropmark plotted by aerial survey

Neolithic feature as excavated

later features as excavated

0                    100 metres

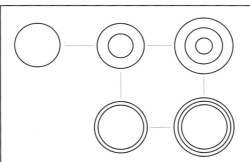

plan of the enclosure at Briar Hill was the eventual outcome of several phases of construction. Furthermore, he argued that it is anachronistic to suggest that the principles of classical and modern architecture and in particular precise mathematical accuracy would have been important to the builders of causewayed enclosures (Evans 1988a, 85–6). By way of comparison, the plans of many later Neolithic stone circles seem to have been laid out by eye (Barnatt and Moir 1984, 204). This technique was evidently sufficiently precise to create the appearance of circularity to those who encountered the monument in reality, rather than on paper as a two-dimensional plan.

*Figure 4.2*
*In 1997–8, construction of a new road across Chalk Hill at Ramsgate in Kent led to the excavation of a segment of a causewayed enclosure identified in 1975 and plotted by RCHME in 1996. The excavation revealed the presence of further causewayed ditches, some so shallow that they had not shown as cropmarks. This highlights both the strengths and weaknesses of archaeological survey: aerial survey was crucial in indicating the extent of the monument, its probable date and, therefore, the nature of the deposits which could be expected. However, reliance on the survey plan alone would in this case have provided a misleading picture of the details. (Based on information supplied by Canterbury Archaeological Trust)*

*Figure 4.3*
*Rog Palmer classified causewayed enclosures according to the number and spacing of their circuits. The fundamental problem with this approach is that it treats the monuments as static entities. There is evidence both in the form of certain plans and from excavations that the plans of causewayed enclosures changed through the modification of existing circuits and the addition of new ones. Palmer's system compares only the final forms of causewayed enclosure and thus does not necessarily compare like with like.*

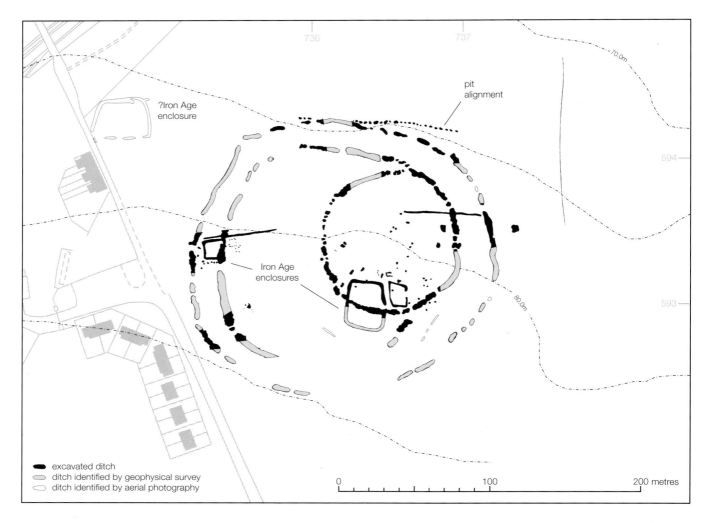

Figure 4.4
*Following extensive excavation of the causewayed enclosure at Briar Hill in Northamptonshire,
the excavators suggested that the ditches represented a single phase of construction, built with
precision according to a plan based on axial symmetry and proportion (Bamford 1985;
Chapman 1985). Both these suggestions have been dismissed (Evans 1988a, 85–6; Bradley
1998b, 79). Only the western half of the inner circuit, referred to by the excavators as the
'spiral arm' seems to show any concern with mathematical geometry and this may represent the
conversion of the original circuit to a more circular enclosure at a later date. In its initial form
the causewayed enclosure may have had a roughly circular or slightly D-shaped plan, the
straighter side perhaps coinciding with the three principal entrances. (Based on Bamford 1985)*

Figure 4.5 (facing page)
*The enclosure around the later Neolithic barrow known as Duggleby Howe in North Yorkshire.
The perimeter is remarkable in that it maintains its circular plan in spite of its large size and the
fairly steep gradient. Fairly precise planning may have been involved. Yet it remains uncertain
whether the enclosure is truly a causewayed enclosure. The plan is dissimilar from typical causewayed
enclosures in several respects; indeed, there are no known typical causewayed enclosures in Yorkshire.
In a local context, the monuments which perhaps have most in common with the Duggleby enclosure
are later Neolithic henges with causewayed ditches, such as that at Newton Kyme. While the location
of the monument, on a slope overlooking the headwaters of the Gypsey Race, has much in common
with some causewayed enclosures, it also has parallels amongst some henges.*

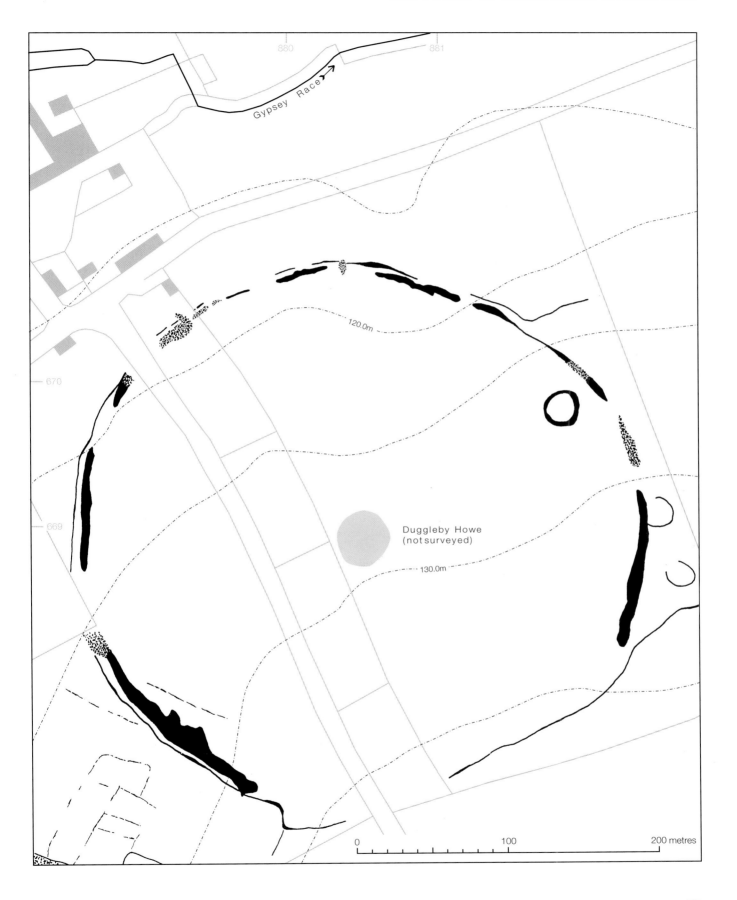

Duggleby Howe
(not surveyed)

Very few causewayed enclosures are actually perfectly circular. Indeed, there are reasons to suspect that some of those that are may represent a rather different type of monument (*see* Chapter 8: A tradition of enclosures?). For example, excavation has shown that the perfectly circular enclosure at Flagstones in Dorset was probably built several hundred years later than the majority of accurately dated causewayed enclosures (Healy 1997, 44 and table 1). Likewise, the perfectly circular enclosure at Duggleby Howe in North Yorkshire (Fig 4.5) is unusually large and may have more in common with later Neolithic henges in that area. The enclosure at Melbourne in Cambridgeshire was initially interpreted as a possible causewayed enclosure (Palmer 1976, table 1), but it too arguably has closer affinities with henges (*see* Fig 8.1).

E C Curwen noted that most causewayed enclosures are oval in plan (Curwen 1930, 48). Whilst this observation still holds true, strictly speaking, there are several certain or very probable causewayed enclosures whose circuits are very nearly circular. Rather than being smoothly curved, however, they generally comprise a series of straight sections. Examples are the middle circuit at Windmill Hill in Wiltshire (Fig 2.8), the pair of circuits at Great Wilbraham in Cambridgeshire (Fig 4.7) and the three closely spaced

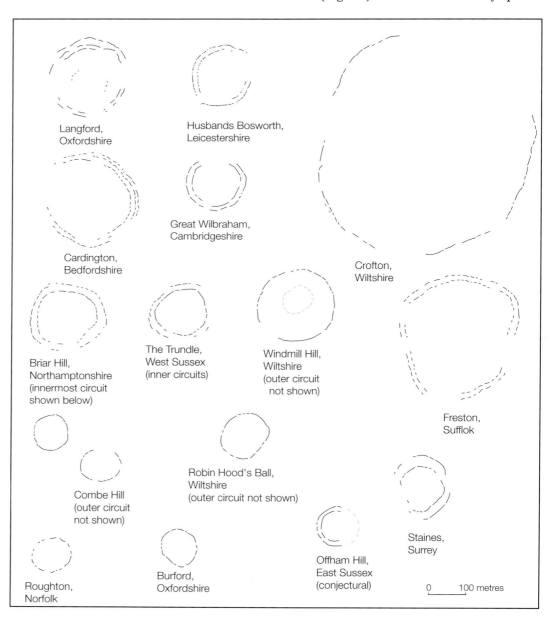

Langford, Oxfordshire

Husbands Bosworth, Leicestershire

Cardington, Bedfordshire

Great Wilbraham, Cambridgeshire

Crofton, Wiltshire

Briar Hill, Northamptonshire (innermost circuit shown below)

The Trundle, West Sussex (inner circuits)

Windmill Hill, Wiltshire (outer circuit not shown)

Freston, Sufflok

Combe Hill (outer circuit not shown)

Robin Hood's Ball, Wiltshire (outer circuit not shown)

Staines, Surrey

Roughton, Norfolk

Burford, Oxfordshire

Offham Hill, East Sussex (conjectural)

0    100 metres

*Figure 4.6*
*A range of near-circular causewayed enclosures demonstrates the nature of planning in the earlier Neolithic. None is perfectly circular, but most could well have appeared circular when encountered on the ground. Even the distinct angles evident in the plan of the enclosure at Freston in Suffolk may not have been apparent on the ground, due to the great size of the monument and the slightly uneven topography.*

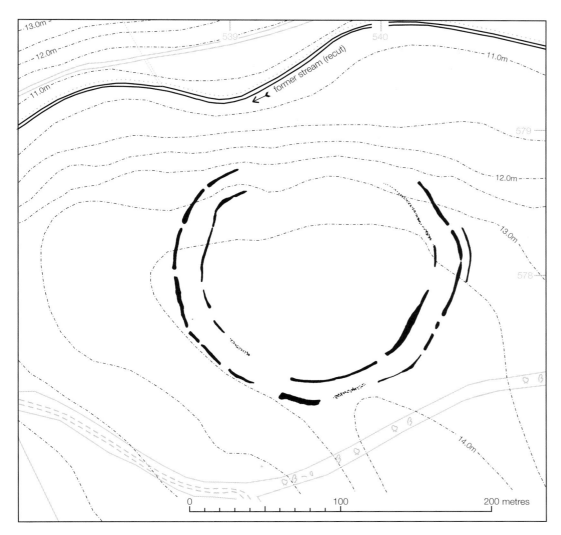

*Figure 4.7*
*The ditch of the*
*causewayed enclosure at*
*Great Wilbraham in*
*Cambridgeshire is very*
*close to being circular, but*
*comprises a series of*
*straight lengths, perhaps*
*constructed by separate*
*gangs of workers. Traces*
*of the ditch are absent*
*closer to the stream valley*
*where geological conditions*
*are unfavourable, but*
*excavations in 1975–6*
*demonstrated that the*
*circuits continue.*

circuits at Langford in Oxfordshire and at Cardington in Bedfordshire (*see* Figs 7.3 and 8.9). If complete, the two circuits on Offham Hill in East Sussex may also have been nearly circular, rather than incomplete as suggested by the excavator of the site (Drewett 1977, 203). It is impossible to be certain, however, since the eastern side of the monument has been entirely destroyed by quarrying (Fig 4.8). The plan of the enclosure at Crofton in Wiltshire is also remarkably near to a circle, given its great size and the undulating topography of its setting (*see* Fig 4.21). All these monuments are sufficiently close to being circular to suggest that their plans were broadly agreed in advance, with the intention of giving the appearance of circularity (Fig 4.6).

Some circuits are more obviously elliptical, for instance the outer one on Windmill Hill and the inner one on Combe Hill in East Sussex (Fig 2.8 and *see* Fig 8.5).

Yet if the view is accepted that earlier Neolithic planning was not greatly concerned by mathematical accuracy, their forms may also have been intended to give the impression of circularity. At Windmill Hill, two parallel lines of topsoil discovered under the bank of the outer circuit were interpreted as guides for its construction, although they were not found elsewhere around the circuit (Smith 1959, 155). It may be appropriate to think of various other oval enclosures as effectively circular: for example, those at Burford in Oxfordshire, Roughton in Norfolk, the inner circuits of Robin Hood's Ball in Wiltshire and The Trundle in West Sussex (*see* Figs 1.3, 6.7, 1.4 and 8.6). Indeed, the outer pair of circuits at Briar Hill (that is, the cause-wayed enclosure disregarding the more perfectly circular inner circuit) exhibit the same kind of approximate circularity (Fig 4.4). Modern surveys show such

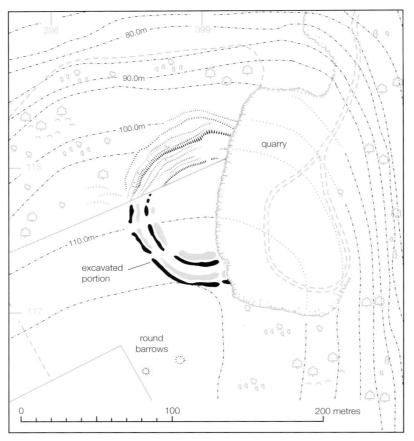

quarry

118

excavated
portion

round
barrows

117

0                100                200 metres

*Figure 4.8*
*Peter Drewett suggested*
*that the plan of the*
*causewayed enclosure at*
*Offham in East Sussex*
*might have been*
*incomplete, terminating at*
*the edge of the steep*
*natural scarp to the east.*
*Although certainty is*
*impossible, the new survey*
*evidence together with a*
*conjectural reconstruction*
*of the topography prior to*
*quarrying suggests that*
*the circuits may have been*
*complete and perhaps very*
*nearly circular. (Based on*
*Drewett 1977)*

enclosures to be less than perfect circles in plan, but the circuits may have appeared quite adequately circular when they survived in three dimensions. In passing, it is interesting to note that a sketch plan of the enclosure at Robin Hood's Ball by E C Curwen – an experienced fieldworker – portrayed the outer circuit as being virtually circular, although it is in fact one of the most angular in England (Curwen 1930, fig 6). In many cases, the probable entrances are the only points where the builders evidently rejected approximate circularity (Evans 1988b, 139).

Not all oval enclosures can have been intended to appear circular. In some instances this can again be attributed to the overriding importance of entrances. As described in Chapter 3, the inner circuits at Eastleach in Gloucestershire and at Windmill Hill in Wiltshire are emphatically kidney shaped, while the enclosure on Court Hill in West Sussex and the inner circuit at Staines in Surrey are D-shaped, apparently in order to emphasise the position of single entrances (Figs 3.3 and 3.17). As with those enclosures with approximately circular plans, some concept of the

plan must have been agreed in advance to achieve the final design. A considerable number of enclosures, such as those on Donegore Hill in County Antrim, on Whitesheet Hill in Wiltshire and at Alrewas in the valley of the River Trent are distinctly egg shaped (Fig 4.9 and *see* Figs 5.3 and 8.3). In the valley of the River Welland, three enclosures clustering within a 5km radius (Etton in Cambridgeshire, Uffington and Barholm in Lincolnshire) all share this plan form, and are also similar in size. In the valley of the River Nene, about 10km to the south, the enclosures at Southwick in Northamptonshire and Upton in Cambridgeshire are also quite similar (*see* Fig 6.3). The possible reasons behind this similarity in plan are discussed in Chapter 6: Regionalism in the British Isles. The egg-like shape does not tend to strike the modern eye as the outcome of planning in the same way as does an approximately circular plan. Yet it is sufficiently widespread amongst causewayed enclosures to suggest that it may have been deliberately intended, perhaps to create obvious axes within the central space. This may have allowed one end of the enclosure to be distinguished immediately, for example, as the front or back (Fleming 1972; Evans 1988c, 92).

Certain enclosures seem to indicate a rather different approach to planning from that evident at the sites discussed so far. At Northborough, for example, the circuits enclose a more or less oval area, but the alignments of the individual ditch segments are much more irregular, so that their course wavers erratically from side to side (*see* Fig 5.16). This may be a consequence of the episodic process of construction described in Chapter 3, which perhaps involved the digging of only a few ditch segments every year or so. Alternatively, it may simply be that the ditches were dug in order to avoid existing features, such as buildings or large trees (or tree stumps). Indeed, it is uncertain whether there was any plan agreed in advance as to what line the perimeter should follow. The recognition of broader chronological sequences in the plans of causewayed enclosures is discussed further below.

A few circuits are so markedly polygonal that it would be impossible to argue that the straight sides and distinct angles would not have been apparent on the ground. Examples are the enclosures at Haddenham in Cambridgeshire, which is roughly triangular, and at West Kington in Wiltshire,

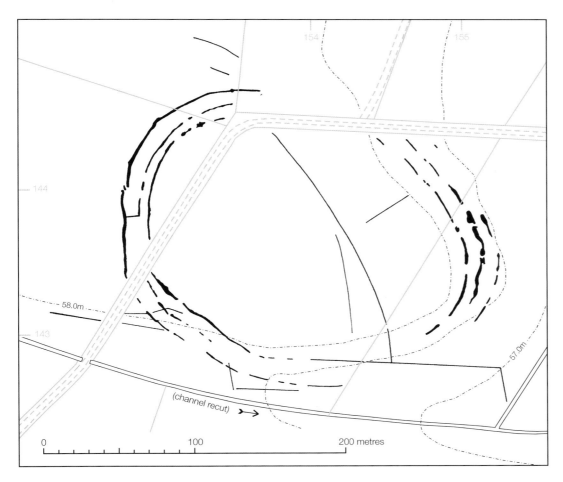

Figure 4.9
The causewayed
enclosure at Alrewas in
Staffordshire. The
egg-shaped plan of the
perimeter is not directly
constrained by the
topography or the course
of the adjacent stream
(which has been
artificially straightened at
a relatively recent date).
A considerable number of
other causewayed
enclosures have a similar
plan. The shape may
therefore have been
deliberately intended,
rather than simply an
accidental consequence of
the attempt to create an
approximate circle.

which appears quite close to being rectangular (Fig 4.11 and *see* Fig 7.2). These distinct changes of angle may also be products of the kind of *ad hoc* construction described above. In some cases, however, other factors were also important, such as the relationship of the enclosure to the topography and the development of the monuments over time. Both of these issues are discussed further below.

In 1978 the excavators of the causewayed enclosure at Orsett pointed out that of the forty-six enclosures identified at the time, only six (13 per cent of the total) had complete circuits (Hedges and Buckley 1978, 248). Since then, the number known to have complete or nearly complete circuits has grown to twenty-four (35 per cent of the present total). Indeed, there are hints that at least the inner circuit at Orsett may have been complete (*see* Fig 3.11). The proportion remains relatively small, however, still apparently supporting the theory that the process of creation may have been more important than the completion of the enclosures. In many cases, however, partial

circuits were completed by natural features such as steep slopes or rivers (*see* below). Uncleared woodland, or even hedges planted deliberately, may also have been used to mark boundaries, although this would be very difficult to detect in

Figure 4.10
The causewayed enclosure
at Cardington in
Bedfordshire. When
recorded by Palmer in
1976, the cropmarks only
allowed the eastern third
of the enclosure to be
mapped. The enclosure
was one of those Hedges
and Buckley (1978)
suggested was incomplete.
The almost circular
perimeter can now be seen
to have occupied a rise
approximately 2m above
the present height of the
nearby stream.
(Cambridge University
Collection of Air
Photographs; copyright
reserved: K17 AM 11)

*Figure 4.11*
*The causewayed enclosure at Haddenham in Cambridgeshire appears to have been orientated towards a former course of the River Ouse, with a broad formal entrance midway along its straighter western side. The excavator noted that the eastern perimeter corresponds to a very slight slope in the gravel rise (Evans 1988b, 139). The topography does seem to have influenced the form of the enclosure, though it did not necessarily 'complete' the broad gap in the perimeter in any physical sense. That the earthworks did not actually form a complete enclosure clearly has implications for how the monument could have been used.*

archaeological terms. Elsewhere, more recent activity such as quarrying has destroyed parts of the enclosures, making any reconstruction speculative. In other cases, such as the causewayed enclosure at Cardington (Fig 4.10), overlying deposits may have masked the archaeological features so as to reduce their ability to produce cropmarks, giving the impression of incomplete circuits. At Chalk Hill, Ramsgate (Fig 4.2) and at Burham in Kent, for example, the curvature of the arcs of causewayed ditch could well indicate that they actually form parts of complete circuits. It seems likely that the enclosure at Haddenham, despite its irregular plan, will in due course be proven to have had a complete circuit (Fig 4.11). If these sites are excluded, only about sixteen enclosures – less than a quarter of the total number – seem quite likely never to have had complete circuits. At Dorney in Buckinghamshire, Landbeach in Cambridgeshire and Eastry in Kent, the curvature of the arcs of causewayed ditch recorded by aerial survey is so slight that the boundaries may never have been

intended to form complete circuits (Fig 4.12). It is possible, therefore, that the use of certain causewayed enclosures did not require the space to be totally enclosed.

## Planning in relation to the topography

Isobel Smith commented that many of the upland enclosures were 'unconformable' in their relationship to the natural topography (Smith 1971, 92). In saying this, she was referring primarily to the causewayed enclosures in upland locations confirmed through excavation by that date, such as The Trundle, Whitehawk Camp and, of course, the enclosure she herself had worked upon at Windmill Hill. The curious relationship of these enclosures to the topography is discussed further in Chapter 5: Upland-oriented causewayed enclosures. The choice of topographical location, however, had some influence on the plans of around a quarter of the sixty-six causewayed enclosures known in England (Fig 4.13).

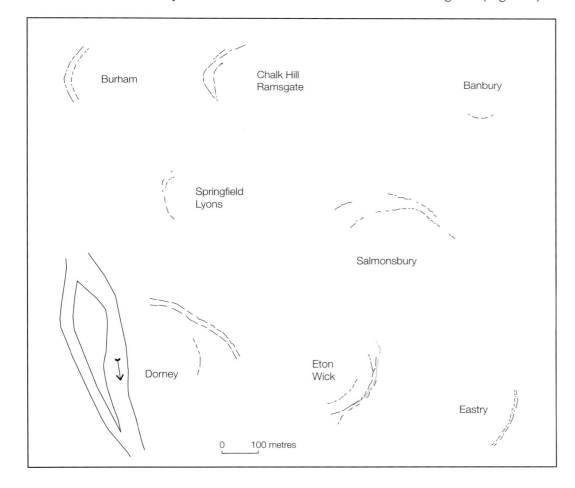

*Figure 4.12*
*At many sites, drift deposits of alluvial silt and colluvium (hillwash) may have partially buried the monuments, reducing the strength of the cropmarks. As at Orsett, it is often the downslope sides of the circuits that are absent, where overlying colluvial deposits might be expected to be thicker. In these examples, arcs of causewayed ditch may prove to represent parts of complete enclosure, but this would not be a safe assumption in every case.*

63

This is particularly true of causewayed enclosures in upland locations (other than those discussed by Smith), such as Birdlip Camp in Gloucestershire (Fig 4.14) and the enclosure on Dorstone Hill in Hereford and Worcester. These were built on steep-sided promontories so that only a relatively short length of earthwork across the neck of the spur was required to form a complete enclosure. Causewayed enclosures in similar locations in France, such as that at Catenoy overlooking the valley of the River Oise, are termed *éperons barrés*, meaning 'cut-off spurs' (*see* eg Blanchet and Martinez 1988, fig 8.3). Yet at both Hembury in Devon and Crickley Hill in Gloucestershire (Figs 2.20 and 4.15), the narrow spurs were not simply cut off by a barrier of the shortest possible length, built across the ridge. Instead, the earthworks seem to have turned well below the edge of the escarpment and run along the contours to form complete circuits. At Crickley Hill, the tip of the spur, which might be expected to be its 'inner sanctum', appears to have lain outside the enclosure. This suggests that in some instances, it was not only considered important that the perimeter should enclose completely, but also that the barriers forming it should be entirely artificial, regardless of the natural barriers available.

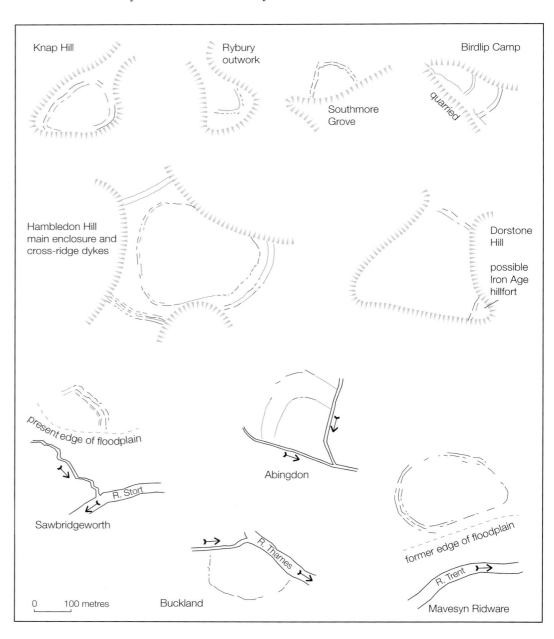

*Figure 4.13*
*The relationships of the plans of selected causewayed enclosures to the topography of their settings. Based on an impression of certain enclosures surviving as earthworks on the chalk uplands, the relationship of the monuments has often been considered bizarre, but a fair proportion relate directly to the topography.*

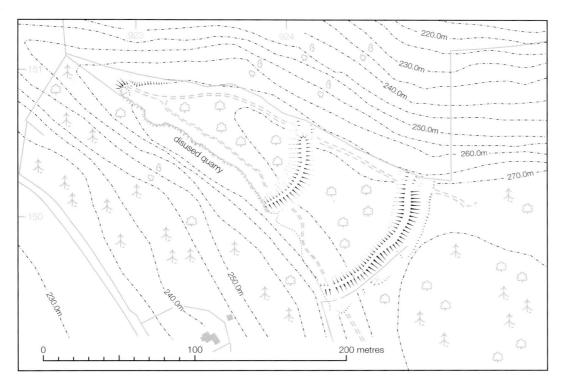

Figure 4.14
*Birdlip Camp (also known as The Peak Camp) in Gloucestershire lies less than 2km from the better known causewayed enclosure on Crickley Hill. The earthworks preserve only slight evidence for causeways in the outer ditch, while no trace of the inner ditch survives at all. The banks appear to have been nearly continuous, the outer probably having a single central entrance.*

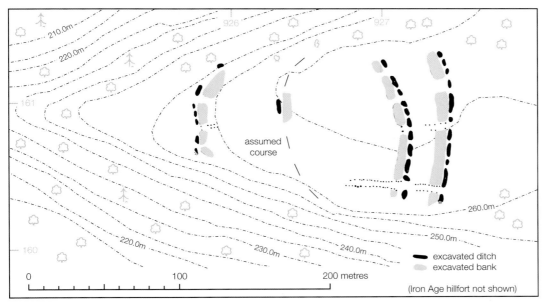

Figure 4.15
*The first phase of the causewayed enclosure at Crickley Hill in Gloucestershire differs strikingly from Birdlip Camp in its relationship to the topography. Despite the similar shape of the promontory, the perimeter does not appear to have incorporated the almost sheer escarpments, but instead formed an enclosure virtually independent of the topography. This seems to have left the tip of the promontory outside the enclosure, although it might be expected to have been the 'inner sanctum'. (Based on Dixon 1988, fig 4.1)*

Like the almost triangular enclosure on Knap Hill in Wiltshire, the somewhat angular plan of the main causewayed enclosure on Hambledon Hill in Dorset broadly respects the shape of the hilltop it occupies (Figs 2.7 and 4.16). Outside this main circuit, the narrow necks of land to the south and east are crossed by double lines of causewayed banks and ditches, which end at the very edges of the steep intervening coombs. These have been described as 'cross-ridge dykes' (Mercer 1988). A parallel can be found in the outlying length of causewayed bank and ditch that crosses the ridge to the east of Rybury Camp in Wiltshire (*see* Fig 8.7). On Whitesheet Hill too, at least one of the cross-ridge dykes on the spurs surrounding the causewayed enclosure might be interpreted as Neolithic on the basis of the form of the earthworks (Fig 8.3), but the dating evidence recovered by trial excavation is not clear-cut (Rawlins *et al* forthcoming).

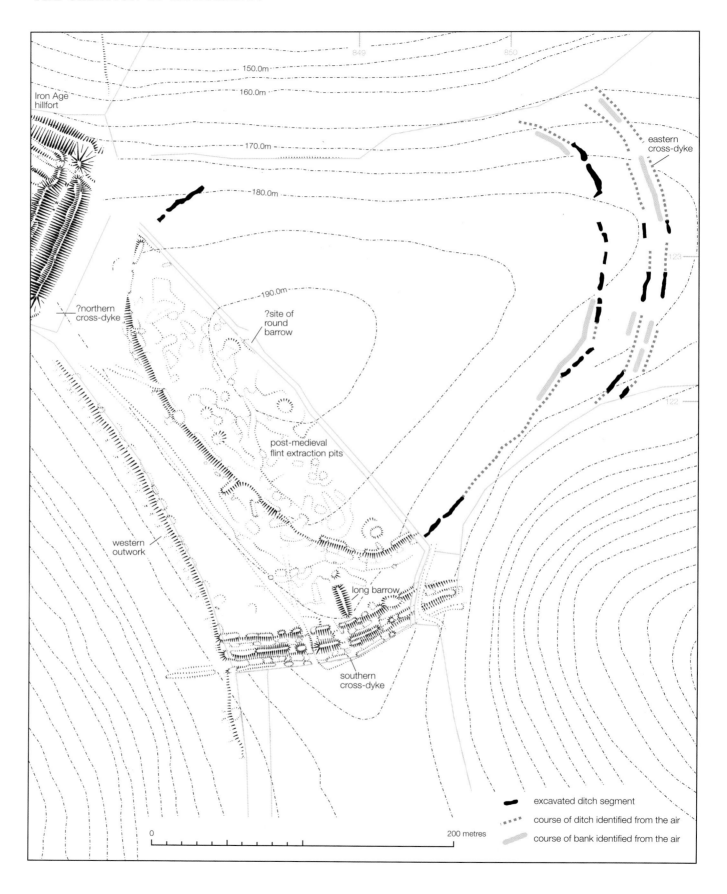

Iron Age
hillfort

150.0m
160.0m
170.0m
180.0m
190.0m

eastern
cross-dyke

?northern
cross-dyke

?site of
round
barrow

post-medieval
flint extraction pits

western
outwork

long barrow

southern
cross-dyke

excavated ditch segment

course of ditch identified from the air

course of bank identified from the air

0                    200 metres

On Hambledon Hill, however, field survey has identified the vestiges of a possible third cross-ridge dyke on the northern spur (Fig 4.16). If it should prove that all three cross-ridge dykes are contemporary, they may effectively have formed a double circuit, roughly concentric with the triangular main enclosure, but interrupted by the topography. Two or three further outworks, sited much lower down the three spurs leading to the central summit, may have defined a third circuit. Alternatively, or perhaps in addition, two of the possible three may have formed part of the linear causewayed earthwork that perhaps runs for almost 3km along the western flank of the massif.

Certain causewayed enclosures in riverine locations were built so as to incorporate watercourses into the circuit (Fig 4.13), for example, at Sawbridgeworth in Hertfordshire, at Buckland and at Broadwell in Oxfordshire and perhaps at Kedington in Suffolk and Dorney in Buckinghamshire (Carstairs 1986, 164). While the plans of the enclosures at Broadwell and Kedington (see Figs 5.17 and 5.21) suggest that some attempt was made to maintain the approximate circularity evident at many other sites, those of the enclosures at Buckland and Sawbridgeworth (Fig 4.17 and see Fig 5.18)

are markedly angular and rectilinear. The circuits at Mavesyn Ridware in Staffordshire and Southwick have the appearance of being 'squashed' along one side, the straighter sides in fact following low natural terraces that mark the edge of the later floodplain (Fig 4.18 and see Fig 8.10).

## Concentric circuits and their spacing

Around two-thirds of all certain and probable causewayed enclosures have more than one circuit of bank and ditch. Where multiple circuits exist, they are usually laid out concentrically. Those that are not concentric are discussed below, for they potentially shed light on the chronological development of other causewayed enclosures. It can seldom be demonstrated that different circuits of the same enclosure were built at the same time. The assumption that they were in use simultaneously has, however, often been the starting point for discussions of how the space may have been used (see Chapter 7: What happened inside causewayed enclosures?). Where the question has not been resolved, it may be more appropriate to treat different circuits almost as separate enclosures.

Figure 4.16 (facing page) *The main causewayed enclosure and its associated 'cross-ridge dykes' and 'outworks' on Hambledon Hill in Dorset all respect the natural topography to a large degree. In the course of Roger Mercer's excavations on the hilltop between 1974 and 1986, fieldwork and aerial photographic analysis by Rog Palmer identified Neolithic earthworks not recognised during the rapid survey carried out by RCHME in 1959. Among the most important are the 'western outwork' and the 'relict spur outwork', so-called because it is almost entirely buried beneath a late Iron Age 'hornwork'. Despite the damage done to the surviving third of the main causewayed enclosure by a brief period of ploughing in the mid-1960s, the earthworks still preserve indications of their original form.*

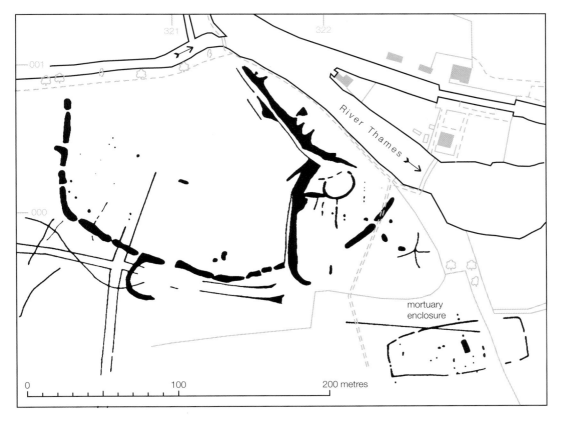

0        100        200 metres

*Figure 4.17*
*The angular plan of the causewayed enclosure at Buckland in Oxfordshire directly reflects its relationship to the River Thames. The C-shaped arc of ditch adjoining the southern side of the enclosure may be a ditch surrounding a large round barrow, perhaps of later Neolithic or Bronze Age date. Further to the south-east, a large 'mortuary enclosure' or short cursus monument may be of earlier Neolithic date. The ditch of this monument also appears to be causewayed.*

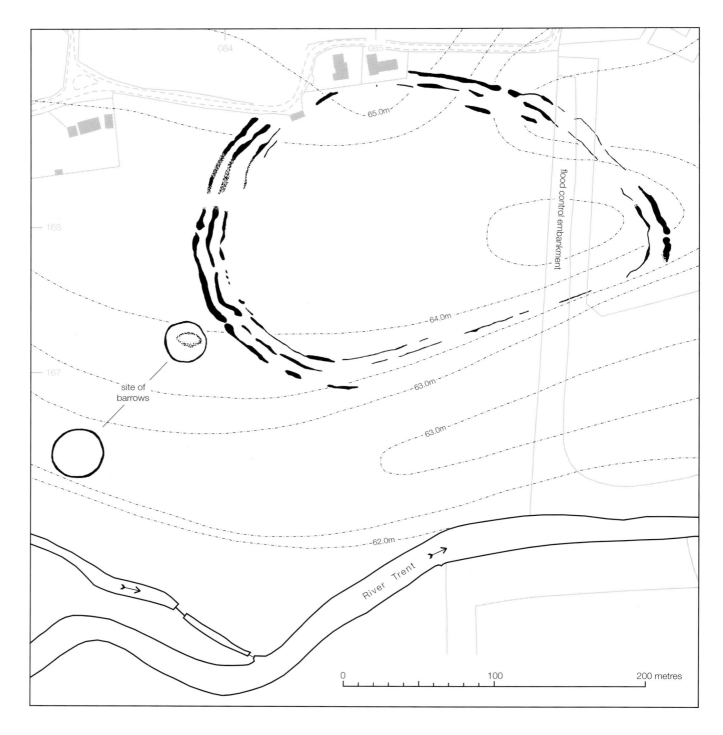

*Figure 4.18*
*The egg-shaped plan of the causewayed enclosure at Mavesyn Ridware in Staffordshire is*
*fairly similar to that of the enclosure 7km to the east at Alrewas. Yet at Mavesyn Ridware,*
*the straight southern edge of the perimeter takes account of a low natural scarp, which*
*defines the limit of seasonal flooding along the River Trent.*

Rog Palmer proposed that causewayed enclosures could be divided into those with widely spaced circuits, found in upland locations in the south of England, and those with closely spaced circuits, found in riverine locations in the Thames Valley and further north (Palmer 1976, 168). There is clearly a strong trend towards closely spaced circuits, the edges of the ditches lying between 5m and 15m apart (Fig 4.19). This space would have been wide enough for a bank (whether the outermost of a pair, or a single central one), perhaps in most cases separated from the edges of the ditches by a level berm several metres wide. This may have allowed sufficient space for groups of people to collect around the ditch segments, but not enough for major gatherings between the circuits or for the corralling of large herds, for example (Evans 1988c, 90). The great majority of enclosures with closely spaced circuits are found in riverine locations as Palmer suggested (Fig 4.20). All those with three closely spaced circuits occupy riverine sites (those at Sawbridgeworth, Broadwell, Langford, Cardington, and at both Alrewas and at Mavesyn Ridware in Staffordshire). A few enclosures with two closely spaced circuits lie on higher ground, including those at Orsett, Freston, Offham Hill and Donegore Hill. If the pairs of ditches at Orsett in Essex and Freston effectively formed single circuits, however, as discussed in Chapter 3, those enclosures might be disregarded. The enclosures on Offham Hill and Donegore Hill may also be unusual, in that excavation has proved that the circuits were not dug at the same time (Drewett 1977, 211; Mallory 1993, 416). Re-interpretation of the earthworks at The Trundle and Whitehawk Camp suggests that both enclosures may have had closely spaced pairs of banks and ditches, although the available radiocarbon dates are inconclusive as to whether one or other circuit was added at a later date (Drewett 1994, table 4). If the cross-ridge dykes surrounding the main causewayed enclosure on Hambledon Hill are regarded as a circuit, as proposed above, then this circuit would also comprise two closely spaced banks and ditches.

On the basis of the graph, widely spaced circuits can be defined as those at least 20m apart. Enclosures with such plans, which include those at Windmill Hill, Staines and Crickley Hill (Figs 1.6, 2.8, 3.17 and 4.15), are clearly in the minority, but have been the subject of a disproportionate amount of

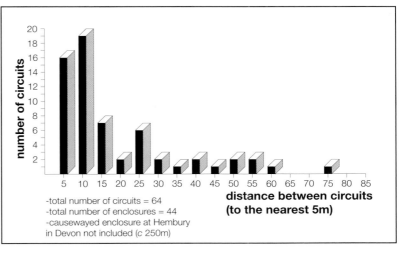

-total number of circuits = 64
-total number of enclosures = 44
-causewayed enclosure at Hembury in Devon not included (c 250m)

research and debate. Among the most widely spaced are those at Birdlip (c 55m apart; Fig 4.14), at Abingdon in Oxfordshire (65m apart; Fig 2.16), and perhaps at Hembury (c 230m apart; Fig 2.20). In all these instances, the enclosures are sited on promontories, which suggests that the distance between the circuits may have been increased in order to enclose a comparable area to those sites where the topography was less of a restriction. At Abingdon, however, the inner circuit seems to have gone out of use at the time when the outer was built (Avery 1982, 12). If it is assumed that widely spaced circuits were in use at the same time, there would have been sufficient space for any number of activities to take place between the circuits, even allowing for the presence of a broad bank adjacent to each ditch (Evans 1988c). Most causewayed enclosures with widely spaced circuits lie on higher ground, as Palmer suggested, but there are again several exceptions, including the enclosures at Abingdon and Staines. The larger of the two non-concentric enclosures at Fornham All Saints, which lies adjacent to the River Lark in Suffolk, also has widely spaced circuits (see Fig 4.25). The pairs of closely spaced ditches at Northborough (see Fig 5.16) and perhaps at Eastleach (Fig 3.18) and at Eton Wick in Berkshire may have had single central banks and, therefore, these enclosures might be regarded as having two widely spaced circuits, comparable to those at Orsett.

Where more than one circuit exists, the outer ditches tend to be broader than the inner ones and, therefore, possibly deeper or with larger banks. The causewayed enclosure at Eastleach in Gloucestershire is the most pronounced example, where parts

*Figure 4.19*
*The spacing of concentric circuits, using average distances between the edges of ditches. Rog Palmer (1976) analysed the ratios between the areas enclosed by the largest and smallest circuit at each enclosure. There are several problems with the use of area ratios to measure the spacing of the circuits. Although that approach gives similar results, the distances between the ditches offer a larger and more robust set of data.*

of the outermost of the four ditch circuits are around 12m wide – about ten times as wide as the innermost, though this might represent a broad palisade trench (Fig 3.18). The outer ditches of the enclosures at Robin Hood's Ball, Windmill Hill, Abingdon, Staines and The Trundle are more typical in being around twice as wide (Figs 1.4, 2.8, 2.16, 3.17 and see Fig 8.6). There are exceptions: excavation has shown that the inner circuits at Offham Hill and Crickley Hill were the more substantial earthworks

(Figs 4.8 and 4.15; Drewett 1977; Dixon 1988). At The Trundle, excavation has shown the broader outer ditch to be almost V-shaped in profile, but elsewhere the deep outer ditches appear to have been simply broader and deeper versions of the more typical U-shape (Curwen 1929a, 46; I Smith 1965, figs 4, 5 and 6; Case 1956, fig 2; Robertson-Mackay 1987, figs 7 and 8). Where excavated, the outer ditches have also proved to contain fewer artefacts. It may be, therefore, that the difference in the size of

*Figure 4.20 (below) The distribution of enclosures with widely spaced and closely spaced circuits.*

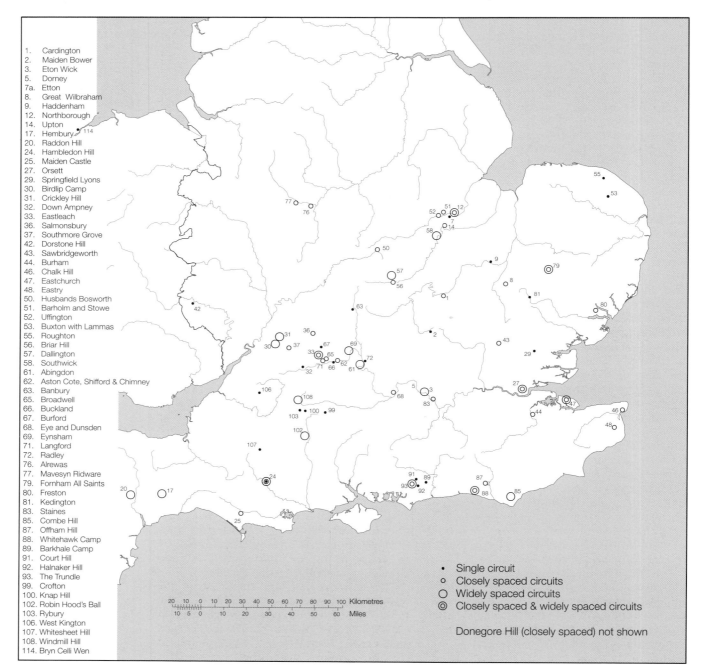

| 1. | Cardington |
| 2. | Maiden Bower |
| 3. | Eton Wick |
| 5. | Dorney |
| 7a. | Etton |
| 8. | Great Wilbraham |
| 9. | Haddenham |
| 12. | Northborough |
| 14. | Upton |
| 17. | Hembury |
| 20. | Raddon Hill |
| 24. | Hambledon Hill |
| 25. | Maiden Castle |
| 27. | Orsett |
| 29. | Springfield Lyons |
| 30. | Birdlip Camp |
| 31. | Crickley Hill |
| 32. | Down Ampney |
| 33. | Eastleach |
| 36. | Salmonsbury |
| 37. | Southmore Grove |
| 42. | Dorstone Hill |
| 43. | Sawbridgeworth |
| 44. | Burham |
| 46. | Chalk Hill |
| 47. | Eastchurch |
| 48. | Eastry |
| 50. | Husbands Bosworth |
| 51. | Barholm and Stowe |
| 52. | Uffington |
| 53. | Buxton with Lammas |
| 55. | Roughton |
| 56. | Briar Hill |
| 57. | Dallington |
| 58. | Southwick |
| 61. | Abingdon |
| 62. | Aston Cote, Shifford & Chimney |
| 63. | Banbury |
| 65. | Broadwell |
| 66. | Buckland |
| 67. | Burford |
| 68. | Eye and Dunsden |
| 69. | Eynsham |
| 71. | Langford |
| 72. | Radley |
| 76. | Alrewas |
| 77. | Mavesyn Ridware |
| 79. | Fornham All Saints |
| 80. | Freston |
| 81. | Kedington |
| 83. | Staines |
| 85. | Combe Hill |
| 87. | Offham Hill |
| 88. | Whitehawk Camp |
| 89. | Barkhale Camp |
| 91. | Court Hill |
| 92. | Halnaker Hill |
| 93. | The Trundle |
| 99. | Crofton |
| 100. | Knap Hill |
| 102. | Robin Hood's Ball |
| 103. | Rybury |
| 106. | West Kington |
| 107. | Whitesheet Hill |
| 108. | Windmill Hill |
| 114. | Bryn Celli Wen |

• Single circuit
○ Closely spaced circuits
◯ Widely spaced circuits
◎ Closely spaced & widely spaced circuits

Donegore Hill (closely spaced) not shown

20 10 0 10 20 30 40 50 60 70 80 90 100 Kilometres
10 5 0 10 20 30 40 50 60 Miles

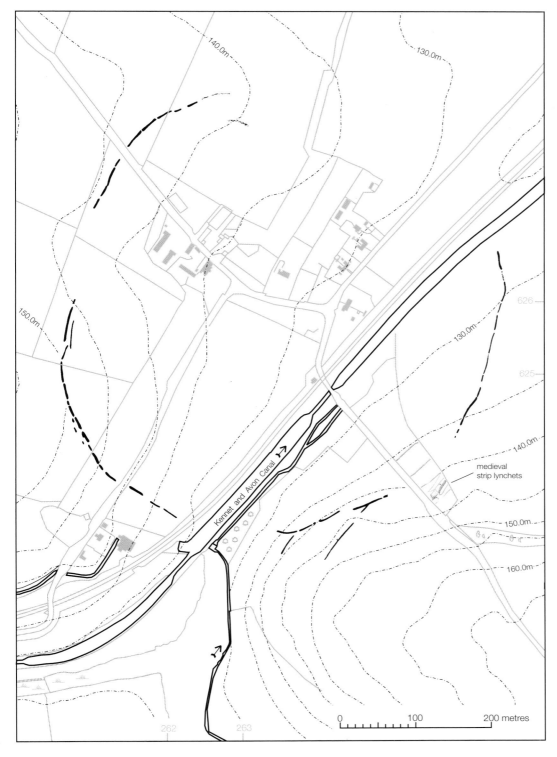

*Figure 4.21*
*The causewayed enclosure at Crofton in Wiltshire is quite simply extraordinary in terms of its size. Though it shares many of the characteristics of causewayed enclosures (Lobb 1995), it was clearly rather different from the norm. The nearly circular circuit takes no account of the topography and may have surrounded the confluence of the River Dunn and a smaller tributary stream, prior to the creation of the Kennet and Avon Canal (note that this plan is reproduced at 1:5 000).*

the ditches (and in some cases their profile) reflects some difference in the function of the enclosing earthworks, or the date of their construction. On the European mainland, the earlier change from V-shaped to U-shaped ditches seems to have accompanied a change in the role of causewayed enclosures from settlement to ceremonial site (Whittle 1977, 226–31). In England, Roger Mercer has argued that the greater size of the linear outworks along the western flank of Hambledon Hill must indicate that the hilltop came to be used as a defensive stronghold (Mercer 1985; 1988, 100–5). The outer circuit of the causewayed enclosure on Raddon Hill in Devon may have been enlarged to similar proportions in the final phase of its use, although this circuit may prove to be of Iron Age date (*see* Fig 5.2; Gent and Knight 1995). Yet if Mercer's theory is correct, it is curious that the causewayed construction technique was still retained for the ditches, leaving them weak in terms of defence. At The Trundle the deep outer ditch is sited halfway down a steep slope. It thus makes poor tactical use of the terrain, at least to a modern eye (but *see* Drewett 1977, 223–4). The size of the earthworks may therefore have been at least partly symbolic of the wealth or power of the community (Bradley 1984b, 25–37; Evans 1988b, 143–4 ).

## Area

The area within the inner lip of the ditch circuits provides a consistent gauge of their size, although it does not allow for the difference that might have been made by any bank that may have existed. Of those proven to be earlier Neolithic by excavation, the smallest is the inner circuit of the enclosure on Windmill Hill at 0.41ha (Fig 2.8). The largest is at Crofton, which lies less than 20km from Windmill Hill (Fig 4.21). At around 27ha, the single circuit is almost three times larger than the next largest enclosure and over sixty-six times larger than the inner circuit on Windmill Hill. The enclosure has other very unusual characteristics: its topographic location, the small quantity of finds recovered from the ditch and the possibility that the ditch was originally V-shaped. On balance, a

534
535
999
998
River Thames
0
100
200 metres

*Figure 4.22*
*The probable causewayed enclosure at Radley in Oxfordshire is one of the smallest known in England. It occupies a small gravel island between the Thames and a tributary channel and this may have influenced its size.*

number of circuits
10
8
6
4
2
1
2
3
4
5
6
7
8
9
10
11
12
area in hectares
-total number of circuits = 100
-total number of enclosures = 54
-causewayed enclosure at Great Bedwyn in Wiltshire not included (c 27ha)
accurate (+/- 0.1ha)
fairly accurate (+/- 0.3ha)
approximate (+/- 1.0ha)

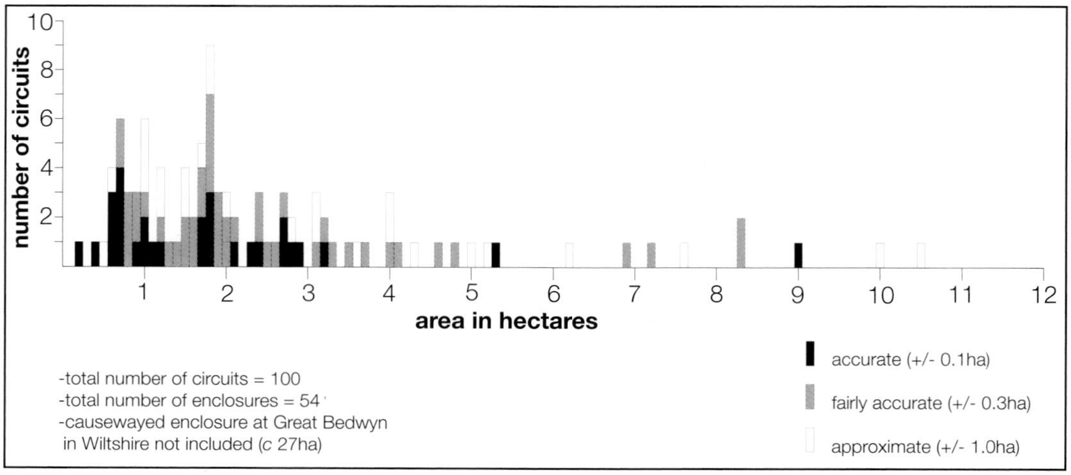

*Figure 4.23*
*The areas of different circuits, treating each as a potential enclosure in its own right. The comparison of minimum areas alone assumes that the innermost circuits were the earliest and that they remained in use throughout the lifetime of the monument. This is not necessarily so. Enclosures of medium size with single circuits are similar in area to the outer and middle circuits of enclosures with two or more widely spaced circuits.*

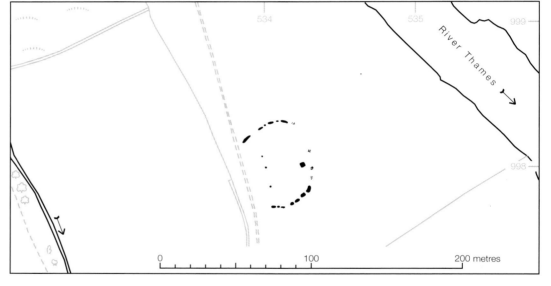

degree of caution is necessary in treating the monument as a causewayed enclosure. Smaller enclosures than Windmill Hill, such as those at Radley in Oxfordshire (Fig 4.22) and Bentley in Suffolk, both around 0.2ha, are known from aerial survey, but neither has been confirmed as a causewayed enclosure. The enclosure at Bentley, in particular, is slightly unusual in terms of other aspects of its form. It may have been a ring-ditch surrounding a large barrow or a circle of pits intended to hold timber uprights, rather than a causewayed enclosure.

Discounting the more dubious examples, there would appear to be three reasonably distinct trends in the areas enclosed by the circuits of causewayed enclosures (Fig 4.23):

1  small circuits enclosing between 0.4ha and 1.2ha, with a strong central tendency around 0.7ha;
2  medium circuits enclosing between 1.4ha and 5.5ha, with a weak central tendency around 1.8ha;

3  large circuits mostly enclosing between $c$ 6ha and $c$ 10ha.

This three-fold division is difficult to interpret: it may reflect differences in date, location, architectural style and social or economic function (*see* Chapter 7). A number of trends can be identified, however (Fig 4.24). The enclosure at Roughton and perhaps those at Sawbridgeworth, Bentley and Buxton in Norfolk are the only ones with small areas which lie north of the Thames Valley. Around half the total number of circuits enclosing small areas lie in riverine locations, but almost all of these are found in the upper reaches of the Thames Valley. Various interpretations have been put forward for this trend (*see* Chapter 6). Almost all those circuits which enclose small areas in upland locations are the inner circuits of causewayed enclosures with two or more widely spaced circuits, for instance, those at Windmill Hill, Combe Hill, Robin Hood's Ball and perhaps Raddon Hill.

*Figure 4.24*
*The distribution of circuits according to their size, excluding those where too little of the plan is known to be fairly sure of the area.*

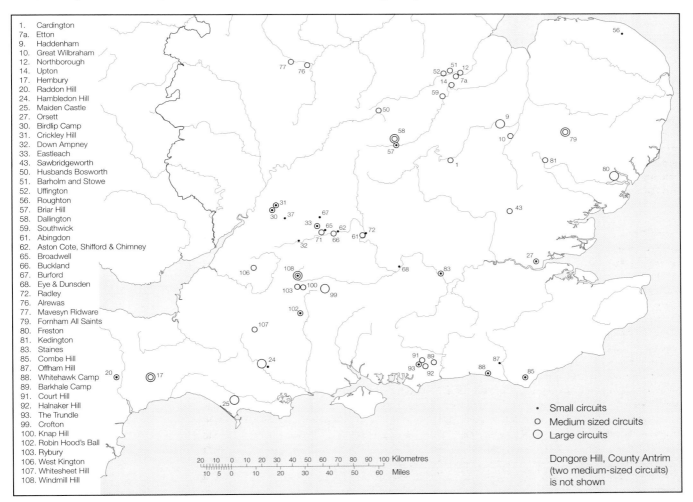

1.   Cardington
7a.  Etton
9.   Haddenham
10.  Great Wilbraham
12.  Northborough
14.  Upton
17.  Hembury
20.  Raddon Hill
24.  Hambledon Hill
25.  Maiden Castle
27.  Orsett
30.  Birdlip Camp
31.  Crickley Hill
32.  Down Ampney
33.  Eastleach
43.  Sawbridgeworth
50.  Husbands Bosworth
51.  Barholm and Stowe
52.  Uffington
56.  Roughton
57.  Briar Hill
58.  Dallington
59.  Southwick
61.  Abingdon
62.  Aston Cote, Shifford & Chimney
65.  Broadwell
66.  Buckland
67.  Burford
68.  Eye & Dunsden
72.  Radley
76.  Alrewas
77.  Mavesyn Ridware
79.  Fornham All Saints
80.  Freston
81.  Kedington
83.  Staines
85.  Combe Hill
87.  Offham Hill
88.  Whitehawk Camp
89.  Barkhale Camp
91.  Court Hill
92.  Halnaker Hill
93.  The Trundle
99.  Crofton
100. Knap Hill
102. Robin Hood's Ball
103. Rybury
106. West Kington
107. Whitesheet Hill
108. Windmill Hill

20  10  0  10  20  30  40  50  60  70  80  90  100 Kilometres
10  5  0      10      20      30      40      50      60 Miles

•  Small circuits
○  Medium sized circuits
◯  Large circuits

Dongore Hill, County Antrim (two medium-sized circuits) is not shown

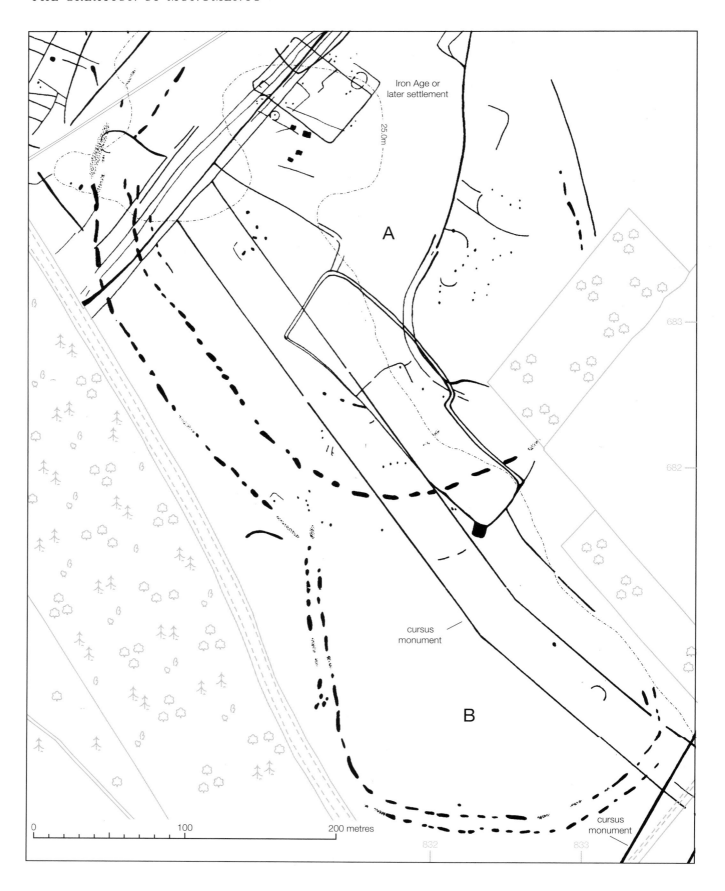

Iron Age or
later settlement

25.0m

A

683

682

cursus
monument

B

cursus
monument

0          100          200 metres

832          833

Circuits enclosing areas of medium size, sometimes with other closely spaced circuits but very seldom with widely spaced circuits, appear to be the norm to the north of the Thames Valley. Above, it was suggested that, until the chronological relationship between concentric circuits is better understood, it would be safer to treat widely spaced circuits essentially as enclosures in their own right. If this is the case, many of the second circuits of enclosures on higher ground, such as those on Crickley Hill and at Orsett, together with many to the south of the Thames Valley, such as those on Windmill Hill, Raddon Hill and Robin Hood's Ball, could be regarded as enclosures of medium size. Among the other medium-sized enclosures on high ground are those with only single circuits, such as Barkhale Camp in West Sussex, Rybury and those on Court Hill and Whitesheet Hill.

## Detecting change over time in plans

Plans produced by surface survey are often like photographic multiple exposures: all the phases of the construction, modification and later use of a monument are represented in a single image. Given what is known of the way in which causewayed enclosures were created and maintained, it cannot simply be assumed that all their circuits were in use at the same time. It has been suggested above that most circuits were demonstrably built according to a plan broadly agreed in advance, but that in some cases even the individual segments of bank and ditch may have been dug in separate episodes. Misalignments and sharp changes in angle around the circuits of the enclosures at Robin Hood's Ball, Northborough and Whitesheet Hill, among others, may indicate that even the initial construction process was discontinuous (see Figs 1.4, 5.16 and 8.3). The greatest problem with Rog Palmer's (1976) scheme of classification is that it implicitly accepts that the causewayed enclosures remained static in the eventual form in which they were recorded from the air. There are very few instances where the modifications that were almost certainly made over the course of time can be detected with confidence. Yet these few perhaps demonstrate the potential for change at the many other causewayed enclosures where the evidence is presently insufficient.

As discussed in Chapter 3, it is possible that the pairs of closely spaced concentric ditches at Orsett, Freston, Northborough and perhaps elsewhere were dug to provide material for single central banks (Hedges and Buckley 1978, 236). In these instances, it may be assumed that the two circuits of ditch were dug at the same time, essentially as one, and remained in use together. On the other hand, at several enclosures that survive as earthworks, and probably at Briar Hill (Bamford 1985, fig 20), equally closely spaced pairs of ditches were accompanied by two separate banks. In these cases, there are no grounds for assuming that both circuits were built at the same time. For instance, the pairs of banks and ditches on Offham Hill and on Donegore Hill are closely spaced, but excavation suggests that they were built a considerable length of time apart: the outer and inner circuits respectively were added at later dates (Drewett 1977, 211; Mallory 1993). In the absence of well dated sequences of pottery styles, the passage of time between phases of construction has usually been deduced from radiocarbon determinations (eg Hambledon Hill; Mercer and Healy in preparation) or inferred changes in the environment (eg Offham Hill; Thomas in Drewett 1977, 238–9). Variations in the densities of artefacts found in the different circuits at Windmill Hill have also been pointed to as evidence of a change in use, although this obviously might have resulted from the different activities carried out within different zones at the same time (Whittle 1996, fig 7.25; Whittle and Pollard 1995; Whittle et al 1999). Even in the few instances where excavation can provide such insights, the intervals between the construction of different circuits are generally uncertain, possibly only a matter of months rather than decades or centuries. The radiocarbon dating techniques currently available do not allow such short time spans to be distinguished.

Where circuits are widely spaced, it is even more uncertain whether they were built and used at the same time. Despite this, discussions of the division of space and activities within the enclosures have often been based upon the assumption that even if circuits were built at different times, the earlier ones would have continued in use with the newly constructed ones (eg Bradley and Holgate 1984, 116; Evans 1988c; Whittle 1996, fig 7.25). Excavation at Abingdon suggested, however, that the

*Figure 4.25 (facing page) The causewayed enclosure at Fornham All Saints overlooking the River Lark in Suffolk comprises two distinct parts. The plan indicates a sequence of development that cannot easily be demonstrated for those enclosures with concentric circuits. The addition of an 'annexe' (B) to the original causewayed enclosure (A) would appear to have created a separate new enclosure. Both enclosures are overlain by a Neolithic cursus monument which is probably of a somewhat later date. This in turn intersects with a second cursus immediately to the south-east of the causewayed enclosure. The small rectangular enclosure, linear field boundaries and other features are probably of Iron Age or later date.*

inner circuit was levelled when the outer circuit was constructed (Avery 1982, 12). Other causewayed enclosures seem to have been used over a fairly lengthy time-scale and the deliberate destruction of the banks is attested at some sites. Therefore, it is not inconceivable that earlier circuits were disused and overgrown by the time later ones were built and that the earlier circuits had effectively ceased to define separate spaces. Clearly their locations were not forgotten, but their importance may have been entirely symbolic. It is tempting to assume that where circuits were added, the innermost were the earliest, as has been shown at Offham Hill and Abingdon. At Crickley Hill and Donegore Hill, however, the fact that the inner circuits were built later (Mallory 1993; Dixon 1988) indicates that contraction of the enclosed area is just as likely.

Those circuits that are not laid out concentrically offer a clue to how other causewayed enclosures may have developed over the course of time. The plan of the enclosure at Fornham All Saints (Fig 4.25) is unusual in that at least two phases of construction can be identified with confidence. In the first phase, or perhaps more than one phase, two or three widely spaced circuits were built (A on plan). Subsequently, a pair of closely spaced circuits, perhaps representing a single episode of construction, was added to one end of the original enclosure to form what could be described as an annexe (B on plan). From this arrangement, it can be inferred that at least one circuit of the original enclosure still survived as an earthwork when the annexe was built. The annexe would seem to have created an additional but separate space, which did not supersede the inner circuit of the existing enclosure. This could perhaps have provided a zone reserved for different activities. This scenario would support the possibility that at enclosures with widely spaced concentric circuits, such as those at Staines, Abingdon, Birdlip Camp and Windmill Hill, new circuits may have been added to the original monuments in order to allow a more complex division of the space (Evans 1988c). In turn, this might offer an explanation for the marked contrasts in the plans of the different circuits at certain enclosures. For example, the unusually angular outer circuits at Robin Hood's Ball and possibly The Trundle may be polygonal because their

plans accentuated the minor changes of angle in the inner circuits (Fig 1.4 and *see* Fig 8.6). The mismatches between causeways in the ditches of more closely spaced circuits might also result from the same kind of addition.

On the other hand, a plausible interpretation of the complex patterns of earthworks at The Trundle and Whitehawk Camp is that certain circuits, or parts of them, were overlain by circuits added at a later date (Fig 4.26). This would seem to imply that the original enclosures had become to some extent redundant as separate spaces, suggesting a rather different sequence of development from the model described above. On the basis of his earthwork survey, E C Curwen suggested that the earthworks at The Trundle formed a spiral, allowing cattle to be herded into the innermost circuit (Curwen 1954, 86; Fig 2.23). It seems more likely, however, that this interpretation confused parts of two separate circuits laid out eccentrically, so that the inner pair impinged upon an earlier pair. Curwen's plan of Whitehawk Camp correctly portrays two major pairs of circuits and the earthworks would appear to confirm his suspicion that there may have been further circuits (Curwen 1936, 69; 1954, 71–2). It has been suggested on the basis of Curwen's plan that the enclosure may have undergone a sequence of expansion (Russell and Rudling 1996, 57–9 and fig 14). This interpretation is plausible, but there are other earthworks, not recorded by Curwen, that may represent parts of at least two more circuits. These may again have been laid out slightly eccentrically, so that in places they impinged on what had been built before. At both sites, however, the innermost circuits remain prominent as earthworks and apparently undisturbed. This may be because they were built first and respected throughout the later sequence of modifications, or because they were built, or rebuilt, towards the end of that sequence. In either case, the inference to be drawn is that the chronological relationships between widely spaced circuits laid out concentrically is perhaps not as straightforward as has often been assumed. At Eastleach, for example, the differences in the positions of the entrances through the inner pair of circuits and the third and fourth circuits may indicate that the eventual plan represents three (or more) phases of destruction and reconstruction (Fig 3.18). Further evidence

*Figure 4.26 (facing page) In contrast to the annexe at Fornham All Saints, re-interpretation of the earthworks at Whitehawk Camp in East Sussex and The Trundle in West Sussex suggests that both causewayed enclosures underwent phases of remodelling in which the original circuits were overlain by new ones. This may have important consequences for the understanding of enclosures with concentric circuits, where it is seldom possible to prove whether or not all were in use at the same time.*

for change over time can be detected in the relationships of certain enclosures to the natural topography; this is discussed further in Chapter 5.

Based on the plan of the cropmarks of the enclosure at Briar Hill (Fig 4.4), the circular inner circuit was initially thought to be different in date from the outer two circuits (Wilson 1975, 180). This theory was rejected by the excavators, who argued that the entire plan represented a single phase of construction (Bamford 1985, 39), but the original interpretation still appears more convincing. Whether the inner circuit or the outer pair is the earlier phase remains open to debate, however (Evans 1988c, 85–6; Mercer 1990, 63–4). On the basis of the plan, Richard Bradley (1998b, 79) has gone so far as to compare the inner circuit with circular monuments built several centuries later, such as the enclosure at Flagstones in Dorset (*see* Chapter 8: A tradition of enclosures?). All the artefacts recovered from the inner circuit by excavation point, however, to an earlier Neolithic date. The evidence of the plan is inconclusive, but on balance it seems more likely that the western half of the inner circuit was a later addition, which incorporated a stretch of the inner of the two pre-existing circuits. The new earth-work seems to have been laid out with greater concern to achieve near-perfect circularity and comprised much shorter pit-like ditch segments and an external bank (Bamford 1985, fig 20). Whether the remaining stretches of the two pre-existing circuits survived this modification, so as to form a separate zone (as at Fornham All Saints), or whether they were filled in to leave a single smaller enclosure (as perhaps at The Trundle and Whitehawk Camp), may never be determined.

## Other monuments with causewayed ditches

The causewayed construction technique is not unique to enclosures. The ditches flanking a small number of earlier Neolithic long barrows, including the first phase of the Wor Barrow in Dorset and the barrow at North Marden in West Sussex, were also apparently constructed as interlinked pits (Fig 4.27). Indeed, as mentioned in Chapter 2, the barrow at Badshot in Surrey was initially interpreted as part of a causewayed enclosure with two circuits (Lowther 1936;

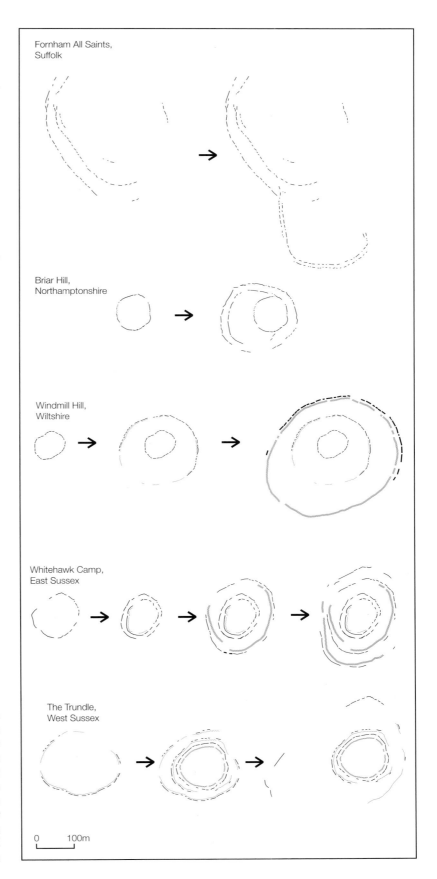

Fornham All Saints, Suffolk

Briar Hill, Northamptonshire

Windmill Hill, Wiltshire

Whitehawk Camp, East Sussex

The Trundle, West Sussex

0    100m

Keiller and Piggott 1939). The two long barrows on Hambledon Hill appear to have segmented ditches, although they are different from each other in form and may have been built at different dates. Several roughly rectangular enclosures, such as those at Normanton Down in Wiltshire,

Long Crichel in Dorset and adjacent to the causewayed enclosure at Buckland also have causewayed ditches. These enclosures, conventionally known as mortuary enclosures, may in fact represent a form of long barrow, or have performed a similar purpose (Ashbee 1984, 49), although the example at Buckland might be interpreted as a small cursus monument.

Such monuments may shed light on the thinking behind the technique of causewayed construction. Above all, they perhaps highlight the extent to which interpretations of causewayed enclosures have been forced to concentrate on the ditches, rather than what occurred within the space they enclosed, because of the virtual absence of surviving evidence there. In considering the function of long barrows, it is unlikely that the flanking ditches should be thought more important than the area that lay within them, due to the physical survival of the mound in many cases. Although the ditch segments may have been invested with symbolic significance, the main focus of ritual activity was clearly the entrances or forecourts of the tombs and the burial chambers themselves. Similarly, it seems likely that only the gap in the ditch at the front of the barrows would have been used for access and, therefore, the causeways in the flanking ditches have to be explained in some other way. It is perhaps the absence of any clear focus for activity within causewayed enclosures that has led attention to be fixed on their perimeters.

## Conformity or diversity?

Modern perceptions of the meaning and use of causewayed enclosures are bound to be substantially different from those of people in the earlier Neolithic. The initial impression of homogeneity in the forms of the enclosures, as they appear today, must quickly give way to the realisation that the class would have comprised an extremely diverse set of individual monuments. This diversity is apparent in all aspects of their form: overall plan, size and the nature of their enclosing circuits. It is also apparent that the causewayed ditch is not the hard-and-fast diagnostic characteristic it first appeared to be and that some enclosures did not in fact fully enclose.

So can causewayed enclosures still be thought of as a single class, or are they best regarded as a series of unique monuments,

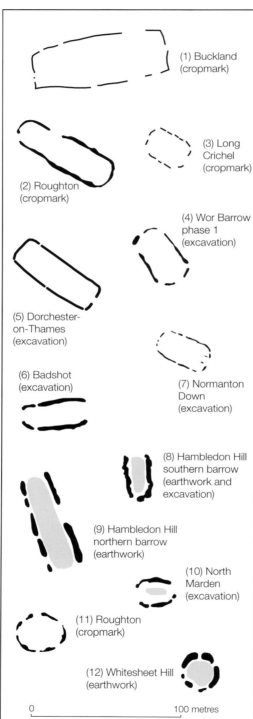

(1) Buckland (cropmark)

(2) Roughton (cropmark)

(3) Long Crichel (cropmark)

(4) Wor Barrow phase 1 (excavation)

(5) Dorchester-on-Thames (excavation)

(6) Badshot (excavation)

(7) Normanton Down (excavation)

(8) Hambledon Hill southern barrow (earthwork and excavation)

(9) Hambledon Hill northern barrow (earthwork)

(10) North Marden (excavation)

(11) Roughton (cropmark)

(12) Whitesheet Hill (earthwork)

0                    100 metres

*Figure 4.27*
*Plans of long barrows and 'mortuary enclosures' of similar size with causewayed ditches. In 1959 RCHME recorded the southern long barrow on Hambledon Hill in Dorset as an earthwork at a large scale immediately prior to its destruction by ploughing. The barrow extended almost the entire width of the space between the circuit of the main causewayed enclosure and the adjacent southern cross-ridge dyke. Mercer's excavations showed that the sequence of recutting and deliberate deposition in the ditches of the barrow mirrored that in the ditch of the enclosure. (Based on Ashbee 1984; Atkinson et al 1951; Barrett et al 1992; Drewett 1986 and Keiller and Piggott 1939)*

grouped together for the convenience of archaeological discussion? The answer is of course 'both'. The extent of the variations around the typical themes is perhaps unsurprising: as the earliest known monuments devised to enclose space, causewayed enclosures apparently had no precedents. The construction technique also seems to have been of widespread and long-lasting importance. Yet, at the same time, differences may be equally significant: the products of specific social, economic, geographical, chronological or functional contexts.

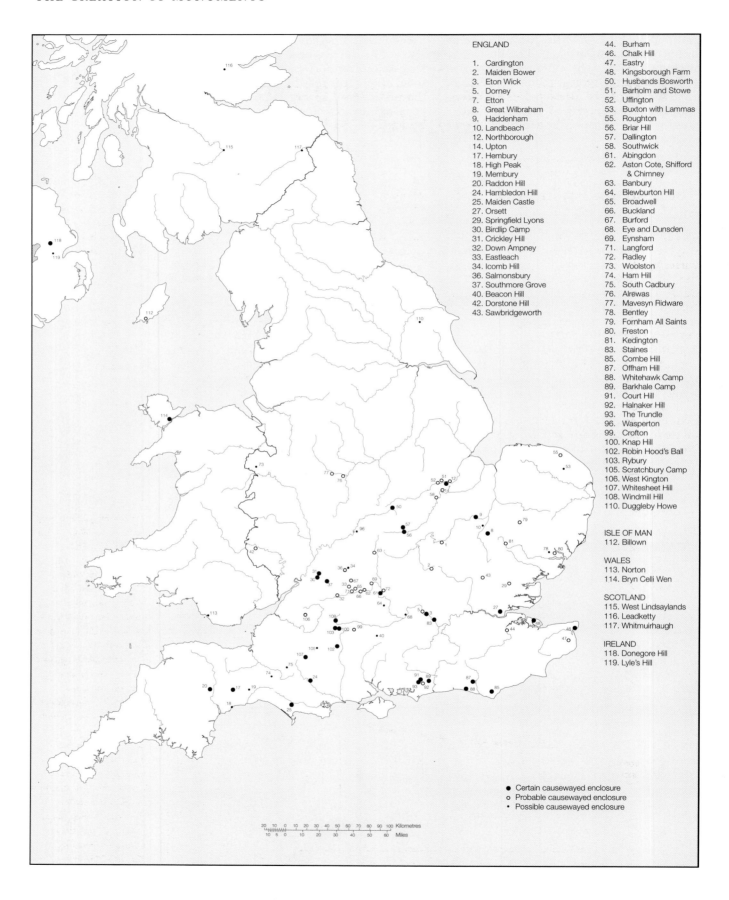

ENGLAND

1. Cardington
2. Maiden Bower
3. Eton Wick
5. Dorney
7. Etton
8. Great Wilbraham
9. Haddenham
10. Landbeach
12. Northborough
14. Upton
17. Hembury
18. High Peak
19. Membury
20. Raddon Hill
24. Hambledon Hill
25. Maiden Castle
27. Orsett
29. Springfield Lyons
30. Birdlip Camp
31. Crickley Hill
32. Down Ampney
33. Eastleach
34. Icomb Hill
36. Salmonsbury
37. Southmore Grove
40. Beacon Hill
42. Dorstone Hill
43. Sawbridgeworth

44. Burham
46. Chalk Hill
47. Eastry
48. Kingsborough Farm
50. Husbands Bosworth
51. Barholm and Stowe
52. Uffington
53. Buxton with Lammas
55. Roughton
56. Briar Hill
57. Dallington
58. Southwick
61. Abingdon
62. Aston Cote, Shifford & Chimney
63. Banbury
64. Blewburton Hill
65. Broadwell
66. Buckland
67. Burford
68. Eye and Dunsden
69. Eynsham
71. Langford
72. Radley
73. Woolston
74. Ham Hill
75. South Cadbury
76. Alrewas
77. Mavesyn Ridware
78. Bentley
79. Fornham All Saints
80. Freston
81. Kedington
83. Staines
85. Combe Hill
87. Offham Hill
88. Whitehawk Camp
89. Barkhale Camp
91. Court Hill
92. Halnaker Hill
93. The Trundle
96. Wasperton
99. Crofton
100. Knap Hill
102. Robin Hood's Ball
103. Rybury
105. Scratchbury Camp
106. West Kington
107. Whitesheet Hill
108. Windmill Hill
110. Duggleby Howe

ISLE OF MAN
112. Billown

WALES
113. Norton
114. Bryn Celli Wen

SCOTLAND
115. West Lindsaylands
116. Leadketty
117. Whitmuirhaugh

IRELAND
118. Donegore Hill
119. Lyle's Hill

● Certain causewayed enclosure
○ Probable causewayed enclosure
• Possible causewayed enclosure

# 5
# Distribution and location in the physical landscape

## The distribution in England and the British Isles

The number of certain and probable causewayed enclosures known in England currently stands at sixty-six. In some areas, the distribution of sites is not much less dense than regions of similar size on the European mainland (Fig 5.1). A further seventeen sites identified in England have as yet produced too little evidence to be regarded as more than possible causewayed enclosures. Rog Palmer's review, published in 1976, recorded forty-three sites in England, of which five can be firmly rejected and two seem unlikely. Two certain, one probable and four possible causewayed enclosures have now been identified in Northern Ireland, Wales, the Isle of Man and

Scotland. Even counting only the certain and probable examples, the corpus of causewayed enclosures in the British Isles can be said to have nearly doubled in number over the quarter of a century since 1976.

Palmer's work demonstrated that the distribution of causewayed enclosures in England stretched well beyond Wessex and Sussex, particularly into East Anglia and the Midlands. Since 1976, there have been further discoveries in East Anglia, in the upper reaches of the Thames Valley and in Kent, a county long thought to lack causewayed enclosures altogether (Barber 1997, 80–3). The most northerly of the conventional causewayed enclosures in England are those discovered through aerial reconnaissance in the Trent Valley, neighbouring each other at Alrewas and

*Figure 5.1 (facing page) The distribution of certain, probable and possible causewayed enclosures in the British Isles.*

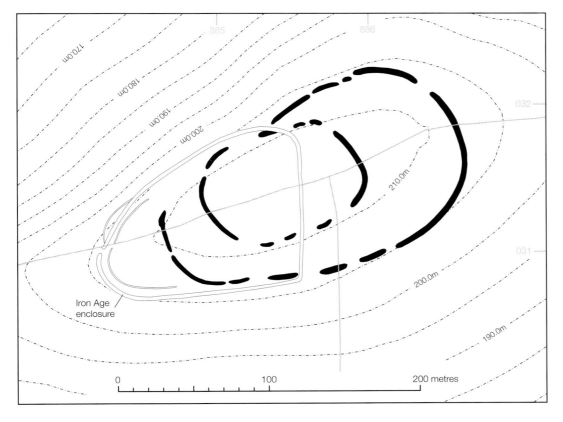

Iron Age enclosure

0        100        200 metres

*Figure 5.2 The causewayed enclosure on Raddon Hill in Devon is the westernmost causewayed enclosure known in England. The western end of the Neolithic enclosure is overlain by a D-shaped enclosure of Iron Age date. The enclosure is one of only a few which occupy a hilltop, rather than the slope just below the summit. The plan, which is known principally from geophysical survey, suggests that the enclosure may have been built in at least two main phases. It is possible, however, that the ditch that appears to represent an outer circuit may be of Iron Age date. (Based on Gent and Knight 1995)*

Figure 5.3
The enclosure on Donegore
Hill in County Antrim,
discovered in 1981 and
excavated in 1983–6. In
terms of its plan and
siting, just below the
summit, the enclosure is
very similar to many in
southern England.
Radiocarbon dates prove
that the first circuit (the
outer one) was dug equally
early in the Neolithic
period, between 4,000 BC
and 3,800 BC. The idea
of building with
causewayed earthworks,
therefore, seems to have
spread rapidly. (Based on
Mallory 1993)

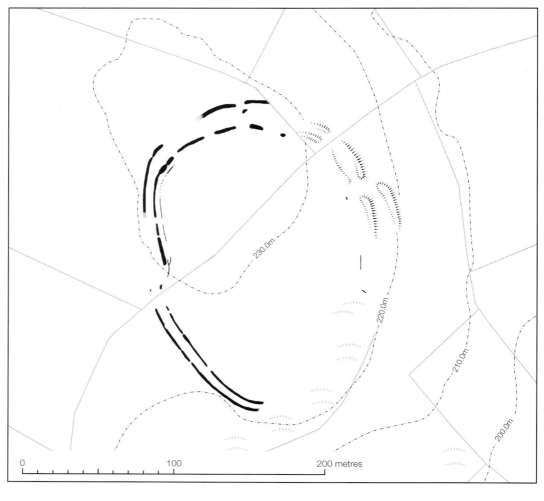

Figure 5.3
The enclosure on Donegore
Hill in County Antrim,
discovered in 1981 and
excavated in 1983–6. In
terms of its plan and
siting, just below the
summit, the enclosure is
very similar to many in
southern England.
Radiocarbon dates prove
that the first circuit (the
outer one) was dug equally
early in the Neolithic
period, between 4,000 BC
and 3,800 BC. The idea
of building with
causewayed earthworks,
therefore, seems to have
spread rapidly. (Based on
Mallory 1993)

Figure 5.4
The cropmark at
Whitmuirhaugh in
Roxburghshire, for long
interpreted as an enclosure
of Dark Age origin, is one
of three possible
causewayed enclosures
identified by the Royal
Commission on the Ancient
and Historical Monuments
of Scotland. Like many
riverine sites, it occupies a
slight rise, which would
have lifted it just above any
seasonal flooding, and is
sited near the confluence of
the major river (the Tweed)
with a much smaller
tributary. (Crown
Copyright: RCAHMS)

Mavesyn Ridware in Staffordshire, together
with those at Roughton and Buxton in
northern Norfolk. In the South-West, few
conventional causewayed enclosures have
as yet been identified. The westernmost
certain example currently known lies on
Raddon Hill in Devon (Fig 5.2).

Since 1976, there have also been several
discoveries and re-interpretations of known
sites elsewhere in the British Isles, which
collectively may be of great significance. In
Northern Ireland, fieldwalking in 1981
identified a possible causewayed enclosure
on Donegore Hill in County Antrim
(Fig 5.3). Subsequent excavation proved it to
be of earlier Neolithic date, producing radiocarbon dates from its earliest phases of
construction which are as early as many in
southern England (Mallory 1993). In 1990,
the excavation of test pits near a Neolithic
chambered tomb at Bryn Celli Wen on the
Isle of Anglesey chanced upon a ditch, which
subsequent excavations have shown to be
part of a causewayed enclosure, also similar

in form to examples found on the chalk uplands of southern England (Edmonds and Thomas 1991; 1992; 1993). In 1995, geophysical survey at Billown near Castletown on the Isle of Man revealed a length of causewayed ditch, which subsequent excavations have proved to be of earlier Neolithic date and quite probably part of an enclosure (Darvill 1996b; 1997a). In 1996, aerial photographic sorties flown by the Royal Commission on the Ancient and Historical Monuments of Wales (RCAHMW) recorded a double-circuited enclosure with causewayed ditches at Norton in Glamorgan, which could well be Neolithic on the basis of its form and location (Driver 1997). In Scotland, research carried out by the Royal Commission on the Ancient and Historical Monuments of Scotland (RCAHMS) has interpreted three enclosures recorded previously through aerial survey as possible causewayed enclosures: at Whitmuirhaugh in Roxburghshire (Fig 5.4), West Lindsaylands in Lanarkshire and Leadketty in Perthshire. Although none has yet been tested by excavation, in terms of their forms and locations, all three seem to have much in common with examples in central and southern England.

## Causewayed enclosures on the European mainland

In 1930, E C Curwen first drew parallels between the causewayed enclosures in England and sites in France and Germany (Curwen 1930). More recently, there have been two major reviews of enclosures in Europe (Burgess *et al* 1988; Andersen 1997), as well as relevant studies of the Neolithic in general (*see* eg Hodder 1990; Whittle 1996). In Denmark, France and Germany, the number of known sites has also risen rapidly since the 1960s, again mainly through programmes of aerial research. In some parts of these countries, the distribution of sites is now far more dense than even the most dense concentrations in southern England. In eastern Europe, where flying was restricted until the 1990s for political reasons, archaeological research is undergoing a rebirth (for examples, see Andersen 1997). The distribution pattern remains patchy, however, both spatially and in terms of the dates at which monuments were built and came to prominence (Whittle 1996, 266–74; Andersen 1997, 277–80). The earliest phase of building causewayed enclosures (though not enclosures more generally)

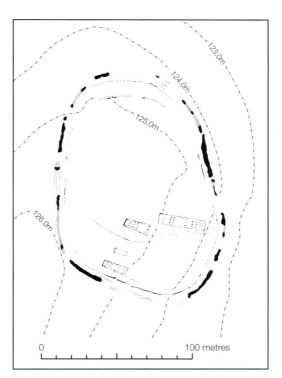

Figure 5.5
*The enclosure at Darion in Belgium is classed as a causewayed enclosure, but is different from those in the British Isles in at least two key respects: its early date and its clear evidence for settlement in terms of long houses and pits (the latter omitted for clarity). Richard Bradley (1993) suggests that this and similar enclosed settlements of early date came to be idealised. This fostered the notion that constructing enclosures with causewayed earthworks was the 'right way' to build a communal monument, an idea which spread across much of north-western Europe. (Based on Keely and Cahen 1989)*

seems to have been the period between 5,000 BC and 4,200 BC. Their appearance in northern Germany, western France, Denmark and the British Isles followed between 500 and 1,000 years later, in the period known on the European mainland as the Middle Neolithic.

Causewayed enclosures on the European mainland usually employ the same structural elements as those in England: banks, ditches and palisades. A significant number enclose much larger, more irregularly shaped areas and appear more elaborate in their designs. Some enclosures in western France, such as that at La Coterelle, have as many as six closely spaced concentric circuits and entrances with complex outworks, reminiscent of certain Iron Age hillforts (Cassen and Boujot 1990, 457; *see also* Andersen 1997, fig 235). In terms of function, the range of artefacts and human and animal remains from many of the enclosures on the European mainland seems to be broadly similar to that from sites in England. A greater number, however, notably earlier sites such as the enclosure at Darion in Belgium, have convincing evidence for long-term settlement, in the form of large numbers of pits and timber structures, including long houses (Fig 5.5; Keely and Cahen 1989). Of all the various causewayed enclosures in Europe, those apparently most similar to the examples in the British Isles are found in Denmark and central/western France and seem to be of broadly similar date (Bradley 1993, 87–9). They are not only closer in plan to the English sites, but often share many of the locational preferences outlined below (Andersen 1997, 281). This need not imply direct cultural links between England and the European mainland, but it may well indicate that there was a broad unity of concept as to how and where causewayed enclosures should be built.

## Geology as a factor in the distribution

In the 1990s, a number of causewayed enclosures were discovered by chance in the course of excavations: those at Husband's Bosworth in Leicestershire (Clay 1999a; b) and at Kingsborough Farm

in Kent being perhaps the most notable. Most sites discovered since 1976, however, have been identified as cropmarks through aerial photographic reconnaissance. It is important to recognise this, because cropmarks develop under specific conditions – conditions which are not found equally throughout the British Isles. The differences in growth which cause cropmarks result from local changes in the moisture content in the soil within and above archaeological features. This variation is more pronounced on certain geological backgrounds, particularly the light, well draining soils found on river gravel terraces and the chalk and limestone landmasses. Even in central and southern England there are large areas where the geological background, together with the current agricultural regimes, is unlikely to produce clear cropmarks. For example, the geologically complex area known as

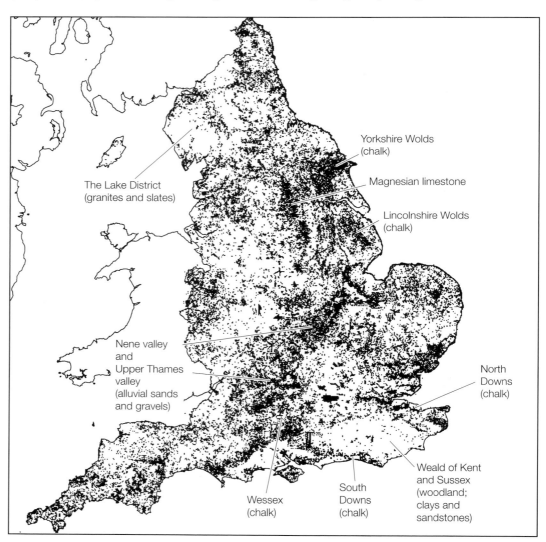

Figure 5.6
The distribution of specialist archaeological air photographs held in English Heritage's National Monuments Record closely matches the areas of chalk, limestone and alluvial sands and gravels, where cropmarks are most visible. It also roughly matches the distribution of causewayed enclosures, which strongly suggests that there are still many sites awaiting discovery.

The Weald lies between the causewayed enclosures known on the chalk South Downs in East Sussex and those on the North Downs in Kent, at Burham, Eastry and Ramsgate. There is plenty of evidence for earlier Neolithic activity in the Weald in the form of worked flints, axes and colluvial deposits suggestive of forest clearance (M Gardiner 1990, 42–3). This suggests that there is potential for the discovery of monuments. Yet the clays that dominate the geology of the area are unproductive of cropmarks and best support woodland and rough pasture which further hampers the identification of sites from the air. A glance at a geological map for the rest of the country, compared to the distribution of specialist archaeological air photographs, indicates how much the geological conditions could distort the picture of the distribution of causewayed enclosures (Fig 5.6).

Along with chalk and limestone, alluvial river gravels and sands are most productive of cropmarks and, at present, over 90 per cent of the certain and probable causewayed enclosures known in the British Isles are found on these geological backgrounds. In Wales and Scotland, ideal geological conditions are relatively scarce. If the newly identified sites in those countries do indeed prove to be Neolithic, it would be logical to conclude that the current distribution map *must* be greatly distorted in favour of central and southern England. The present picture may be a reflection of the partial impression accepted prior to the 1970s, when sites identifiable as cropmarks in low-lying locations first began to be identified. In the British Isles as a whole, taking into account sites which may have been concealed by the construction of later monuments (discussed in Chapter 8), by present-day woodland and urban development, together with land in the south-east lost through the rise in sea level since the Neolithic period, there may be a massive bias in the distribution map of causewayed enclosures. As a result, any impression of patterning, whether at a national or local level, still needs to be treated with caution.

## 'Tor enclosures': causewayed enclosures built in stone?

As mentioned in Chapter 2, the possibility that two stone-built enclosures in Cornwall, at Carn Brea and Trencrom Hill, might be of Stone Age date was raised by Charles Henderson some years before causewayed enclosures were recognised as the principal form of earlier Neolithic enclosure (Henderson MSS 'Antiquities of Cornwall', Courtney Library, Royal Institution of Cornwall, Truro). The excavation of the enclosures at Carn Brea in 1970–3 (Mercer 1981) and at Helman Tor in 1986 (Fig 5.7; Mercer 1986a) confirmed that both these sites were of earlier Neolithic date. A further fifteen stone-built enclosures, including the one on Trencrom Hill, are now regarded as being potentially of earlier Neolithic date on the grounds that they share some of the characteristics of Carn Brea (Fig 5.8; Silvester 1979, 188–9 and fig 5; Mercer 1981, 190–1; 1986b, 51–2). Most have low, irregular banks built of weathered granite blocks, often retained by slabs of stone set upright or on edge. Some have narrow entrances set at relatively frequent intervals (Fig 5.9), and almost all surround and incorporate tors and smaller natural outcrops of granite. This last trait has earned them the name 'tor enclosures'. It has also prompted comparison with certain 'cliff castles' in Cornwall: though generally thought to be of Late Bronze Age and Iron Age date, in some cases these too may have originated in the Neolithic (Sharpe 1992, 66–7). On the other side of the Bristol Channel, certain stone-built enclosures in South Wales, such as that at Clegyr Boia, are also comparable in form to the tor enclosures (Tilley 1994, 87–90; Williams 1952).

Despite the fact that conventional upland causewayed enclosures made use of the locally available rock (that is, sedimentary chalk in most cases) in their banks, the granite-built tor enclosures have not generally been treated as direct counterparts of the causewayed enclosures. There is very seldom evidence for ditches accompanying their stony banks and their association with natural outcrops has no obvious parallel amongst causewayed enclosures. Yet long cairns built in stone are agreed to be counterparts of the earthen and chalk-built long barrows. In view of the mutually exclusive distributions of the two forms of enclosure, is it legitimate to consider the tor enclosures of the South-West simply as causewayed enclosures built in igneous, rather than sedimentary geological situations?

There are certainly general similarities to the causewayed enclosures in terms of the dating evidence and range of artefacts obtained from the two excavated tor enclosures. One of the major obstacles to making direct comparisons between the finds is the fact that human and animal bone is very seldom preserved in the acid soil conditions found at the tor enclosures. In terms of the form of the monuments, the segmented ditches so characteristic of conventional causewayed enclosures are apparently absent from tor enclosures (but *see* Mercer 1981, fig 24). There are nonetheless other points of similarity. Certain tor enclosures, such as those at Carn Brea and Whittor in Devon, are defined by multiple, more or less concentric circuits. At The Dewerstone in Devon (Fig 5.10), the two low banks are closely spaced, reminiscent of the circuits of many causewayed enclosures. They are interrupted by three

and possibly as many as five original gaps, all of which may have been entrances. These are spaced at intervals which are certainly less frequent than the causeways in the ditches of most causewayed enclosures, but which are perhaps comparable to the intervals between the gaps in their banks (*see* Chapter 3: Banks).

The excavations at Carn Brea and Helman Tor may turn out to have opened a Pandora's Box of stone-built enclosures of Neolithic date elsewhere in Britain. One such occupies the highest point of the escarpment known as Gardom's Edge in the Derbyshire Peak District (Fig 5.11). The enclosure has been provisionally dated to the Neolithic on the grounds that it is anomalous

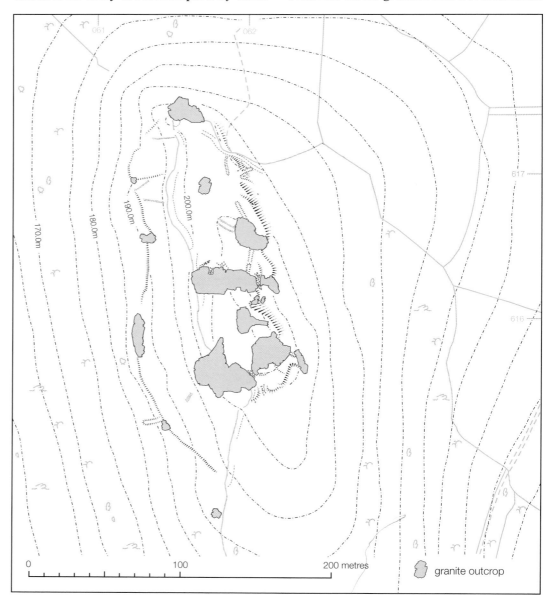

*Figure 5.7*
*The stone-built enclosure surrounding Helman Tor in Cornwall is one of the two 'tor enclosures' proven to be of earlier Neolithic date. The modern field wall joining the western sides of the main granite outcrops may overlie a Neolithic wall and probably reused much of the stone from it. Note how the outer circuit on the western slope runs between relatively small outcrops of a rock, a characteristic common to all the tor enclosures in the South-West.*

0          100          200 metres

granite outcrop

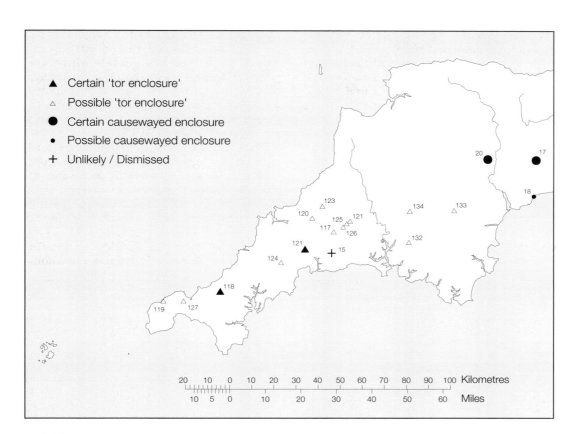

*Figure 5.8*
*The distribution of causewayed enclosures and tor enclosures in the South-West. A circuit of discontinuous ditch surrounding an Iron Age fort at Bury Down near Lanreath is the only possible conventional causewayed enclosure identified to date in Cornwall. The form of the earthwork has little in common with known causewayed enclosure, however; trial excavation also revealed a number of points of difference, including an absence of any datable artefacts.*

Legend:
▲ Certain 'tor enclosure'
△ Possible 'tor enclosure'
● Certain causewayed enclosure
• Possible causewayed enclosure
+ Unlikely / Dismissed

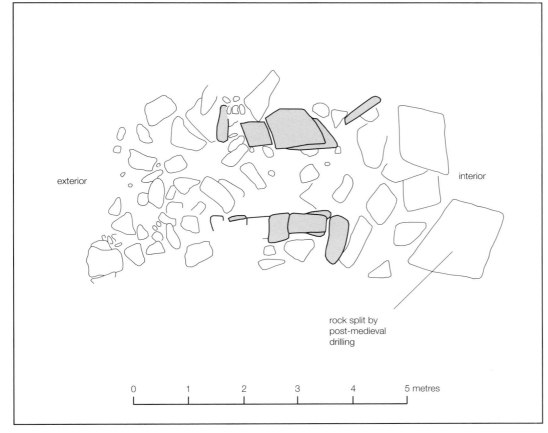

*Figure 5.9*
*The narrow gateway of the tor enclosure at De Lank in Cornwall is one of the features that suggests it is of earlier Neolithic date. Similar entrances were identified at Carn Brea. The use of large facing blocks set on edge, with only limited evidence for coursed walling, is another characteristic of tor enclosures.*

*Figure 5.10*
*The plan of the tor*
*enclosure at The*
*Dewerstone in Devon and*
*its relationship to the*
*topography have aspects in*
*common with the*
*conventional causewayed*
*enclosures found further to*
*the east. The smaller*
*enclosure and the*
*associated circular house*
*platforms are thought to be*
*of later Bronze Age date.*
*There is slight evidence in*
*the pattern of stone*
*clearance on the spur that*
*the tor enclosure predates*
*the smaller enclosure, but*
*that is the only dating*
*evidence currently*
*available for the*
*monument. The granite*
*outcrop at the tip of the*
*promontory has been much*
*reduced by quarrying, but*
*would once have been a*
*striking feature in the*
*landscape.*

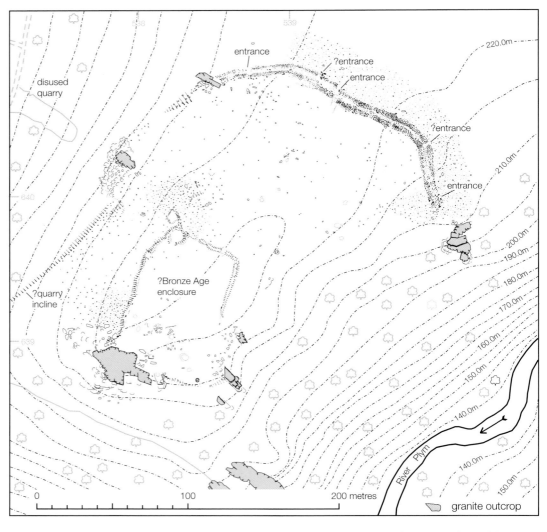

*Figure 5.11 (facing page)*
*The stone-built enclosure*
*adjacent to the Gardom's*
*Edge escarpment in the*
*Derbyshire Peak District.*
*Although the overall plan*
*has little in common with*
*either conventional cause-*
*wayed enclosures or the tor*
*enclosures of the South-*
*West, the frequency of*
*entrances and blocked*
*entrances may share some*
*of the constructional logic*
*of the other types of earlier*
*Neolithic enclosure.*

in form and can be shown to predate field clearance of earlier Bronze Age date, although a later Neolithic or very Early Bronze Age date for the enclosure cannot yet be ruled out (Ainsworth 1997; Ainsworth and Barnatt 1998; Barnatt *et al* 1998; 1999). Though its overall plan has little in common with any known causewayed enclosures, the perimeter is formed by a low stone bank interrupted in several places. It may also have surrounded a tor-like natural outcrop prior to intensive quarrying of the millstone grit.

Since the granite uplands of the Cheviots in Northumberland are comparable in geological terms to the uplands of the South-West, the same issues arise. On the Milfield Plain immediately to the east of the Cheviots, a major group of later Neolithic henges survived as earthworks until the 1960s, but has since been levelled by ploughing (Harding 1981; Waddington 1996). In the Cheviots themselves, on the other hand,

while hundreds of undated prehistoric monuments are well preserved as earthworks, not a single example of an earlier Neolithic enclosure has been securely identified. It remains to be seen whether this reflects a genuine absence of causewayed enclosures, or whether a preconceived idea of the appearance of earlier Neolithic enclosures, based on a stereotype established in southern England, has prevented their recognition in the North (Topping 1997a, 118).

Enclosures built in igneous and metamorphic rock elsewhere in England have been suspected of being Neolithic in date, including those in Cumbria on the summit of Carrock Fell and adjacent to the possible long cairn at Skelmore Heads. However, field survey has usually only served to confirm that such enclosures are unusual in some aspect of their siting or construction.

If the tor enclosures of the South-West and perhaps stone-built enclosures elsewhere can indeed be seen as counterparts of causewayed enclosures, it must then be legitimate to question whether it is actually correct to treat interrupted ditches as the defining characteristic of earlier Neolithic enclosures and whether the current definition of the class should be revised. As has been pointed out in Chapter 3, the unequal survival of the banks of causewayed enclosures and the much smaller quantity of artefactual evidence they preserve has traditionally led attention to be focussed on the role of the ditches in defining the boundary. The remarkable deposits found in the ditches indicate that they cannot be dismissed as mere quarries (Evans 1988c, 89), yet some form of digging was virtually unavoidable to obtain material for the adjacent banks. In areas of igneous and metamorphic rock, building material is generally easily available on the surface in the form of scree and clitter, so that a bank could have been constructed without any form of digging. Field survey indeed suggests that the majority of the tor enclosures are composed of the large irregularly shaped weathered blocks and smaller fragments typical of those available on the surface in the immediate vicinity (Fig 5.12). At these sites, the construction of the bank alone seems to have been of primary importance; it was not felt necessary to dig a ditch for symbolic or ritual purposes. Turning once again to conventional causewayed enclosures, this may reinforce the suggestion made in Chapter 3 that banks, for which so little evidence survives, were of great importance in defining the boundaries. Perhaps it is the phenomenon of enclosure, rather than the technique of causewayed construction, that should be seen as the defining characteristic of the class of monument.

In the gazetteer (Appendix, 149), all the tor enclosures suggested to be of Neolithic date are listed separately. Until trial excavation of one or two of the sites in northern England can confirm or deny that their unusual qualities can be equated to an earlier Neolithic date, as the excavations at Carn Brea and Helman Tor have done in the South-West, further discussion will remain unfounded. Equally, the discovery of even a single 'conventional' causewayed enclosure in an upland context in northern England would have important implications: it might be inferred that the scarcity of such monuments in the North is genuine after all and that the stone-built enclosures may represent something altogether different.

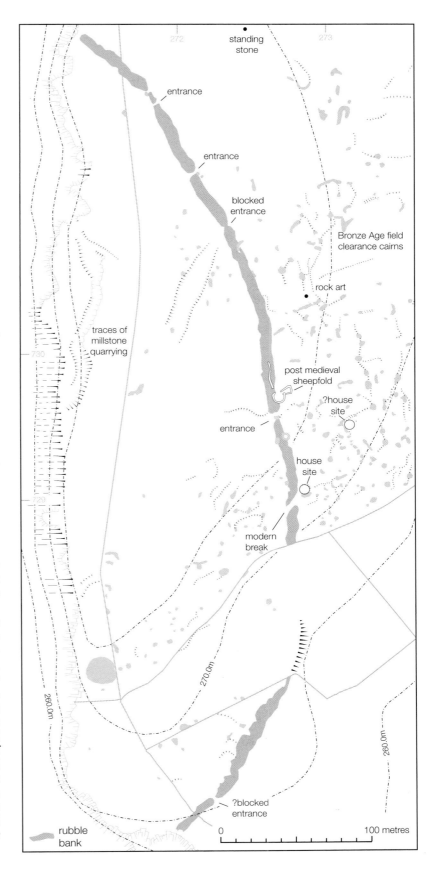

*Figure 5.12*
*The enclosure on Trencrom Hill in Cornwall was perceptively surveyed by Charles Henderson in 1914–7 (see Fig 2.5) and the key observation on which he based his suggestion of a Neolithic origin still stands up to scrutiny, that is, the similarity of some parts of the perimeter to the excavated enclosure at Carn Brea. This section of walling in the south-west corner of the enclosure was exposed by erosion following a brush fire in 1994. The barrier appears unsophisticated, but may have secured the base of a timber superstructure. (Copyright: Trevor Pearson)*

*Figure 5.13*
*Statistical analysis can reduce the landscape to a neutral backdrop. A range of graphs shows how statistics can appear to demonstrate differing patterns. Graph A suggests that most enclosures were built between 100m and 500m from water, while graph B suggests that there is no pattern at all in the altitude at which they were sited. Graph C, which attempts to compensate for the differing sizes of enclosures and the varying nature of their topographic settings, reveals three fairly distinct trends: enclosures whose perimeters are in very close proximity to streams or rivers, those which lie at a moderate height and distance from the nearest stream and those that lie a much greater distance and/or height from the nearest watercourse.*

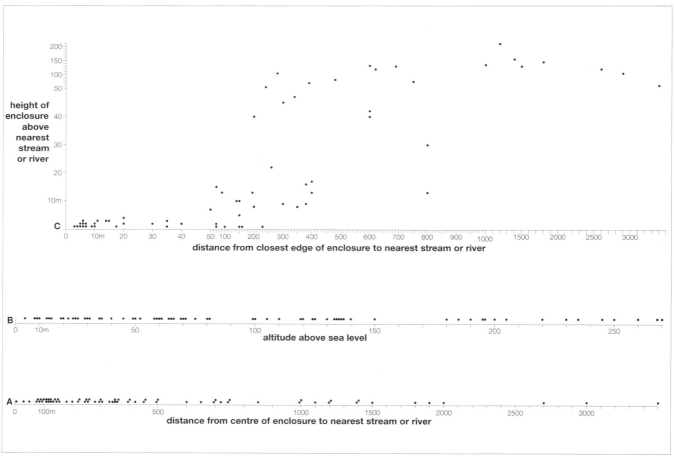

# Patterns of location in the physical landscape

The differential survival of enclosures, in which earthworks are preserved on higher ground (where agriculture has been less intensive) and only cropmarks in riverine situations, at first created the impression that there was a basic distinction between two types of location. Isobel Smith (1971, 90) suggested that the growing number of riverine sites should be seen as 'complementary'; upland sites, however, particularly those on chalk, have been the subject of far more excavations and continue to colour perceptions of the riverine sites, perhaps unfairly (Barber 1997, 77–8). Palmer (1976) used statistical analyses to test whether the monuments themselves could be treated as a single class and concluded that they could. Ironically, in achieving this crucial step forward, he also cemented the perception of a straightforward two-fold division between *riverine* and *upland* locations, and glossed over more subtle differences within both categories (Fig 5.13).

The statistical approach favoured in the 1970s appeared to offer an objective analytical tool with which to make sense of the patterning that genuinely exists in the locations of causewayed enclosures. Treating the physical landscape as a 'neutral backdrop' actually hinders a full understanding of the location of a monument (Tilley 1994, 23; Thomas 1996a, 83–91). The key to where Neolithic people chose to build their monuments must have been, to some degree, what might be called their 'sense of place' – how people perceived, in ideological and social terms, the hills, rivers, forests and clearings which made up their physical surroundings. This approach has been explored at various different levels (Thomas 1991, 29–32; Bradley 1993, 22–44; Tilley 1994; Darvill 1997b). Modern concepts of the environment are bound to differ from those of people in the Neolithic: it is far from simple to reconstruct the appearance of the Neolithic landscape and even more difficult to understand how people perceived it at the time.

Analysis in the field of the siting of causewayed enclosures in relation to the topography suggests that the long-accepted riverine/upland division needs to be refined. In very bald terms, it is possible to distinguish between two types of location amongst the riverine sites: those occupying slight rises in the valley floor and those on valley sides. Among the upland causewayed enclosures, it is possible to distinguish between sites on the basis of their orientation. Almost all are located on sloping ground, but in some cases the topography restricts the view from the interior so that only lower ground is visible (here termed *lowland-oriented*), while in other cases only higher ground can be seen (*upland-oriented*). The sites located on rises in valley floors could perhaps be further sub-divided into those which lie next to minor tributaries and those where major rivers were preferred; enclosures associated with springs and with confluences may also be significant minorities. The categories used below are therefore not intended to impose a typological straitjacket, nor to classify for the sake of classifying; rather the distinctions between what seem to be meaningful differences are intended to open avenues for future research (Fig 5.14).

## Rises in valley floors

Causewayed enclosures built in such a way that watercourses were incorporated into their plans have already been discussed in Chapter 4. More than one-third of all certain and probable enclosures occupy the edges of slight rises in valley floors, on the very margin of what could today be termed river floodplains (Fig 5.15). It is widely agreed, however, that the regular occurrence of seasonal flooding postdates the building of most causewayed enclosures (Brown 1997, 210–18). The development of floodplains was brought about by various factors and was accelerated over the course of prehistory through silting brought about

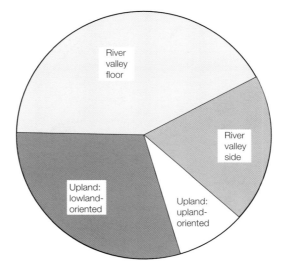

*Figure 5.14*
*The division of causewayed enclosures according to their topographic setting can only be approximate, since the divisions between the categories are not strict.*

*Figure 5.15*
*The causewayed*
*enclosure at Buckland in*
*Oxfordshire, adjacent to*
*the River Thames. As the*
*broad hedgeline in the*
*bottom right corner of the*
*photograph follows the*
*course of a ditch which*
*carries a tributary stream,*
*it is possible that the circuit*
*terminated at the edge of*
*the minor watercourse.*
*It is possible, however, that*
*the cropmarks have not yet*
*revealed the full plan of the*
*site. (NMR 4694/12)*

*Figure 5.16*
*The causewayed enclosure*
*at Northborough in*
*Cambridgeshire occupies a*
*slight rise in the gravel*
*subsoil, which later*
*deposits of alluvium have*
*made barely perceptible to*
*the eye. The course of the*
*Roman canal or drain*
*known as the Car Dyke*
*cuts across the middle of*
*the site.*

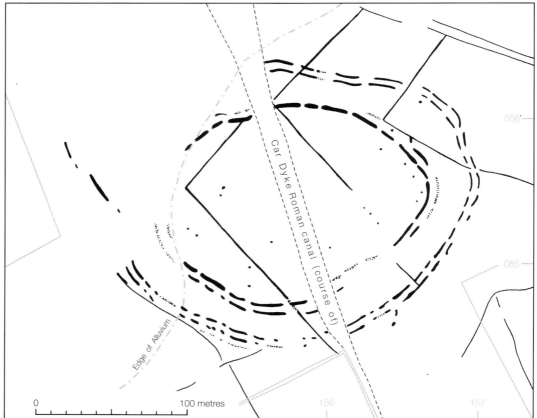

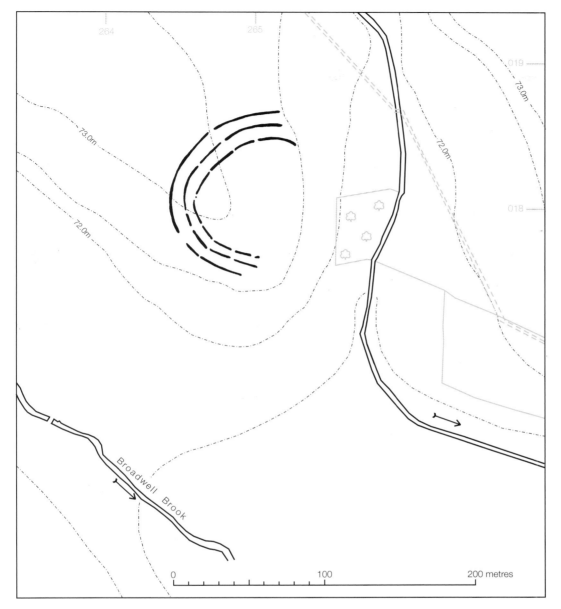

*Figure 5.17*
*Detailed topographic survey shows how the semicircular plan of the causewayed enclosure at Broadwell in Oxfordshire relates to the line of the terrace along the edge of the adjacent stream channel. Today, the stream itself is narrow enough to step across and it seems unlikely to have been much broader in the Neolithic. As such, it cannot have played a role in completing the circuit in any strictly functional sense.*

by increasingly intensive clearance of the forests and subsequent agriculture. At Abingdon in Oxfordshire, however, it has been suggested that water tables may have risen before 4,000 BC, that is, slightly prior to the construction of the monument. This may have partly resulted from human activity such as deliberate clearance of woodland and subsequent agriculture (Parker 1997, 101–2; *see also* Leeds 1928, 461). Elsewhere, the choice of location is so consistent that the intention seems to have been to place the monument just above the potential high water mark, even if flooding seldom or never occurred. Modern appearances can be deceptive: the causewayed enclosure at Northborough in Cambridgeshire lies 850m from the present channel of the River Welland, but at what may have been the very edge of the former floodplain, as testified by the alluvial deposits which have shrouded part of the site (Fig 5.16). There are more typical examples, which lie between 30m and 200m from present-day water courses, at Barholm in Lincolnshire, Staines in Surrey, Alrewas in Staffordshire, Cardington in Bedfordshire, Broadwell and Aston Cote in Oxfordshire, Down Ampney in Gloucestershire (Figs 3.6, 3.17, 4.9, 4.10, 5.17 and *see* Fig 8.11). In a few instances, such as at Mavesyn Ridware in Staffordshire and Southwick in

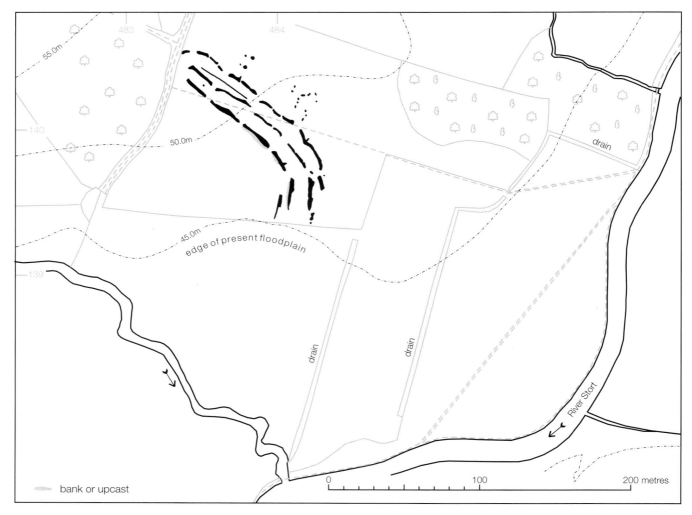

bank or upcast

0    100    200 metres

*Figure 5.18*
*At their southern end,*
*the ditches of the*
*causewayed enclosure at*
*Sawbridgeworth in*
*Hertfordshire continue as*
*far as the edge of what is*
*now boggy ground,*
*regularly flooded by the*
*River Stort. Assuming the*
*floodplain has developed*
*since the Neolithic, they*
*may once have continued*
*further still. At the other*
*end, their course remains*
*uncertain: they seem to be*
*turning back towards the*
*stream, but no traces can*
*be identified in the wood.*

Northamptonshire, the perimeter of the causewayed enclosure itself follows the edge of the rise (Fig 4.18 and *see* Fig 8.10). At Great Wilbraham in Cambridgeshire the nearly circular circuit seems to have been deliberately laid out so that its perimeter only just meets the edge of the higher ground (Fig 4.7). Its slight tilt towards the water's edge recalls the siting of many enclosures in upland locations.

The difference in height between the centre of the causewayed enclosure and the present watercourse is often less than 2m. At Staines, a detailed contour survey showed that the highest point of the interior of the enclosure was only a metre above a former stream, while the outer ditch lay immediately adjacent to its modern channel (Fig 3.17; Robertson-Mackay 1987). From the roots of rushes preserved within the silt in the base of the ditch segments at Etton in Cambridgeshire, it was deduced that the ditches may have held

standing water for some of the year while the causewayed enclosure was still in active use. Deposits of alluvium in the interior of the enclosure suggest that by the beginning of the third millennium BC, the site was subject to regular flooding, presumably in late winter or spring (French 1990; 1998b). At Abingdon, the excavator also suggested that flooding may have occurred while the enclosure was in use (Leeds 1928, 461). At Haddenham, however, which lies little more than a metre above the valley floor, the absence of preserved organic material suggests that the enclosure was built on fairly dry ground (Hall *et al* 1987, 189). The same conclusion has been reached at various sites in similar locations in the valley of the Seine in northern France (eg at Noyen-sur-Seine: Mordant and Mordant 1988, 231). Environmental evidence may well be preserved at several enclosures that have not been excavated, such as those at Broadwell (Fig 5.17) and Buckland in

Oxfordshire (Fig 5.15), where parts of the ditches could have flooded seasonally. It is remarkable that at sites such as Abingdon, Mavesyn Ridware and Sawbridgeworth, ground within a stone's throw which is several metres higher was not chosen as the site of the enclosure. This suggests a deliberate link with the water itself, which undoubtedly combined both functional and symbolic considerations (Field 1998).

There is a marked difference in the kinds of watercourse favoured for the siting of the causewayed enclosures on rises in valley floors. Some, such as those at Mavesyn Ridware, Buckland and Fornham All Saints lie adjacent to major rivers (respectively the Trent, the Thames and the Lark). Since these watercourses would almost certainly have been navigable in the Neolithic, the possibility that access was gained by boat may well explain the concentration of causewayed enclosures along certain river valleys, such as the Thames, the Welland and the Nene. Although relatively few of the many logboats discovered in the British Isles have been dated, none has been found to be any earlier than the Bronze Age (McGrail 1978, table 5.1). Boats must have been used, however, in the exchange of people and artefacts between Great Britain, Ireland and mainland Europe. The distribution of probable prehistoric logboats in England indicates that many of the river systems along which causewayed enclosures

*Figure 5.19*
*The causewayed enclosure at Great Wilbraham in Cambridgeshire was sited at the centre of this photograph, close to a narrow stream. The meandering line of the channel probably indicates that its course has remained unchanged since at least the medieval period. Due to drought and modern drainage for agriculture, the channel only rarely becomes wet, even over the winter months. (NMR AA00/6703)*

are found would probably have been used for transport in the Neolithic (McGrail 1978, fig 207; *see also* Case 1969, 178–80). Other causewayed enclosures, such as those at Down Ampney, Langford, Cardington, Barholm and Great Wilbraham relate to very minor tributaries. In most cases, these cannot have been navigable themselves, but the causewayed enclosures usually lie less than 5kms away from the confluence of the stream with a larger river. The points of confluence of minor streams with larger rivers were themselves also apparently favoured locations as, for example, at Buckland in Oxfordshire and Sawbridgeworth in Hertfordshire (Fig 5.18). These are the enclosures closest in design to the *méandres barrés* found in the river valleys of northern France (for examples, *see* Mordant and Mordant 1988, fig 13.2).

In some cases, it is possible that water levels may have changed significantly since the Neolithic: the streams at Abingdon in Oxfordshire are now small, but may have fed a body of open water at the time the causewayed enclosure was in use (Parker 1997, 101). Some minor streams have been culverted in modern times to improve drainage, so that only slight changes in the topography indicate their original course. Others have been so severely affected by natural drought and artificial drainage that they are no longer streams, but merely dry, meandering channels (Fig 5.19).

## Valley-side locations

Enclosures in valley-side locations have much in common with those upland sites which are oriented towards low-lying

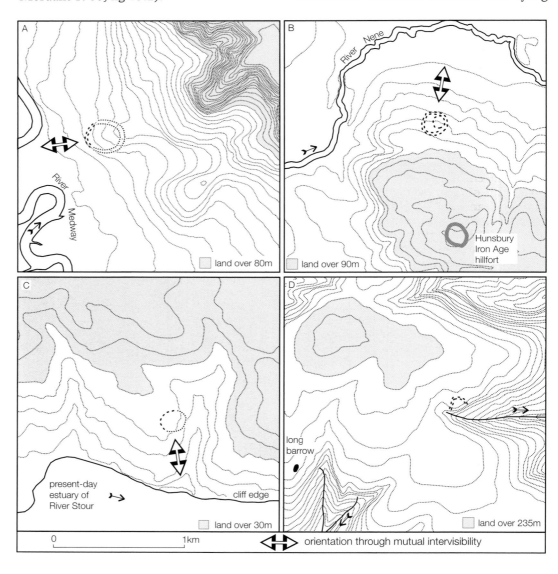

*Figure 5.20
Since causewayed enclosures sited on the sides of river valleys clearly avoid the highest ground, they seem to be quite closely connected with the rivers they overlook. Like most of the enclosures on higher ground however, they occupy sloping ground so that that they 'tilt' across the contours (A Burham, Kent; B Briar Hill, Northamptonshire; C Chalk Hill, Ramsgate, Kent; D Southmore Grove, Gloucestershire).*

ground, in that they overlook lowland areas and are physically 'tilted' in that direction by their siting on sloping ground. Unlike the upland sites, however, they emphatically avoid genuine upland nearby (which is in some cases up to 120m higher) and overlook the valleys of rivers or streams, rather than more extensive low-lying expanses. On these criteria, causewayed enclosures which are as much as 25m above water courses, such as those at Briar Hill in Northamptonshire, Orsett in Essex, Burham in Kent, and Uffington in Lincolnshire fall into the valley-side category (Fig 5.20). The causewayed enclosure at Kedington in Suffolk occupies the tip of a spur that slopes steeply down to the River Stour, so that it is very similar to those sites located on valley floors in terms of its proximity to the watercourse (Fig 5.21).

A few sites show a clear affinity with watercourses, but do not clearly fall into either of the categories outlined above. Crofton in Wiltshire, which was mentioned in Chapter 4 for its unusual size, is equally strange in terms of its topographic setting (Fig 5.22). Prior to creation of the Kennet and Avon Canal, the enclosure would appear to have surrounded a stretch of the River Dunn, a minor tributary of the River Kennet, and perhaps its confluence with another small stream. Being almost circular in plan and exceptionally large in area, the perimeter encloses an irregular segment of both sides of the valley of the stream. The minor streams at Abingdon in Oxfordshire may have been similarly encompassed, although only the promontory at the point of confluence is known to have been enclosed. At Freston in Suffolk the enclosure surrounds the head of a shallow dry valley. This holds a spring now barely sufficient to feed an agricultural pond, though it may once have fed a nearby tributary of the River Stour. At Southmore Grove in Gloucestershire, the causewayed enclosure abuts the edge of a steep-sided valley, overlooking a

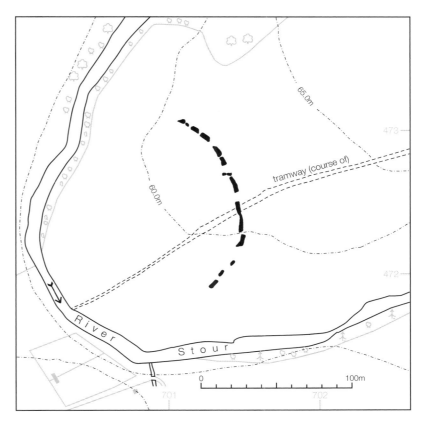

spring (Fig 5.23). The stream valley overlooked by the enclosure at West Kington in Wiltshire is also extremely steep-sided; it is conceivable that erosion has considerably altered the profile of the valley since the Neolithic.

## Lowland-oriented causewayed enclosures

Examples of lowland-oriented causewayed enclosures in upland settings include those at Robin Hood's Ball and Windmill Hill in Wiltshire, Maiden Castle in Dorset, Barkhale Camp and Court Hill in West Sussex and Chalk Hill near Ramsgate in Kent. There are two main differences

*Figure 5.21*
*The causewayed enclosure at Kedington in Suffolk is similar to sites located on rises in valley floors in terms of its proximity to the edge of the River Stour, but has more in common with sites on valley sides in terms of the steepness of the spur it occupies. This underlines the point that none of the locational characteristics can be regarded as entirely exclusive.*

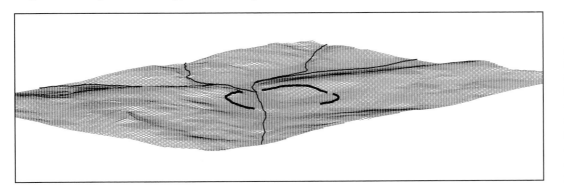

*Figure 5.22*
*Digital ground models offer one way of depicting the setting of a monument in three dimensions. Here, the causewayed enclosure at Crofton in Wiltshire is seen obliquely, as though from the air, in order to highlight the relationship of the exceptionally large perimeter to the valley sides.*

between these enclosures and those sited on the sides of river valleys. The first is that the upland enclosures exhibit a much closer association with the highest ground. They do not actually occupy the *tops* of hills, however, but are instead typically centred on gently sloping ground up to 10m below the summit. The very tops, so close to the heavens, may have been revered as sacred places (Pryor 1998a, 50; *see also* Field 1998). As a result, they too, like the valley-side enclosures, tilt in the direction of the lower-lying ground (Fig 5.24; *see also* Smith 1971, 111). This has been noted as a typical characteristic of many causewayed enclosures in Europe (Andersen 1997, 282). It should be emphasised that this 'orientation', like that of the entrances (*see* Chapter 4: Planning in relation to the topography) relates only to the local topography and does not reflect any cosmological direction.

The second difference is that there is no explicit link between the causewayed enclosure and a river or stream. Although it has been noted that most lie about 2km from a watercourse (Palmer 1976, table 1; Drewett 1994, fig 14), enclosures such as those at Barkhale Camp and Windmill Hill in fact lie on the side of the hill facing away from the nearest stream. The nearest sources of water to Crickley Hill and Birdlip Camp lie at the foot of the escarpment and are, therefore, the least accessible (Dixon 1994, 23). The enclosure at Robin Hood's Ball is an extreme example in lying *c* 4km away as the crow flies from the nearest watercourse. Enclosures such as those at Offham in East Sussex and the Stepleton enclosure on Hambledon Hill in Dorset are more typical in that they seem to overlook low-lying ground through which a stream or river flows, rather than looking directly towards the watercourse itself. The link with water is thus less explicit than that of the valley-side locations, though not necessarily unimportant.

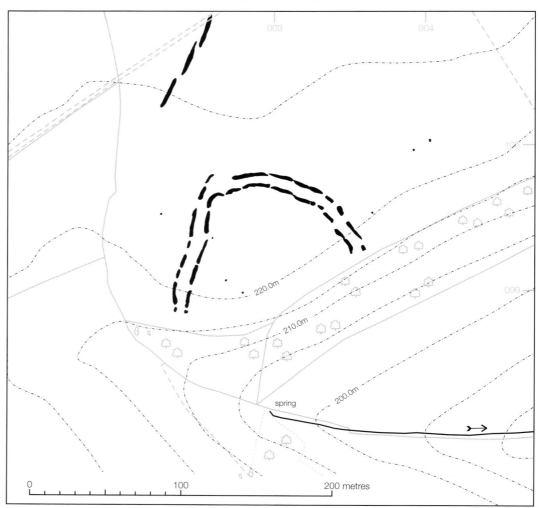

*Figure 5.23*
*The enclosure at Southmore Grove in Gloucestershire seems to be deliberately sited to overlook the source of a minor stream. The escarpment along the northern edge of the valley is steep, but not so steep as to prevent access altogether. The possible 'screened' entrance on the northern side faces up the gentle slope.*

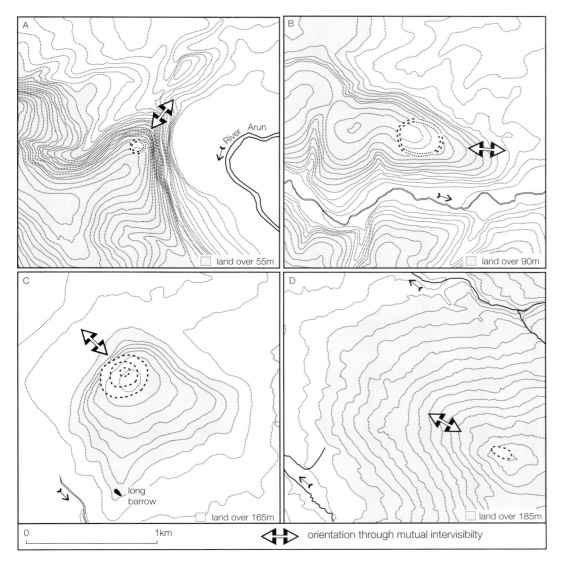

*Figure 5.24*
*Some upland enclosures*
*seem to be oriented towards*
*a low-lying area, in what*
*seems a fairly simple*
*visual relationship: the*
*enclosure commands an*
*oblique view across the*
*lower ground and, because*
*it tilts across the contours,*
*is in turn visible at a*
*similar oblique angle from*
*the lower ground*
*(A Offham Hill, East*
*Sussex; B Maiden Castle,*
*Dorset; C Windmill Hill,*
*Wiltshire; D Green How,*
*Cumbria). Note that the*
*enclosure on Green How*
*was discovered after the*
*completion of the project*
*(see back cover).*

## Upland-oriented causewayed enclosures

The most immediately apparent characteristic of upland-oriented settings is their proximity to eye-catching natural landforms, or to striking elements of larger landmasses that are naturally dramatic. Examples of such settings include some of the best known causewayed enclosures in the country: Rybury Camp, Knap Hill and Whitesheet Hill in Wiltshire and The Trundle, Whitehawk Camp and Combe Hill in Sussex (Fig 5.25). This co-location must be interpreted as a conscious choice, though not one simply triggered by any unusual piece of topography. There is no suggestion that the pattern was strictly determined by the geography, since no single type of topographic feature was

favoured exclusively. Rather it seems that a spectrum of different settings was considered appropriate, but all involving some form of precipitous scarp slope – a hillside, a promontory or a coomb. To a degree, this variability in the choice of topography accounts for the wide range in the altitudes at which the upland enclosures lie.

In most instances of such dramatic locations, the orientation of the enclosure is ambiguous, this characteristic contrasting strikingly with the valley-side and lowland-oriented sites. From one side of the perimeter of the enclosure, there is often a spectacular vista across a broad tract of lower-lying land, which tends to attract the attention of anyone visiting the site. Yet the enclosure lies on ground that falls away in the opposite direction, towards the upland, as though turning its back on the vista.

*Figure 5.25
The orientation of
upland-oriented sites is
ambiguous. Like the
lowland-oriented
causewayed enclosures,
they offer a view across a
low-lying area, but from
that lower ground it is the
topography rather than the
enclosure itself that can be
seen. The earthworks can
only be seen from the
higher ground in the
opposite direction
(A Combe Hill, East
Sussex; B Rybury,
Wiltshire; C Whitehawk
Camp, East Sussex;
D Knap Hill, Wiltshire).*

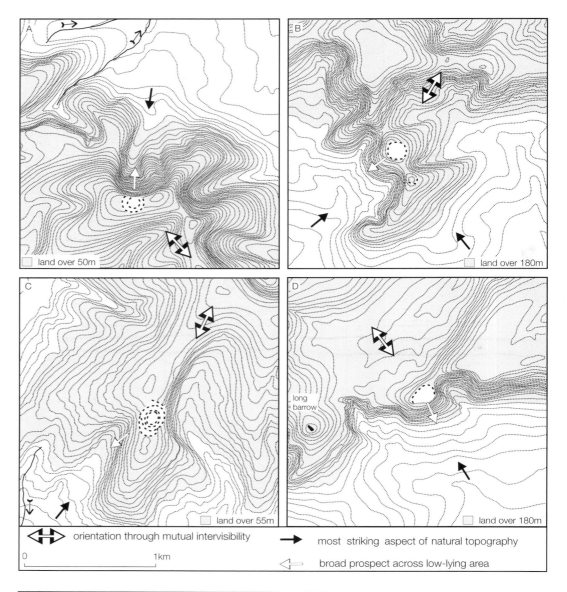

*Figure 5.26
The setting of the
causewayed enclosure at
Combe Hill in East
Sussex, on the edge of the
northern escarpment of the
South Downs, is one of the
most dramatic in England
when seen from the lower
ground to the north. Like
the enclosures at The
Trundle and Whitehawk
Camp on the southern
escarpment, however, the
ground on which the
enclosure lies tilts towards
the massif of the Downs, so
that the earthworks and
interior are only visible
from that direction.*

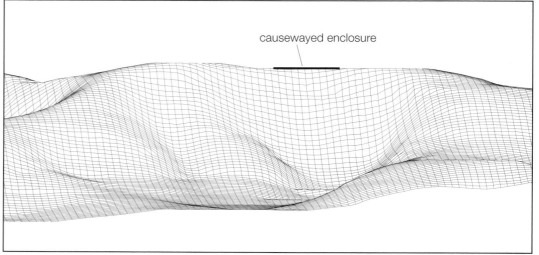

*Figure 5.27 (above)*
*At Rybury in Wiltshire, the causewayed enclosure tilts northwards so that the interior would have*
*been clearly visible from the higher ground in that direction. Seen from the north, this relationship to*
*the topography is highlighted by the siting of the rampart of the overlying Iron Age hillfort, which*
*follows the natural contour far more closely. (NMR AA96/2986)*

*Figure 5.28 (below)*
*A length of causewayed bank and ditch skirting the edge of an eminence to the east of the main*
*causewayed enclosure at Rybury does not entirely make sense as a defensive outwork. It may have*
*been deliberately sited so as to make an element of the monument visible from the low-lying ground*
*to the south-east. The enclosure itself is, however, typical of upland-oriented sites in tilting away*
*from the low ground with the result that it can be overlooked from the crest of the main massif.*

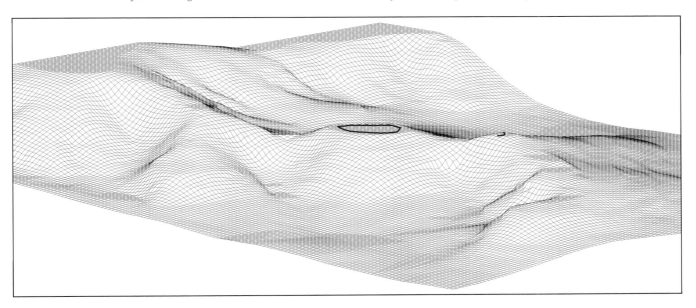

*Figure 5.29*
*The causewayed enclosure*
*on Knap Hill in Wiltshire.*
*Like the enclosure at*
*Rybury nearby, this*
*enclosure seems to be*
*oriented northwards*
*towards the upland. In*
*this case, however, that*
*impression is given not by*
*the siting of the enclosure*
*on a slope, but by the*
*apparent absence of*
*earthworks along the*
*southern escarpment.*
*(NMR 15290/06)*

As a result, there is a kind of polarity to the orientation of these sites. On the one hand, they seem to be sited so that the striking topography signals their position when seen from the adjacent lower-lying ground. On the other hand, the earthworks themselves and the interiors of the enclosures are only visible from the higher ground. It must be assumed that the siting of such important monuments was not haphazard, but was conceived and thought through in advance; the distinctive trait could therefore be significant.

For instance, the enclosures on Combe Hill (Fig 5.26), Rybury Hill and Whitesheet Hill overlook the heads of natural coombs which cut particularly deeply into chalk escarpments. These 'gigantic bowls', to paraphrase Colt Hoare's description in 1812 of the topography at Whitesheet (Hoare 1812, 41), are conspicuous from a great distance across the adjacent low-lying ground and may have signalled the position of the monument when seen from that direction. Equally, when looking away from the monuments across the low-lying ground, the sudden drop of the scarp slopes creates a sense of standing

at the edge of the world. In both cases, however, the earthworks themselves are very difficult to distinguish when seen from below, because the ground slopes gently away in the opposite direction. Excavation has not provided any hint that there was a timber superstructure to make the earthworks more prominent. On the other hand, because the enclosures tilt towards the upland, their plans and interiors are clearly visible from that direction (Figs 5.27, 5.28 and 5.29).

Prior to the expansion of suburban Brighton, the promontory which White-hawk Camp in East Sussex occupies would have been a visually striking landform when seen from the coastal plain to the south. Yet the enclosure itself is only visible from the chalk uplands to the north. The Trundle is sited on St Roche's Hill in West Sussex, a dramatic isolated summit, which is visible from all directions, but is most imposing and eye-catching from a far greater distance when seen from the coastal plain to the south. The Trundle has usually been described as a 'hilltop' site (for example Palmer 1976, table 1; Drewett 1994, table 5), but in fact the inner circuit of the causewayed enclosure is centred on the sloping ground just off the summit, quite typically, and tilts northwards towards the main range of the South Downs.

## The tor enclosures

While the tor enclosures in the South-West do seem to have been deliberately sited with respect to specific topographic features in the landscape, they share few of the characteristics of the conventional causewayed enclosures. Like many of the settings of the upland-oriented sites, Carn Brea and Helman Tor in Cornwall are visually striking, due partly to the isolation of the massifs and partly to the dramatic form of the rock outcrops which the enclosures surround and incorporate. As described above, this direct association with striking natural rock formations is a defining characteristic of the whole group of tor enclosures. While many command an impressive view, it is usually panoramic, apparently without any specific orientation. This contrasts strongly with almost all the conventional causewayed enclosures in upland settings, the most important exception being the site on Raddon Hill, which is the nearest known site to the tor enclosures.

*Nr 2.*      *Feby 5 1821.*

*hawk hill shewing the ... of the camp and the ... in the valleys —.*

*Nr 41. East side of White Hawk Hill Camp*

## Detecting change over time in the settings of causewayed enclosures

Isobel Smith's (1971, 92) observation that causewayed enclosures have '. . . the appearance of predetermined plans carried out regardless of topography' echoed the comments of fieldworkers from Hadrian Allcroft onwards and has become something of a mantra in discussions of the monuments. By contrast, the siting of long barrows has long been agreed to show that the builders were fully aware of the nature of the topography and carefully considered how to use it to best effect (eg Ashbee 1984, 21–4; Tilley 1994, 121–42). As has been shown in this chapter, Smith's conclusion does not hold good for a significant proportion of the causewayed enclosures now known to have existed. There is also a degree of consistency in the siting of most enclosures on higher ground, even if the logic evident in the choice of location seems strange to a modern mind. Turning to those enclosures to which Smith was directly referring, it has already

been suggested that there is evidence in the plan forms of Whitehawk Camp and the enclosure at The Trundle that they were modified over time. Such changes may account convincingly for the 'strangeness' evident in the relationship of the eventual plans of certain enclosures to the topography.

The most striking example of this phenomenon is at Windmill Hill in Wiltshire, where the outer circuit plunges down the hillside, seemingly heedless of the slope; the overall vertical range between the highest and lowest points is almost 20m. A similar situation exists at the Trundle where the gradient is steeper in places, although the overall vertical range is slightly less. The location of Whitehawk Camp has sometimes been referred to as an unusual saddle-like situation (eg Drewett 1994, table 5). On the northern side of the enclosure, the outermost circuit does not drop down the side of a hill, but instead extends across an area of level ground and reaches as far as the ascending slope beyond it (Figs 5.30 and 5.31). At all these sites, however, the innermost circuit is located on gently sloping ground, just below the

*Figure 5.30*
*View from the east of Whitehawk Camp in East Sussex, as sketched by the Revd Skinner in 1821. Despite his over-simplified depiction of the earthworks in plan (see Fig 2.3), Skinner's view gives a good impression of the setting of the causewayed enclosure prior to the expansion of housing developments on the slopes. Note the tilt of the earthwork (that is, the larger outer circuits) northwards to the right. (Revd J Skinner Collection; MS 33, 658, 40;41 reproduced by kind permission of the British Library)*

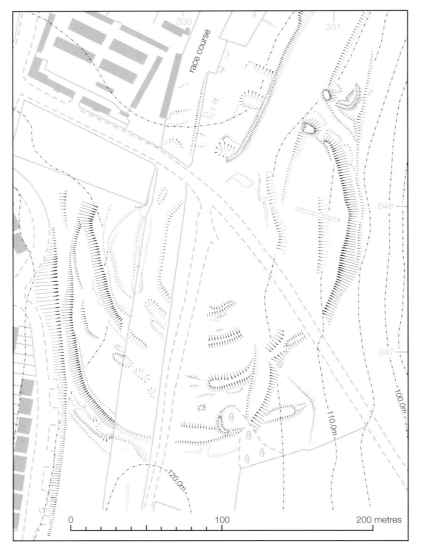

outer circuit is seriously at odds with the topography. On the basis of the overall plan, however, and its relationship to the topography, it is not impossible that the monument was constructed in three phases, the three circuits built in sequence from inner to outer. These few examples may serve to indicate the potential for change in the form and extent of the many other causewayed enclosures where the evidence cannot be detected.

## Visibility and vegetation

In the mid 1990s, visibility became an important topic of research in the study of various types of prehistoric monument (Tilley 1994; Drewett 1994, fig 15; Cleal and Allen in Cleal *et al* 1995, 34–40; Woodward and Woodward 1996; Bradley 1997, 82–8; Topping 1997a and b). This is partly because it can be safely assumed that the natural topography in the environs of most sites has remained more or less constant, holding out the hope that one aspect of a given monument can be viewed – if not strictly experienced – in much the same way as it was by the people who built and used it. The exceptions in this respect are the monuments in riverine and fenland locations, where major environmental change has occurred in some instances. As a result, this avenue of research has further promoted disproportionate interest in the upland sites of Wessex and Sussex, where the visual attributes of the topography seem to have been harnessed deliberately.

In discussing visibility, the key factor that has changed greatly over the last 5,000 years is vegetation. The majority of causewayed enclosures on high ground were probably at first located in fairly small clearings in woodland, although certain sites, including Whitehawk Camp and The Trundle, may have occupied more open country from an early stage (Thomas 1982; Drewett *et al* 1988, 35–6). This conclusion is based on the evidence of snails and other environmentally sensitive mollusca, since pollen is very seldom preserved on the sites found on the chalk uplands. As a result, the full range of species and their relative proportions are not clear, though charcoal from various sites indicates the probable presence of oak, elm, lime, ash, pine and hazel. It may be that slightly sloping ground was chosen for the causewayed enclosures on high ground so as to improve the view to or from their interiors (Smith 1965, 19). Vegetation could have

*Figure 5.31*
*The earthworks of Whitehawk Camp in East Sussex remain fairly well preserved, despite the damage done by development and the use of the northern part of the site as part of Brighton racecourse. The central circuits occupy a typical position on gently sloping ground and are not particularly awkward in their relationship to the topography. The outer circuits, on the other hand, are at odds with the lie of the land, perhaps indicating that the enclosure expanded beyond the area originally intended for it.*

summit, in the position typical for causewayed enclosures on higher ground.

It could be inferred from this evidence alone that the extent of these enclosures may have increased over time through the addition of new circuits. With each addition, the original slight displacement from the summit would have been amplified, culminating in the extraordinary placement of the outermost perimeters. The apparent awkward fit of the eventual plans to the natural topography may, therefore, result in part from the expansion of the enclosures far beyond the area that was initially envisaged for them. At Windmill Hill, the excavated evidence suggests that the inner and middle circuits may have been built at the same time and that the outer circuit was added somewhat later (Whittle *et al* 1999). This is quite conceivable, given that only the been cleared initially by felling, given the use of large quantities of oak for the structural timbers at causewayed enclosures such as those on Hambledon Hill in Dorset (*see* Chapter 3: Timber structures). There is also widespread evidence for burning in proximity to causewayed enclosures, indicated by the presence of 'catholic' species of snails and microscopic charcoal fragments (Moore 1997). In some cases, the clearance of trees to make space for the causewayed enclosure and sometimes to build palisades must have had the effect of drawing attention to the position of the monument, even more obviously than the construction of the earthworks themselves. Upland-oriented causewayed enclosures, located on the very edges of steep scarp slopes, such as those on Combe Hill and Whitesheet Hill, must have been made conspicuous from the low-lying ground below by the absence of trees as much as by the topography. Both sites, seen from a distance, could have been identified easily as gaps in the treeline along the horizon. Genuine hilltop sites such as the causewayed enclosure on Raddon Hill and the main enclosure on Hambledon Hill could have stood out like bald patches in the tree canopy. The visual impact of moving out of the woodland and into the cleared ground occupied by the causewayed enclosure may have been as great as that of the earthworks themselves (Fig 5.32).

With regard to sites in Sussex, it has been suggested that as long as the clearing extended to a minimum of 15m from the perimeters of the causewayed enclosures, visibility would have been at least a possible issue (Drewett *et al* 1988, 35–6). With so many variables involved, however, it is difficult to be confident in such an estimate for enclosures elsewhere in the country. The various species which are attested in the vicinity of the monuments all have different heights and densities of foliage, varying according to season. The topography of the South Downs in Sussex is also generally fairly abrupt, much more so than the rolling landscape of eastern England in particular. Causewayed enclosures such as those at Robin Hood's Ball in Wiltshire, Orsett in Essex and Freston in Suffolk occupy slight slopes in gently undulating terrain (Figs 1.4, 3.11, 3.14). The clearance of much larger areas would have been necessary for the site to be visible at all.

Turning to the causewayed enclosures in riverine locations, analyses of alluvial deposits and soil micromorphology suggest that the channels of watercourses generally remained constant until around 3,000 BC. This was presumably due to the presence of woodland stabilising the banks (Burrin and Scaife 1984; French 1990; Needham and Macklin 1992; Brown 1997, 210–15). Alluvial deposits at Daisy Banks Fen, near the

*Figure 5.32*
*Reconstruction of the process of forest clearance in the earlier Neolithic. This drawing gives a good impression of the sudden visual impact that would have been the result of forest clearance prior to the building of a monument. Where causewayed enclosures were built in such an environment, the edge of the clearings may even have been seen as their outermost perimeters. (Courtesy of the Museum of London)*

causewayed enclosure at Abingdon, preserve seeds and pollen that offer one of the most useful records of vegetation change to be found in southern England (Parker 1997; Barclay *et al* 1996, 6–8). Similar species are present to those known from higher ground: elm, oak, ash, lime, birch, pine and hazel. Pine and birch have together, however, been estimated to represent only 5 per cent of the trees, with elm and lime between them accounting for 73 per cent. Small quantities of willow and alder may have been confined to the banks of the stream. Pollen from cereal crops and grasses suggest that open clearings nearby were being used for agriculture and grazing. The composition of the woodland would therefore have differed slightly, but the vegetation cover around many causewayed enclosures located on valley floors may have had much in common with that in the environs of the upland sites. Given the lack of topographic variation, however, visibility cannot have been an issue at all, except perhaps where it was possible to approach the causewayed enclosure by boat along the open corridor created by a major river. At Haddenham on the former bank of the River Ouse in Cambridgeshire, the monument may have been oriented towards the river through the elaboration of the architecture (Evans 1988b, 139).

## Human geography

The relationships of causewayed enclosures to the physical landscape have been discussed at length, primarily because the evident patterns may reveal some of the factors that influenced the siting of the monuments. Visibility has been a central topic, because the apparently deliberate orientation of causewayed enclosures on higher ground seems to link them to specific sectors of the landscape, hinting at the involvement of the monuments in the human geography of the area (Drewett 1994, fig 15). Since the 1970s, there have been several attempts to identify 'territories' with which individual causewayed enclosures may have been associated. These studies, which are the subject of the next chapter, have generally disregarded the topographic settings of causewayed enclosures and other monuments and have thereby reduced the dynamics of the physical landscape to a two-dimensional board. Far from being a neutral backdrop, the form of the physical landscape may prove a strand of evidence that has much to contribute to this research. In Chapter 6, the conclusions that can be drawn from the patterns evident in the siting of causewayed enclosures will be discussed.

# 6
# Making sense of the human landscape

## The Mesolithic and earliest-Neolithic background

The builders of causewayed enclosures inhabited a physical landscape already deeply permeated with memories and beliefs. The existing associations of particular places with seasonal resources, with people and myths may well have been factors in the location of causewayed enclosures (Thomas 1991; Bradley 1993; 1998b; Edmonds 1999, 11–31). On the European mainland, there may have been direct continuity from a Mesolithic settlement at the causewayed enclosure at Noyen-sur-Seine in the Paris basin (Mordant and Mordant 1992). In England, only at certain causewayed enclosures in the west of the country, such as the one on Dorstone Hill in Hereford and Worcester (Pye 1967–9), does the density of Mesolithic flints indicate that the area may already have been visited repeatedly or quite intensively used and perhaps even extensively deforested. Elsewhere, the presence of Mesolithic worked flints at or near enclosures is not unusual, but seldom in sufficient quantities to suggest that the places were foci for long-term or repeated activity prior to the construction of the monument.

The location of certain causewayed enclosures does hint that the use of the landscape in the Mesolithic may have been a more indirect influence on their siting. Those on rises in the floors of river valleys and on the valley sides may have derived from the typical siting of much earlier Mesolithic hunting camps in similar locations (Whittle 1996, 29–34). The easy pickings of the rich flora and fauna in the rivers and their environs are very likely to have remained as attractive to the builders of causewayed enclosures as to the earlier hunter-gatherers (Brown 1997, 208–9).

Actual activity is clearly not the only means by which places could have acquired a status that may have influenced the siting of causewayed enclosures (Bradley 1993, 22–44; Edmonds 1999). The inevitable reliance of prehistoric archaeology on structural and artefactual evidence does not, however, make it easy to recognise the many possible forms of social or cultural significance that would have left no physical trace at all. The striking landforms adjacent to the upland-oriented causewayed enclosures and tor enclosures in particular may have been quite literally landmarks; that is, memorable and recognisable fixed points that could have denoted specific places or symbolised larger areas, with little or no actual activity occurring there. Ethnographic research and place-name studies in many societies have drawn attention to the importance of natural features in inspiring place-names and mental maps of the landscape (eg Tuan 1977; Gelling 1984; Chapman 1988; Tilley 1994). These are often linked with real or mythical individuals or events. Rivers and their valleys must have been important in guiding movement around the forested landscape throughout the Mesolithic (Ingold 1986). The concentration of causewayed enclosures, long barrows and cursus monuments along river valley systems must indicate that the importance of these routes continued well into the Neolithic (Richards 1996). Various physical features of long-standing significance may, therefore, have been chosen as the sites of causewayed enclosures, perhaps to enshrine their importance.

Neolithic activity predating the building of causewayed enclosures is almost as difficult to discern as Mesolithic activity. Due to the problems in obtaining precise dates and the lengthy periods over which certain types of artefact were used, clear stratigraphic relationships have usually been relied upon. The causewayed enclosure at Crickley Hill in Gloucestershire has produced less equivocal evidence of Neolithic activity predating the construction of the earthworks. This comprised features, including three or four small post-built 'huts', sealed beneath the bank of the outer circuit, which is thought to be the earlier of the two (Dixon 1988, 78). Elsewhere, the evidence is less clear-cut. At Windmill Hill and at Robin Hood's Ball in Wiltshire, Neolithic features (including a human burial at Windmill Hill) were discovered beneath the banks of the outer circuits (Whittle 1990; Thomas 1964, 8). If, as suggested above, these circuits are later additions, however, the activity could have been contemporary with the construction or use of the inner circuits. At Bryn Celli Wen on the Isle of Anglesey, the ditch of the causewayed enclosure appears to have been aligned on a standing stone, which had been broken and deliberately buried. Neither feature has been accurately dated as yet (Edmonds and Thomas 1991a).

## Regionalism in the British Isles

The distribution and forms of causewayed enclosures, along with other types of monuments and artefacts, have repeatedly been used as evidence in the search for social and cultural groups (eg Curwen 1930; Piggott 1954; Renfrew 1973; Palmer 1976; Barker and Webley 1978; Cunliffe 1993, fig 2.6). Conversely, understanding these groups may provide the key to interpretating how the monuments themselves were used and why they were located in specific places. Rog Palmer's (1976) influential analysis proposed four subdivisions of the distribution in England, which he termed the Sussex, Thames, South-West and Midlands regions (Fig 6.1). The starting point for this work was the observation that each grouping seemed to be delimited by areas where causewayed enclosures were absent, even though the conditions were suitable for the production of cropmarks (Palmer 1976, 162–3 and fig 8). Palmer also sought to demonstrate that there were similarities in the forms of the causewayed enclosures within each region and concluded that enclosures with 'simple' single circuits tended to lie in the south, with more complex forms further north.

Since 1976 the discovery of more sites has gradually extended the boundaries of some of the groupings proposed by Palmer to the point where they merge with each other and are no longer convincing as regions. For example, the eastern end of his Thames group can no longer be clearly distinguished from sites in northern Kent nor from the southern limit of the scatter of

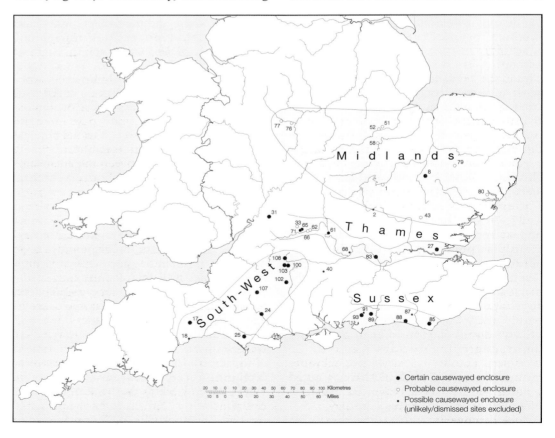

*Figure 6.1*
*Regional groups of causewayed enclosures, excluding those sites that have subsequently been dismissed. The current distribution pattern, together with a consideration of the forms and landscape settings of the enclosures, suggests that there are relatively few instances where large groupings can be identified. Some apparent groups may represent the activity of a single small community over several generation. (Redrawn from Palmer 1976)*

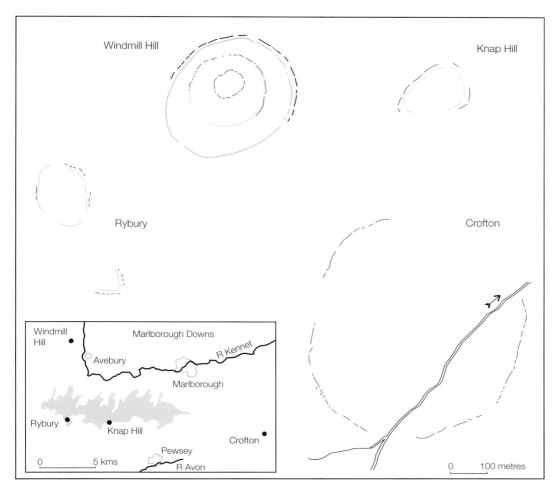

*Figure 6.2*
*The cluster of causewayed enclosures on the southern range of the Marlborough Downs seems convincing as a group when seen simply as points on the map, but begins to look much less so when the very different forms and locations of the monuments are considered.*

sites in the Midlands. Other sites, especially some of those in Palmer's Midland group such as Alrewas and Mavesyn Ridware in Staffordshire, remain conspicuously isolated as pairs or individuals and are now equally unconvincing as parts of larger regions. The distribution of enclosures in East and West Sussex could now, as in 1976, be interpreted as two smaller groups rather than as a single region (Russell 1997, 70–3). Small clusters of sites may appear convincing as a region when seen simply as points on the map, but they seldom comprise monuments of very similar form. In Wiltshire, for example, the causewayed enclosures on Windmill Hill, Rybury, Knap Hill and at Crofton lie within a few kilometres of each other, yet are very diverse in terms of their plan forms and topographic settings (Fig 6.2). In considering outlying causewayed enclosures such as those on Donegore Hill in County Antrim and on Chalk Hill at Ramsgate in Kent, it may be unreasonable to expect that future discoveries will show them to be

parts of larger groupings. Individual causewayed enclosures may have constituted 'regions' and sparse scatters of sites, such as those which for the most part comprise Palmer's South-West and Midland groups, may represent not one region, but many. Differences in form between the enclosures in different areas can, therefore, be seen as quite predictable variation in the reaction of disparate communities in giving expression to a new idea of an alien form of monument, which was still vague and variable. Regionalism, if this is indeed the correct term, seems to have operated on a much smaller scale than Palmer suggested.

There are exceptions that prove the rule, where small numbers of causewayed enclosures with similar characteristics cluster on river systems. Each is usually within easy walking distance of the next. As described in Chapter 4, in the valley of the River Welland, five causewayed enclosures lie within 5km of each other (one certain and one probable at Etton, and very probable sites at Northborough in Cambridgeshire

*Figure 6.3*
*The concentration of causewayed enclosures in the valleys of the rivers Nene and Welland is all the more remarkable in that they all seem to share a similar plan form and size. Only at Southwick does the topography seem to have influenced the plan, for the eastern side of the enclosure follows the course of a stream. The sites are also generally similar in their locations, most lying on very slight rises in what subsequently became the Fenland.*

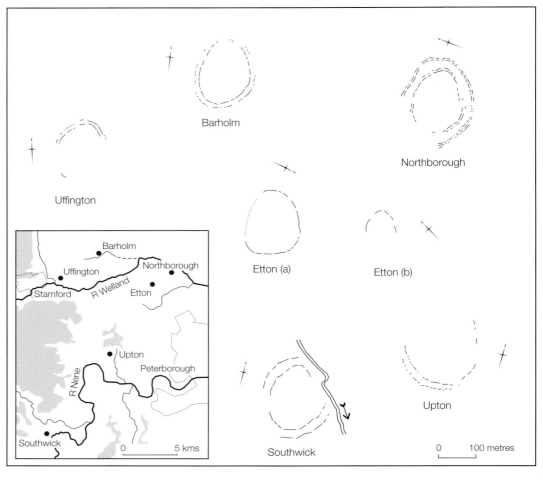

*Figure 6.3*
*The concentration of causewayed enclosures in the valleys of the rivers Nene and Welland is all the more remarkable in that they all seem to share a similar plan form and size. Only at Southwick does the topography seem to have influenced the plan, for the eastern side of the enclosure follows the course of a stream. The sites are also generally similar in their locations, most lying on very slight rises in what subsequently became the Fenland.*

*Figure 6.4 (facing page)*
*The concentration of causewayed enclosures and other earlier Neolithic monuments and sites in the upper and middle reaches of the Thames Valley arguably offers far greater potential for research into the nature and extent of earlier Neolithic territories than any other part of England. Gravel extraction on a vast scale has led to an increase in archaeological work since 1976, both through aerial survey (Fenner and Dyer unpublished 1994) and fieldwork (eg Barclay et al 1997; Hey 1997).*

and at Barholm and Uffington in Lincolnshire) and seem to share a similar plan and size (Fig 6.3). They also share similar locations: the first four lie on slight rises on the margins of the present floodplains of streams and rivers, while the enclosure at Uffington is only a little different, occupying a gentle slope on a valley side. In the valley of the River Nene, about 10km to the south, the causewayed enclosures at Upton and Southwick in Cambridgeshire are similar. Likewise, in the valley of the River Trent, the enclosures at Alrewas and Mavesyn Ridware in Staffordshire, only 4km apart, again share a common plan, size and similar locations on low rises in the valley floor.

Along the middle and upper reaches of the River Thames, at least fifteen enclosures cluster in an area of less than 3,000km² (Fig 6.4). Those on the northern edge of the concentration, at Burford and Southmore Grove, occupy relatively high ground overlooking streams. The remainder all lie on low rises within 2km of either the

Thames or its tributary streams (Case 1986, 19). The proportions with closely spaced and widely spaced circuits are roughly equal and there are no pronounced similarities in their forms. With the exception, however, of the outer circuit of the enclosure at Staines in Surrey and perhaps the enclosures at Dorney in Buckinghamshire and Eton Wick in Berkshire (which lie on the eastern limit of the concentration) all the circuits seem to have enclosed small or medium sized areas. Similarly, many of the numerous cursus monuments in the area, which may be broadly contemporary with the causewayed enclosures, are also relatively small. Julian Thomas (1991, 154–5) has suggested that the patterns evident in the forms of the monuments may reflect low population densities within a dispersed form of social organisation. In contrast, Jan Harding (1995) has argued on the basis of the same evidence that the area was densely settled, although perhaps still within a dispersed society.

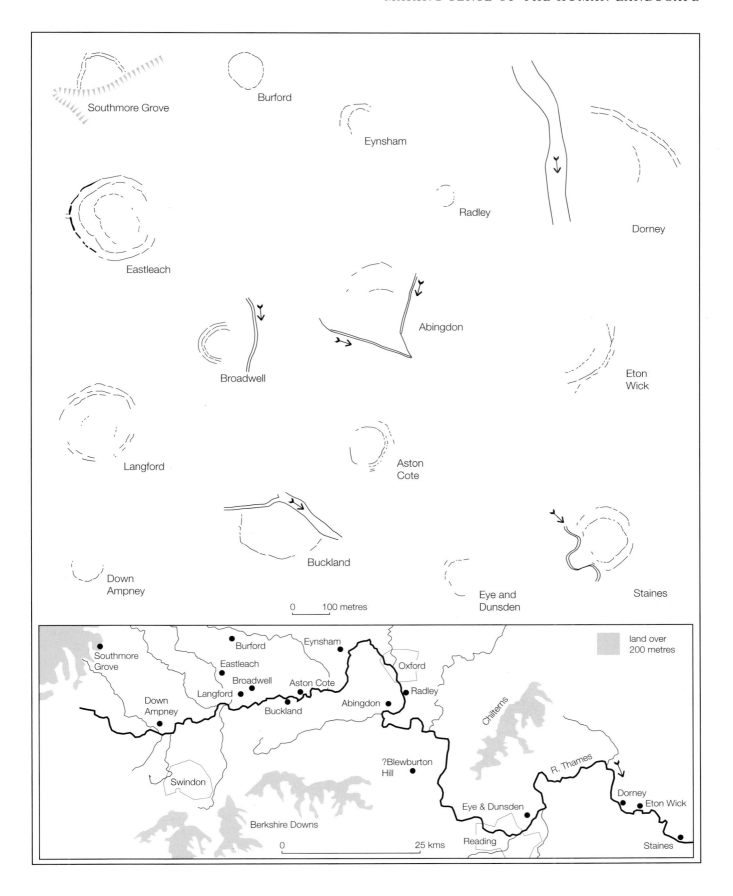

Southmore Grove

Burford

Eynsham

Radley

Dorney

Eastleach

Abingdon

Broadwell

Eton Wick

Langford

Aston Cote

Buckland

Down Ampney

Eye and Dunsden

Staines

0    100 metres

Southmore Grove

Burford

Eynsham

Eastleach

Oxford

Broadwell

Aston Cote

Radley

Langford

Down Ampney

Buckland

Abingdon

Swindon

?Blewburton Hill

Chilterns

R. Thames

Eye & Dunsden

Dorney

Eton Wick

Reading

Berkshire Downs

Staines

land over 200 metres

0    25 kms

111

Of the seven causewayed enclosures in the valleys of the Rivers Nene and Welland, only the first enclosure discovered at Etton has yet been excavated and accurately dated (Pryor 1998b). Without better understanding of the period when causewayed enclosures were in use, it remains impossible to know how the sites within each apparent group interacted with each other, if at all. Each of the other monuments may have belonged to a separate group, or a sub-division of the same social group, or several groups may have used two or more enclosures at different seasons of the year (Fig 6.5). Alternatively, the enclosures may have been built decades or even generations apart, as groups abandoned their original territory for whatever reason and moved on to start afresh. As with the analysis of the plan forms of causewayed enclosures carried out in Chapter 4, an incomplete knowledge of their chronology presents a major problem in interpreting the social landscape.

## Pairs of causewayed enclosures?

There are a few instances of two causewayed enclosures lying in close proximity to each other, hinting that they may have been 'paired' in some sense. On higher ground, the enclosures at Crickley Hill and Birdlip Camp in Gloucestershire lie within 2km of each other and are visible from each other, as well as overlooking the same lowland area. The enclosures at Rybury

and Knap Hill lie within 4km apart and are both apparently oriented towards the same upland massif. In Northamptonshire, the enclosures on valley sides at Briar Hill and Dallington lie within sight of each other, at a distance of around 4km, the former overlooking the River Nene and the latter a tiny tributary stream. Among the enclosures in the Upper Thames Valley, those in Oxfordshire at Langford and Broadwell, Buckland and Aston Cote, Abingdon and Radley, together with those at Dorney and Eton Wick all lie within 6km of each other (Fenner and Dyer 1992, 68; Fig 1.8). A similar pattern may have existed in the valleys of the Rivers Nene and Welland and the Rivers Aisne and Seine in northern France (Dubouloz et al 1988, figs 11.2–11.5; Andersen 1997, fig 259). Considering the distribution pattern simply as points on the map, there would seem to be quite a strong case for thinking that pairs of enclosures could have functioned together as single units. This has led to a bias in the search for enclosures, and in turn to a number of misidentifications in the vicinity of certain or probable causewayed enclosures: at Cherhill and at Overton near Windmill Hill, at Hainford near Roughton and at East Bedfont near Staines.

The evidence for pairings is far from conclusive, however. Looking at the pattern in the Thames Valley, Humphrey Case (1986, 22) has taken the contrary view, arguing that the enclosures which make up each apparent pairing are unlikely to have been contemporary and are, therefore, not really pairs at all. Certainly, both there and in

*Figure 6.5*
*Possible models for earlier Neolithic territories and patterns of mobility. It may well be that different groupings of causewayed enclosures represent different forms of territory and mobility. Gabriel Cooney (1997) has warned against the establishment of a 'new orthodoxy' through the acceptance of a stereotypical Neolithic lifestyle in which uniform sedentariness is simply replaced by uniform mobility.*

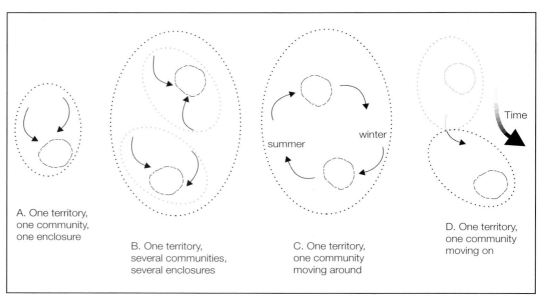

A. One territory, one community, one enclosure

B. One territory, several communities, several enclosures

C. One territory, one community moving around

summer   winter

D. One territory, one community moving on

Time

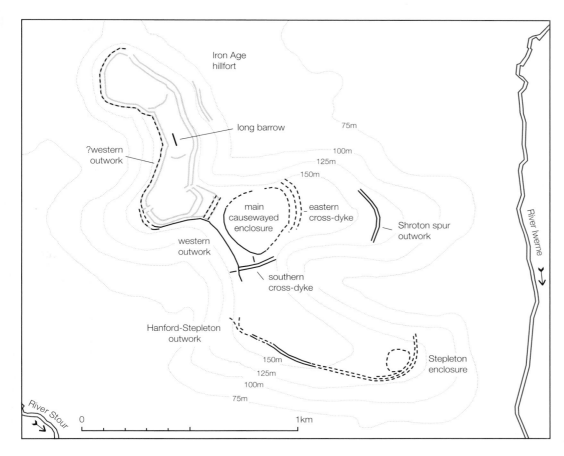

Figure 6.6
*The principal earlier Neolithic monuments on Hambledon Hill in Dorset. Radiocarbon determinations suggest that the main causewayed enclosure is the earliest element of the complex and that the western outwork and Hanford/Stepleton outwork are the latest additions.*

northern France, the enclosures in question are generally quite dissimilar from each other in form. This may support Case's argument, especially considering that, in some cases (for example, the enclosure at Abingdon), their forms would probably have changed over time.

Alternatively, it may be that causewayed enclosures were genuinely paired and that the differences evident in their forms are because they had different functions, each perhaps complementing the role of the other. More probably, the differences evident in their forms may indicate that the precise plans simply did not matter, as long as they retained the basic characteristics recognised as typical of the class. Going further still, it is possible that causewayed enclosures complemented unenclosed sites, or sites that were enclosed solely by palisades or uncleared woodland. There may also have been complementary differences in the siting of the monuments. It may be significant that in the Nene and Welland valleys and at Alrewas and Mavesyn Ridware in the valley of the River Trent, one of each pairing lies next to a major river and the other next to a small tributary. A similar pattern may have existed in the valley of the Seine (*see* Andersen 1997, fig 259).

At Hambledon Hill in Dorset, the main causewayed enclosure on the central summit lies less than 1km from a smaller causewayed enclosure built at a somewhat later date on the Stepleton spur. In a late phase of the use of the two enclosures, they were physically linked to each other by the construction of two lengths of double bank and ditch, also of causewayed construction, called the 'western outwork' and 'Hanford/ Stepleton outworks' by the excavators (Mercer and Healy in preparation). Field survey now suggests that the western outwork may have extended along the whole western flank of the hill (Fig 6.6). There is some evidence to support the suspicion that two enclosures may have been equally closely juxtaposed at Whitesheet Hill (Cunliffe 1993, 57), but only one of the two that can be identified with confidence is certainly of Neolithic date.

## Regions without causewayed enclosures

It was suggested in Chapter 5 that the absence of causewayed enclosures from the extreme south-west of England may be apparent rather than real, perhaps a consequence of geological conditions and the search exclusively for enclosures with interrupted ditches. It has also been observed, however, that there are genuine differences in form and location evident among the tor enclosures. It is, therefore, possible, particularly given the absence of conventional causewayed enclosures on the lower ground, that the South-West and parts of northern England were genuinely different in the way people put into effect the new idea of enclosure. The absence of typical causewayed enclosures might then represent a social difference rather than a geological one.

There are also regions where the absence of causewayed enclosures certainly cannot be argued away as a consequence of the geology or modern land-use and must reflect a genuine absence of the type of monument. The chalk uplands of the Yorkshire Wolds, for example, provide conditions that are highly productive of cropmarks. The area has also been thoroughly recorded through aerial reconnaissance (Manby 1988; Stoertz 1997). Yet not a single conventional causewayed enclosure has been discovered. It has been suggested that the relatively large, circular enclosure with interrupted ditches at Duggleby Howe in North Yorkshire is a local adaptation of the typical design. As noted in Chapter 5, however, the form of the enclosure has as much in common with the causewayed circuits of certain later Neolithic henges on the Wolds and elsewhere in Yorkshire.

It might be inferred from this that there was a dense core of more conventional causewayed enclosures in central and southern England, with a small number of 'abnormal' forms around the periphery of this area. In terms of the spread of the idea of the new form of monument in the earlier Neolithic, it might be concluded that the concept of how a causewayed enclosure should be designed simply 'degenerated' as it was transferred northwards. This conclusion would, to a great extent, echo the migration scenario favoured by advocates of the 'culture-historical' approach in the first half of the 20th century (eg Piggott 1954). In this context, the identification of enclosures in Northern Ireland, on the Isle of Anglesey, the Isle of Man and perhaps in South Wales and Scotland that seem to be comparable to typical causewayed enclosures in central and southern England is extremely important. Their existence in this form argues strongly that the 'diffusionist' model of the communication of ideas is oversimplified. Instead, it would seem that the concept of how enclosures should be built was passed more or less intact throughout the British Isles, but was purposefully modified in certain areas and rejected outright elsewhere.

## Territories: causewayed enclosures, long barrows and flint mines

To be effective, the analysis of regionalism cannot rely on a single source of evidence. Yet with scant understanding of the nature of settlement and society (as discussed below), interpretations are still forced to rely heavily on the distribution of monuments: causewayed enclosures, long barrows and the flint mining complexes that developed to monumental proportions.

Causewayed enclosures have frequently been linked with long barrows (*see* eg Ashbee 1984; Renfrew 1973; Cunliffe 1993, fig 2.6; Fig 6.7), and Palmer made proximity to long barrows one of his criteria in comparing the upland and lowland sites (Palmer 1976, 176–7). There are two main reasons for linking the two forms of monument. Firstly, there are several sites where the two types of monument are found in contact, or in very close proximity to each other. The long barrows adjacent to the enclosures at Hambledon Hill and Knap Hill are amongst those which survive as earthworks, while those at Haddenham and Roughton have been levelled by ploughing (Fig 6.7). The so-called 'mortuary enclosure' at Buckland may also represent a similar form of monument (Figs 4.17 and 4.27).

In two cases, at Hambledon Hill and at Barrow Hills near Abingdon in Oxfordshire, shorter long barrows, or oval barrows, appear to be broadly contemporary with the causewayed enclosures (Mercer and Healy in preparation; Bradley 1992; Barclay *et al* 1996, 17). At Hambledon Hill, the barrow extended across most of the space between the main causewayed enclosure and the southern cross-ridge dyke and there are slight indications from the plan relationship that it might have been built before the southern cross-ridge dyke. At Barrow Hills, the barrow is situated on the opposite side of a small stream from the inner circuit of the enclosure. The barrow contained two inhumations, while that on Hambledon

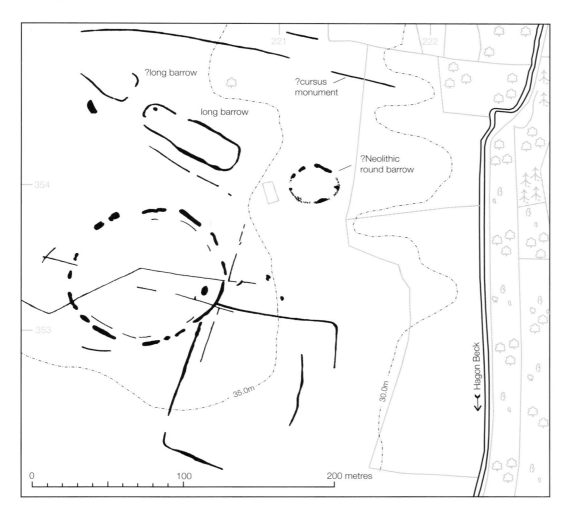

Figure 6.7
The complex of cropmarks associated with the causewayed enclosure at Roughton in Norfolk seems to represent two long barrows, a round barrow with a causewayed ditch, which may be of Neolithic date, and perhaps a cursus monument to the north. Note how the long barrows appear to have been kept apart from the causewayed enclosure by a line of pits that may represent a substantial palisade or some other setting of timber uprights.

Hill contained a maximum of three, rather than a single individual as was first thought (Mercer 1980a, 43; Bradley 1984, 23). Deposits in the ditches of both barrows were similar in character to those found in the ditches of the enclosures, suggesting that the barrows were involved in at least some of the activities which took place in the causewayed enclosures.

Secondly, as discussed below in Chapter 7, some causewayed enclosures are thought to have functioned as arenas for the exposure of corpses for excarnation prior to burial in the barrows. This seems unlikely to represent a full explanation of their proximity, but the association between the two forms of monument does seem to be fairly consistent (Fig 6.8). For example, the causewayed enclosure at Maiden Castle seems to be associated with the concentration of long barrows conventionally termed the Dorset Ridgeway Group. Further, the extent of the North Wiltshire (Avebury) group of barrows overlaps closely with the area encompassed by the causewayed enclosures on Windmill Hill, Rybury and Knap Hill. The cluster of causewayed enclosures in the Upper Thames Valley mirrors the distribution of chambered tombs of the Cotswold-Severn type on the higher ground 10km to the north (Barclay et al 1996, fig 1). These monuments may not be the single distinctive type they at first appear, however, and more localised trends in their forms can be identified (Bestley 1993). As far as can currently be detected, clusters of long barrows generally lie at a slight distance from the causewayed enclosures. Where programmes of fieldwalking have taken place, the scarcity of struck flint suggests that these areas were not intensively used, despite – or perhaps because of – the concentrations of funerary monuments (eg Barrett et al 1991, 34–5). Most concentrations of barrows lie within a radius of 10km (that is, a relatively short walk) of an enclosure; a similar pattern has been noted in Denmark (Madsen 1988, fig 17.10).

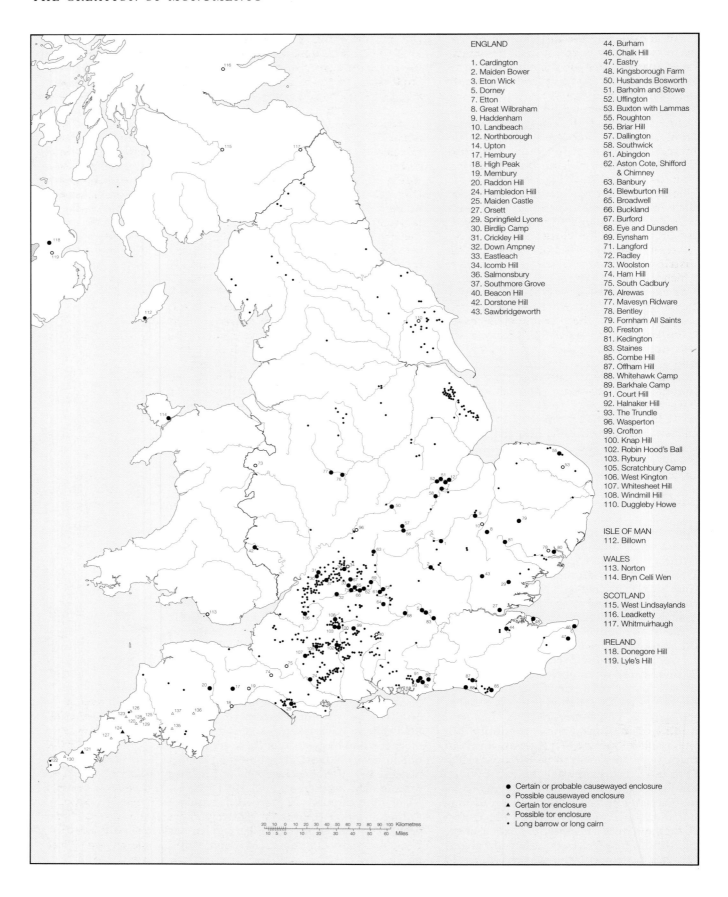

ENGLAND

1. Cardington
2. Maiden Bower
3. Eton Wick
5. Dorney
7. Etton
8. Great Wilbraham
9. Haddenham
10. Landbeach
12. Northborough
14. Upton
17. Hembury
18. High Peak
19. Membury
20. Raddon Hill
24. Hambledon Hill
25. Maiden Castle
27. Orsett
29. Springfield Lyons
30. Birdlip Camp
31. Crickley Hill
32. Down Ampney
33. Eastleach
34. Icomb Hill
36. Salmonsbury
37. Southmore Grove
40. Beacon Hill
42. Dorstone Hill
43. Sawbridgeworth

44. Burham
46. Chalk Hill
47. Eastry
48. Kingsborough Farm
50. Husbands Bosworth
51. Barholm and Stowe
52. Uffington
53. Buxton with Lammas
55. Roughton
56. Briar Hill
57. Dallington
58. Southwick
61. Abingdon
62. Aston Cote, Shifford
    & Chimney
63. Banbury
64. Blewburton Hill
65. Broadwell
66. Buckland
67. Burford
68. Eye and Dunsden
69. Eynsham
71. Langford
72. Radley
73. Woolston
74. Ham Hill
75. South Cadbury
76. Alrewas
77. Mavesyn Ridware
78. Bentley
79. Fornham All Saints
80. Freston
81. Kedington
83. Staines
85. Combe Hill
87. Offham Hill
88. Whitehawk Camp
89. Barkhale Camp
91. Court Hill
92. Halnaker Hill
93. The Trundle
96. Wasperton
99. Crofton
100. Knap Hill
102. Robin Hood's Ball
103. Rybury
105. Scratchbury Camp
106. West Kington
107. Whitesheet Hill
108. Windmill Hill
110. Duggleby Howe

ISLE OF MAN
112. Billown

WALES
113. Norton
114. Bryn Celli Wen

SCOTLAND
115. West Lindsaylands
116. Leadketty
117. Whitmuirhaugh

IRELAND
118. Donegore Hill
119. Lyle's Hill

● Certain or probable causewayed enclosure
○ Possible causewayed enclosure
▲ Certain tor enclosure
△ Possible tor enclosure
• Long barrow or long cairn

20 10 0 10 20 30 40 50 60 70 80 90 100 Kilometres
10 5 0 10 20 30 40 50 60 Miles

In considering the distribution of long barrows and long cairns, it must be remembered that any analysis is confronted by the same bias towards the uplands, especially the chalk and limestone areas, which distorts the picture of causewayed enclosures. It is quite possible that the number of barrows known from lowland areas will gradually increase and that the eventual pattern of their distribution may be rather different from its present state (eg *see* Jones 1998). The apparently close relationship between the two types of monument has itself led to more intensive searches for long barrows in the areas around enclosures. This reconnaissance strategy is bound to bias the distribution of new discoveries, some of which may prove to have been too optimistic. For example, at Halnaker Hill in West Sussex, a long barrow was identified less than 100m from the possible causewayed enclosure (Bedwin 1983). Excavation was not conclusive, but a more sceptical consideration of the evidence on the ground and from the air suggests that the mound and its flanking depression are of fairly modern origin.

It has long been noted that certain causewayed enclosures lie near flint mining complexes (Curwen 1929b, 25) and other enclosures suggested to be of earlier Neolithic date may have lain near the sources of

raw material for stone axes (Edmonds 1993, 117). This observation too has led to misidentifications of both causewayed enclosures and flint mines (eg Dyer and Hales 1961, 51; Mercer 1987; *see also* Barber *et al* 1999).

Discussion of possible interrelationships between causewayed enclosures and flint mines can only really be applied effectively to Sussex, where there are relatively large numbers of both forms of monument (Fig 6.9). It has been suggested that there may have been three distinct zones in the landscape, separated from each other by the valleys of the rivers Arun and Adur. The central block may have been characterised by a cluster of major flint mining complexes and the blocks to either side dominated by clusters of causewayed enclosures (Russell 1997, 73 and fig 7.1). The pattern is not at all clear-cut, however, for there are flint mines in the western block; indeed, the probable causewayed enclosure on Halnaker Hill in West Sussex overlooks the flint mining complex at Long Down. In the eastern block, severe coastal erosion has occurred since the Neolithic and this may have destroyed sites on the southern edge of the South Downs. Furthermore, the dating evidence currently available for the flint mining complexes in Sussex suggests that they may have originated considerably

*Figure 6.8 (facing page)*
*The distribution of causewayed enclosures, long barrows, chambered tombs and other Neolithic burial monuments. Note the dense distribution of burial monuments on the chalk uplands north and south of the Humber, where causewayed enclosures are noticeable by their absence.*

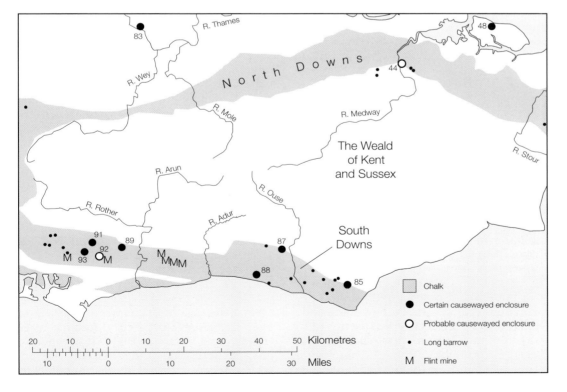

*Figure 6.9*
*The distribution of causewayed enclosures, long barrows and flint mines in East and West Sussex. Together with analysis of the surface finds (Gardiner 1984), Sussex offers potential for a reassessment of Palmer's proposal that the area might represent a single region.*

earlier than the causewayed enclosures, though they may well have continued in sporadic use until the Early Bronze Age (Field 1997, 63; Barber *et al* 1999, 81–2). The nature of any interrelationships, therefore, remains unclear.

## Territories: settlement, mobility and resources

For most of the 20th century, studies of the earlier Neolithic have attempted to understand the nature of the settlements and territories of the period through analysis of its monuments and the resources represented by the artefacts and ecofacts discovered at them. For example, Case (1982, 2–3) inferred a territory around the causewayed enclosure at Abingdon comprising both arable and grazing land, occupied by a group of six nuclear families. This was calculated on the basis of the artefacts discovered and the minimum number of adults required to build the earthworks.

From the mid-1980s, the tables have gradually turned: the key to understanding causewayed enclosures is now seen to be an improved knowledge of how the wider landscape was being used (eg Barclay *et al* 1996). A more secure foundation for this reappraisal has been provided by the broad coverage of aerial reconnaissance (eg Fenner and Dyer unpublished 1994) and programmes of systematic field walking (eg Gardiner 1984; Brown and Edmonds 1987; Schofield 1987; Hall *et al* 1987; Holgate 1988; Barrett *et al* 1991; papers in Schofield (ed) 1991; Hall and Coles 1994). The opportunity provided by gravel extraction to investigate large areas through excavation has also become increasingly important (eg Hey 1997; Evans and Knight forthcoming). In some low-lying areas where artefacts have been buried deep beneath alluvial and colluvial deposits, fieldwalking can be less effective. These deposits began to accumulate rapidly in the wake of the more intensive deforestation and agriculture of the Early Bronze Age, in some cases, as at Etton, burying the Neolithic ground surfaces and thus preserving them intact (Pryor 1998b). Systematic investigation of such buried landscapes requires innovative techniques, but can reveal how intensively the Neolithic landscape was being used away from monumental sites (eg Evans and Knight forthcoming). All this archaeological effort is beginning to show that there is

abundant evidence for widespread settlement of later Neolithic date in southern Britain (Clark and Schofield 1991, 104). Concentrations of earlier Neolithic flintwork remain few and far between, however: the quantities found are sometimes far smaller than those of Mesolithic date.

There have been few discoveries of possible settlement structures. In the British Isles as a whole, fewer than forty long houses are known, not all of which are well dated and not all of which were necessarily dwellings (Thomas 1996b; Topping 1996). The scarcity of recorded long houses may be because less substantial temporary structures, better suited to a more mobile lifestyle, have been overlooked or are now impossible to identify (Healy 1988). If this is the case, these dwellings may have been erected both within causewayed enclosures and at widely scattered locations around the landscape. The permanence of the causewayed enclosures and long barrows may have counterbalanced the impermanence of the settlement pattern (Sherratt 1990, 149)

The increasing acceptance that in the earlier Neolithic the population may have remained as mobile as the hunter-gatherers of the Mesolithic is fundamental to the study of regions and territories in England. There is little agreement as to what form that mobility may have taken, however, or whether it was uniform throughout the British Isles (Whittle 1997; Cooney 1997, 26–30). Exotic artefacts from enclosures, such as stone axes from various sources around the British Isles and the European mainland, or pottery made from gabbroic clay originating on the Lizard peninsula in Cornwall (Grimes 1979; Peacock 1969), initially gave the impression that there was unrestricted movement over wide areas and perhaps even long-distance trade (*see* Chapter 7). This idea led to suggestions that the enclosures were central places at the heart of territories, from which some form of control could be exerted over people and the redistribution of commodities (Renfrew 1973; Barker and Webley 1978). Yet such exotic items are likely to have been transferred over greater than average distances from their sources, perhaps from hand to hand within a highly formal process of exchange and perhaps over the course of several generations (Bradley and Edmonds 1993). If society was not sedentary and activity at causewayed enclosures was intermittent, the monuments may have been peripheral in terms of the everyday lives of individuals and communities (Bradley 1978, 103; J P Gardiner 1984, 21; 1990; Holgate 1984; 1988; Evans *et al* 1988). Analysis of snails and other molluscs is beginning to suggest that in contrast to the wooded environments of the causewayed enclosures on higher ground, the lower ground was perhaps relatively open with scattered concentrations of human activity (Whittle 1993, 40–2; Allen 1997a, 183–4; 1997b, 278–9). The remote positions of the monuments may have been deliberately chosen to underline their role as neutral ground for groups to come together.

The sources of more mundane resources may offer a more reasonable impression of the extent of the territories exploited by the groups who built and used causewayed enclosures. The large regions identified by Palmer were also thought to correspond to patterns in the distribution of decorated pottery styles (Gardiner 1984, 34), supporting the idea that the groupings represented large territorial units. Yet it is possible that the distribution pattern of different styles of decorated pottery masks more localised distributions of subtly different forms and types of clay (Cleal 1992). A large proportion of the pottery found at most excavated causewayed enclosures was made using clay available from local sources. For example, analysis of the pottery found on Hambledon Hill indicated that much of it utilised a type of clay found predominantly within a few kilometres of the hilltop (Brown in Mercer and Healy in preparation). Almost all the pottery excavated at the causewayed enclosure on Briar Hill could have been manufactured within a few kilometres of the site, the only uncommon clay type being found around 35km away – that is, within one day's walk (Bamford 1979, 107–9).

A variety of food resources were also in plentiful supply within relatively short distances of most enclosures, but this need not imply that the enclosures themselves were used as permanent bases. Contrary to the belief held for much of the 20th century, the cultivation of cereals does not necessarily imply a wholly sedentary lifestyle and it is quite likely that the earliest farmers moved on either every few years or according to the seasons (Thomas 1991, 28; but *see* Cooney 1997). Arable agriculture could have been carried out in an archipelago of small clearings scattered around very loosely defined territories. Wild food resources would also have been available throughout the landscape. It may be in one sense irrelevant to the purpose of causewayed enclosures that many were sited on thresholds between geological and environmental zones (Barker and Webley 1978), if the monuments were not after all centres from which local resources were exploited and controlled. Yet the different zones would have offered different foodstuffs and other natural resources at different times of year. Wooded river plains, together with the watercourses themselves, must have provided a spectrum of environmental conditions rich in natural resources, again differing according to the season (Brown 1997, 282–3; Hey 1997, 109–10). It may be that causewayed enclosures fitted into a wider pattern of settlement and land-use around the landscape, ordered according to the changing seasons. This may support the theory, discussed further in Chapter 7, that the use of some, if not all, causewayed enclosures was seasonal. Monuments, both causewayed enclosures and long barrows, may have been peripheral to the principal areas of everyday activity but acted as staging posts in an annual cycle of movement around loosely defined territories. Such a way of life would conform to a model elegantly expressed by Alasdair Whittle as 'tethered mobility' (Whittle 1997, 21). What actually took place on the occasions when the causewayed enclosures themselves were in active use is the subject of the next chapter.

# 7
# Uses and meanings

## The nature of the evidence

Interpretations of the purposes of cause-wayed enclosures and what the monuments might have meant to the people who built and used them have tended to focus on two main strands of evidence: the intriguing form of the perimeters and the structures, artefacts and human and animal remains discovered by excavation. Inferences drawn from both sources of evidence have been influenced by (and have in turn been influential upon) contemporary ideas about the Neolithic as a whole. Although no single function or explanation that can be applied to the entire class of monument has yet been agreed, certain themes are common to many current theories.

This book has been concerned primarily with pursuing the first strand of evidence. Although many past theories have been based upon the form of the causewayed earthworks, the plans of the enclosures have generally been treated as if all conformed to a single stereotype and as if they remained unchanged throughout their use. Until the 1970s, the common technique of cause-wayed construction was also widely thought to imply a narrow unity of purpose for the whole class. As has been shown in Chapters 3 and 4, however, although the technique is widespread, the form of the perimeters was by no means uniform and the degree of variation in overall plan is considerable. Some enclosures seem to have changed dramatically in form over the course of their use and, therefore, possibly in purpose too. By comparing the plan forms, the contexts of the local landscape of each site and the potentially varied sequences of development it is hoped that this study will provide a more secure basis for future research.

If the diverse plan forms of causewayed enclosures have often been reduced to a stereotype, discussion of the excavated evidence has also repeatedly concentrated upon the handful of sites, mostly in upland locations, where large-scale excavations have taken place. Among the most influential

*Figure 7.1 (facing page) Reconstruction of how the concentric circuits of the causewayed enclosure on Windmill Hill may have served to define separate zones of activity in the interior. The model derived from Windmill Hill has been highly influential in the interpretation of causewayed enclosures as a class. As noted in Chapter 5, however, enclosures with widely spaced concentric circuits represent a small minority, since there are indications that the multiple circuits may not all have been built or used at the same time. (Reproduced from Whittle and Pollard 1998)*

causewayed enclosures in this respect are those at Windmill Hill in Wiltshire (Fig 7.1; Smith 1965; Whittle and Pollard 1995; Whittle *et al* 1999) and more recently Crickley Hill in Gloucestershire (Dixon 1988) and Hambledon Hill in Dorset (Mercer 1980a; 1988; 1989a and b; Mercer and Healy in preparation). Despite this heavy reliance on data from a small number of sites, excavations at these and other cause-wayed enclosures, of varying scale and quality, have brought to light a tremendous diversity of evidence. Structural and artefactual remains and the quantity and kinds of material recovered vary both between sites and within individual enclosures. At Staines in Surrey, for example, while the inner circuit of ditch was noticeably more prolific in finds, the types of artefacts and the quantities present varied between different segments (Robertson-Mackay 1987). The diversity of the excavated evidence has been underlined by the attention directed towards certain unique and particularly striking discoveries. For example, a low gravel mound excavated in a ditch segment at Haddenham in Cambridgeshire had part of a polished stone axe set into its upper surface and was found to be covering a small group of human skull fragments (Evans 1988b, 134). At the partly waterlogged enclosure at Etton in Cambridgeshire, coppice stools had evidently grown in the ditches and been harvested, while pollen samples may indicate that cereal crops were grown within the circuit (Pryor *et al* 1985, 294; 1987; 1988b; 1998b). A wide range of interpretations can be supported by the excavated evidence, according to the prevailing theoretical framework.

## Creation and re-creation: a function of causewayed enclosures?

As the earliest recorded monuments designed to enclose open space, causewayed enclosures represent an unprecedented phenomenon in the archaeological record of the British Isles. The deliberate deposition of artefacts and other cultural material into features dug into the ground represents another important new departure. The creation of the monuments – especially the initial act of defining a place as separate from the outside world – has therefore increasingly been stressed as a key aspect of their function (eg Smith 1971; Bradley 1984a; 1993; Evans 1988b; 1988c; Edmonds 1993).

Debate has repeatedly focussed on the discontinuous form of the circuits. Does the construction technique represent simply a pragmatic response to the tools available in the earlier Neolithic? Or was it the product of a set of beliefs, through which the nature of Neolithic society can perhaps be understood better, even though the builders were probably unaware that they were expressing those beliefs through what they created?

If the former is true, this might explain why there is so much variation in the length of the ditch segments and why other monuments, including some long barrows, also have discontinuous ditches, as demonstrated in Chapters 3 and 4. It has been suggested that the discontinuous form of the ditches is in effect irrelevant, because they were simply convenient quarries dug to provide material for continuous banks (eg Mercer 1988, 89). The new surveys of the enclosures that survive as earthworks show that this was not usually the case, however, and that the banks were sometimes just as discontinuous as the ditches. In addition, more or less the same tools were available throughout the Neolithic. Despite the variation in the frequency of the causeways, causewayed enclosures genuinely stand apart from most other monuments of the period in almost always having discontinuous earthworks. For instance, almost all the cursus monuments, the earliest of which are roughly contemporary with the causewayed enclosures, have virtually continuous earthworks (Evans 1988c, 89). This suggests that discontinuous earthworks were to some extent simply a method of construction, but a method that was considered more appropriate to this form of enclosure than to other monuments (Bradley 1993, 69–90). This is the starting point for attempts to understand the underlying meaning of the technique and the process of creation.

One theory suggests that the discontinuous circuits were the product of a communal act of creation on the part of a dispersed or fragmented society (Megaw and Simpson 1979, 80; Startin and Bradley 1981, 291; Mercer 1990, 28–9). Following this line of argument, the frequency of causeways in the earthworks might shed light on the social relations of the builders. For instance, the circuit of Barkhale Camp in West Sussex, where the causewayed form of both ditch and bank was strictly maintained, may have been built by a more dispersed or fragmented community than the more continuous circuit nearby on Court Hill.

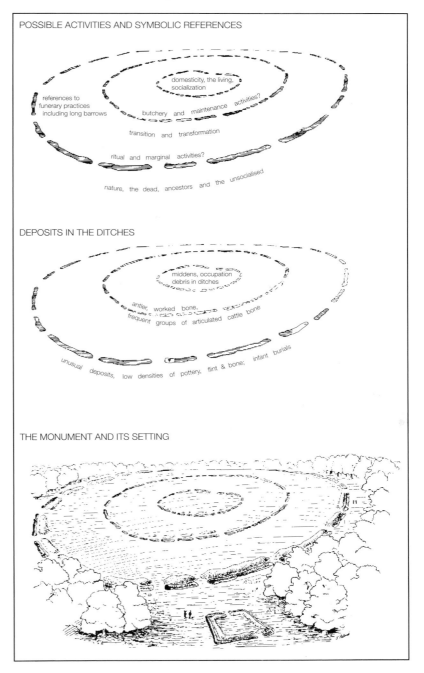

POSSIBLE ACTIVITIES AND SYMBOLIC REFERENCES

references to funerary practices including long barrows

domesticity, the living, socialization

butchery and maintenance activities?

transition and transformation

ritual and marginal activities?

nature, the dead, ancestors and the unsocialised

DEPOSITS IN THE DITCHES

middens, occupation debris in ditches

antler, worked bone, frequent groups of articulated cattle bone

unusual deposits, low densities of pottery, flint & bone; infant burials

THE MONUMENT AND ITS SETTING

Yet complete causeways were clearly not an inevitable consequence of working in small groups. As Francis Pryor has pointed out, separate work gangs are perfectly capable of cooperating to dig continuous earthworks (Pryor *et al* 1985, 307). There has never yet been a convincing argument as to why the nature of society should be so simply and precisely replicated in the form of the earthworks.

It was observed in Chapter 4 that although many causewayed enclosures must have been built according to a plan broadly agreed in advance, others may have been constructed in a more piecemeal fashion. These last sites may indicate that the initial act of construction, like the later recutting, was episodic, that is, one or more groups returning year after year, rather than many groups working at the same time. This may be the case, but it does not of itself explain the causewayed construction, for just as separate groups are capable of cooperating to dig a continuous earthwork, so a group returning at intervals could have taken up the construction at the point it left off. If gaps were deliberately left between episodes of construction, this might suggest that different elements of the perimeters were linked with certain events or acts of deposition, and subsequently with people's memories of those specific occasions. In this way, the creation and recreation of each circuit as a whole may have charted the passage of time.

Another theory suggests that the numerous causeways in the ditches may have been intended to show that the boundaries could be crossed by people approaching from any direction (Evans 1988c, 92; Hodder 1990, 161; Edmonds 1993, 111; 1995, 69). As discussed in Chapter 3, however, a significant proportion of enclosures appear to have had only one formal entrance and in general there were probably fewer entrances than the number of causeways in the ditch circuits would at first seem to suggest. In practice, the settings of enclosures sited adjacent to steep slopes or to major rivers would also have limited the range of approaches, a point that is not immediately clear when the plans of the perimeters are divorced from their landscape contexts. The patterning in the choice of location discussed in Chapter 5 indicates that, as the siting of the monuments was not accidental, the limitations to access must equally have been taken into account when the sites were chosen.

One of the most promising current theories argues that the discontinuous earthworks of causewayed enclosures may derive from an idealised 'folk memory' of the form of very early enclosed settlements on the European mainland, such as that at Darion in Belgium (Bradley 1993; *see also* Fig 5.5). There was evidently great variety in the plans of such early settlements and the way their perimeters were constructed. As time passed, however, causewayed earthworks were apparently singled out as their characteristic feature and the plan forms and construction techniques were gradually standardised. As the concept spread further to areas that lacked a tradition of sedentary settlement, including the British Isles, the relatively mobile communities might or might not choose to adopt the new idea of building enclosures. As there were probably no drawn plans of the original enclosures, the form would have been passed through peoples' memories and by word of mouth. It is easy to imagine how the common technique of causewayed construction might have stuck in the mind, but also how variation in form would naturally have occurred. People would also have made use of the enclosed space in ways that suited their own established social and economic practices. Seen in this light, the local circumstances of each enclosure are perhaps even more significant than the common technique, for they account for all variations in the form, setting and function. In Ireland, where the existence of sedentary settlements seems more likely (Cooney 1997), causewayed enclosures were apparently hardly adopted at all.

By providing a focus for people to come together on specific occasions, the creation and re-creation of the monuments may have helped to confirm links between groups and individuals, simultaneously establishing a place of lasting significance to all (Bradley 1998a and b, 71–2). Each recut ditch segment may have provided a receptacle for the deliberate placement or disposal of cultural material (*see* below). These acts were perhaps intended to reaffirm the importance of the boundary and the enclosed area, or to mark the participation of individuals and small groups in the larger enterprise. The relatively short intervals that may have separated such episodes cannot be established by current dating techniques, nor on the basis of the forms of the excavated artefacts. Differences in the composition and quantity of material recovered from different circuits at Windmill Hill, Hambledon Hill and Staines may indicate that a considerable length of time elapsed between the construction of each. Smith noted, however, that joining potsherds were recovered from different circuits at Windmill Hill (Smith 1965, 14), hinting that 'commemorative' acts may have taken place in different parts of the monument at broadly the same time. It remains unclear why some enclosures were rebuilt repeatedly in the same form, while new circuits were added to others. Such expansion may have been the direct result of a rise in the local or regional importance of the monument in question, or its frequency or longevity of use. It may reflect a straightforward increase in the number of people using the enclosure, or changes in the nature of the activities that occurred there. There may have been competitive or prestigious aspects to such modifications (Evans 1988b, 143–4).

# What happened inside causewayed enclosures?

Archaeological features identified inside causewayed enclosures are far from plentiful. Where they exist they tend to be poorly preserved and consequently present a greater problem for interpretation. The contents of excavated ditch segments around the perimeter are, therefore, the principal evidence on which interpretations of the activities that took place in the interior have been based. In many cases, these deposits are prolific and well preserved. The emphasis placed on them generally follows from an implicit assumption that the material derives from and, therefore, directly represents the activities that took place in the interior.

'Reading' this evidence is not so straightforward, however. For example, the presence of banks (and perhaps palisades) inside the ditch circuits would have placed a barrier between the interior and the places where the material was being deposited. Any deposition in a ditch may, therefore, actually reflect activities occurring outside the enclosed area.

The gradual realisation that the presence of potsherds, animal bones, struck flints and other less commonplace items found within ditches was not simply a product of silting, but would have required some

human action, helped to focus greater attention on the structure and nature of the deposits. Isobel Smith's (1965) discussion of the evidence from the ditches of the enclosure on Windmill Hill was the first to make the crucial step forward. Subsequently, the presence of recuts within ditch fills, evidence for the deliberate levelling of banks and the rapid backfilling of ditches, and the purposeful and sometimes highly organised deposition of cultural material into the ditch segments have become a recognised characteristic of most excavated causewayed enclosures.

## Feasting

Smith regarded much of the cultural material in the ditches as the remains of communal feasts, buried ceremonially in the course of the episodic visits. The main evidence for feasting is the dark, midden-like deposits comprising the remains of slaughtered animals, and the pottery in which food might have been stored, prepared and eaten. In the ditches of the enclosure at Staines, there were separate dumps comprising only a single kind of material, such as animal bone or pottery (Robertson-Mackay 1987). At Hambledon Hill in Dorset, Tony Legge (1981) noted the overwhelming dominance of cattle among the animal bones, suggesting extravagance in consumption and wastefulness in deposition.

## Exchange and manufacturing

The theory that enclosures represented places to which many different things – finished objects and raw materials, some of distant or exotic origin, together with domesticated livestock, agricultural produce and human remains – were brought to be used, exchanged or deposited in some way, is understandable given the apparent periodic or episodic nature of the use of the enclosures (Smith 1965, 19; Edmonds 1995, 68–73; Pryor 1998a, 66–7). Occasional gatherings at specific places that were perhaps regarded as neutral ground represent an obvious opportunity to acquire or exchange, or to perform rites appropriate to those transactions. It does not follow from this, however, that exchange was the primary function of causewayed enclosures.

The presence of numerous objects of non-local stone among the material excavated by Keiller at Windmill Hill was a major stimulus for the inception of what became the Council for British Archaeology's Implement Petrology Programme (Grimes 1979). This project aimed to establish the sources of the various kinds of stone used in manufacturing tools in the Neolithic. Similar research has focussed on pottery, most notably that found on sites in the South-West manufactured from gabbroic clay, which probably originated on the Lizard peninsula in Cornwall (Peacock 1969). While material of distant origin was certainly being taken to some enclosures, however, it was evidently not all being taken away, for everything recovered by excavation had been deposited in a ditch or pit (Drewett 1977, 224). This need not imply that no exchange took place at all: there is no reason to assume that everything brought to an enclosure was intended exclusively either for exchange or for deposition. Since some at least was clearly intended or chosen for deliberate deposition, the way objects were being chosen and carefully placed and organised at causewayed enclosures emphasises the fact that they were not just treated simply as tools or prestige items, but held greater significance. Many of the stone implements were apparently deliberately broken, as though to demonstrate that their useful lives had come to an end (Bellamy and Edmonds 1991).

There are a few instances where sources of flint occur close to causewayed enclosures, while evidence that flint knapping may have taken place at the enclosures themselves has been found. This has also prompted suggestions that enclosures may have been involved in the control of the supply and circulation of flint and other workable stone (Case 1982). The most frequently cited examples include the causewayed enclosures on Hambledon Hill, on Offham Hill in East Sussex, at Robin Hood's Ball in Wiltshire and at Maiden Castle in Dorset. In each case, however, the flint that was exploited is not of the highest quality and occurs in minor surface exposures. Numerous similar sources exist across much of southern and eastern Britain (Barber et al 1999). They are not comparable in terms of the quality of the stone or the scale of exploitation with the flint mines and stone axe 'factories'. Instead they may simply represent sources whose raw material came to be worked, or at least deposited, within the enclosures during episodes when they were being used. In the case of Hambledon Hill, the possible flint mines identified during excavations in the 1970s almost certainly postdate the use of the enclosures (Mercer and Healy in preparation; Barber et al 1999; contra Mercer 1987).

The flint assemblage from Maiden Castle suggests that most of the flint was of local origin, with a small quantity of flint gravel imported from more distant sources (Evans et al 1988; Sharples 1991a, 227). Much of the flint gravel appears to have been brought to the enclosure in the form of prepared cores for the manufacture of flakes and blades. The local flint was worked on site on quite a scale to produce large core tools, such as axes. While the enclosure seems to have been the site of considerable productive activity, however, few of the by-products of axe manufacture are to be found in the landscape surrounding the enclosure. The proximity of the local flint sources may lie behind the importance attached to the place prior to the construction of the causewayed enclosure. In addition, the finished objects manufactured within the enclosure may have acquired a special status or role because of their provenance. This is some way, however, from proving that the link between the siting of the enclosure and the location of flint sources was of overriding importance.

## Settlement

The theory that causewayed enclosures represented some form of settlement – places where people lived or were based for at least part of the time – has been raised intermittently ever since the 1920s. As noted in Chapter 2, the lack of evidence for permanent structures within the enclosures at first appeared to contradict this idea. Yet as mentioned in Chapter 6, if long houses were not commonplace and lightweight structures much more difficult to detect were the norm (Healy 1988), perhaps it is unwise to rule out causewayed enclosures completely as places of settlement. It has been suggested that enclosures of small and medium size might represent settlements (Mercer 1980a, 60–1; Evans 1988b, 143–4). Despite the wealth of excavated evidence now available, however, there is still little indication that individual episodes of occupation at causewayed enclosures were anything other than short-lived.

The few pits and postholes noted during the early excavations on enclosures forced the idea of substantial structures and permanent settlement to be set aside.

The instances of house-like buildings such as that discovered by Dorothy Liddell (1931) at Hembury in Devon allowed the possibility that some kind of long-term presence had been maintained within certain enclosures. The evidence is generally far from straightforward, however. The irregular array of postholes clearly represents some kind of structure, but Darvill's (1996a, fig 6.4, no. 9) re-interpretation of the ground plan makes a rather more convincing house than Liddell's original excavation plan (Liddell 1931, 97 and fig 3). More recent excavations at the enclosures at Hambledon Hill (Mercer 1980a; 1988; Mercer and Healy forthcoming), Etton (Pryor 1987; 1988a; 1988b; 1998b; Pryor *et al* 1985), Crickley Hill (Dixon 1988), Briar Hill (Bamford 1985) and Staines (Robertson-Mackay 1987) have revealed scatters and concentrations of pits and postholes, although the date of such features in relation to the earthworks can seldom be fixed with any certainty. At Crickley Hill, three rectangular houses have been assigned to the later phases of the use of the causewayed enclosure (Dixon 1988, 82). At Etton, the best evidence for a structure comprised gullies and post holes arranged in an L-shape, associated with a

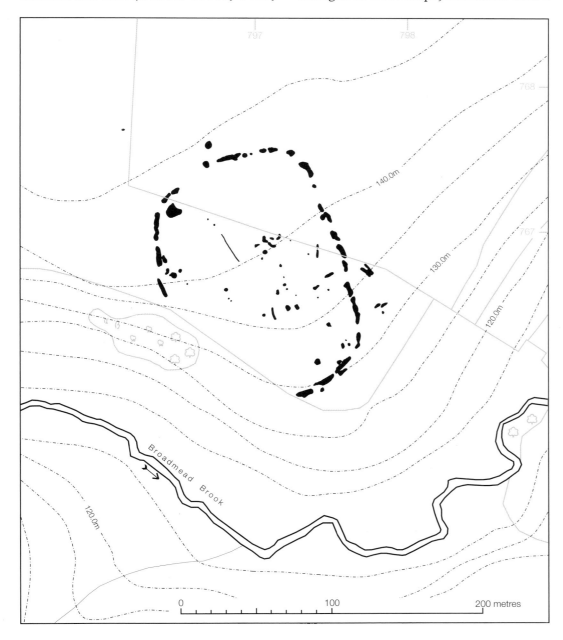

Figure 7.2
*The causewayed enclosure at West Kington in Wiltshire does not appear to have been overlain by Iron Age or later settlement as certain other enclosures were. It is, therefore, a reasonable inference that the pits and postholes recorded as cropmarks could well be contemporary with the enclosure itself. Note the unusually rectangular plan of the circuit, and the pronounced misalignments in the course of the ditch, which may hint at an episodic process of construction.*

darker 'floor' some 4m square. This deposit proved rich in flint debris and some of the associated features contained potsherds. The proximity of this structure to the western entrance of the enclosure led Francis Pryor to interpret it as a possible guardhouse (Pryor 1998b, 81–2, 106, 356).

Evidence for buildings within causewayed enclosures recorded through survey is equally slight, comprising clusters of pits or ditches whose date in relation to the enclosure cannot be established without excavation. Just inside the perimeter of the enclosure at Freston in Suffolk, a rectangular arrangement of large postholes defines a building approximately 34m long by 8m wide (Fig 3.14). This is the most convincing example of a possible Neolithic long house, but certain Saxon 'halls' are similar in plan (eg *see* Fowler 1976, figs 2.15–16). In general, definite Neolithic buildings remain scarce, as indeed they do for the Neolithic more generally throughout the British Isles (Thomas 1996b).

Pits are more commonly evident as cropmarks, though only where the enclosure has not been overlain by later settlement, as at West Kington in Wiltshire (Fig 7.2), can they reasonably be linked with the use of the enclosure. At Langford in Oxfordshire, for example, a scatter of pits seems to relate to an innermost circuit of ditch, but this circuit is sufficiently different in form from the outer circuits to hint that it may be of quite different date (Fig 7.3). The contents of pits excavated within enclosures are broadly the same as those encountered in ditch segments, although some variety may exist within individual sites. More problematically, the contents of these enclosed pits are not obviously different from the contents of pits encountered elsewhere in the landscape, away from known enclosures. A range of pottery, flint and stone artefacts, human and animal remains have been recovered, suggesting that such features may have been used as, or intended to be, receptacles for deliberate deposition in a manner comparable to the ditch segments. As Ian Kinnes (1994, 96) concludes, pits appear to have been used for the deliberate placement of objects, not for functional storage or disposal of rubbish. There is, therefore, nothing concrete to link either long houses or pits with typical everyday settlement.

Excavation of the enclosure at Etton has revealed that there were two distinct 'halves' to the interior, divided from each other at first by a fenceline and later by a shallow ditch as well. Francis Pryor (1998b, 368) has argued that this east–west division must have been of fundamental importance, since it marked a clear difference in the distribution of pottery and worked flints, as well as pits, postholes and ritual deposits. It was suggested that one half of the interior contained some form of seasonal or episodic settlement, represented by numerous small postholes and pits. The other half was characterised by a quantity of small funerary deposits together with small pits containing a variety of placed deposits, including stone axes, pots, a complete quernstone and numerous charred hazelnuts and acorns. The excavator of the site has concluded that the enclosure had clearly defined funerary and non-funerary halves and that the funerary activity was probably episodic and brief (Pryor 1987; 1998b).

## Funerary ritual

The roles that causewayed enclosures may have played in funerary ritual are equally problematic. The presence of human remains, often fragmentary and disarticulated, but occasionally represented by complete inhumations and cremations, has been cited as evidence for the use of the interiors for funerary rites. Again, there is the issue of chronology to consider, since the burials of complete bodies, as opposed to body parts and bone fragments, tend to come later in the sequence at each site. The main causewayed enclosure on Hambledon Hill has figured strongly in this debate. The presence of human skulls placed on the bottoms of ditches, as well as a range of human bones and bone fragments from other contexts, combines with the presence of two long barrows in the immediate vicinity to strengthen the argument for a funerary connection. Roger Mercer's evocative description of the main enclosure as a 'vast, reeking open cemetery, its silence broken only by the din of crows and ravens' (Mercer 1980a, 63) has often been quoted. The assertion of a direct link between the enclosure as an area for excarnation and preparation of skeletal remains, however, and the adjacent long barrows as the final destinations for those remains, is not without difficulties. Assuming that the deposition of human remains in the barrows was contemporary with the main use of the enclosures, significant parts of the skeleton, including skulls and other

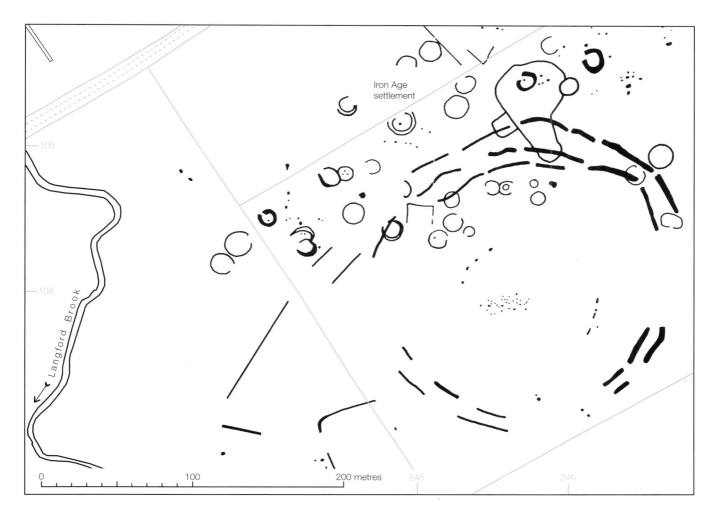

Iron Age
settlement

109

108

Langford Brook

0    100    200 metres    245    246

*Figure 7.3*
*The northern side of the*
*causewayed enclosure at*
*Langford in Oxfordshire is*
*overlain by a settlement,*
*probably of Iron Age date,*
*comprising circular houses,*
*pits and palisade trenches.*
*The dense scatter of pits*
*near the centre of the*
*causewayed enclosure*
*seems to be separate from*
*the Iron Age settlement.*
*It appears to lie within the*
*innermost circuit of ditch,*
*but it remains uncertain*
*whether this apparently*
*more circular circuit (on*
*the basis of the two short*
*arcs that can be traced) is*
*actually contemporary with*
*the rest of the causewayed*
*enclosure.*

bones, were clearly not being taken to the barrows. Instead, they were being deposited within ditch segments or pits, in a manner quite similar to other types of cultural material. Furthermore, the bones deposited in the ditches need not have been derived from bodies exposed within the enclosure, but may have been brought to the site from elsewhere, and need not have arrived as complete bodies.

Since the preservation of bone is particularly good on enclosures on chalk uplands like Hambledon Hill, these sites have dominated discussion. Human bone was also found, however, at Staines in Surrey and at Abingdon in Oxfordshire (Robertson-Mackay 1987, 36–8; Leeds 1928, 476). It has been suggested that, as rivers were not only important for transporting the living, but as routes for passing into the afterworld, they were, therefore, used for the disposal of bodies and cremated remains (Bradley and Edmonds 1993; Edmonds 1999). Assuming a relatively mobile population that gathered

periodically at enclosures, it may be that some of the human remains at these sites represent token or partial disposal of individuals who died at a distance from the enclosure, at a different time of year. Such deposition would further strengthen the links between the enclosure, the people who used it and their ancestors (Edmonds 1999). Alternatively, the suggestion that the presence of human remains must represent the performance of some kind of funerary activity may be as ethnocentric in its assumptions as are ideas of enclosures as defended sites. Instead, it may have been other symbolic values of human remains being harnessed at places such as Hambledon Hill.

## Defence

Discussion of the defensive capabilities of causewayed enclosures and of Neolithic warfare in general was revived in the 1970s by the discoveries at two sites then undergoing long term programmes of excavation:

Crickley Hill in Gloucestershire (Dixon 1988) and the Stepleton enclosure on Hambledon Hill in Dorset (Mercer 1980a; 1988; 1989a; 1989b). Both seem to have been attacked by archers and partly destroyed by fire, leaving thick and easily recognisable deposits of carbonised wood (Fig 7.4). On Hambledon Hill, the timber palisade appears to have collapsed while still ablaze, burying the body of a young man with an arrowhead embedded in his chest cavity (Mercer 1980a, 51 and figs 29 and 30). At Crickley Hill, arrowheads littered the ground around the entrance, bearing silent witness to an intense battle. The evidence from both sites received support from similar discoveries at the tor enclosure at Carn Brea in Cornwall, where 800 flint arrowheads were recovered during excavation, as well as evidence for burning (Mercer 1981).

These discoveries were reminiscent of Dorothy Liddell's (1930; 1931; 1932; 1935) much earlier excavations at Hembury in Devon. Her more limited trenching had also revealed much evidence of burning, as well as around 146 flint leaf-shaped arrowheads. In this case, however, doubts have been expressed about whether the burning was genuinely closely associated

with the arrowheads (Brown 1989, 47–8). The arrowheads were actually found in a range of different contexts across the excavated areas. Some were found in the causewayed ditches, but many came from the pits at the tip of the promontory and were associated with a range of less warlike material including other flint implements, pottery, hazelnut shells and some cereal remains. Even those found in the ditch segments tended to lie in layers above those which contained burnt material. In other words, many of the arrowheads at Hembury are likely to represent the sort of 'ritual' deposits discussed above, rather than an attack on the enclosure.

The quantity and distribution of the flint arrowheads at Crickley Hill seems to indicate an attack, although analysis of the material is still in progress (Dixon 1988). The numbers at Hambledon Hill are considerably smaller and the scale of the event (or events) which led to their presence is consequently more difficult to determine, although clearly some violence was involved. Nonetheless, these sites remain a small minority among the total of excavated enclosures, despite their prominence in discussions of the purposes of the monuments. The evidence for conflict

*Figure 7.4*
*Reconstruction of the 'innermost outwork' and 'Hanford/Stepleton outwork' at the point where they join the causewayed enclosure on the Stepleton spur of Hambledon Hill in Dorset. The timber-laced earthwork prompted comparisons with the 'box ramparts' of certain Iron Age hillforts. Although the discoveries at Hambledon Hill have heavily influenced perceptions of the Neolithic as a whole, the complex is exceptional in many respects, and there are few structures that can have been as massive or extensive. Note that Roger Mercer's reconstruction of the perimeter portrays the timber-faced banks as continuous barriers, although earthwork survey both at Hambledon Hill and elsewhere would suggest that they were causewayed to some extent. (Reproduced from Mercer 1985)*

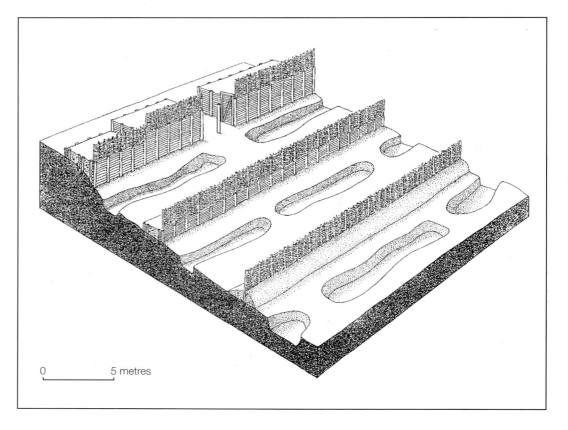

0     5 metres

appears to be restricted to a few enclosures in the South-West, which may indicate that the region was more prone to conflict. Alternatively, the destruction of these sites might point to a regional ritual practice of periodically destroying the enclosures, either as part of a cycle of recreation or as part of the process of abandonment. Warfare itself may have been a highly ritualised activity (Sharples 1991b).

In all four cases discussed above (Carn Brea, Crickley Hill, Hambledon Hill and Hembury), the evidence for violence and destruction occurs quite late in the history of the sites. Only at Carn Brea does an attack seem to have been followed by a complete cessation of activity. At the other enclosures, pits and recuts continued to be dug in the ditches after apparent episodes of destruction and midden-like debris continued to be deposited. This may have been done to commemorate the monument or the act of its destruction, but it can be interpreted equally well as part of the long-established process of deliberate deposition in causewayed enclosure ditches. At both Crickley Hill and Hambledon Hill, the subsequent recutting and deposition appears to have continued for some time.

That violence occurred at some sites is, however, some way from proving that cause-wayed enclosures were primarily intended to fulfil a defensive role. Objections have usually stemmed from the inherently weak nature of the discontinuous perimeters and the topographic settings chosen for their construction. As described in Chapter 4, survey suggests that some enclosures may not actually have comprised complete circuits. Even the imposing outworks at Hambledon Hill seem only to have extended along the western flank of the massif. Furthermore, there is good evidence, from both survey and excavation, that construction was episodic and prolonged. In a few cases, construction may have begun without a fixed plan in mind, and the eventual plan may have differed greatly from what was initially conceived. In short, there is little to indicate that the need for defence was a prime mover in the creation and early use of many causewayed enclosures. On the other hand, it may well be that the gathering of disparate groups at the enclosures, perhaps with livestock and exotic goods in their possession, proved the cause of raids or outbreaks of violence.

It has been argued that the later embell-ishment of particular enclosures, through the construction of additional earthwork circuits or palisades, might represent the transformation of the earlier monuments in response to competition and perhaps an increasing threat of violence (Bradley 1984a, 25–37). Certainly at Hambledon Hill, the evidence for attack postdates the addition of the outworks. There are possibilities other than a greater risk of attack that might explain these additions, however. They may instead have been intended: to provide greater restriction on movement into and around the enclosed area; to enhance the visual impact of the existing earthworks, or to emphasise further the division between inside and outside. These are all ideas which have been considered in interpreting the ways in which later Neolithic henge monuments and stone circles were used and experienced (eg Barrett 1994). It may be that the ideas embodied in the construction and use of the first henge monuments were already present to some degree in the later use of some causewayed enclosures.

To some extent, the ideas of Neolithic society and of warfare underpinning some of the defensive arguments represent a back projection of ideas about the assumed role of Iron Age hillforts. The incidences of hillforts constructed over the remains of causewayed enclosures, discussed further in Chapter 8, have probably strengthened the analogy. Ironically, the re-emergence of support for a Neolithic with aspects in common with the supposedly warlike Iron Age comes at the very time when hillforts are increasingly being interpreted as cult centres which were not necessarily primarily defensive strong-holds (eg Stopford 1987; Bowden and McOmish 1987; 1989).

Discussions concerning the nature of warfare and conflict in the Neolithic have shown a tendency towards ethnocentric assumptions which may not be appropriate to the period (Drewett 1977, 222–4; Orme 1981). Anthropological and archaeological evidence suggests that social conflict and violence can take many different forms and occur for many different reasons and need not be the only means of resolving disputes between or within communities (Carman 1997). The nature of earlier Neolithic society, the scale of the enclosure earth-works, the manner and duration of their creation and use and the lack of evidence for anything other than intermittent, episodic activity make it difficult to regard more than a few causewayed enclosures as strongholds. The appearance of more complex earthworks and the construction of palisades might suggest that some sites acquired a more socially prestigious position with time, perhaps associated with greater restrictions on use and access. In these instances, some form of conflict may have ensued. In other words, enclosures such as those at Hambledon Hill and Crickley Hill may have become the focus of conflict during periods of local unrest arising from particular circumstances precisely because gatherings were taking place there. They were probably not generally designed and used with the possibility of conflict in mind, within a society that was inherently prone to warfare and violence. Certainly the perimeters may have indirectly offered the potential for defence and the importance of the enclosures may from time to time have made that characteristic useful. It is clear that conflict did occur in the earlier Neolithic, but there is little to suggest that this was an important factor in the construction of causewayed enclosures as a class.

## What happened outside causewayed enclosures?

In contrast to the profusion of evidence recovered from the monuments themselves, the immediate environs of causewayed enclosures have seldom been investigated by excavation. At Windmill Hill, Keiller had used various surveying and probing techniques to search for archaeological features, including the earthworks themselves, but his sole success beyond the confines of the outer circuit was a shallow ditch enclosing a small rectangular area, the date and purpose of which is uncertain. Material of earlier Neolithic date has been collected from the ground surface, both by chance and more systematically, in the vicinity of certain causewayed enclosures, including those at Knap Hill in Wiltshire, Kedington in Suffolk, Hambledon Hill, Robin Hood's Ball and Maiden Castle (Charge 1982; Mercer and Healy forthcoming; Richards 1990, 61–5; Woodward et al in Sharples 1991a, 21–36). In some cases, this may indicate that activity of broadly contemporary date was taking place in close proximity to the enclosures. At Maiden Castle, these activities may have included the quarrying of flint exposures along the Roman Road Ridge to the north. The complex of monuments at Barrow Hills near the Abingdon causewayed enclosure includes the long barrow and oval barrow mentioned in Chapter 6. In addition, radiocarbon dating has confirmed that a small group of flat graves were also contemporary with the enclosure (Barclay et al 1996, 17). There is, however, very little other material of earlier Neolithic date in that area (Barclay and Halpin 1999).

At Etton, two lengths of ditch around 130m long in total were identified some 80m to the north-west of the causewayed enclosure. Beyond this boundary was a concentration of small pits and postholes, some of the latter possibly representing rectangular structures. This broadly contemporary site, known as Etton Woodgate I, was also separated from the causewayed enclosure by a former watercourse (Pryor et al 1985, 278–81). The lengths of ditch can perhaps be compared to a crescent-shaped length of bank and ditch immediately to the north of the enclosure on Court Hill in West Sussex (Fig 3.3). There, a concentration of burnt flint and pottery recovered by fieldwalking hints that different activities may have been carried out beyond this boundary (Holden 1951, 184). A trial excavation was unable to clarify the date of either the crescent-shaped earthwork or the scatter of finds on the surface (Bedwin 1984). Similarly, at Bentley in Suffolk, possible traces of an arc of ditch lie 60m to the south of the enclosure, although the cropmarks may represent much later quarrying.

The lack of exploration of the immediate environs of causewayed enclosures may in part be due to perceptions about the nature of these sites. Interpretations of their functions have tended to focus on what may have happened inside them, while the ditches are an established source both of artefacts and, via their silting, evidence for the longer-term history both of the site and its immediate environment. The possibility that significant activity may have been occurring outside the ditch circuits needs to be considered.

## Seasonal gatherings?

Smith regarded the complex deposits in the ditches of causewayed enclosures as the eventual products of repeated seasonal or periodic gatherings, comparable to a rural fair of the more recent past (Smith 1965, 19). Her ideas remain the foundation of many current theories concerning the purpose of causewayed enclosures, because the concept of occasional gatherings of

scattered groups offers the most convincing scenario for understanding the diversity of the various activities attested (Fig 7.5).

Most of the cattle bones recovered at Hambledon Hill were from mature females, with very few bones from calves. This pattern was interpreted as representing the slaughter of surplus animals from a predominantly dairy economy, which would presumably have occurred in the autumn (Legge 1981, 179–80). The scarcity of young males was taken to indicate that they were being consumed elsewhere and perhaps at a different season. The imperatives of the pastoral cycle suggested a similar season to Francis Pryor, excavator of the causewayed enclosure at Etton (Pryor 1998a, 67). Together with the widespread occurrence of hazelnut shells, crab apples, sloe pips and the more unusual discoveries of charred grain at causewayed enclosures, for example, at Hambledon Hill, there is some evidence that the feasting may have been linked to a celebration of the harvest

(Piggott 1954, 28, 92–3). The evidence from Etton suggests that the principal gatherings probably occurred in the late summer or early autumn (Pryor 1998b, 364) and similar sites near rivers on low rises in valley floor may have been completely unusable in late winter and spring. None of the evidence is incontestable, however. The most significant objection is that the biological indicators of autumn mentioned above are more abundant and easy to detect in archaeological terms than indicators of other seasons. In other words, gatherings may have been taking place at other times, but could be even more difficult to recognise.

## Conclusions

Even a brief study of the evidence derived from both excavation and survey firmly underlines the difficulties involved in pinning one specific function onto causewayed enclosures as a class. While evidence is not plentiful, theories based upon it can be

*Figure 7.5*
*Reconstruction of the causewayed enclosure at Staines in Surrey. The portrayal epitomises the idea that causewayed enclosures were meeting places to which livestock and commodities for exchange were brought from all directions. As noted in Chapter 4, however, the form of the plan suggests that there may actually have been only a single entrance and that the two circuits were not necessarily in contemporary use. (Courtesy of the Museum of London)*

diametrically opposed. If a single explanation for the purpose of the monuments can be put forward, it is that they were arenas which allowed the scattered population to gather and conduct ongoing projects which demanded and gave focus to their gatherings. In this light, causewayed enclosures can be seen as both fulfilling and creating a need. The diversity of artefactual remains suggests that people carried out the whole spectrum of different activities that such meetings permitted. Along with other earlier Neolithic monuments such as long barrows, causewayed enclosures may represent the first detectable evidence for the interaction of larger communities. This picture certainly accords well with current perceptions of the nature of the earlier Neolithic. Yet since so much of what is understood about the period remains tied to the interpretation of causewayed enclosures, advances in the understanding of the wider landscape may well revolutionise the understanding of causewayed enclosures.

# 8
# The afterlife of causewayed enclosures

## The end of causewayed enclosures

The episodic nature of the use of causewayed enclosures generally makes it difficult to trace any decrease in activity on the sites, or to pinpoint the moment at which their use was finally at an end. In all likelihood, there would not have been any uniform 'decline and fall' of all the enclosures. Most seem to have been abandoned before 3,000 BC, but probably in different ways and at different times, in much the same way as they came into use. At a number of sites, excavation has revealed evidence for 'terminal events', which may have deliberately marked the abandonment of the monuments. These include the erection of four posts around the ditch circuit at Briar Hill (Bamford 1985, 136), and the filling of a final recut of the ditch of the main causewayed enclosure at Hambledon Hill with large flint nodules (Mercer 1980a, 36–7). The evidence for the destruction of the banks at Crickley Hill, which culminated in all the material of the bank being piled into the ditch has been discussed in Chapter 7 (Dixon 1988, 81). In some cases, however, these acts may have been carried out as late as the Early Bronze Age. They perhaps represent reuse of a monument that was even then already ancient, after a long period of abandonment.

## A tradition of enclosures?

Stonehenge, which lends its name to the whole class of later Neolithic henge enclosures, is actually very different from the norm for that type of monument. The earliest phase of the monument (Stonehenge I) is the circular circuit of bank and ditch that enclosed the space where the megalithic circle was later built. The closest parallel to it is the enclosure excavated at Flagstones, on the outskirts of Dorchester in Dorset. In terms of date, Stonehenge I, at around 2,950 BC and Flagstones, at *c* 3,100 BC, are later than the majority of accurately dated causewayed enclosures and earlier than the majority of henges. They have some characteristics in common with causewayed enclosures and others with henges. It is, therefore, tempting to try to trace the evolution of a tradition in the building of enclosures (Whittle 1996, 275).

Stonehenge I and the Flagstones enclosure are, however, sufficiently different from what had come before to suggest that they represent a new or re-invented concept. On one hand, both are nearly perfectly circular in plan, unlike causewayed enclosures, which are more approximately circular or oval. Excavation of the ditches has not recovered the large quantity of feasting debris and other artefacts that most excavations at causewayed enclosures have produced. On the other hand, the ditches of both Stonehenge I and the Flagstones enclosure were dug as a series of small interlinked pits, in a similar way to those of certain causewayed enclosures (Cleal *et al*

*Figure 8.1*
*The enclosure at Melbourne in Cambridgeshire differs from causewayed enclosures in having a nearly perfectly circular plan and in occupying a level plateau. The nature of the smaller circular ring-ditches is unclear. On balance, it perhaps has more in common with enclosures such as Stonehenge (phase I) and at Flagstones in Dorset than it has with causewayed enclosures.*

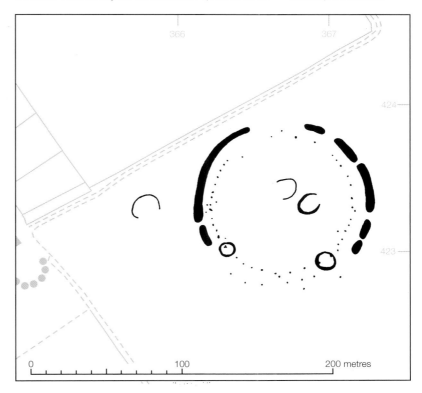

*Figure 8.2 (facing page)*
*Schematic plans of the*
*arrangement of cursus*
*monuments in relation*
*to the causewayed*
*enclosures at Etton in*
*Cambridgeshire and*
*Fornham All Saints in*
*Suffolk. At a number of*
*sites, cursus monuments*
*lie near causewayed*
*enclosures, but only at*
*these two sites do they*
*appear to have physically*
*impinged on each other.*

1995, 113–4). Stonehenge has an internal bank with at least three gaps around the circuit, but the evidence for a bank at Flagstones is inconclusive. Both enclosures lie on gentle slopes, slightly below the brow of the hill, as do so many causewayed enclosures on higher ground (Cleal and Allen in Cleal *et al* 1995, 34–40 and figs 22–3).

The issues surrounding these later enclosures are unlikely to be answered until more sites have been investigated, but as yet very few other possible examples have been identified. The circular inner circuit of the enclosure on Briar Hill in Northamptonshire has been pointed to as one such (Mercer 1990, 63–4). The plan of the circuit (Fig 4.4) probably does suggest that the circuit is of a later date than the others, although the sequence of development remains debatable (Evans 1988a, 85–6; Bradley 1998b, 79). In either case, the plentiful artefacts recovered tend to suggest that the modification took place in the earlier Neolithic (Bamford 1985). The enclosure at Melbourne in Cambridgeshire (Fig 8.1), which Rog Palmer (1976) included in his gazetteer of causewayed enclosures but regarded as doubtful, may represent another possible example. The apparently nearly circular circuit of ditch within the causewayed enclosure at Langford in Oxfordshire seems at odds with the other circuits and may also be a later addition (Fig 7.3).

# The reuse of causewayed enclosures later in the Neolithic

The effect of later activity on any monument once it has first gone out of use does not always reflect the attitudes underlying that activity. In some cases, the original form of the monument is consciously acknowledged out of a kind of respect, but the activity itself is destructive to some degree. One example might be the act of archaeological excavation itself. On the other hand, later activity may preserve the form of the monument, contribute to its destruction or disregard it completely, for reasons of convenience or lack of awareness. The attitudes of later people to earlier monuments are seldom easy to discern in archaeological terms, especially through survey techniques, but the question is particularly relevant to an understanding of the siting of monuments and land-use in general later in the Neolithic. At that time, many causewayed enclosures would still have

been quite prominent as earthworks, but the places they occupied may have become as important or more important than the actual monuments themselves.

## Cursus monuments

Colin Renfrew's study, among others, suggested that causewayed enclosures were effectively replaced as social and territorial expressions by new forms of enclosure, often bigger and more formally structured in design, such as cursus monuments and certain henges (Renfrew 1973; *see also* Thomas 1991, 143–77). Cursus monuments, like causewayed enclosures, vary greatly in form – from rectangular enclosures only a few hundred metres long, to great avenues flanked by high embankments that stretch for kilometres and cross streams and rolling terrain. At present, there is little firm evidence about how cursus monuments related to causewayed enclosures. It is now clear that they overlapped chronologically, with cursus monuments in use between 3,600 BC and 3,000 BC (Barclay and Bayliss 1999). In some cases, cursus monuments lie fairly close to causewayed enclosures. For example, the 'lesser cursus' near Stonehenge lies around 2.5km from Robin Hood's Ball; radiocarbon determinations from antler placed on the base of the cursus ditch indicate that it was constructed around 3,400 BC (Richards 1990). Other examples of juxtaposition are to be found at Cardington in Bedfordshire and at Aston, Cote, Shifford and Chimney in Oxfordshire. The mortuary enclosure at Buckland in Oxfordshire might also be interpreted as a small cursus monument (Fig 4.17). Elsewhere, the cursus monuments were entirely separate, in terms of both location and time. The Dorset cursus, the longest in the country, has been linked with Hambledon Hill, the largest causewayed enclosure complex (Tilley 1994, 200–1), but the connection between the two is tenuous. They lie 8km apart and radiocarbon dates suggest that the cursus was built towards the end of the main use of the causewayed enclosure.

At Etton in Cambridgeshire, new evidence suggests that the so-called Maxey cursus may have bent slightly to pass about 60m to the south-west of the causewayed enclosure and terminated about 100m beyond it. The terminal of a second cursus, known as the Etton cursus, seems to have lain almost entirely within the enclosure. Its southern ditch more or less bisected the interior, passing through a gap in the central fenceline. From the causewayed enclosure, the cursus headed south-eastwards on almost the same alignment as the Maxey cursus (Pryor 1998b). This not only suggests that the cursus monument is later, but that its builders were concerned to preserve the physical integrity of the causewayed enclosure (Fig 8.2). At Fornham All Saints in Suffolk, a cursus monument apparently replaced the causewayed enclosure, cutting across the centre of both the main enclosure (A) and the horseshoe-shaped annexe (B), apparently without heeding their existence. Immediately to the south-east of the enclosures, however, the terminal of a second possible cursus has been identified, with the terminal of a third somewhat further to the south-east. It is as though the causewayed enclosures served as inter-sections or focal points for the routes followed by the cursus monuments. This relationship suggests that there may have been a major change in the way people encountered the causewayed enclosures (Thomas 1991, 46). It is possible, however, that cursus monuments were intended to fix routes already long in use and that an existing respect for the causewayed enclosures was simply formalised (Harding 1999; Last 1999). It has also been observed that many cursus monuments, particularly in East Anglia and the Upper Thames Valley, approximately follow the lines of rivers (Last 1999). The course of the river may have influenced their routes more than the existence of the earlier monuments (Richards 1996).

## Henges

Disregarding Stonehenge I and the Flag-stones enclosure, there is little to link causewayed enclosures with conventional henges. A roughly circular enclosure with a single entrance which lies within the causewayed enclosure at Dallington in Northamptonshire may be a henge, but as yet there is no firm evidence (Bamford 1985, 136). Certain henges in Yorkshire, like the one at Newton Kyme, are surrounded by circular circuits of causewayed ditch that may represent a different, perhaps earlier, phase of construction. In view of the total absence of conventional causewayed enclosures elsewhere in the region, however, it seems more likely that this represents a local tradition in the construction of henges, rather than in adapting earlier monuments.

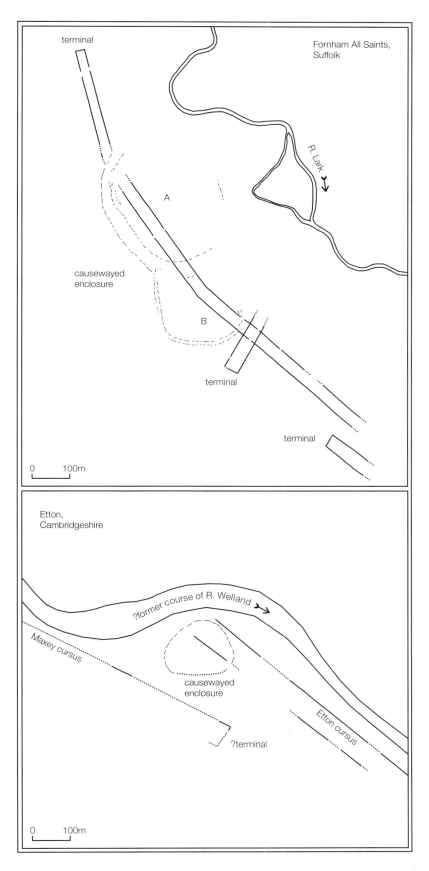

*Figure 8.3*
*On Whitesheet Hill in*
*Wiltshire, the smaller*
*barrows dispersed along the*
*scarp edge are almost*
*certainly of Bronze Age*
*date. Ironically, it was*
*probably the assumption*
*that the larger barrow was*
*also of Bronze Age date*
*which initially led to the*
*suggestion that the under-*
*lying causewayed enclosure*
*might be earlier still. Note*
*the cross-ridge dyke to the*
*east of the enclosure, which*
*may prove to be of Neolithic*
*date, although excavation*
*has proved inconclusive*
*(Rawlins et al forthcoming).*

## Later Neolithic barrows

At Whitesheet Hill in Wiltshire, a large round barrow is centred directly above the ditch of the causewayed enclosure (Fig 8.3). The barrow has a surrounding ditch which appears, from the surface traces, to be constructed as a series of pits (Piggott 1952, 406). In this it resembles several examples lying less than 50km to the south, which excavation has shown to be of later Neolithic date: Handley Barrow 27 in Cranborne Chase and Dorchester Site 2, Phase 1 (Barrett, *et al* 1991, fig 3.16; *see also* Kinnes 1979). It seems an unlikely coincidence that the Whitesheet barrow stands directly on top of the causewayed earthwork of the enclosure and itself has a ditch that is causewayed. The barrow lies separate from a group of smaller barrows,

which are characteristic of the Early Bronze Age in size and form; Colt Hoare (1812) recorded that excavation of one yielded a Beaker. This group occupies a position which relates primarily to the topography, again more typical of the Bronze Age, strung out along the very edge of the scarp slope. This contrast suggests that the larger barrow may have been sited with awareness and direct respect for the earlier monument.

Another large barrow with a causewayed ditch may be represented by a very faint cropmark 75m outside the causewayed enclosure at Roughton in Norfolk (Figs 4.27 and 6.7). A smaller example, also with a causewayed ditch, lies near Robin Hood's Ball. Three even smaller barrows may have impinged on the banks and ditches of this enclosure, though these are not necessarily

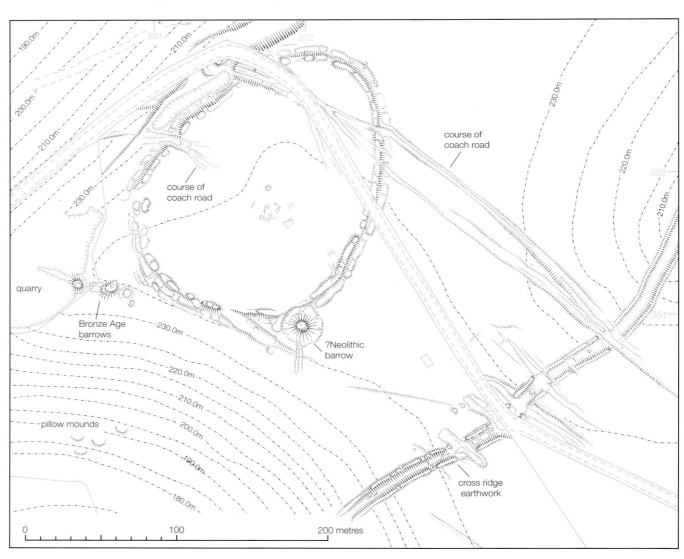

Neolithic or Bronze Age – barrows of similar size have proved to be of Anglo-Saxon date. One is now hardly visible as an earthwork, although it was recorded in the course of an earlier survey by the Royal Commission (Thomas 1964, 13). Recent geophysical survey at Whitehawk Camp in East Sussex contradicts the appearance of the earthworks by suggesting that an oval mound, first recorded by E C Curwen in the 1920s, overlies the ditch of the enclosure (Geophysical Surveys of Bradford, unpublished).

At Crickley Hill in Gloucestershire and Maiden Castle in Dorset, long mounds or 'bank barrows' were built across the circuits of the disused causewayed enclosures. In these cases, the elongated form of the barrows suggests a more dynamic relationship with the disused enclosures, perhaps involving a processional movement from the outside to the inside (or vice versa; Bradley 1984b). In both cases, the bank barrows were built at some time after the enclosure itself had fallen into disuse (Dixon 1988, fig 4.6; Sharples 1991a, 255–6).

All these new monuments would thus seem to have placed a 'full stop' on the main period of use of the enclosures. Yet in another sense, they are perhaps the first distinct acts of commemoration in the afterlife of the original monuments (Bradley 1993, 113).

## The reuse of causewayed enclosures in the Bronze and Iron Ages

Beaker pottery has been found in the upper levels of the ditches of several causewayed enclosures on higher ground, including Windmill Hill, Hambledon Hill, Maiden Castle and Barkhale Camp. Until the 1990s, this material was interpreted as deliberate reuse of causewayed enclosures by people in the later Neolithic and Early Bronze Age, a sign of their respect for the earlier monuments (Bradley 1984a, 79–81). Yet new research argues that the material has perhaps received undue attention, that the well preserved layers in the ditches can be seen as elements of broader spreads of Beaker pottery which have been disturbed by ploughing and other factors (Hamilton in Whittle et al 1999). If so, the distribution as a whole may be better interpreted as the result of reuse of the site, without any regard for the monument itself. In contrast to the upland sites, those

in riverine locations, such as Staines in Middlesex, seldom produce more than a handful of sherds.

There are, nonetheless, certain instances of Beaker activity which appears to acknowledge both the existence and the form of the earlier monument. At Briar Hill, postpits containing Beaker pottery and dated to around 2,140 BC indicate that four vertical timbers were placed in a symmetrical arrangement around the inner circuit of the enclosure. At least twelve Beakers had apparently been placed quite deliberately in relation to the earlier ditches (Bamford 1985, 47). In contrast to the numerous fragments of bone found in ditches in earlier Neolithic contexts, the crouched complete inhumations found in the ditches of Whitehawk Camp (Fig 8.4) and the causewayed enclosures at The Trundle and on the Stepleton spur of Hambledon Hill may well be of Beaker date (Curwen 1936, 70; 1929b, 46–9; Mercer and Healy in preparation). Whether these burials really show respect for the monuments themselves, or for some less well defined concept of the place or the past remains open to debate.

There are many instances where relatively small round barrows, which are generally assumed to be of Early Bronze Age rather than later Neolithic date, are sited in close proximity to causewayed enclosures. On Barrow Hills near the causewayed enclosure at Abingdon in Oxfordshire, a number of round barrows were built adjacent to the Neolithic oval barrow to form a linear cemetery aligned approximately on the centre of the enclosure (Barclay and Halpin 1999). This juxtaposition might, from a sceptical point of view, be dismissed as to all intents and purposes coincidental. For example, two of the three barrows on Knap Hill in Wiltshire, two of the three on Combe Hill (Fig 8.5), two on Offham Hill in East Sussex and one at Eastry in Kent occupy the highest ground (like many other round barrows along the chalk escarpments) and have no explicit relationship with the nearby causewayed enclosure. At Windmill Hill, where one of the barrows appears to be sited deliberately on the line of the causewayed enclosure ditch, the topography may have been the primary, if not the sole, influence on the choice of its location. Even the two barrows near Barkhale Camp in West Sussex, or the two outside the causewayed enclosure at Mavesyn Ridware in Staffordshire are not explicitly linked with the earlier monument.

Although the boundary between the later Neolithic period and the earliest Bronze Age has become blurred, the presence of Bronze Age material on the sites of most causewayed enclosures must still be interpreted as renewed activity on the site after a lengthy interval, rather than a later mani-festation of continuous acitivity. After periods of disuse lasting several centuries, the earthworks of some causewayed enclosures may have been completely overgrown. Those under grass, especially those that were being regularly grazed, may have remained quite prominent as earthworks.

*Figure 8.4*
*At The Trundle in West Sussex, the grave of a young adult woman was cut into the upper levels of the Neolithic ditch. Although no artefacts were found to conclusively date the burial, its stratigraphic position and the flexed position of the body are characteristic of the Beaker period. (Photo E C Curwen 1928; Sussex Archaeological Society)*

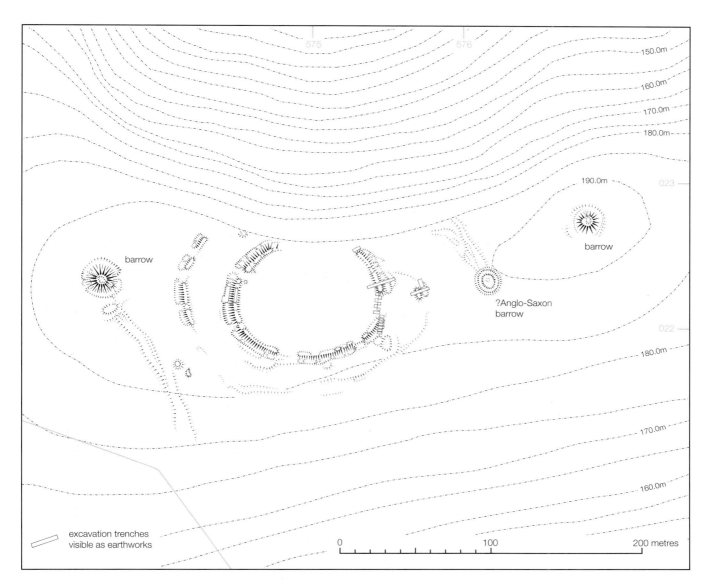

barrow

barrow

?Anglo-Saxon
barrow

excavation trenches
visible as earthworks

0        100        200 metres

People of the Beaker period may have identified and re-excavated these earthworks – the ancient monuments of the day – in an almost archaeological way (Hingley 1996, 241–2). The circumstances that led them to do so can only be imagined. Perhaps the monuments had acquired mythical status and were seen as the creations of powerful gods or ancestors. There may also have been much more practical reasons, which it could be too simplistic to reduce to a nominal 'respect' for the past. The absence of evidence that can be detected through archaeological techniques should not lead to the conclusion that the earlier monuments went unrecognised in later prehistory. On the contrary, where ancient earthworks were recognised, their presence must have contributed greatly to the later character

and importance of the places they occupied (Bradley 1993; Thomas 1991, 30).

The theory that Iron Age hillforts were analogous to causewayed enclosures has now been generally rejected. It has been replaced, however, by the suspicion that the siting of some hillforts may result from an attachment to the locations occupied by the earlier monuments (Cunliffe 1974, 302; Wainwright 1975, 60–71). The evidence to support this theory is not great: there are in fact only eight known instances of juxta-position, representing around 20 per cent of the upland causewayed enclosures, but a negligible percentage of hillforts.

In isolated cases, however, specifically Maiden Castle in Dorset and Hembury in Devon, the Iron Age ramparts were built directly on top of the existing earthworks. It

*Figure 8.5*
*The causewayed enclosure at Combe Hill in East Sussex is flanked by barrows that are presumably of Bronze Age date, but these occupy the highest ground and do not necessarily relate directly to the enclosure. More intriguing is the small disc-like barrow which appears to be sited on top of a slight earthwork; this may be Bronze Age, but could also be of Anglo-Saxon date.*

*Figure 8.6*
*The causewayed enclosure*
*underlying the Iron Age*
*hillfort known as The*
*Trundle in West Sussex.*
*Note how the polygonal*
*line of the Iron Age circuit*
*seems to reflect the much*
*slighter angles in the inner*
*circuit of the Neolithic*
*enclosure. The mound on*
*the summit, which was*
*occupied in the medieval*
*period by the chapel of*
*St Roche, may have*
*originated as a Bronze*
*Age barrow; a linear ditch*
*which may be of later*
*Bronze Age date appears*
*to be aligned on the*
*mound.*

could simply be argued that less effort would have been required to construct the ramparts as a result. At Maiden Castle, however, the primary rampart was actually constructed on top of the Neolithic ditch, rather than the bank. The greater length of the perimeter required by following the course of the earlier earthwork must have largely negated any economy there may have been in incorporating the slight earthwork. The decision to adhere to the plan of the ancient enclosure suggests that there may have been some more complex motivation. Some similar motivation is hinted at by the plan of The Trundle hillfort in West Sussex (Fig 8.6). The polygonal plan, which is unusual when compared to other hillforts in Sussex, echoes the slighter angles in the inner circuit of the causewayed enclosure. Today, the inner circuit remains the most massive of the Neolithic earthworks visible

on the surface, even though Curwen's excavations suggested that it may have been partially levelled at some point in the Iron Age (Curwen 1929b, 37). Interestingly, the hillfort, which has traditionally been termed a 'contour' fort, in fact tilts slightly to the north across the contours, as does the causewayed enclosure.

As mentioned in Chapter 5, it is possible that a number of causewayed enclosures may have been destroyed or buried by the construction of hillforts. The concentration of Neolithic artefacts in the vicinity of the hillforts on Ham Hill and South Cadbury in Somerset has prompted speculation (Smith 1971, 90; Cunliffe 1993, fig 2.6). A length of ditch containing a little earlier Neolithic material was discovered beneath the hillfort on Blewburton Hill in Oxfordshire, seeming to lend weight to the theory (Harding

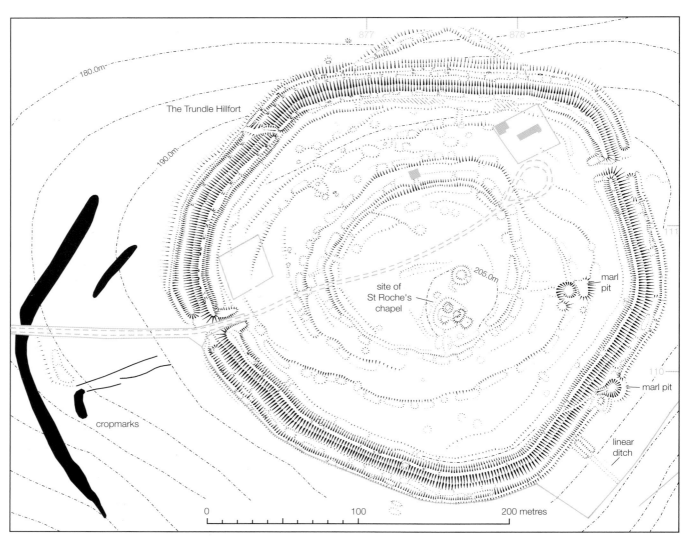

*Figure 8.6*
*The causewayed enclosure underlying the Iron Age hillfort known as The Trundle in West Sussex. Note how the polygonal line of the Iron Age circuit seems to reflect the much slighter angles in the inner circuit of the Neolithic enclosure. The mound on the summit, which was occupied in the medieval period by the chapel of St Roche, may have originated as a Bronze Age barrow; a linear ditch which may be of later Bronze Age date appears to be aligned on the mound.*

1976, 141–2; Holgate 1988, 340). There were, however, arguably far fewer finds than might be expected if the ditch were part of a causewayed enclosure and there is no firm supporting evidence from the other sites. It is noticeable that the three causewayed enclosures found to be completely buried beneath Iron Age hillforts all lie in the south-west of England, perhaps reflecting a local trend in the siting of the Iron Age monuments.

Away from the South-West, there are grounds for doubting whether there will prove to be many more discoveries of causewayed enclosures masked by hillforts. At a considerable number of sites, causewayed enclosures are detectable through earthwork survey despite the superimposition or juxtaposition of a hillfort. The presence of earlier earthworks is even evident in the unusual plan of the Iron Age ramparts at Hembury in Devon and at

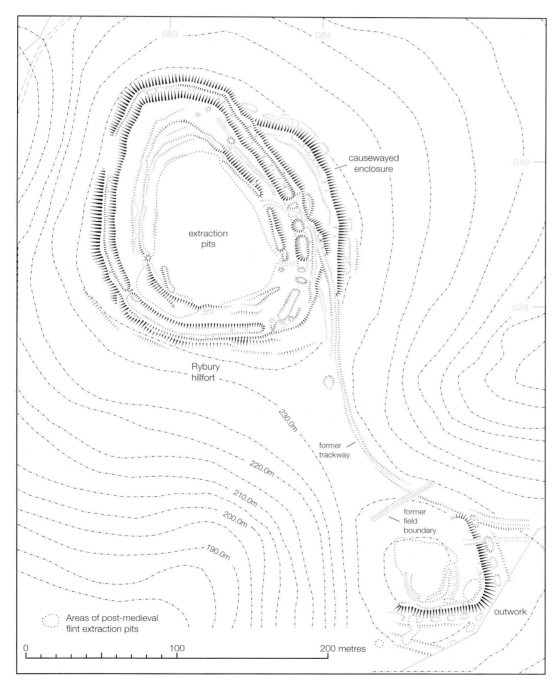

Figure 8.7
The causewayed enclosure underlying the hillfort known as Rybury in Wiltshire. In the interior of the hillfort, only slight traces of the course of the circuit of the causewayed enclosure can be identified by earthwork survey, due in part to the intensive digging for flint that has pock-marked the summit. Sufficient can be recognized, however, to show that the circuit encircled the summit, but in such a way as to tilt down the northern slope in a manner typical of causewayed enclosures on high ground.

141

*Figure 8.8*
*The sequence of*
*development of the southern*
*cross-ridge dyke and*
*western outwork on*
*Hambledon Hill, based*
*upon the earthwork*
*evidence. The date of the*
*final recut of the outer ditch*
*of the cross-ridge earthwork*
*is uncertain, but a short*
*stretch of the ditch of the*
*main causewayed enclosure*
*has been similarly recut,*
*again with a slight counter-*
*scarp bank. A Bronze Age*
*or Iron Age date seems*
*plausible.*

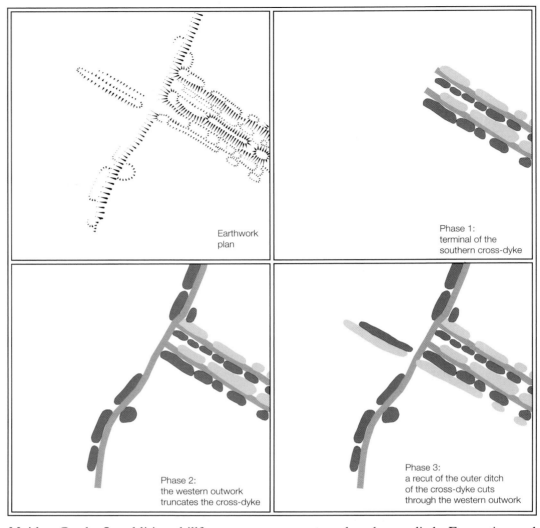

Earthwork plan

Phase 1:
terminal of the
southern cross-dyke

Phase 2:
the western outwork
truncates the cross-dyke

Phase 3:
a recut of the outer ditch
of the cross-dyke cuts
through the western outwork

Maiden Castle. In addition, hillforts were, with certain exceptions, sited on the tops of hills, unlike causewayed enclosures. As a result, in certain cases where causewayed enclosures are overlain by hillforts, the earlier earthworks emerge from beneath one side of the Iron Age ramparts. This throws the contrast in their designs in relation to the topography into sharp relief, as at Rybury Camp in Wiltshire (Fig 8.7) and the outer circuit of The Trundle in West Sussex. At Maiden Bower in Bedfordshire, though the full plan of the causewayed enclosure is unknown, the position and orientation of the known segment of its ditch suggests that it too may have been only partially overlain by the hillfort.

One of the last modifications of the main causewayed enclosure on Hambledon Hill seems to have involved the recutting of the outer ditch of the southern cross-ridge earthwork and perhaps a short section of the main causewayed enclosure ditch. Excavation and earthwork survey indicate that the original U-shaped ditch of the cross-ridge earthwork was recut with a shallow V-shaped profile, and the material used to form an almost continuous bank along its outer edge (Fig 8.8). It is thought that these recuts might result from the reuse of the Neolithic earthworks as outworks of the great Iron Age hillfort on the northern spur of the hill. The recuts contain only pottery of earlier Neolithic date, but this may be residual material from the original earthwork, which became incorporated into the silts of the later ditch (Mercer and Healy in preparation). A possible parallel for this is to be found at Whitehawk Camp in East Sussex. There, a ditch follows the northern side of the outer circuit for most of its length, but breaks away from it at each end to continue tangentially to the edge of the natural scarp. A similar ditch may have existed at the southern end of

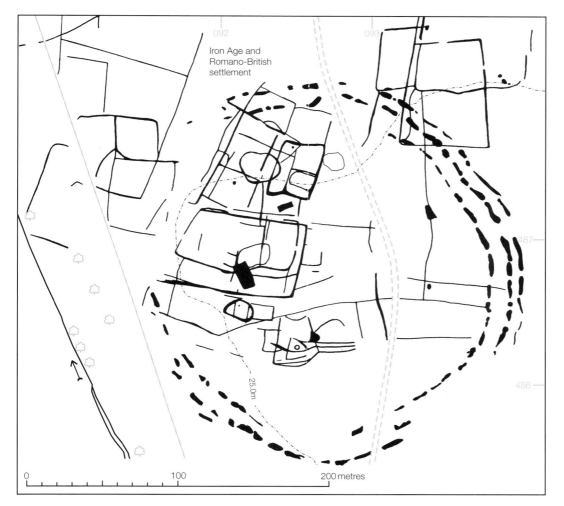

Iron Age and
Romano-British
settlement

0    100    200 metres

*Figure 8.9*
*The causewayed enclosure*
*at Cardington in*
*Bedfordshire is overlain by*
*a dense spread of late Iron*
*Age and Romano-British*
*occupation. Trial*
*excavation (Johnston*
*1955–6, 94) recovered*
*only Romano-British*
*pottery, prompting initial*
*concern that the site had*
*been incorrectly identified.*
*In the course of the new*
*investigation, however,*
*moderate quantities of*
*worked flint were also*
*noted on the surface.*

the site. Both were portrayed on the Revd Skinner's plan of 1821 (Fig 2.3) and detected by geophysical survey (Geophysical Surveys of Bradford unpublished). Trial excavation has proved inconclusive (Russell 1997), but in form, both ditches have much in common with later prehistoric cross-ridge dykes and may well be of later Bronze Age or early Iron Age date.

Some enclosures located on rises in valley floor and on valley sides, such as those at Cardington in Bedfordshire, Orsett in Essex and Langford in Oxfordshire were overlain by dense Iron Age and Roman settlements, which show no sign whatsoever of having respected or reused the earlier monument (Figs 8.9, 3.11 and 7.3). Indeed, after centuries of alluviation, and perhaps ploughing, it is doubtful whether the Neolithic earthworks would have survived to any appreciable degree on many of these floodplain sites. At Eastleach in Gloucestershire, however, there is a hint that the later settlement may have respected the line of the

largest of the four ditch circuits of the causewayed enclosure, suggesting that it may have still survived as a substantial earthwork. As mentioned in Chapter 4, at Southwick in Northamptonshire a palisade runs between the ditches at the southern end of the causewayed enclosure (Fig 8.10). This seems to be part of a later and smaller timber-built enclosure, whose perimeter followed a section of the earlier earthwork. Indeed, small-scale excavations across one of the causeways at this point recovered only Iron Age material from the ditches (Hadman 1973). At Down Ampney in Gloucestershire, most of the causewayed enclosure seems to have been disregarded when a series of small compounds was built on the site, perhaps in the late Bronze Age or Iron Age. There too, however, a short length of one of the later boundary ditches may have been influenced by the course of the Neolithic circuit (Fig 8.11). At Springfield Lyons in Essex, a small circular enclosure with multiple entrances lies immediately

*Figure 8.10*
*The causewayed enclosure at Southwick in Northamptonshire. Like the enclosure at Cardington, trial excavation at the southern end of the enclosure recovered only Iron Age pottery from the upper levels of the ditch (Hadman 1973). Aerial survey puts this discovery into context: the southern half of the causewayed enclosure appears to have been reused as the site of a palisaded enclosure. The alignment of the palisade between the widely spaced ditches of the Neolithic enclosure suggests that the causewayed earthworks may have survived to some degree.*

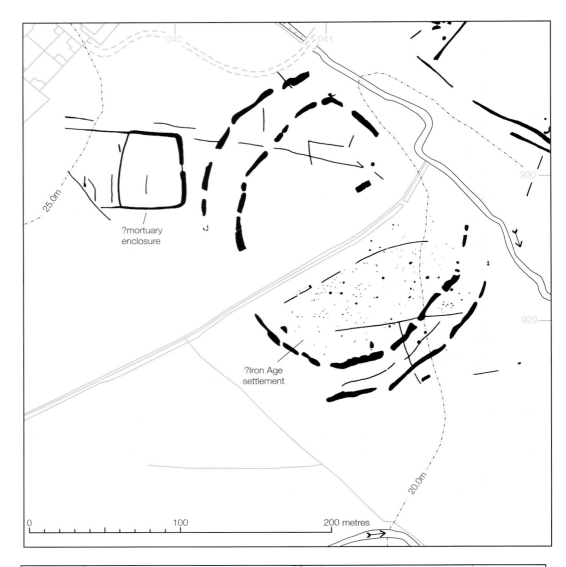

*Figure 8.11*
*The causewayed enclosure at Down Ampney in Gloucestershire is typical of a site in a fertile valley bottom, where intensive agriculture and settlement were already under way by the later Iron Age. The survey evidence suggests that the enclosure earthworks may already have been so degraded by that date as to be unrecognisable on the ground.*

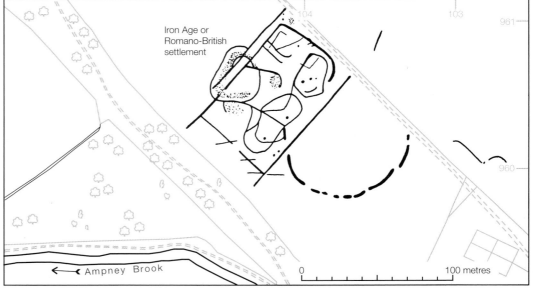

adjacent to the causewayed enclosure. Excavation has proved that it is of late Bronze Age date and might be interpreted variously as a defended settlement or a ritual monument. Its siting and form both hint that it could have been a conscious imitation of, or re-invention of, the perceived form of the earthworks of the Neolithic enclosure (Brown 1996, 30).

## The historic period: causewayed enclosures come full circle

In Essex, the causewayed enclosure at Orsett and the possible example at Springfield Lyons were both the sites of pagan Anglo-Saxon cemeteries (Buckley and Hedges 1982). It is uncertain, however, whether either enclosure would have remained visible as an earthwork by that time and it may be that their presence was essentially coincidental. In the 7th and 8th centuries AD, Saxons were buried in the banks of the Stepleton enclosure on Hambledon Hill (Mercer and Healy in preparation). This isolated example, however, needs to be seen in the context of other burials at that period: many other earthworks – including Neolithic long

barrows and Bronze Age round barrows – were reused in this way (Williams 1998; Semple 1998). There is, therefore, little to suggest that causewayed enclosures in general or the Stepleton enclosure in particular were revered more than any other ancient monument. There is certainly no firm evidence that causewayed enclosures were accorded any special treatment later in the medieval period.

In modern times, the sites of causewayed enclosures have been reused for many purposes (Fig 8.12), but instances of such commemorative acts have been scarce. In the 1930s, chalk rubble was used to create a hill-figure near the centre of the innermost circuit of the causewayed enclosure on Windmill Hill in Wiltshire (Fig 2.8). The slight surviving earthwork suggests an animal shape, but only aerial photographs testify to its true form – a pig! Yet archaeological excavation itself can be seen as an act of reuse and, without documentary records, trenches would probably be interpreted as such by future generations of archaeologists (Fig 8.13). Furthermore, the reverence which has been accorded to these monuments from the days of Stukeley onwards should remind us how many other forms of 'reuse', in the broadest sense of the word, are simply not detectable archaeologically. Of the ten

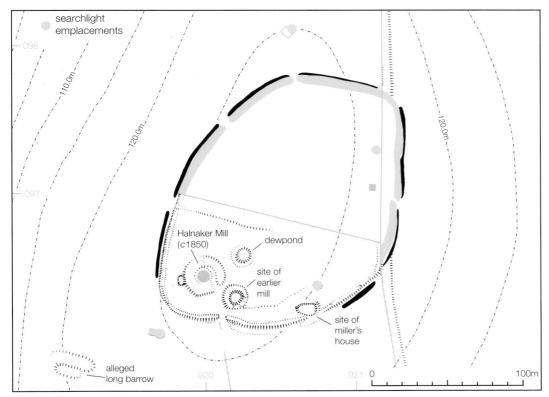

*Figure 8.12*
*On Halnaker Hill in West Sussex, almost by coincidence, a sequence of later monuments occupied the site of a probable causewayed enclosure. Trial excavation recovered Iron Age and Roman pottery, although the source of this is uncertain (Bedwin, 1982; 1983; 1984–5). A windmill may first have been built on the hilltop in the mid-16th century. In the 19th century, the miller's house was sited on the bank of the enclosure and the rest of the perimeter appears to have defined the limits of a yard. In the Second World War, the good visibility from the hilltop made it an ideal location for a searchlight battery.*

*Figure 8.13*
*The most visible earthworks*
*at Windmill Hill today are*
*as much the work of*
*Alexander Keiller and of the*
*National Trust as they are of*
*the Neolithic communities*
*which created the monument.*
*During the 1930s, a second*
*campaign of work directed by*
*Keiller was centred around*
*the restoration of the earth-*
*works and their presentation*
*to the public. This involved*
*re-excavating those ditches*
*previously dug, as well as*
*re-turfing the mound and*
*ditches of the some of the*
*overlying Bronze Age*
*barrows (shown here).*
*Initially, the causewayed*
*enclosure and barrow ditches*
*were left open, their inner*
*faces lined with turf. In*
*1959–60, the ditches were*
*once again refilled, this time*
*with soil and rubble brought*
*from elsewhere, and then*
*sown with grass. Shallow*
*depressions were deliberately*
*left in order to mark the*
*location of these segments*
*and to show the intervening*
*causeways. (NMR*
*AA77/2913)*

enclosures which are still well preserved as earthworks, three (Windmill Hill, White-sheet Hill and Barkhale) are now owned by the National Trust, while the remainder are protected under the auspices of English Nature and other conservation bodies, in partnership with English Heritage. Carefully managed regimes of grazing and scrub clearance are designed to preserve the downland environment essential to the continued survival of the monuments.

Yet these measures, on the basis of the physical evidence alone, may be virtually undetectable to future generations of archaeologists.

In the course of his excavations at Whitehawk Camp in East Sussex, Cecil Curwen commented on the parallels between modern reuse of the monuments and the events which characterised their use nearly six thousand years earlier '. . . the ditches became once more receptacles for local rubbish . . . nearly filled with an incredible quantity of scrap iron, including bedsteads, baths, stoves, parts of motor-cars and bicycles etc.' (Curwen 1934, 104).

Today, in one way or another, we continue to participate actively in the after-life of causewayed enclosures.

# 9
# Looking ahead – where next for research?

Understanding of causewayed enclosures has relied heavily on the evidence from the handful of sites that have been extensively excavated. Several of these, such as the vast enclosures at Haddenham in Cambridgeshire and on Hambledon Hill in Dorset or the unusually designed enclosure on Windmill Hill, are so unusual that it may be unwise to treat them as templates for understanding causewayed enclosures as a class. By directing attention towards sites that have seldom figured in previous discussions, in particular those in lowland locations that no longer survive as earthworks, this book has attempted to broaden the foundations of future research. In this respect, the corpus of detailed plans at comparable scales to a large degree speaks for itself.

The survey evidence has shown that certain long-held beliefs about causewayed enclosures are erroneous or partial truths. Too little emphasis has been placed on the role of the banks in defining the perimeters. The diversity in the forms of individual monuments is clearly evident, but so too is the regular occurrence of certain characteristics that may point towards a norm: a single complete circuit, or two closely-spaced circuits, with relatively infrequent causeways through the banks and a single main entrance. Potential for change over time has been shown to be the 'Achilles heel' of past attempts to distinguish between causewayed enclosures on the evidence of their plan alone. Yet at the same time, there are a few instances where analysis of the plan provides more compelling evidence for the evolution of the monument than excavation is generally able to do. Far from being 'unconformable' in their relationships to their topographic settings, fieldwork has revealed a remarkable consistency in the locations of the monuments, although based upon a logic which is quite alien to modern principles. Again, this is perhaps most striking among those sites in lowland locations where the tiny changes in relief might long have been overlooked as a locational factor. Yet it must be admitted that, while the survey evidence presented in this book has led to significant advances in the understanding of individual monuments, it has left unanswered many of the more intractable questions about the roles and functions of causewayed enclosures as a class.

The principal aim has been to provide a foundation for future research. As Chapter 2 has made clear, new discoveries from fieldwork, aerial survey and excavation on the one hand and advances in thinking on the other continually leapfrog each other while pushing forward knowledge and understanding of causewayed enclosures. There are many interrelated avenues along which research may advance, some dealing with questions about causewayed enclosures themselves and others addressing aspects of the wider landscape.

## Dating

Causewayed enclosures can now generally be dated to the Neolithic with some confidence on the basis of survey evidence alone. In some cases even this basic question remains unanswered, however, and it is uncertain whether there was any regional patterning in the dates at which causewayed enclosures were built and used. Perhaps more importantly, accurate dating of individual enclosures and their component parts will help to answer how causewayed enclosures related to their sur-rounding landscapes. Were those causewayed enclosures that lie in close proximity to each other in use at the same time, or centuries apart? Were different circuits of individual enclosures in use contemporaneously? These issues go beyond simply improving our knowledge of individual sites. They may shed light on the nature and development of the class of monument as a whole, and indeed of Neolithic society itself. Of the causewayed enclosures excavated so far, only a few have been dated using the modern techniques that can offer the degree of accuracy necessary to begin to answer these key questions.

## Distribution

Aerial reconnaissance will undoubtedly continue to have an important role in the discovery of causewayed enclosures, but survey techniques currently in development may eventually transform knowledge of the areas of the distribution map less likely to produce good cropmarks. Equally, causewayed enclosures currently dominate the distribution of earlier Neolithic enclosures, because they are relatively easy to identify through survey. Until knowledge of other forms of earlier Neolithic enclosure is improved, including the tor enclosures, the broader picture of their distribution is obscured. If causewayed enclosures form only part of a larger and less distinct class, it may be necessary to reassess much of what is currently thought.

## Landscape contexts

What really was the nature of the earlier Neolithic environment? Where were the settlements and areas of day-to-day activity with which causewayed enclosures were linked? What are the sources of the raw materials – plants, stones and clay – found at causewayed enclosures? These questions have repercussions for almost every aspect of our understanding of Neolithic monuments and society. The answers are to be found not only through investigation of the monuments themselves, but also through work in the wider landscape. A larger body of data may in due course transform the understanding of the ancient landscape and of the place of individual sites and monuments within it. Systematic fieldwalking in the immediate vicinity of causewayed enclosures may be the first step, but the evidence for everyday activity of the earlier Neolithic is notoriously difficult to identify. An improved knowledge of other forms of monument – particularly cursus monuments – may also contribute to the understanding of causewayed enclosures.

## Form

Continued aerial survey will also probably go a long way towards understanding the form of causewayed enclsoures, but geophysical survey and, where appropriate, small-scale trial excavation may also contribute.

## Function

In the past, large-scale excavations have often been touchstones for the re-evaluation of long-held ideas; they are certain to so remain. Theories born in the causewayed enclosures on the southern chalk uplands have, however, dominated thinking for too long. Further work is needed at sites located on valley floors, particularly those where waterlogging may have preserved organic remains. It is important to measure and control the preservation of these sites, which, despite their evident value, have seen so little work to date.

## Making the most of existing data

It is seldom easy to use the finds and paper records of old excavations to answer questions that have only recently become important. Yet many of the questions being asked by archaeologists today are the same as those asked by the likes of Alexander Keiller and E C Curwen in the 1920s. There is work to be done in revisiting the finds and paper records produced by excavations carried out up to three generations ago.

# Appendix:
## Gazetteer of causewayed enclosures in the United Kingdom

All those causewayed enclosures whose existence was known up to January 2000 are listed. This includes not only certain and probable causewayed enclosures, but also a number of suggested sites that can only be regarded as possible candidates on the strength of current evidence. Also included are a few sites that were once alleged to have been causewayed enclosure, but have since been re-interpreted. So-called 'tor enclosures' have been treated as possible variants of the class, but are listed separately from conventional causewayed enclosures.

Entries in the gazetteer are ordered alphabetically, first by county and then by the name of the site. Most sites discovered through aerial reconnaissance are here named after the parish in which they lie, while the majority of the sites surviving as earthworks (and a few others) have conventionally been named after later monuments in the immediate vicinity (eg The Trundle, Maiden Bower), or some other feature in the environs (eg Combe Hill, Robin Hood's Ball). The name of the civil parish and district are given in every case. The National Monuments Record (NMR) reference number of each site is given. Further information and archival material can be obtained from English Heritage's public archive by quoting these numbers. The National Grid Reference (NGR) for the centre of each enclosure is given, except where only a short arc of the circuit can be traced. In such cases, the grid reference is centred on the feature itself and is noted as such after the reference.

Cross-references to large scale plans in this book are given in bold next to the relevant gazetteer entry. Other major published sources are also listed.

## Causewayed enclosures in England

1 Cardington, Bedford, Bedfordshire
**8.9** *Status* very probable.
*NGR* TL 0926 4870
*NMR number* TL 04 NE 25
*Excavations* 1951–2
*Main published sources* Johnston, 1955–6, 94; Palmer 1976 (10)
*Comments* Plough-levelled enclosure, discovered during aerial reconnaissance by Cambridge University Committee for Aerial Photography (UCAP) in 1951. Trial excavations by two Cambridge University undergraduates encountered features relating to Romano-British settlement, but did not confirm the date of the enclosure.

2 Maiden Bower, Houghton Regis,
**2.18** South Bedfordshire, Bedfordshire
*Status* probable.
*NGR* SP 9966 2247
*NMR number* SP 92 SE 42
*Excavations* Cook 1913
*Main published sources* Smith 1915; Dyer 1955; Matthews 1976; Palmer 1976 (33)
*Comments* Ditch segments with a characteristic shallow U-shaped profile, partially overlain by an Iron Age hillfort and only visible in section in the side of a chalk quarry, which has presumably destroyed much of the circuit. The location would appear to have been typical of lowland oriented sites.

3 Eton Wick, Eton, Windsor and Maidenhead, Berkshire
*Status* certain.
*NGR* SU 9503 7810
*NMR number* SU 97 NE 110
*Excavations* Ford 1984–5
*Main published sources* Ford 1986; 1991–3
*Comments* Plough-levelled enclosure, first recognised on vertical aerial photographs by the East Berkshire Archaeological Survey in 1983. Small-scale excavation confirmed the identification.

4 Uffton Nervet, West Berkshire, Berkshire
*Status* dismissed.
*NGR* SU 617 690
*NMR number* SU 66 NW 7
*Excavations* Reading Museum 1961–3
*Main published sources* Anon 1960, 286
*Comments* Part of a cropmark complex was initially suggested by J K St Joseph to be a possible causewayed ditch, but subsequent excavations encountered no features earlier than the late Iron Age.

5 Dorney, South Buckinghamshire, Buckinghamshire
*Status* probable.
*NGR* SU 9178 7907
*NMR number* SU 97 NW 88
*Excavations* none
*Main published sources* Carstairs 1986, 164 and fig 3
*Comments* Stretches of two or three plough-levelled parallel causewayed ditches, probably forming part of an enclosure, discovered during aerial reconnaissance by RCHME in July 1975. Fieldwalking on the site recovered only later Neolithic and Bronze Age flints.

6 Pitstone Hill, Pitstone, Aylesbury Vale, Buckinghamshire
*Status* unlikely.
*NGR* SP 9496 1420 (feature centred)
*NMR number* SP 91 SW 56
*Excavations* none
*Main published sources* Dyer and Hales 1961, 51
*Comments* A stretch of ditch with a continuous bank lying outside it. The curving course suggests that it may have formed part of an enclosure, the rest of which has been levelled by ploughing. The earthwork is probably prehistoric, but the suggested causeways in the ditch are more likely to represent post-medieval damage. The identification was based partly on the proximity of alleged Neolithic flint mines, which have also been discredited.

7a Etton, Maxey, Peterborough, Cambridgeshire
*Status* certain.
*NGR* TF 1385 0735
*NMR number* TF 10 NW 51
*Excavations* Pryor 1982–6
*Main published sources* Pryor and Kinnes 1982; Pryor *et al* 1985; Pryor 1987; Pryor 1998b
*Comments* Plough-levelled enclosure, discovered during aerial reconnaissance by S Upex (on behalf of the Nene Valley Research Committee) in 1976. Partial waterlogging allowed the recovery of organic remains during large scale excavations.

7b Etton, Maxey, Peterborough, Cambridgeshire
*Status* probable.
*NGR* TF 1379 0656
*NMR number* TF 10 NW 96
*Excavations* none
*Main published sources* none
*Comments* Plough-levelled enclosure, superficially similar in appearance to the certain site immediately to the north, discovered during aerial reconnaissance by R Palmer in 1998.

8 Great Wilbraham, South
**4.7** Cambridgeshire, Cambridgeshire
*Status* certain.
*NGR* TL 5395 5780
*NMR number* TL 55 NW 8
*Excavations* Alexander and Clarke 1975; Alexander and Kinnes 1976
*Main published sources* Palmer 1976 (26); Anon 1977
*Comments* Plough-levelled enclosure discovered by CUCAP during aerial reconnaissance in July 1972. Publication of the excavations is in preparation.

9 Haddenham, East Cambridgeshire,
**4.11** Cambridgeshire
*Status* certain.
*NGR* TL 4120 7365
*NMR number* TL 47 SW 47
*Excavations* Evans and Hodder 1981–4
*Main published sources* Evans 1988b;
Hodder 1992; Evans and Hodder
forthcoming
*Comments* Plough-levelled enclosure
discovered during aerial reconnaissance
in 1953. Fairly small-scale excavations
revealed evidence for particularly
complex recutting.

10 Landbeach, South Cambridgeshire,
Cambridgeshire
*Status* possible.
*NGR* TL 4830 6545 (feature centred)
*NMR number* TL 46 NE 59
*Excavations* none
*Main published sources* none
*Comments* Length of plough-levelled
causewayed ditch. The site was first
photographed by RCHME in August
1982 and first identified as a possible
causewayed enclosure by CUCAP in
June 1995.

11 Melbourne, South Cambridgeshire,
**8.1** Cambridgeshire
*Status* unlikely.
*NGR* TL 3668 4235
*NMR number* TL 34 SE 38
*Excavations* none
*Main published sources* Palmer 1976
(39)
*Comments* Plough-levelled enclosure,
discovered by CUCAP during aerial
reconnaissance in March 1956. The
ditch is interrupted, but the site is
otherwise unusual in form and
location. Possibly a henge.

12 Northborough, Peterborough,
**5.16** Cambridgeshire
*Status* very probable
*NGR* TF 1557 0845
*NMR number* TF 10 NE 34
*Excavations* none
*Main published sources* none
*Comments* Plough-levelled enclosure,
discovered during aerial reconnaissance
by J Pickering in July 1996.

13 Stapleford, South Cambridgeshire,
Cambridgeshire
*Status* unlikely.
*NGR* TL 4893 5306
*NMR number* TL 45 SE 35
*Excavations* none
*Main published sources* none
*Comments* Plough-levelled enclosure
discovered during aerial reconnaissance
by CUCAP in June 1950. It is
somewhat unusual in terms of its form
and location.

14 Upton, Peterborough, Cambridgeshire
**3.2** *Status* very probable.
*NGR* TF 0998 0058
*NMR number* TF 00 SE 45
*Excavations* none
*Main published sources* none
*Comments* Plough-levelled enclosure
discovered during aerial reconnaissance
by RCHME in July 1995.

15 Bury Down Camp, Lanreath, Caradon,
Cornwall
*Status* unlikely.
*NGR* SX 1880 5940
*NMR number* SX 15 NE 1
*Excavations* Ray 1994
*Main published sources* Ray 1998
*Comments* A circuit of bank and ditch,
apparently causewayed, has usually
been interpreted as an unfinished outer
circuit relating to the Iron Age circular
fort which lies within its circumference.
Excavations recovered no diagnostic
artefacts, but the sharply V-shaped
profile may support the original
interpretation.

16 Western Grange Farm, Aston upon
Trent, South Derbyshire, Derbyshire
*Status* dismissed.
*NGR* SK 428 285
*NMR number* SK 42 NW 51
*Excavations* none
*Main published sources* Gibson in Evans
1988b, 145
*Comments* The enclosure was initially
identified on the basis of aerial
photographic evidence. Although the
enclosure is quite possibly prehistoric,
the appearance of causewayed
construction was caused by medieval
ridge and furrow cultivation.

17 Hembury, Payhembury, East Devon,
**2.20** Devon
*Status* certain.
*NGR* ST 1125 0298
*NMR number* ST 10 SW 28
*Excavations* Liddell 1930–5; Todd
1980–3
*Main published sources* Liddell 1930;
1931; 1932; 1935; Palmer 1976 (15);
Todd 1984
*Comments* The enclosure was
discovered during the excavation of the
ramparts of the overlying Iron Age
hillfort. Timber buildings and 'cooking
pits' were identified. The enclosure
may have been attacked.

18 High Peak, Otterton, East Devon,
Devon
*Status* possible.
*NGR* SY 1035 8595
*NMR number* SY 18 NW 26
*Excavations* Pollard 1961–4
*Main published sources* Pollard 1966;
Palmer 1976 (37)

*Comments* A length of ditch associated
with settlement debris, underlying the
earthworks of an early medieval
enclosure. Most of the presumed
enclosure has been destroyed by
coastal erosion.

19 Membury, Membury, East Devon,
Devon
*Status* possible.
*NGR* ST 273 034
*NMR number* ST 20 SE 32
*Excavations* Berridge 1986; Tingle
1994
*Main published sources* Mercer 1990,
fig 1; Tingle 1995
*Comments* Excavations and
fieldwalking have recovered a concentration of earlier Neolithic artefacts
and perhaps the butt end of a ditch.
This may prove to be a pit, however,
and so the identification of the site as
a causewayed enclosure currently
remains unconfirmed.

20 Raddon Hill, Stockleigh Pomeroy
**5.2** (and Shobrooke), Mid Devon, Devon
*Status* certain.
*NGR* SS 8855 0313
*NMR number* SS 80 SE 67
*Excavations* Exeter Museums Archaeological Field Unit (EMAFU) 1994
*Main published sources* EMAFU 1995
*Comments* Plough-levelled causewayed
enclosure, overlain by an Iron Age
enclosure, discovered during aerial
reconnaissance by Frances Griffith in
1986. Geophysical survey and limited
excavation in 1994 (Gent and Knight
1996) confirmed the date of the inner
circuit, but the outer may be Iron Age.

21 Buzbury Rings, Tarrant Keyneston,
North Dorset, Dorset
*Status* dismissed.
*NGR* ST 9185 0590
*NMR number* ST 90 NW 13
*Excavations* 1957; Dorset County
Council 1964
*Main published sources* Curwen 1930,
41; Forde-Johnston 1958; Radley
1964
*Comments* Excavations have recovered
some Neolithic material, but the
enclosure itself has been shown to be
of Iron Age and Romano-British date.

22 Flagstones, Dorchester, West Dorset,
Dorset
*Status* unlikely.
*NGR* SY 7040 8995
*NMR number* SY 78 NW 67
*Excavations* Trust for Wessex
Archaeology 1987–8
*Main published sources* Woodward
1988; Healy 1997
*Comments* Plough-levelled enclosure,
discovered by geophysical survey and

confirmed by excavation by the TWA in 1987–8. The unusual form of the enclosure and its considerably later date suggest that it may represent a different class of monument.

23 Green Hill, Burton Bradstock, West Dorset, Dorset
*Status* dismissed.
*NGR* SY 5117 8865
*NMR number* SY 58 NW 43
*Excavations* none
*Main published sources* Radcliffe 1995
*Comments* Curvilinear features visible on air photographs were initially interpreted as a causewayed enclosure, but are now considered to be mainly geological in origin.

24a Hambledon Hill (main causewayed
**4.16** enclosure), Child Okeford (and Iwerne Courtney or Shroton), North Dorset, Dorset
*Status* certain.
*NGR* ST 8492 1226
*NMR number* ST 81 SW 17
*Excavations* Sieveking and Erskine 1951; Bonney 1959–60; Mercer 1974–1986
*Main published sources* Erskine 1951; RCHME 1970, 131; Palmer 1976 (17); Mercer 1980a; 1985; 1988; Mercer and Healy in preparation
*Comments* Mostly plough-levelled enclosure on the summit of Hambledon Hill, with associated cross-dykes and outworks, some of which survive as earthworks. Large-scale excavations suggested that the site may have been used for excarnation. *See* 24b and 24c for the two possible associated enclosures.

24b Hambledon Hill (Stepleton
**3.20** enclosure), Iwerne Courtney or Shroton, North Dorset, Dorset
*Status* certain.
*NGR* ST 8492 1226
*NMR number* ST 81 SE 52
*Excavations* Mercer 1974–86
*Main published sources* Palmer 1976 (17); Mercer 1980a; 1985; 1988
*Comments* Plough-levelled enclosure on the tip of a spur of Hambledon Hill, with outworks linking it to the main causewayed enclosure (24a). Complete excavation of the enclosure revealed a well preserved section of the timber defences and evidence for timber structures in the interior. The site may have been a settlement, built somewhat later than the main enclosure but in use concurrently with it.

24c Hambledon Hill (hillfort spur enclosure), Child Okeford, North Dorset, Dorset
*Status* unlikely.
*NGR* ST 8492 1226
*NMR number* ST 81 SW 59
*Excavations* Mercer 1985
*Main published sources* Mercer 1988
*Comments* An enclosure surviving as an earthwork underlying the Iron Age hillfort at the north end of Hambledon Hill was suspected to be a counterpart of the Stepleton enclosure at the south (24b). A single radiocarbon determination from Mercer's trial excavation seems to indicate a Bronze Age date, but there may have been a Neolithic precursor to this.

25 Maiden Castle, Winterborne St Martin, West Dorset, Dorset
*Status* certain.
*NGR* SY 6693 8848
*NMR number* SY 68 NE 151
*Excavations* Wheeler 1934–8, Sharples 1985–6
*Main published sources* Wheeler 1943; Palmer 1976 (25); Sharples 1991
*Comments* The enclosure entirely underlies the western ramparts of the first phase of the Iron Age hillfort. It was discovered during Wheeler's excavations there, but poorly recorded at the time. Later research by Sharples interpreted a ditch discovered by Wheeler at the eastern end of the fort, but not recorded in any detail, as a continuation of the enclosure, suggesting that it formed a complete circuit.

26 Lawford, Tendring, Essex
*Status* dismissed.
*NGR* TM 0885 3087
*NMR number* TM 03 SE 25
*Excavations* Blake 1962–3; Peterson and Shennan 1971
*Main published sources* Jessup 1970, 73; Shennan *et al* 1985
*Comments* A later Neolithic ring ditch, initially interpreted as a henge or causewayed enclosure.

27 Orsett, Thurrock, Essex
**3.11** *Status* certain.
*NGR* TQ 6515 8055
*NMR number* TQ 68 SE 21
*Excavations* Essex County Council Archaeological Section 1975
*Main published sources* Palmer 1976 (30); Hedges and Buckley 1978
*Comments* Plough-levelled enclosure, discovered during aerial reconnaissance by CUCAP in June 1961. Fairly small-scale excavations revealed evidence for an elaborate timber entrance.

28 Saffron Walden, Uttlesford, Essex
*Status* unlikely.
*NGR* TL 539 379
*NMR number* TL 53 NW 156
*Excavations* Maynard 1882
*Main published sources* Bassett 1982, 5
*Comments* A series of pits up to 2.4m deep containing decayed red deer antlers was discovered during building work in 1882. The description is not convincing as a causewayed enclosure, but the topography would be typical of a valley-side location.

29 Springfield Lyons, Springfield, Chelmsford, Essex
*Status* probable.
*NGR* TL 7357 0818 (feature centred)
*NMR number* TL 70 NW 105
*Excavations* Essex County Council 1987–91
*Main published sources* Priddy 1988; Gilman 1989; 1991
*Comments* Plough-levelled enclosure discovered by excavation in 1989–90. The identification could not be absolutely confirmed.

30 Birdlip Camp, Birdlip Hill, Cowley,
**4.14** Cotswold, Gloucestershire
*Status* certain.
*NGR* SO 9243 1502
*NMR number* SO 91 NW 10
*Excavations* Darvill 1980–1
*Main published sources* Darvill 1981–2
*Comments* Promontory enclosure still surviving in part as an earthwork. There is only slight evidence for numerous causeways.

31 Crickley Hill, Coberly, Cotswold (and
**4.15** Badgeworth, Tewkesbury), Gloucestershire
*Status* certain.
*NGR* SO 9265 1610
*NMR number* SO 91 NW 43
*Excavations* Dixon 1969–93
*Main published sources* Palmer 1976 (13); Dixon 1988
*Comments* The enclosure entirely underlies the ramparts of an Iron Age hillfort and was discovered during large-scale excavations. The enclosure underwent a sequence of modification and was apparently attacked towards the end of its use.

32 Down Ampney, Cotswold,
**8.11** Gloucestershire
*Status* very probable.
*NGR* SU 1023 9601
*NMR number* SU 19 NW 6
*Excavations* none
*Main published sources* RCHME 1976; Leach 1977
*Comments* Plough-levelled enclosure, discovered during aerial reconnaissance by CUCAP in August 1975.

33 Eastleach, Cotswold, Gloucestershire
**3.18** *Status* very probable.
*NGR* SP 2156 0472
*NMR number* SP 20 SW 21
*Excavations* none
*Main published sources* Palmer 1976
(3); Oxford Archaeological Unit 1982
*Comments* Plough-levelled enclosure
discovered during aerial
reconnaissance by RCHME in June
1970. Field walking undertaken by
OAU recovered flints, prehistoric
pottery and a stone pounder from the
surface.

34 Icomb Hill, Icomb, Cotswold,
Gloucestershire
*Status* possible.
*NGR* SP 2050 2315
*NMR number* SP 22 SW 1
*Excavations* none
*Main published sources* Savile 1978;
Darvill 1987, 42–3
*Comments* Plough-levelled enclosure,
initially interpreted as an Iron Age
hillfort. Stretches of interrupted ditch
and palisade trench, more reminiscent
of a causewayed enclosure, were
discovered during aerial
reconnaissance by CUCAP in July
1964. Neolithic artefacts have been
recovered from the hill during
fieldwalking. Darvill (1987) identified
a smaller enclosure in the interior,
which has been dismissed as
geological in origin.

35 Rodmarton, Cotswold,
Gloucestershire
*Status* unlikely.
*NGR* ST 9405 9852
*NMR number* ST 99 NW 51
*Excavations* none
*Main published sources* none
*Comments* A length of plough-levelled
elongated pits or ditch segments,
discovered during aerial
reconnaissance by RCHME in July
1983.

36 Salmonsbury, Bourton-on-the-Water,
Cotswold, Gloucestershire
*Status* probable.
*NGR* SP 1730 2090
*NMR number* SP 12 SE
*Excavations* none
*Main published sources* Marshall 1995
*Comments* Plough-levelled enclosure
discovered by magnetometer survey in
1994.

37 Southmore Grove, Rendcomb,
**5.23** Cotswold, Gloucestershire
*Status* very probable.
*NGR* SP 0025 0990
*NMR number* SP 00 NW 50
*Excavations* none
*Main published sources* Trow 1985

*Comments* Plough-levelled enclosure,
discovered during aerial reconnaissance
by RCHME in July 1983. Fieldwalking
around the site in 1985 recovered large
quantities of worked flint.

38 East Bedfont, Hounslow,
Greater London
*Status* dismissed.
*NGR* TQ 0806 7367
*NMR number* TQ 07 SE 13
*Excavations* Department of Greater
London Archaeology 1988–1991
*Main published sources* Palmer 1976
(41); David *et al* 1988; Pathy-Barker
1988
*Comments* Plough-levelled enclosure
first recognised on aerial photographs
by the Ordnance Survey in 1966. The
site was initially interpreted as a
causewayed enclosure, but excavated
evidence indicates a late Bronze Age
date.

39 West Wickham Common, Bromley,
Greater London
*Status* dismissed.
*NGR* TQ 3985 6522
*NMR number* TQ 36 NE 1
*Excavations* Hogg 1937
*Main published sources* Hogg and O'Neil
1937; Hogg *et al* 1941; Hogg 1981
*Comments* Fairly well preserved
earthwork enclosure, initially thought
to be a causewayed enclosure on the
basis of the discontinuous form of the
earthworks, but much more plausibly
interpreted as an unfinished Iron Age
hillfort.

40 Beacon Hill, Burghclere, Basingstoke
and Deane, Hampshire
*Status* possible.
*NGR* SU 4585 5727
*NMR number* SU 45 NE 39
*Excavations* none
*Main published sources* Palmer 1976
(35); Eagles 1991
*Comments* Two short arcs of extant
interrupted ditch traced by earthwork
and geophysical survey within an Iron
Age hillfort. The evidence is
inconclusive, but these features may
relate to a causewayed enclosure.

41 Butser Hill, Eastmeon, East
Hampshire, Hampshire
*Status* dismissed.
*NGR* SU 7120 2000
*NMR number* SU 72 SW 11
*Excavations* none
*Main published sources* Piggott 1930,
193
*Comments* Piggott suggested that an
apparently discontinuous earthwork on
Butser Hill might be a Neolithic
causewayed enclosure. Earthwork
survey suggests that the earthwork may

be prehistoric, but that its discontinuous form results from military
diggings (perhaps Napoleonic) along
its length.

42 Dorstone Hill, Dorstone, South
Herefordshire,
Hereford and Worcester
*Status* probable.
*NGR* SO 3260 4230
*NMR number* SO 34 SW 18
*Excavations* Pye 1965–9
*Main published sources* Pye 1967; 1968;
1969
*Comments* Plough-damaged earth and
stone-built enclosure, excavation
suggested it is an earlier Neolithic and
Bronze Age enclosed settlement. A
better preserved earthwork usually
interpreted as an Iron Age promontory
fort may represent an inner circuit.

43 Sawbridgeworth, East Hertfordshire,
**5.18** Hertfordshire
*Status* very probable.
*NGR* TL 4830 1396
*NMR number* TL 41 SE 27
*Excavations* none
*Main published sources* Palmer 1976
(11)
*Comments* Plough-levelled enclosure,
discovered during aerial
reconnaissance by CUCAP in July
1962.

44 Burham, Tonbridge and Malling, Kent
*Status* probable.
*NGR* TQ 7166 6238 (feature centred)
*NMR number* TQ 76 SW 68
*Excavations* none
*Main published sources* none
*Comments* Plough-levelled arc of
causewayed double ditch, discovered
during aerial reconnaissance by
RCHME in June 1982.

45 Chalk, Gravesend, Kent
*Status* unlikely.
*NGR* TQ 67 73
*NMR number* TQ 67 SE 207
*Excavations* none
*Main published sources* Jessup 1970, 73;
Holgate 1981, fig 3
*Comments* Jessup refers to a
causewayed enclosure destroyed (?by
development or quarrying) shortly
prior to 1970. No location is given and
no evidence has been found to support
the claim.

46 Chalk Hill, Ramsgate, Thanet, Kent
**4.2** *Status* certain.
*NGR* TR 3615 6465
*NMR number* TR 36 SE 24
*Excavations* Canterbury Archaeological
Trust 1997–8
*Main published sources* Shand 1998
*Comments* Plough-levelled enclosure,

discovered during aerial reconnaissance by CUCAP in June 1975. Excavations by CAT in 1997–8 revealed several more circuits than the cropmarks had suggested and recovered a typical range of deposits and finds.

47  Eastry, Dover, Kent
*Status* probable.
*NGR* TR 3038 5237 (feature centred)
*NMR number* TR 35 SW 180
*Excavations* none
*Main published sources* none
*Comments* Plough-levelled arc of causewayed ditch which may well represent part of a large enclosure. The site was discovered during aerial reconnaissance by CUCAP in June 1976.

48  Kingsborough Farm, Eastchurch, Swale, Kent
*Status* certain.
*NGR* TQ 9765 7205
*NMR number* TQ 97 SE 36
*Excavations* Archaeology South-East 1999
*Main published sources* none
*Comments* Plough-levelled causewayed enclosure discovered during excavation in advance of a housing development. Approximately a third of the perimeter was investigated.

49  Margate, Thanet, Kent
*Status* unlikely.
*NGR* TR 3485 6989 (feature centred)
*NMR number* TR 36 NW 227
*Excavations* none
*Main published sources* none
*Comments* Plough-levelled stretch of interrupted ditch of uncertain date, possibly early medieval, photographed by CUCAP in 1956–7 and plotted by RCHME in 1986.

50  Husband's Bosworth, Harborough, Leicestershire
*Status* certain
*NGR* SP 635 825
*NMR number* SP 68 SW 47
*Excavations* University of Leicester Archaeological Services 1999
*Main published sources* Clay 1999a and b
*Comments* Plough-levelled causewayed enclosure discovered through geophysical survey of a surface scatter of flints and subsequently confirmed by trial excavation.

51  Barholm and Stowe, South Kesteven,
**3.6** Lincolnshire
*Status* very probable.
*NGR* TF 0904 1029
*NMR number* TF 01 SE 7
*Excavations* none
*Main published sources* St Joseph 1970;

Palmer 1976 (8)
*Comments* Plough-levelled causewayed enclosure, discovered during aerial reconnaissance by CUCAP in July 1962.

52  Uffington, South Kesteven, Lincolnshire
*Status* very probable.
*NGR* TF 0536 0795
*NMR number* TF 00 NE 37
*Excavations* none
*Main published sources* Palmer 1976 (7)
*Comments* Plough-levelled enclosure discovered during aerial reconnaissance by CUCAP in July 1962.

53  Buxton with Lammas, Broadland, Norfolk
*Status* possible.
*NGR* TG 2514 2194
*NMR number* TG 22 SE 24
*Excavations* none
*Main published sources* none
*Comments* Plough-levelled enclosure, discovered during aerial reconnaissance by CUCAP in May 1956. The site was first interpreted as a causewayed enclosure by Norfolk Archaeological Unit in 1992. Only a few potential causeways can be positively identified, however, and, therefore, its date remains uncertain.

54  Hainford, Broadland, Norfolk
*Status* dismissed.
*NGR* TG 2297 1833
*NMR number* TG 21 NW 25
*Excavations* none
*Main published sources* Healy 1984
*Comments* A plough-levelled enclosure visible on vertical air photographs taken in 1946. The ditch does not appear to be causewayed and there is no firm evidence to suggest a Neolithic date.

55  Roughton, North Norfolk, Norfolk
**6.7** *Status* very probable.
*NGR* TG 2200 3534
*NMR number* TG 23 NW 20
*Excavations* none
*Main published sources* Edwards 1978
*Comments* Plough-levelled enclosure in close proximity to two possible long barrows and a possible round barrow with a causewayed ditch, discovered during aerial reconnaissance by Norfolk Landscape Archaeology in July 1977.

56  Briar Hill, Northampton,
**4.4** Northamptonshire
*Status* certain.
*NGR* SP 7362 5923
*NMR number* SP 75 NW 41
*Excavations* Northamptonshire Development Corporation 1973–8
*Main published sources* Palmer 1976 (14); Bamford 1979; Bamford 1985
*Comments* Plough-levelled enclosure

discovered during aerial reconnaissance by CUCAP in 1972, now destroyed by housing developments. Large-scale excavation revealed evidence for extremely complex recutting. The so-called 'spiral arm' seems more likely to represent the superimposition of a later hengiform monument.

57  Dallington, Northampton,
**3.4** Northamptonshire
*Status* certain.
*NGR* SP 7254 6350
*NMR number* SP 76 SW 53
*Excavations* Oxford Archaeological Unit 1991
*Main published sources* Keevill 1992
*Comments* Plough-levelled enclosure, in association with a possible henge and pit alignment, discovered during aerial reconnaissance by CUCAP in July 1962. Field walking in 1988 and 1991 recovered prehistoric flints and geophysical survey and trial excavation were carried out in 1992.

58  Southwick, East Northamptonshire,
**8.10** Northamptonshire
*Status* very probable.
*NGR* TL 0410 9296
*NMR number* TL 09 SW 35
*Excavations* Middle Nene Archaeological Group 1972
*Main published sources* Hadman 1973; Palmer 1976 (9)
*Comments* Plough-levelled enclosure, photographed during aerial reconnaissance by CUCAP in June 1959 and identified by Arnold Baker and Jim Pickering in 1971. A trial trench dug in 1972 recovered only Iron Age material, but this may be associated with an overlying palisaded enclosure.

59  Tansor, East Northamptonshire, Northamptonshire
*Status* dismissed.
*NGR* TL 052 915
*NMR number* TL 09 SE 116
*Excavations* none
*Main published sources* Palmer 1976 (38)
*Comments* Aerial photographs show only swirls of geological marks, with no evidence for an enclosure.

60  Tuxford, Bassetlaw, Nottinghamshire
*Status* dismissed.
*NGR* SK 7143 6995
*NMR number* SK 76 NW 1
*Excavations* none
*Main published sources* Oswald 1939
*Comments* A length of interrupted ditch, identified as a possible causewayed enclosure in the 1930s, which is more likely to be of Roman or medieval date.

61 Abingdon, Vale of White Horse,
**2.16** Oxfordshire
*Status* certain.
*NGR* SU 5112 9825
*NMR number* SU 59 NW 30
*Excavations* Leeds 1926–7; Case 1954;
Avery 1963
*Main published sources* Leeds 1927;
1928; Case 1956; Avery and Brown
1972; Palmer 1976 (22); Avery 1982
*Comments* Plough-levelled enclosure,
largely destroyed by modern housing
and gravel extraction, discovered
during gravel extraction in 1926.

62 Aston Cote Shifford and Chimney,
West Oxfordshire, Oxfordshire
*Status* very probable.
*NGR* SP 3485 0070
*NMR number* SP 30 SW 10
*Excavations* none
*Main published sources* Benson and
Miles 1974 (map 13); Palmer 1976 (6)
*Comments* Plough-levelled enclosure,
discovered during aerial
reconnaissance by RCHME in July
1969.

63 Banbury, Cherwell, Oxfordshire
*Status* probable.
*NGR* SP 4521 3831 (feature centred)
*NMR number* SP 43 NE 43
*Excavations* none
*Main published sources* none
*Comments* Plough-levelled arc of
causewayed ditch, possibly part of an
enclosure, discovered during aerial
reconnaissance by RCHME in July
1996.

64 Blewburton Hill, Aston Upthorpe (and
Blewbury), South Oxfordshire,
Oxfordshire
*Status* possible.
*NGR* SU 5455 8610
*NMR number* SU 58 NW 53
*Excavations* Harding 1967
*Main published sources* Holgate 1988,
map 33; Mercer 1990
*Comments* Excavation of the Iron Age
hillfort in 1967 revealed a ditch
containing Neolithic artefacts, on the
basis of which the site was listed by
Holgate as a possible causewayed
enclosure.

65 Broadwell, West Oxfordshire,
**5.17** Oxfordshire
*Status* very probable.
*NGR* SP 2650 0182
*NMR number* SP 20 SE 14
*Excavations* none
*Main published sources* Benson and
Miles 1974 (map 4); Palmer 1976 (5)
*Comments* Plough-levelled enclosure,
discovered during aerial
reconnaissance by J K St Joseph in July
1969.

66 Buckland, Vale of White Horse,
**4.17** Oxfordshire
*Status* very probable.
*NGR* SP 3213 0001
*NMR number* SP 30 SW 57
*Excavations* none
*Main published sources* none
*Comments* Plough-levelled enclosure,
discovered during aerial
reconnaissance by RCHME in June
1970.

67 Burford, West Oxfordshire,
**1.3** Oxfordshire
*Status* very probable.
*NGR* SP 2319 1071
*NMR number* SP 21 SW 31
*Excavations* none
*Main published sources* none
*Comments* Plough-levelled enclosure,
discovered during aerial
reconnaissance by RCHME in July
1994.

68 Eye and Dunsden, South Oxfordshire,
Oxfordshire
*Status* probable.
*NGR* SU 7530 7746
*NMR number* SU 77 NE 91
*Excavations* Oxford Archaeological
Unit 1974
*Main published sources* OAU 1974;
Palmer 1976 (36)
*Comments* Cropmarks, apparently
representing a plough-levelled
causewayed enclosure, were discovered
during aerial reconnaissance by
RCHME in July 1970. Although trial
excavations by OAU in 1974 revealed
no features which might account
for the cropmarks, they remain
quite convincing as a causewayed
enclosure.

69 Eynsham, West Oxfordshire,
Oxfordshire
*Status* very probable.
*NGR* SP 4259 0806
*NMR number* SP 40 NW 353
*Excavations* none
*Main published sources* Harding and Lee
1987 (No. 147)
*Comments* Plough-levelled enclosure,
discovered during aerial
reconnaissance by CUCAP in June
1953.

70 Goring, South Oxfordshire,
Oxfordshire
*Status* unlikely.
*NGR* SU 6045 7970
*NMR number* SU 67 NW 33
*Excavations* Oxford Archaeological
Unit 1985–92
*Main published sources* Allen 1995
*Comments* A plough-levelled enclosure
discovered by excavation and
geophysical survey. The site is probably

of Middle Neolithic date, and is
morphologically very different from
most causewayed enclosures.

71 Langford, West Oxfordshire,
**7.3** Oxfordshire
*Status* very probable.
*NGR* SP 2458 0080
*NMR number* SP 20 SW 39
*Excavations* none
*Main published sources* Palmer 1976 (4)
*Comments* Plough-levelled causewayed
enclosure, discovered through aerial
reconnaissance by CUCAP in July
1959.

72 Radley, Vale of White Horse,
**4.22** Oxfordshire
*Status* probable.
*NGR* SU 5341 9980
*NMR number* SU 59 NW 65
*Excavations* none
*Main published sources* none
*Comments* Plough-levelled small
enclosure, discovered during aerial
reconnaissance by RCHME in May
1990.

73 Woolston, West Felton, Oswestry,
Shropshire
*Status* possible.
*NGR* SJ 3274 2358
*NMR number* SJ 32 SW 44
*Excavations* none
*Main published sources* none
*Comments* Plough-levelled stretch of
causewayed ditch, potentially part of
an enclosure, discovered during aerial
reconnaissance by RCHME in July
1971.

74 Ham Hill, Stoke-sub-Hamdon,
Somerset
*Status* possible.
*NGR* ST 483 164
*NMR number* ST 41 NE 118
*Excavations* none
*Main published sources* Smith 1971, 90
*Comments* Earthwork survey and
geophysical survey have not found any
evidence to support Smith's
suggestion, but the setting and concen-
tration of earlier Neolithic finds from
the vicinity remain good circumstantial
evidence.

75 South Cadbury, South Somerset,
Somerset
*Status* possible.
*NGR* ST 628 251
*NMR number* ST 62 NW 29
*Excavations* Alcock 1966–70
*Main published sources* Alcock 1972;
Mercer 1981, 189; Cunliffe 1993,
fig 2.6
*Comments* Earthwork survey and
excavation have not found any hard
evidence to support Mercer's

suggestion, but the setting and concentration of earlier Neolithic finds from the vicinity remain good circumstantial evidence.

76 Alrewas, Lichfield, Staffordshire
**4.9** *Status* very probable.
*NGR* SK 1540 1435
*NMR number* SK 11 SE 18
*Excavations* none
*Main published sources* Palmer 1976 (2)
*Comments* Plough-levelled enclosure, discovered during aerial reconnaissance by CUCAP in June 1960.

77 Mavesyn Ridware, Lichfield,
**4.18** Staffordshire
*Status* very probable.
*NGR* SK 0850 1680
*NMR number* SK 01 NE 33
*Excavations* none
*Main published sources* Palmer 1976 (1)
*Comments* Plough-levelled causewayed enclosure, discovered during aerial reconnaissance by CUCAP in June 1959.

78 Bentley, Babergh, Suffolk
*Status* possible.
*NGR* TM 1146 3922
*NMR number* TM 13 NW 23
*Excavations* none
*Main published sources* none
*Comments* Plough-levelled enclosure, discovered during aerial reconnaissance by CUCAP in May 1968.

79a Fornham All Saints, St Edmundsbury,
**4.25** Suffolk
*Status* very probable.
*NGR* TM 8310 6830
*NMR number* TL 86 NW 38
*Excavations* none
*Main published sources* St Joseph 1964; Palmer 1976 (40)
*Comments* Larger and earlier of two conjoined plough-levelled enclosures, in close association with three cursus monuments. The complex was discovered during aerial reconnaissance by CUCAP in June 1960.

79b Fornham All Saints, St Edmundsbury,
**4.25** Suffolk
*Status* very probable.
*NGR* TM 8323 6807
*NMR number* TL 86 NW 38
*Excavations* none
*Main published sources* St Joseph 1964; Palmer 1976 (40)
*Comments* Smaller and later of two conjoined plough-levelled enclosures, in close association with three cursus monuments. The complex was discovered during aerial reconnaissance by CUCAP in June 1960.

80 Freston, Babergh, Suffolk
**3.14** *Status* very probable.
*NGR* TM 1680 3795
*NMR number* TM 13 NE 19
*Excavations* none
*Main published sources* Palmer 1976 (12)
*Comments* Plough-levelled causewayed enclosure, discovered during aerial reconnaissance by CUCAP in June 1969.

81 Kedington, St Edmondsbury, Suffolk
**5.21** *Status* very probable.
*NGR* TL 7010 4725
*NMR number* TL 74 NW 19
*Excavations* none
*Main published sources* Charge 1982
*Comments* Plough-levelled enclosure, discovered during aerial reconnaissance by CUCAP in June 1976. The single arc of causewayed ditch completes the curve formed by a meander of the River Stour. Fieldwalking in the area has produced large quantities of Mesolithic and Neolithic flint, with a concentration outside the enclosure.

82 Bourne Mill, Farnham, Waverley, Surrey
*Status* dismissed.
*NGR* SU 8528 4792
*NMR number* SU 84 NE 7
*Excavations* Keiller and Piggott 1937–8
*Main published sources* Lowther 1936; Keiller and Piggott 1939; Harding 1976
*Comments* The Badshot long barrow was initially interpreted as parts of two concentric circuits forming part of a causewayed enclosure. This early confusion later led Joan Harding to revive the suggestion.

83 Staines, Spelthorne, Surrey
**3.17** *Status* certain.
*NGR* TQ 0241 7261
*NMR number* TQ 07 SW 14
*Excavations* Robertson-Mackay 1961–63
*Main published sources* Palmer 1976 (27); Healey and Robertson-Mackay 1983; Robertson-Mackay 1987
*Comments* Plough-levelled enclosure first photographed during aerial reconnaissance by Fairey Surveys in March 1956. First identified as a causewayed enclosure by D Spencer in July 1959. Large-scale excavations revealed evidence for complex structured deposition. The site has now been destroyed by gravel extraction.

84 Cockroost Hill, Hove, Sussex (East)
*Status* unlikely.
*NGR* TQ 2456 0845
*NMR number* TQ 20 NW 84
*Excavations* none
*Main published sources* none
*Comments* A possible causewayed enclosure was recorded on photographs taken in 1989, held in the Sussex Sites and Monuments record (ref: 5165). The marks interpreted as a causewayed ditch may be of geological origin and the course of the feature is inconsistent. The overall shape and location are atypical.

85 Combe Hill, Eastbourne, Sussex (East)
**8.5** *Status* certain.
*NGR* TQ 5750 0222
*NMR number* TQ 50 SE 12
*Excavations* Musson 1949; Seton-Williams 1962
*Main published sources* Curwen 1930; Musson 1950; Palmer 1976 (29); Drewett 1994
*Comments* Well preserved earthwork causewayed enclosure. Excavation suggests that deposition may have been structured differently across the site.

86 Malling Hill, Lewes, Sussex (East)
*Status* unlikely.
*NGR* TQ 424 112
*NMR number* TQ 41 SW 111
*Excavations* Richard Lewis 1973
*Main published sources* Lewes Archaeological Group 1974; Palmer 1976 (43)
*Comments* Seven depressions on Malling Hill were thought by Lewis to be suggestive of a causewayed enclosure. A small trench was excavated and considerable quantities of worked flint were recovered. No features are visible on aerial photographs but a short length of surviving earthwork may be the one recorded in 1973. Around twenty waste flakes and two sherds of pottery were noted in spoil from rabbit burrows along its line.

87 Offham Hill, Hamsey, Lewes, Sussex
**4.8** (East)
*Status* certain.
*NGR* TQ 3988 1175
*NMR number* TQ 31 SE 23
*Excavations* Sussex Archaeological Field Unit 1976
*Main published sources* Drewett 1977
*Comments* Enclosure partly destroyed by a 19th-century chalk pit, though a short length still survives as an earthwork. Total excavation of the remaining part prior to its destruction by ploughing suggested that the inner circuit was a later addition.

88 Whitehawk Camp, Brighton, Sussex
**5.31** (East)
*Status* certain.
*NGR* TQ 3303 0477
*NMR number* TQ 30 SW 1
*Excavations* Curwen 1929; 1932–3;
1935
*Main published sources* Ross Williamson
1930; Curwen 1934; 1936; Palmer
1976 (28)
*Comments* Fairly well preserved
earthwork causewayed enclosure
earthwork on Brighton racecourse. The
outer circuit is joined by linear
earthworks, possibly of later date.
Large-scale excavations in the 1930s
revealed evidence for timber gate
structures and perhaps settlement.

89 Barkhale Camp, Bignor Hill, Arundle,
**3.10** Arun (and Bignor, Chichester), Sussex
(West)
*Status* certain.
*NGR* SU 9758 1261
*NMR number* SU 91 SE 31
*Excavations* Ryle 1929; Seton-Williams
1958–61; Leach 1978
*Main published sources* Palmer 1976
(24); Leach 1983
*Comments* Well preserved earthwork
causewayed enclosure. Fairly small-
scale excavations have confirmed the
date of the enclosure.

90 Bury Hill, Houghton, Arun, Sussex
(West)
*Status* unlikely.
*NGR* TQ 0023 1203
*NMR number* TQ 01 SW 28
*Excavations* Bedwin 1979
*Main published sources* Bedwin 1981
*Comments* Plough-levelled enclosure
discovered by CUCAP in May 1964.
The earlier Neolithic date was
confirmed through excavation, but the
enclosure is continuously ditched and
sufficiently different from most
causewayed enclosures to suggest that
it is a different kind of monument.

91 Court Hill, Singleton, Chichester,
**3.3** Sussex (West)
*Status* certain.
*NGR* SU 8977 1375
*NMR number* SU 81 SE 5
*Excavations* Bedwin 1982
*Main published sources* Bedwin 1984
*Comments* Plough-damaged
causewayed enclosure, part of which
survives well as an earthwork. The
enclosure was initially thought to be
continuously ditched but has several
certain and potential causeways. An
outlying arc of ditch with a single
potential causeway may be
contemporary.

92 Halnaker Hill, Boxgrove, Chichester,
**8.12** Sussex (West)
*Status* probable.
*NGR* SU 9200 0965
*NMR number* SU 90 NW 2
*Excavations* Bedwin 1981–3
*Main published sources* Bedwin 1992
*Comments* Plough-damaged enclosure,
part of which survives fairly well as an
earthwork. Excavation suggested that
the enclosure is Neolithic or Bronze
Age, but the existence of several
potential causeways and the form of the
entrance seem to support a Neolithic
date.

93 The Trundle (St Roche's Hill),
**8.6** Chichester, Sussex (West)
*Status* certain.
*NGR* SU 8774 1107
*NMR number* SU 81 SE 52
*Excavations* Curwen 1928, 1930?;
Bedwin and Aldsworth 1980
*Main published sources* Curwen 1929;
1931; Bedwin and Aldsworth 1981;
Palmer 1976 (23)
*Comments* Well preserved complex of
earthworks, partly overlain by The
Trundle Iron Age hillfort. Excavation
by Curwen suggests that the enclosure
is relatively early and similar to
Whitehawk Camp.

94 Hasting Hill, Sunderland, Tyne and
Wear
*Status* possible.
*NGR* NZ 3551 5409
*NMR number* NZ 35 SE 10
*Excavations* A Harding 1980
*Main published sources* Newman 1976
*Comments* Plough-levelled small
enclosure lying close to a probable
cursus monument, discovered during
aerial reconnaissance by N McCord in
August 1972. Excavation in 1980 and
geophysical survey in 1989 were unable
to confirm the date of the enclosure.
Only two of the causeways can be
verified. The circuit appears to respect
a round barrow, but a Neolithic date
cannot be discounted.

95 Hampton Lucy, Stratford-on-Avon,
Warwickshire
*Status* dismissed.
*NGR* SP 2550 5765
*NMR number* SP 25 NE 42
*Excavations* none
*Main published sources* Palmer 1976 (32)
*Comments* Cropmarks of agricultural
origin, initially interpreted as a
Neolithic causewayed enclosure.

96 Wasperton, Warwick, Warwickshire
*Status* possible.
*NGR* SP 2698 5845
*NMR number* SP 25 NE 40
*Excavations* Birmingham University

Field Archaeology Unit 1980–5
*Main published sources* Hughes and
Crawford 1995
*Comments* Enclosure with only a few
distinct causeways, discovered during
aerial reconnaissance undertaken by
RCHME in July 1969. Dated to the
Middle Neolithic on the evidence of
sherds of pottery in the Ebbsfleet
tradition, but the form of the circuit
may support an earlier origin.

97 Beckhampton, Avebury
*Status* unlikely.
*NGR* SU 0892 6938
*NMR number* SU 07 NE 200
*Excavations* Newport, Leicester and
Southampton Universities 1999–2000
*Main published sources* Gillings, Pollard
and Wheatley 2000
*Comments* Plough-levelled enclosure
discovered during aerial survey by
RCHME in 1982. Although described
as a causewayed enclosure, the finds
reported from the excavation suggest it
is of Middle Neolithic date, with more
in common with Flagstones and
Stonehenge I.

98 Cherhill, North Wiltshire, Wiltshire
*Status* dismissed.
*NGR* SU 0311 7005
*NMR number* SU 07 SW 19
*Excavations* MOPBW (Evans and
Smith) 1967
*Main published sources* Evans and Smith
1983
*Comments* Originally thought to be a
causewayed enclosure, this irregular
linear feature has since been re-
interpreted as a possible quarry, but is
potentially of Neolithic date. The area
is now occupied by a housing estate.

99 Crofton, Great Bedwyn, Kennet,
**4.21** Wiltshire
*Status* very probable.
*NGR* SU 2632 6260
*NMR number* SU 26 SE 53
*Excavations* Lobb 1984
*Main published sources* Lobb 1995
*Comments* Plough-levelled exceptionally
large causewayed enclosure, discovered
during aerial reconnaissance by
RCHME in 1976. Excavation
recovered a few flints compatible with
an earlier Neolithic date, but the
enclosure is unusual in its size,
landscape setting and the fact that it
appears to have had V-shaped ditches
in an early phase of its use.

100 Knap Hill, Alton, Kennet, Wiltshire
**2.7** *Status* certain.
*NGR* ST 1210 6365
*NMR number* SU 16 SW 22
*Excavations* Cunnington 1908–9;
Connah 1961

*Main published sources* Cunnington 1909; 1911–12; Connah 1965; Palmer 1976 (21)
*Comments* Well preserved earthwork causewayed enclosure. On the basis of fairly small-scale excavations, the enclosure was the first in England to be confirmed.

101 Overton Hill, Avebury, Kennet, Wiltshire
*Status* dismissed.
*NGR* SU 1145 6845
*NMR number* SU 16 NW 37
*Excavations* none
*Main published sources* Curwen 1930, 41; Palmer 1976 (34); Malone 1989, 47–8
*Comments* Cropmarks of geological origin, initially interpreted as a causewayed enclosure.

102 Robin Hood's Ball, Shrewton (and
1.4 Figheldean) Salisbury, Wiltshire
*Status* certain.
*NGR* SU 1011 4604
*NMR number* SU 14 NW 3
*Excavations* N Thomas 1956; J Richards 1983
*Main published sources* Thomas 1964; Palmer 1976 (20); Richards 1990, 61–5
*Comments* Well preserved earthwork causewayed enclosure. Fairly small-scale excavations revealed pits of broadly contemporary date outside the enclosure.

103 Rybury, All Cannings, Kennet,
8.7 Wiltshire
*Status* certain.
*NGR* SU 0832 6397
*NMR number* SU 06 SE 14
*Excavations* Bonney 1963
*Main published sources* Bonney 1964; Palmer 1976 (18)
Comment: Fairly well preserved earthwork causewayed enclosure, partly overlain by Rybury Iron Age hillfort. The excavations are not fully published.

104 Stonehenge I, Amesbury, Salisbury, Wiltshire
*Status* unlikely.
*NGR* SU 1224 4218
*NMR number* SU 14 SW 4
*Excavations* Gowland 1901; Hawley 1919–26; Atkinson 1950–64 and 1978; Pitts 1979–80
*Main published sources* Kinnes 1979, 18; Cleal *et al* 1995, 113–4
*Comments* Excavation has revealed the existence of causeways and semi-causeways which suggest that the first phase of the enclosure around the megaliths may be a hybrid between causewayed enclosures and henges. Similar to the Flagstones enclosure in Dorset.

105 Scratchbury Camp, Norton Bavant, West Wiltshire, Wiltshire
*Status* unlikely.
*NGR* ST 9116 4424
*NMR number* ST 94 SW 1
*Excavations* W F Grimes 1957
*Main published sources* Curwen 1930, 38; Annable 1958, 17
*Comments* A probable prehistoric enclosure surviving as an earthwork within the ramparts of Scratchbury Camp Iron Age hillfort. Trial excavations which only investigated the upper fills of the ditch were inconclusive and the causewayed appearance of the earthwork seems to result from post-medieval ploughing.

106 West Kington, Nettleton, North
7.2 Wiltshire, Wiltshire
*Status* very probable.
*NGR* ST 7970 7670
*NMR number* ST 77 NE 36
*Excavations* none
*Main published sources* none
*Comments* Plough-levelled causewayed enclosure, with an unusual rectangular plan, discovered during aerial reconnaissance by RCHME in May 1990.

107 Whitesheet Hill, Kilmington,
8.3 Salisbury, Wiltshire
*Status* certain.
*NGR* ST 8017 3519
*NMR number* ST 83 NW 6
*Excavations* Stone and Piggott 1951; Wessex Archaeology 1986; 1989–90
*Main published sources* Piggott 1952; Palmer 1976 (16); Rawlins forthcoming
*Comments* Well preserved earthwork causewayed enclosure, overlain by a possible later Neolithic round barrow. Excavation suggests that the profile of the ditch varies greatly around the circuit.

108 Windmill Hill, Avebury, Kennet,
2.8 Wiltshire
*Status* certain.
*NGR* SU 0867 7144
*NMR number* SU 07 SE 22
*Excavations* Keiller 1925–39; Smith 1957–8; Whittle 1988
*Main published sources* Smith 1959; 1965; Palmer 1976 (19); Malone 1989, 46–66; Anon 1990; Whittle and Pollard 1995; Whittle *et al* 1999
*Comments* Well preserved earthwork causewayed enclosure, for many years regarded as the type-site for upland causewayed enclosures. Large-scale excavations have produced evidence for many different activities, which have influenced the interpretation of other sites.

109 Yarnbury Castle, Berwick Saint James, Salisbury, Wiltshire
*Status* dismissed.
*NGR* SU 0355 4038
*NMR number* SU 04 SW 6
*Excavations* M E Cunnington 1932
*Main published sources* Curwen 1930, 37; Cunnington 1932–4
*Comments* Excavations demonstrated that the curious ditch within the ramparts is of Middle Iron Age date. The form of the earthwork is in any case very different from any known causewayed enclosure.

110 Duggleby Howe, Kirby Grindalythe,
4.5 Ryedale, Yorkshire (North)
*Status* possible.
*NGR* SE 8804 6688
*NMR number* SE 86 NE 2
*Excavations* none
*Main published sources* Kinnes *et al* 1983
*Comments* Cropmarks of a large sub-circular oval enclosure lying concentric to Duggleby Howe, discovered during aerial reconnaissance by CUCAP in March 1956. The enclosure ditch appears to be partially segmented, but the size and shape of the enclosure suggests that it is as likely to be a henge as a causewayed enclosure, or a unique type.

111 South Kirkby and Moorthorpe, Wakefield, Yorkshire (West)
*Status* dismissed.
*NGR* SE 435 105
*NMR number* –
*Excavations* none
*Main published sources* Palmer (31)
*Comments* Listed in Palmer's gazetteer as 'traces said to be showing around South Kirkby hillfort on air photographs taken by Eric Houlder'. Palmer considered the site highly suspect and Houlder considers any marks are associated with the hillfort. No evidence for a causewayed enclosure could be identified by RCHME on the available photographs.

Green How, Ireby and Uldale, Allerdale, Cumbria
*Status* very probable
*NGR* NY 2574 3746
*NMR number* NY 23 NE 12
*Excavations* none
*Main published sources* none
*Comments* Discovered while this book was in the final stages of preparation during aerial reconnaissance by English Heritage in June 2000. The form and location of the enclosure are closely comparable to proven causewayed enclosures in southern England.

## Causewayed enclosures in the Isle of Man

(Information provided by Professor Tim Darvill, Bournemouth University)

112 Billown, Malew, Rushden
*Status* probable.
*NGR* SC 2674 7018 (feature centred)
*NMR number* –
*Excavations* Bournemouth University 1996–7
*Main published sources* Darvill 1997a; 1998
*Comments* Plough-levelled shallow arc of causewayed ditch, probably part of an enclosure, discovered by geophysical survey and test-pitting in 1996; dated by leaf-shaped arrowheads.

## Causewayed enclosures in Wales

(Information provided by the Royal Commission on the Ancient and Historical Monuments of Wales and Dr Julian Thomas, Southampton University)

113 Norton, Glamorgan
**3.19** *Status* possible.
*NGR* SS 8748 7578
*NMR number* SS 87 NE
*Excavations* none
*Main published sources* Driver 1997
*Comments* Plough-levelled enclosure discovered during aerial reconnaissance by RCAHMW in 1997.

114 Bryn Celli Wen, Llandaniel Fab, Anglesey
*Status* certain.
*NGR* SH 5117 7029
*NMR number* –
*Excavations* Southampton and Sheffield Universities 1990–3
*Main published sources* Edmonds and Thomas 1991a; b; 1992; 1993
*Comments* Plough-levelled causewayed enclosure discovered during test-pitting by Southampton University in 1990. Subsequent area excavations revealed that the form of the ditch was similar to certain sites in England and recovered sufficient lithic artefacts to demonstrate an earlier Neolithic date.

## Causewayed enclosures in Scotland

(Information provided by the Royal Commission on the Ancient and Historical Monuments of Scotland and Historic Scotland)

115 West Lindsaylands, Biggar, Clyde, Lanarkshire
*Status* possible.
*NGR* NT 0156 3656
*NMR number* NT 03 NW 35
*Excavations* none
*Main published sources* none
*Comments* Plough-levelled enclosure 0.65ha in area discovered during aerial reconnaissance by CUCAP in 1940.

116 Leadketty, Perthshire
**3.7** *Status* possible.
*NGR* NO 0207 1612
*NMR number* NO 01 NW 21
*Excavations* none
*Main published sources* none
*Comments* Plough-levelled, almost circular, enclosure discovered during aerial reconnaissance by CUCAP in 1971. Fieldwalking has recovered Neolithic material from the surface.

117 Whitmuirhaugh, Sprouston, Roxburgh, Roxburghshire
*Status* possible.
*NGR* NT 7571 3609
*NMR number* NT 73 NE 22.01
*Excavations* none
*Main published sources* Reynolds 1980, fig 7; Smith 1982; 1992
*Comments* Plough-levelled enclosure discovered during aerial reconnaissance by CUCAP in 1936. Initially interpreted as a promontory fort.

## Causewayed enclosures in Ireland

(Information provided by Dr Jim Mallory, the Queen's University, Belfast)

118 Donegore Hill, Freemanstown,
**5.3** County Antrim
*Status* certain.
*NGR* (3)2144 (3)8915
*NMR number* n/a
*Excavations* The Queen's University of Belfast 1983–6
*Main published sources* Mallory and Hartwell 1984; Mallory 1993; in preparation
*Comments* Almost entirely plough-levelled enclosure discovered during fieldwalking by Queen's University in 1981. Excavations revealed large quantities of earlier Neolithic material and many of the constructional features characteristics of the causewayed enclosures found in southern England.

119 Lyle's Hill, Ballynabarnish, County Antrim
*Status* possible
*NGR* (3)2478 (3)8285
*NMR number* n/a
*Excavations* E Evans 1937; B Proudfoot 1951; The Queen's University of Belfast 1987–8
*Main published sources* Simpson and Gibson 1989
*Comments* Palisaded enclosure finally confirmed by excavation in 1987–8. The palisade may have been the only element of the perimeter, but it is not impossible that earthworks once existed.

## Tor enclosures and related types

120 Berry Castle, St Neot, Caradon, Cornwall
*Status* possible.
*NGR* SX 1970 6890
*NMR number* SX 16 NE 5
*Excavations* none
*Main published sources* none
*Comments* none

121 Carn Brea, Kerrier, Cornwall
*Status* certain.
*NGR* SW 6850 0760
*NMR number* SW 064 SE 5
*Excavations* Mercer 1970–3
*Main published sources* Mercer 1981
*Comments* Well preserved complex stone-built tor enclosure, shown by excavation to have been a settlement in its later phases and burnt down in a probable attack.

122 Carn Galver, Zennor, Penwith, Cornwall
*Status* possible.
*NGR* SW 4273 3600
*NMR number* SW 43 NW 121
*Excavations* none
*Main published sources* none
*Comments* Fairly well preserved stone-built enclosure incorporating a tor.

123 De Lank, St Breward, North Cornwall, Cornwall
*Status* possible.
*NGR* SX 1010 7530
*NMR number* SX 17 NW 118
*Excavations* none
*Main published sources* none
*Comments* Poorly preserved stone-built enclosure, partly destroyed by quarrying. The form of the bank and one of the entrances is comparable to Carn Brea.

124 Helman Tor, Lanlivery, Restormel,
5.7 Cornwall
*Status* certain.
*NGR* SX 0618 6164
*NMR number* SX 06 SE 33
*Excavations* Mercer 1986
*Main published sources* Mercer 1986
*Comments* Well preserved stone-built tor
enclosure.

125 Notter Tor, Linkinhorne, Caradon,
Cornwall
*Status* possible.
*NGR* SX 2715 7377
*NMR number* SX 27 SW 111
*Excavations* none
*Main published sources* none
*Comments* Fairly well preserved stone-
built enclosure, incorporating the
outcrops which form Notter Tor.

126 Roughtor, St Breward, North Cornwall,
Cornwall
*Status* possible.
*NGR* SX 1472 8087
*NMR number* SX 18 SW 38
*Excavations* none
*Main published sources* none
*Comments* Fairly well preserved stone-
built enclosure incorporating the
outcrops which form Roughtor.

127 St Stephen's Beacon, St Stephen in
Brannel, Restormel, Cornwall
*Status* possible.
*NGR* SW 9597 5452
*NMR number* SW 95 SE 15
*Excavations* none
*Main published sources* none
*Comments* Poorly preserved stone-built
enclosure surrounding the tor which
forms St Stephen's beacon.

128 Stowe's Pound, Linkinhorne, Caradon,
Cornwall
*Status* possible.
*NGR* SX 2579 7247
*NMR number* SX 27 SE 7
*Main published sources* Fletcher 1989;
Johnson and Rose 1994
*Comments* Well preserved stone-built
enclosure, used in the Bronze Age but
possibly of Neolithic origin, enclosing a
spring.

129 Tregarrick Tor, St Cleer, Caradon,
Cornwall
*Status* possible.
*NGR* SX 2416 7417
*NMR number* SX 27 SW 105
*Excavations* none
*Main published sources* none
*Comments* none.

130 Trencrom Castle, Ludgvan,
Cornwall
*Status* possible.
*NGR* SW 5180 3621
*NMR number* SW 53 NW 18
*Main published sources* none
*Comments* Fairly well preserved stone
built enclosure incorporating a
number of major outcrops, most of
which have been intensively
quarried. Some sections of the
walling are comparable to Carn
Brea, but the two gateways and hut
circles are more likely to be of Iron
Age date. This may indicate that the
enclosure was reused.

131 Carrock Fell, Caldbeck, Allerdale
(and Mungrisdale), Eden, Cumbria
*Status* unlikely.
*NGR* NY 3425 3364
*NMR number* NY 33 SW 1
*Excavations* none
*Main published sources* none
*Comments* Well preserved stone-built
enclosure at an unusually high
altitude. Although the stony bank of
the enclosure is discontinuous and
the location is unusual, the site may
equally be interpreted as an Iron Age
univallate hillfort.

132 Howe Robin, Asby, Eden, Cumbria
*Status* possible.
*NGR* NY 6245 1045
*NMR number* NY 61 SW 75
*Excavations* none
*Main published sources* none
*Comments* Fairly well preserved
stone-built enclosure of unusual
form, which has been interpreted as
earlier Neolithic on the basis of finds
in the vicinity. The enclosure may be
of later prehistoric date.

133 Skelmore Heads, Urswick, South
Lakeland, Cumbria
*Status* possible.
*NGR* SD 2742 7517
*NMR number* SD 27 NE 2
*Excavations* none
*Main published sources* none
*Comments* Fairly well preserved
stone-built enclosure, which has
been suggested as Neolithic on the
basis of a long cairn in close
proximity. There is no explicit link
between the two monuments,
however, and the enclosure may
equally be of later prehistoric date.

134 Gardom's Edge, Baslow and
5.11 Bubnell, Derbyshire
Dales, Derbyshire
*Status* possible.
*NGR* SK 2720 7290
*NMR number* SK 27 SE 37
*Excavations* Edmonds 1990s, Sheffield
University.
*Main published sources* Hart 1985;
Barnatt 1986; Ainsworth and Branatt
1998
*Comments* Well preserved stone-built
enclosure of unusual form which
RCHME survey suggests to Neolithic
or Early Bronze Age. The enclosure
may have surrounded a rock outcrop on
the scarp edge which has been quarried
away.

135 The Dewerstone, Meavy, West Devon,
5.10 Devon
*Status* possible.
*NGR* SX 5395 6406
*NMR number* SX 56 SW 14
*Excavations* none
*Main published sources* none
*Comments* Well preserved stone-built
enclosure, with several possible
entrances. The banks may have
incorporated several outcrops and a tor
prior to quarrying activity.

136 Hound Tor, Manaton, Teignbridge,
Devon
*Status* possible.
*NGR* SX 7430 7897
*NMR number* SX 77 NW 99
*Excavations* none
*Main published sources* none
*Comments* Poorly preserved stone built
enclosure incorporating the two
outcrops which form Hound Tor.

137 Whittor, Peter Tavy, West Devon,
Devon
*Status* possible.
*NGR* SX 5428 7864
*NMR number* SX 57 NW 8
*Excavations* none
*Main published sources* none
*Comments* Well preserved stone-built
enclosure surrounding and incorpo-
rating the outcrops which form Whittor.

138 Rough Haw, Flasby with Winterburn,
Craven, Yorkshire (North)
*Status* unlikely
*NGR* SD 9621 5664
*NMR number* SD 95 NE 70
*Excavations* none
*Main published sources* none
*Comments* Fairly well preserved stone-
built enclosure of unusual form,
discovered during aerial reconnaissance
by RCHME in 1996. The enclosure
incorporates stone outcrops, but may
equally be of later prehistoric date.

# List of references

Abercromby, J 1912 *A Study of the Bronze Age Pottery of Great Britain and Ireland and its Associated Grave-Goods* (2 vols). Oxford: Clarendon Press

Ainsworth, S 1997 'Neolithic "trading centre" found in Peak District'. *Brit Archaeol* **23**, 4

Ainsworth, S and Barnatt, J 1998 'A scarp-edge enclosure at Gardom's Edge, Baslow, Derbyshire', *Derbyshire Archaeol J* **118**, 5–23

Alcock, L 1972 *'By South Cadbury is that Camelot': excavations at Cadbury Castle 1966–70*. London: Thames and Hudson

Allcroft, A H 1908 *Earthworks of England: Prehistoric, Roman, Saxon, Danish, Norman, and Mediaeval*. London: Macmillan

Allcroft, A H 1916 'Some earthworks of West Sussex'. *Sussex Archaeol Collect* **58**, 65–90

Allen, M J 1997a 'Environment and economy: exploitation and farming of the downland' *in* Smith, R J C, Healy, F, Allen, M J, Morris, E L, Barnes, I and Woodward, P J, *Excavations along the route of the Dorchester By-pass, Dorset, 1986–8* (Wessex Archaeol Rep **11**) Salisbury: Trust for Wessex Archaeology, 162–99

Allen, M J 1997b 'Landscape, Land-use and Farming' *in* Smith, R J C, Healy, F, Allen, M J, Morris, E L, Barnes, I and Woodward, P J, *Excavations along the route of the Dorchester By-pass, Dorset, 1986–8* (Wessex Archaeol Rep **11**) Salisbury: Trust for Wessex Archaeology, 277–83

Allen, T G 1995 *Lithics and Landscape: archaeological discoveries on the Thames Water pipeline at Gatehampton Farm, Goring, Oxfordshire 1985–92* (Oxford Archaeol Unit Thames Valley Landscapes Monogr 7). Oxford: Oxford Archaeology Unit and Oxford University Committee for Archaeology

Andersen, N H 1997 *The Sarup Enclosures: the funnel beaker culture of the Sarup site, including two causewayed camps, compared to the contemporary settlements in the area and other European enclosures*, Vol 1. Aarhus: Aarhus University Press

Annable, F K 1958 'Excavation and Field-Work in Wiltshire: 1957'. *Wiltshire Archaeol Nat Hist Mag* **57**, 2–17

Anon 1960 'Recent archaeological discoveries in Berkshire: report of the Field Research Group of the Berkshire Archaeological Society. *The Archaeol Newsletter* **6** (12), 284–7

Anon 1977 'Causewayed camps'. *Curr Archaeol* **58**, 335–40

Anon 1990 'Avebury: Windmill Hill' *in* 'Excavations and fieldwork in Wiltshire 1988'. *Wiltshire Archaeol Mag* **83**, 218–223

Ashbee, P 1984 *The earthen long barrow in England*, 2 edn. Norwich: Geo

Atkinson, R J C, Piggott, C M and Sandars, N K 1951 *Excavations at Dorchester, Oxon*. Oxford: Department of Antiquities, Ashmolean Museum

Avery, M 1982 'The Neolithic causewayed enclosure, Abingdon' *in* Case, H J and Whittle, A W R (eds), *Settlement patterns in the Oxford region: excavations at the Abingdon causewayed enclosure and other sites* (Counc Brit Archaeol Res Rep **44**). Oxford: Ashmolean Museum and Counc Brit Archaeol, 10–50

Avery, M and Brown, D 1972 'Saxon features at Abingdon'. *Oxoniensia* **37**, 66–81

Bamford, H N 1979 'Briar Hill Neolithic causewayed enclosure: second interim report, April 1976 – October 1978. *Northamptonshire Archaeol* **14**, 3–9

Bamford, H N 1985 *Briar Hill* (Northamptonshire Development Corporation Archaeol Monogr **3**). Northampton: Belmont Press

Barber, M 1997 'Landscape, the Neolithic, and Kent '*in* Topping, P (ed), *Neolithic landscapes*. Oxford: Oxbow Books, 77–86

Barber, M, Field, D and Topping, P 1999 *The Neolithic flint mines of England*. London: English Heritage

Barclay, A and Bayliss, A 1999 'Cursus monuments and the radiocarbon problem' *in* Barclay, A and Harding, J (eds), *Pathways and ceremonies. The cursus monuments of Britain and Ireland* (Neolithic Studies Group Seminar Pap **4**). Oxford: Oxbow Books, 11–29

Barclay, A, Bradley, R, Hey, G and Lambrick, G 1996 'The Earlier Prehistory of the Oxford Region in the Light of Recent Research (The Tom Hassall Lecture for 1995)'. *Oxoniensia* LXI, 1–20

Barclay, A and Halpin, C 1999 *Excavations at Barrow Hills, Radley, Oxfordshire, Volume 1: The Neolithic and Bronze Age monument complex*. Oxford: Oxford Archaeological Unit and Oxford Univ Comm Archaeol

Barker, G and Webley, D 1978 'Causewayed camps and Earlier Neolithic economies in central southern England'. *Proc Prehist Soc* **44**, 161–86

Barnatt, J 1986 'Bronze Age remains on the east moors of the Peak District'. *Derbyshire Archaeol J* **106**, 18–100

Barnatt, J and Moir, G 1984 'Stone circles and megalithic mathematics'. *Proc Prehist Soc* **50**, 197–216

Barnatt, J, Bevan, B and Edmonds, M R 1998 *A Prehistoric landscape at Gardom's Edge, Baslow, Derbyshire: excavations in 1997*. Peak District National Park and Sheffield University, unpublished report

Barnatt, J, Bevan, B and Edmonds, M R 1999 *A Prehistoric landscape at Gardom's Edge, Baslow, Derbyshire: excavations in 1998*. Peak District National Park and Sheffield University, unpublished report

Barrett, J C 1994 *Fragments from Antiquity: an archaeology of social life in Britain, 2900–1200 BC*. Oxford: Blackwell

Barrett, J C, Bradley, R J and Green, M 1991 *Landscape, monuments and society: the prehistory of Cranborne Chase*. Cambridge: Cambridge University Press

Bassett, S R 1982 *Saffron Walden: excavations and research 1972–80* (Chelmsford Archaeol Trust Rep **2**/Counc Brit Archaeol Res Rep **45**). London: Counc Brit Archaeol

Bedwin, O 1981 'Excavations at the Neolithic enclosure on Bury Hill, Houghton, W. Sussex 1979'. *Proc Prehist Soc* **47**, 69–86

Bedwin, O 1982 'Excavations at Halnaker Hill, Boxgrove, West Sussex'. *Bull Inst Archaeol* **19**, 92–95

Bedwin, O 1983 'Excavations at Halnaker Hill, Boxgrove, West Sussex (second season)'. *Bull Inst Archaeol* **20**, 80–83

Bedwin, O 1984 'The Excavation of a small hilltop enclosure on Court Hill, Singleton, West Sussex, 1982'. *Sussex Archaeol Collect* **122**, 13–22

Bedwin, O 1984–5 'Excavations at Halnaker Hill, Boxgrove, West Sussex (third season)' *Bull Inst Archaeol* **21–2**, 34–6

Bedwin, O 1992 'Prehistoric earthworks on Halnaker Hill, West Sussex: excavations 1981-1983'. *Sussex Archaeol Collect* **130**, 1–12

Bedwin, O R and Aldsworth, F 1981 'Excavations at The Trundle, 1980'. *Sussex Archaeol Collect* **119**, 208–14

Bell, M, Fowler, P J and Hillson, S W 1996 *The Experimental Earthwork Project 1960–1992* (Counc Brit Archaeol Res Rep **100**). London: Counc Brit Archaeol

Bellamy, P and Edmonds, M R 1991 'Lithic technology and spatial patterning' *in* Sharples, N, *Maiden castle: Excavations and Field Survey 1985–6*. London Historic Buildings and Monuments Commission for England, 32–4

Benson, D and Miles, D 1974 *The Upper Thames Valley. An archaeological survey of the river gravels* (Oxford Archaeol Unit Survey **2**). Oxford: Truexpress

Bersu, G 1940 'Little Woodbury, Wiltshire. Part 1: the settlement as revealed by excavation'. *Proc Prehist Soc* **6**, 30–111

Bestley, N J 1993 'Type and typology and writing the past: the case of the Cotswold-Severn monuments'. *Archaeol Rev Cambridge* **12**(1), 91–103

Bewley, R 1993 'Survey and excavation at a crop-mark enclosure, Plasketlands, Cumbria'. *Trans Cumberland Westmorland Antiq Archaeol Soc* **93**, 1–18

Blanchet, J-C and Martinez, R 1988 'Les camps Néolithiques Chasséens dans le nord-est du Bassin Parisien' *in* Burgess, C, Topping, P, Mordant, C and Maddison, M (eds), *Enclosures and defences in the Neolithic of Western Europe*. Oxford: Brit Archaeol Rep, 149–65

Bonney, D J 1964 'All Cannings: Rybury Camp'. *Wiltshire Archaeol Nat Hist Mag* **59**, 185

Bowden, M 1991 *Pitt Rivers: the life and archaeological work of Lieutenant-General Augustus Henry Lane Fox Pitt Rivers, DCL, FRS, FSA*. Cambridge: Cambridge University Press

Bowden, M and McOmish, D 1987 'The Required Barrier'. *Scott Archaeol Rev* **4** (part 2), 76–84

Bowden, M and McOmish, D 1989 'Little Boxes: more about hillforts'. *Scott Archaeol Rev* **6**, 12–15

Boyd Dawkins, W 1894 'On the Relation of the Palaeolithic to the Neolithic Period'. *J Anthropol Inst* **23**, 242–257

Bradley, R J 1969 'The Trundle Revisited'. *Sussex Notes Queries* **17** (November), 133–4

Bradley, R J 1978 *The Prehistoric Settlement of Britain*. London: Routledge and Kegan Paul

Bradley, R J 1984a *The Social Foundations of Prehistoric Britain: Themes and Variations in the Archaeology of Power*. London: Longmans

Bradley, R J 1984b 'The bank barrows and related monuments of Dorset in the light of recent fieldwork'. *Proc Dorset Nat Hist Archaeol Soc* **105**, 15–20

Bradley, R J 1989 'Herbert Toms – a pioneer of analytical field survey' *in* Bowden, M, Mackay, D and Topping, P (eds), *From Cornwall to Caithness: some aspects of British field archaeology – papers presented to Norman V Quinnell* (Brit Archaeol Rep, Brit Ser **209**). Oxford: Brit Archaeol Rep, 29–47

Bradley, R J 1992 'The Gravels and British Prehistory from the Neolithic to the Early Iron Age' *in* Fulford, M and Nichols, E (eds), *Developing Landscapes of Lowland Britain. The archaeology of the British gravels: a review* (Occas Pap Soc Antiq London **14**). London: Society of Antiquaries of London, 15–22

Bradley, R J 1993 *Altering the Earth. The origins of monuments in Britain and continental Europe. The Rhind Lectures 1991–2* (Soc Antiq Scotl Monogr Ser **8**). Edinburgh: Soc Antiq Scotl

Bradley, R J 1997 *Rock Art and the Prehistory of Atlantic Europe*. London: Routledge

Bradley, R J 1998a 'Interpreting Enclosures' *in* Edmonds, M R and Richards, C (eds), *Understanding the Neolithic of North-Western Europe*. Glasgow: Cruithne Press, 188–203

Bradley, R J 1998b *The significance of monuments*. London: Routledge and Kegan Paul

Bradley, R J and Edmonds, M R 1993 *Interpreting the axe trade: production and exchange in Neolithic Britain*. Cambridge: Cambridge University Press

Bradley, R J and Holgate, R 1984 'The Neolithic sequence in the upper Thames Valley' *in* Bradley, R and Gardiner, J (eds), *Neolithic Studies: a Review of Some Current Research* (Brit Archaeol Rep, Brit Ser **133**). Oxford: Brit Archaeol Rep, 107–134

Brown, A G 1989 'The Social Life of Flint at Neolithic Hembury'. *Lithics* **10**, 46–9

Brown, A G 1997 *Alluvial geoarchaeology: floodplain archaeology and environmental change*. Cambridge: Cambridge University Press

Brown, A G and Edmonds, M R 1987 *Lithic analysis and later British prehistory* (Brit Archaeol Rep, Brit Ser **162**). Oxford: Brit Archaeol Rep

Brown, N 1996 'The archaeology of Essex c 1500–500BC' *in* Bedwin, O (ed), *The Archaeology of Essex. Proceedings of the 1993 Writtle conference*. Chelmsford: Essex County Council, 26–37

Buckley, D and Hedges, J D 1987 *The Bronze Age and Saxon Settlements at Springfield Lyons, Essex: an interim report* (Essex County Council Occas Pap **5**). Chelmsford: Essex County Council

Bulleid, A and Gray, H St G 1911 *The Glastonbury Lake Village. A full description of the excavations and the relics discovered, 1892–1907*, Vol I. Glastonbury Antiquarian Society

Bulleid, A and Gray, H St G 1917 *The Glastonbury Lake Village. A full description of the excavations and the relics discovered, 1892–1907*, Vol II. Glastonbury Antiquarian Society

Bulleid, A and Gray, H St G 1948 *The Meare Lake Village: a full description of the excavations and the relics from the eastern half of the west village, 1910–33*, Vol I. Taunton: privately printed at Taunton Castle

Burgess, C, Topping, P, Mordant, C and Maddison, M (eds), 1988 *Enclosures and defences in the Neolithic of Western Europe* (Brit Archaeol Rep, Int Ser **403**). Oxford: Brit Archaeol Rep

Burl, A 1981 ' "By the light of the cinerary moon": chambered tombs and the astronomy of death' *in* Ruggles, C L N and Whittle A W R (eds), *Astronomy and society in Britain in the period 4000–1500 BC* (Brit Archaeol Rep, Brit Ser **88**). Oxford: Brit Archaeol Rep, 243–74

Burnez, C 1993 'Les camps à enceintes interrompues' *in* Guide de la Musée des tumulus de Bougon. Bougon, 72–81

Burrin, P J and Scaife, R G 1984 'Aspects of Holocene valley sedimentation and floodplain development in southern England'. *Proc Geol Ass* **95**, 81–96

Carman, J (ed) 1997 *Material Harm: archaeological studies of war and violence*. Glasgow: Cruithne Press

Carstairs, P 1986 'An archaeological study of the Dorney area'. *Rec Buckinghamshire* **28**, 163–8

Case, H J 1956 'The Neolithic causewayed camp at Abingdon, Berks'. *Antiq J* **36**, 1–30

Case, H J 1969 'Neolithic explanations'. *Antiquity* **43**, 176–86

Case, H J 1982 'Introduction' *in* Case, H J and Whittle, A W R (eds), *Settlement patterns in the Oxford region: excavations at the Abingdon causewayed enclosure and other sites* (Counc Brit Archaeol Res Rep **44**). Oxford: Ashmolean Mus and Counc Brit Archaeol, 1–9

Case, H J 1986 'The Mesolithic and Neolithic in the Oxford region' *in* Briggs, G, Cook, J and Rowley, T (eds), *The archaeology of the Oxford region*. Oxford: Oxford Univiversity Department of External Studies, 18–37

Cassen, S and Boujot, C 1990 'Grabenumfriedungen im Frankreich der 5. Bis 3.Jahrtausends v. u. Z.'Jornal M V **73**, 455–68

Chapman, A 1985 'The Geometry of the Briar Hill causewayed enclosure' *in* Bamford, H N, *Briar Hill*. Northampton: Belmont Press, 133–144

Chapman, J 1988 'From "space" to "place": a model of dispersed settlement and Neolithic society' *in* Burgess, C, Topping, P, Mordant, C and Maddison, M (eds), *Enclosures and defences in the Neolithic of Western Europe*. Oxford: Brit Archaeol Rep, 21–46

Charge, B 1982 'Fieldwork at a Neolithic cropmark site, Hall Farm, Kedington, Suffolk'. *Haverhill District Archaeol Group J* **3** (part 1), 4–25

Childe, V G 1931 'The Continental Affinities of British Neolithic Pottery'. *Archaeol J* **88**, 37–66

Clark, G T 1880 'Some Remarks Upon Earthworks'. *Archaeol J* **37**, 217–226

Clark, J G D 1936 *The Mesolithic Settlement of Northern Europe*. Cambridge: Cambridge University Press

Clark, J G D and Piggott, S 1933 'The Age of the British Flint Mines'. *Antiquity* **7**, 166–183

Clark, R H and Schofield, A J 1991 'By experiment and calibration: an integrated approach to the archaeology of the ploughsoil' *in* Schofield, A J (ed), *Interpreting artefact scatters: contributions to ploughzone archaeology* (Oxbow monogr **4**). Oxford: Oxbow Books, 93–105

Clay, P 1999a 'A first causewayed enclosure for Leicestershire'. *Past: the newsletter of the Prehistoric Society* **32** (July), 3–4

Clay P 1999b 'The Neolithic and Bronze Age of Leicestershire and Rutland'. *Leicestershire Archaeol Hist Soc Trans* **73**, 1–18

Cleal, R M J 1992 'Significant Form: Ceramic Styles in the Earlier Neolithic of Southern England' *in* Sharples, N and Sheridan A (eds), *Vessels for the Ancestors*. Edinburgh: Edinburgh University Press, 286–304

Cleal, R M J, Walker, K E and Montague, R 1995 *Stonehenge in its Landscape. Twentieth-century Excavations* (Engl Heritage Archaeol Rep **10**). London: HMSO

Clift, J G N 1907 'Maiden Castle, Dorchester'. *J Brit Archaeol Ass, new ser* **13**, 157–168

Coles, J M 1987 *Meare Village East: The Excavations of A Bulleid and H St George Gray 1932–1956* (Somerset Levels Pap **13**). Taunton: Somerset Levels Project/Somerset County Council Museums Service

Coles, J M and Minnitt, S 1995 *Industrious and fairly civilized: the Glastonbury Lake Village*. Taunton: Somerset Levels Project/Somerset County Council Museums Service

Colt Hoare, R C 1812 *The Ancient History of South Wiltshire*, reprinted 1975. East Eardsley: EP Publishing and Wiltshire County Library

Connah, G 1965 'Excavations at Knap Hill, Alton Priors'. *Wiltshire Archaeol Nat Hist Mag* **60**, 1–23

Connah, G 1969 'Radiocarbon Dating for Knap Hill'. *Antiquity* **43**, 304–5

Cooney, G 1997 'Images of settlement and the landscape in the Neolithic' *in* Topping, P (ed), *Neolithic landscapes*. Oxford: Oxbow Books, 23–31

Copley, G J 1958 *An archaeology of south-east England: a study in continuity*. London: Phoenix House

Crawford, O G S 1927 'Windmill Hill, Wiltshire'. *Antiquity* **1**, 104–5

Crawford, O G S 1937 'Causewayed Settlements'. *Antiquity* **11**, 210–2

Crawford, O G S 1953 *Archaeology in the Field*. London: J M Dent and Sons

Crawford, O G S and Keiller, A 1928 *Wessex from the Air*. Oxford: Clarendon Press

Cunliffe, B W 1974 *Iron Age Communities in Britain: an account of England Scotland and Wales from the seventh century BC until the Roman conquest*, 1 edn. London: Routledge and Kegan Paul

Cunliffe, B W 1992 'Preface' *in* Fulford, M and Nichols, E (eds), *Developing Landscapes of Lowland Britain. The archaeology of the British gravels: a review* (Occas Pap Soc Antiq London **14**). London: Society of Antiquaries of London

Cunliffe, B W 1993 *Wessex to AD 1000*. London and New York: Longman

Cunnington, M E 1909 'On a remarkable feature in the entrenchments of Knap Hill Camp, Wiltshire'. *Man* **9**, 49–52

Cunnington, M E 1911–12 'Knap Hill Camp'. *Wiltshire Archaeol Nat Hist Mag* **37**, 42–65

Cunnington, M E 1932–4 'Excavation in Yarnbury Castle Camp, 1932'. *Wiltshire Archaeo Nat Hist Mag* **46**, 198–205

Curwen, E C 1929a *Prehistoric Sussex*. London: The Homeland Association

Curwen, E C 1929b 'Excavations in The Trundle, Goodwood, 1928'. *Sussex Archaeol Collect* **70**, 33–85

Curwen, E C 1930 'Neolithic Camps'. *Antiquity* **4**, 22–54

Curwen, E C 1931 'Excavations in The Trundle'. *Sussex Archaeol Collect* **72**, 100–49

Curwen, E C 1934 'Excavations in Whitehawk Neolithic Camp, Brighton, 1932–3'. *Antiq J* **14**, 99–133

Curwen, E C 1936 'Excavations in Whitehawk Camp, Brighton, Third Season, 1935'. *Sussex Archaeol Collect* **77**, 60–92

Curwen, E C 1938 'The early development of agriculture in Britain'. *Proc Prehist Soc* **4**, 27–51

Curwen, E C 1946 *Plough and Pasture*. London: Cobbett Press

Curwen, E C 1954 *The Archaeology of Sussex*, 2 rev edn. London: Methuen

Darvill, T 1981 'Excavations at the Peak Camp, Cowley: an interim note'. *Glevensis* **15**, 52–56

Darvill, T 1982 'Excavations at the Peak Camp, Cowley, Gloucestershire'. *Glevensis* **16**, 20–25

Darvill, T 1987 *Prehistoric Gloucestershire*. Gloucester: Sutton and Gloucestershire County Library

Darvill, T 1996a 'Neolithic Buildings in England, Wales and the Isle of Man' *in* Darvill, T and Thomas, J (eds), *Neolithic Houses in Northwest Europe and Beyond* (Neolithic Studies Group Seminar Pap 1; Oxbow Monogr **57**). Oxford: Oxbow Books, 77–111

Darvill, T 1996b *Billown Neolithic Landscape Project, Isle of Man, 1995* (Bournemouth Univ Sch Conservation Sci Res Rep **1**). Bournemouth and Douglas: Bournemouth University and Manx National Heritage

Darvill, T 1997a *Billown Neolithic Landscape Project, Isle of Man, 1996* (Bournemouth Univ Sch Conservation Sci Res Rep **3**). Bournemouth and Douglas: Bournemouth University and Manx National Heritage

Darvill, T 1997b 'Neolithic Landscapes: identity and definition' *in* Topping, P (ed), *Neolithic landscapes*. Oxford: Oxbow Books, 1–14

Darvill, T 1998 *Billown Neolithic Landscape Project, Isle of Man, 1997* (Bournemouth Univ Sch Conservation Sci Res Rep **3**). Bournemouth and Douglas: Bournemouth University and Manx National Heritage

David, A, Lewis, J and Cotton, J 1988 'Mayfield Farm, East Bedfont'. *London Archaeol* **5** (15), 412

Dixon, P 1988 'The Neolithic Settlements on Crickley Hill' *in* Burgess, C, Topping, P, Mordant, C and Maddison, M (eds), *Enclosures and defences in the Neolithic of Western Europe*. Oxford: Brit Archaeol, 75–87

Dixon, P 1994 *Crickley Hill, volume 1: the hillfort defences*. Nottingham: Crickley Hill Trust/University of Nottingham, Department of Archaeology

Drewett, P 1977 'The Excavation of a Neolithic Causewayed Enclosure on Offham Hill, East Sussex, 1976'. *Proc Prehist Soc* **43**, 201–41

Drewett, P 1980 'The Sussex plough damage survey' *in* Hinchcliffe, J and Schadla-Hall, R T 1980 *The Past Under the Plough* (DoE Occas Pap 3). London: DoE

Drewett, P 1994 'Dr V Seton-Williams' excavations at Combe Hill, 1962, and the role of Neolithic causewayed enclosures in Sussex'. *Sussex Archaeol Collect* **132**, 7–24

Drewett, P L, Rudling, D and Gardiner, M 1988 *The South-East to AD 1000*. London: Longman

Driver, T 1997 'Norton: the first interrupted ditch enclosure in Wales?'. *Aerial Archaeol Res Group News* **15**, 17–19

Dubouloz, J, Lebolloch, M and Ilett, M 1988 '*Middle Neolithic enclosures in the Aisne valley*' *in* Burgess, C, Topping, P, Mordant, C and Maddison, M (eds), *Enclosures and defences in the Neolithic of Western Europe*. Oxford: Brit Archaeol Rep, 209–26

Dyer, J F 1955 'Maiden Bower near Dunstable. Part 1'. *Bedfordshire Archaeol* **1** (part 1), 47–52

Dyer, J F and Hales, A J 1961 'Pitstone Hill: a study in field archaeology'. *Rec Buckinghamshire* **17** part 1, 49–56

Eagles, B N 1991 'A new survey of the hillfort on Beacon Hill, Burghclere, Hampshire'. *Antiq J* **148**, 98–103

Edmonds, M R 1993 'Interpreting causewayed enclosures in the past and the present' *in* Tilley, C (ed), *Interpretative Archaeology*. Oxford: Berg, 99–142

Edmonds, M R 1995 *Stone tools and society*. London: Batsford

Edmonds, M R 1999 *Ancestral Geographies of the Neolithic: Landscapes, monuments and memory*. London: Routledge

Edmonds, M and Thomas, J 1991a *The Anglesey Archaeological Landscape Project. First Interim Report*. Lampeter: St David's University College

Edmonds, M and Thomas, J 1991b *The Anglesey Archaeological Landscape Project. Second Interim Report, 1991*. Lampeter: St David's University College

Edmonds, M and Thomas, J 1992 *The Anglesey Archaeological Landscape Project. Third Interim Report, 1992*. Lampeter: St David's University College

Edmonds, M and Thomas, J 1993 *The Anglesey Archaeological Landscape Project. Fourth Interim Report, 1993*. Lampeter: St David's University College

Edwards, D 1978 'An interrupted ditched enclosure and oval enclosure at Roughton'. *E Anglian Archaeol* **8**, 93–4

Erskine, R W H 1951 'A Neolithic causewayed enclosure at Hambledon Hill, Parishes of Childe Okeford and Iwerne Courtney, National Grid Reference ST 848 122'. *Proc Dorset Nat Hist Archaeol Soc* **73**, 105–6

Evans, C 1988a 'Monuments and analogy: the interpretation of causewayed enclosures' *in* Burgess, C, Topping, P, Mordant, C and Maddison, M (eds), *Enclosures and defences in the Neolithic of Western Europe*. Oxford: Brit Archaeol Rep, 47–73

Evans, C 1988b 'Excavations at Haddenham, Cambridgeshire: a "planned" enclosure and its regional affinities' *in* Burgess, C, Topping, P, Mordant, C and Maddison, M (eds), *Enclosures and defences in the Neolithic of Western Europe*. Oxford: Brit Archaeol Rep,127–148

Evans, C 1988c 'Acts of enclosure: a consideration of concentrically-organised causewayed enclosures' *in* Barrett, J C and Kinnes, I (eds), *The archaeology of context in the Neolithic and Bronze Age: recent trends*. Sheffield: J R Collis and Univ Sheffield Dep of Archaeol Prehist, 85–96

Evans, C and Hodder, I forthcoming *The Haddenham Project volume 1: the emergence of a Fenland landscape*. Cambridge: MacDonald Institute Research Papers

Evans, C and Knight, M forthcoming 'A Fenland delta: later prehistoric land-use in the lower Ouse regions' *in* Dawson, M (ed), *The Archaeology of the Ouse Valley* (Counc Brit Archaeol Res Rep). London: Counc Brit Archaeol

Evans, J G 1966 'Land Mollusca from the Neolithic Enclosure on Windmill Hill'. *Wiltshire Archaeol Nat Hist Mag* **61**, 91–2

Evans, J G 1967 'Cherhill'. *Archaeol Rev* **2**, 8–9

Evans, J G 1972 *Land Snails in Archaeology*. London: Seminar Press

Evans, J G, Rouse, A J and Sharples, N M 1988 'The landscape setting of causewayed camps: some recent work on the Maiden Castle enclosure' *in* Barrett, J C and Kinnes, I (eds), *The archaeology of context in the Neolithic and Bronze Age: recent trends*. Sheffield: J R Collis and Univ Sheffield Dep of Archaeol Prehist

Evans, J G and Smith, I F 1983 'Excavations at Cherhill, North Wiltshire, 1967' *Proc Prehist Soc* **49**, 43–117

Farrar, R (ed) 1951 'Archaeological Fieldwork in Dorset in 1951'. *Proc Dorset Nat Hist Archaeol Soc* **73**, 85–115

Fell, C I and Davis, R V 1988 'The petrological identification of stone implements from Cumbria' *in* Clough, T H McK and Cummins, W A (eds), *Stone axe studies*, Vol 2 (Counc Brit Archaeol Res Rep **67**). London: Counc Brit Archaeol, 71–7

Fenner, V E P and Dyer, C A 1994 'The Thames Valley Project. A report for the National Mapping Project'. RCHME unpublished report held in the NMR

Field, D 1997 'The landscape of extraction: aspects of the procurement of raw material in the Neolithic' *in* Topping, P (ed), *Neolithic landscapes*. Oxford: Oxbow Books, 55–67

Field, D 1998 'Round barrows and the harmonious landscape: placing Bronze Age burial monuments in south-east England'. *Oxford J Archaeol* **17** (3), 309–26

Fleming, A 1972 'Vision and design approaches to ceremonial monument typology'. *Man* **7**, 57–73

Fletcher, M 1989 'Stowe's Pound' *in* Bowden, M, Mackay, D, and Topping, P (eds), *From Cornwall to Caithness. Some aspects of British field archaeology, Papers presented to Norman V Quinell* (Brit Archaeol Rep, Brit Ser **209**). Oxford: Brit Archaeol Rep, 71–8

Ford, S 1986 'A newly-discovered causewayed enclosure at Eton Wick, near Windsor, Berkshire'. *Proc Prehist Soc* **52**, 319–320

Ford, S 1991–3 'Excavations at Eton Wick'. *Berkshire Archaeol J* **74**, 27–36

Forde-Johnston, J L 1958 'A note on excavation at Buzbury Rings'. *Proc Dorset Nat Hist Archaeol Soc* **80**, 107–8

Fowler, P J 1976 'Agriculture and rural settlement' *in* Wilson D M (ed), *The archaeology of Anglo-Saxon England*. London: Methuen, 23–98

Fox, C 1932 *The Personality of Britain: its influence on inhabitant and invader in prehistoric and early historic times*. Cardiff: National Museum of Wales

French, C A I 1990 'Neolithic Soils, Middens and Alluvium in the Lower Welland Valley'. *Oxford J Archaeol* **9**, 305–11

Gardiner, E 1925 'Hambledon Hill'. *Proc Dorset Nat Hist Antiq Fld Club* **46**, 73–4

Gardiner, J P 1984 'Lithic distributions and settlement patterns in Central Southern England' *in* Bradley, R J and Gardiner, J (eds), *Neolithic studies. A review of some current research* (Brit Archaeol Rep, Brit Ser **133**). Oxford: Brit Archaeol Rep, 315–40

Gardiner, J P 1990 'Flint procurement and Neolithic axe production on the South Downs: a re-assessment' *Oxford J Archaeol* **9**, 119–40

Gardiner, M 1990 'The archaeology of the Weald – a survey and review'. *Sussex Archaeol Collect* **128**, 33–53

Gelling, M 1984 *Place-Names in the Landscape. The geographical roots of Britain's place-names*. London: J M Dent

Gent, T H and Knight, M 1995 'Excavation and survey of a multi-period enclosure site, Raddon Hill, Stockleigh Pomeroy: interim report'. Exeter Archaeology unpublished site report no. 95.68

Gillings, M, Pollard J and Wheatley, D 2000 'The Beckhampton Avenue and a "new" Neolithic enclosure: an interim report on the 1999 excavations'. *Wiltshire Archaeol Nat Hist Mag* (Wiltshire Heritage Studies) **93**, 1–8

Gilman, P (ed) 1989 'Excavations in Essex 1988'. *Essex Archaeol Hist* **20**, 157–71

Gilman, P (ed) 1991 'Excavations in Essex 1990'. *Essex Archaeol Hist* **22**, 148–61

Gould, I C 1901 'Early Defensive Earthworks' *J Brit Archaeol Ass*, new ser **7**, 15–38

Gray, H St G 1935 'The Avebury Excavations 1908–1922'. *Archaeologia* 84, 99–126

Gray, H St G and Bulleid, A 1953 *The Meare Lake Village. A full description of the excavations and the relics from the eastern half of the west village, 1910–1933*, Vol II . Taunton: privately printed at Taunton Castle

Gray, H St G and Cotton, M A 1966 *The Meare Lake Village. A full description of the excavations and the relics from the eastern half of the west village, 1910–1933*, Vol III. Taunton: privately printed at Taunton Castle

Grimes, W F 1979 'The history of implement petrology in Britain' *in* Clough T H McK and Cummins W A (eds), *Stone Axe Studies: archaeological, petrological, experimental, and ethnographic* (Counc Brit Archaeol Res Rep 23). London: Counc Brit Archaeol, 1–4

Hadman, J A 1973 'Southwick'. *Northamptonshire Archaeol* **8** (June), 5

Hall, D, Cameron, F, Gurney, D and Coles, J M 1987 *The Fenland Project no. 2: Fenland landscape and settlement between Peterborough and March* (E Anglian Archaeol Rep **35**). Cambridge: Fenland Project Committee and Cambridgeshire Archaeological Committee

Hall, D and Coles, J 1994 *Fenland survey: an essay in landscape and persistence* (Engl Heritage Archaeol Rep 1). London: English Heritage

Harding, A F 1981 'Excavatons at the prehistoric ritual complex near Milfield, Northumberland'. *Proc Prehist Soc* **47**, 87–136

Harding, A F and Lee, G E 1987 *Henge monuments and related sites of Great Britain* (Brit Archaeol Rep, Brit Ser **175**). Oxford: Brit Archaeol Rep

Harding, D W 1976 'Blewburton Hill, Berkshire: Re-excavation and Re-appraisal' *in* Harding, D W (ed), *Hillforts: Later Prehistoric Earthworks in Britain and Ireland*, 133–46. London: Academic Press

Harding, J 1976 'Badshot Lea long barrow and its settlement site'. *Bull Surrey Archaeol Soc* **129**, 2

Harding, J 1995 'Social histories and regional perspectives in the Neolithic of Lowland England'. *Proc Prehist Soc* **61**, 117–136

Harding, J 1999 'Pathways to new realms: cursus monuments and symbolic territories' *in* Barclay, A and Harding, J (eds), *Pathways and ceremonies. The cursus monuments of Britain and Ireland* (Neolithic Studies Group Seminar Pap 4). Oxford: Oxbow Books, 30–8

Hart, C 1985 'Gardom's Edge, Derbyshire: settlements, cairnfields and hillforts' *in* Spratt, D and Burgess, C (eds), *Upland settlement in Britain. The second millennium B.C. and after* (Brit Archaeol Rep, Brit Ser **143**). Oxford: Brit Archaeol Rep, 71–5

Hawkes, J 1935 'The Place of Origin of the Windmill Hill Culture'. *Proc Prehist Soc* **1**, 127–9

Hawkes, J 1982 Mortimer *Wheeler: Adventurer in Archaeology*. London: Weidenfeld and Nicolson

Hawkins, G S 1963 *Stonehenge decoded*. London: Souvenir Press

Healey, E and Robertson-Mackay, R 1983 'The lithic industries from Staines causewayed enclosure and their relationship to other earlier Neolithic industries in southern Britain'. Lithics **4**, 1–27

Healy, F 1984 'Farming and field monuments: the Neolithic in Norfolk' *in* Barringer, C (ed), *Aspects of East Anglian Pre-history (twenty years after Rainbird Clarke): a collection of essays*. Norwich: Geo, 84–5

Healy, F 1988 *The Anglo-Saxon Cemetery at Spong Hill, North Elmham, Part VI: Occupation during the Seventh to Second Millennia BC* (E Anglian Archaeol Rep **39**). Dereham: Norfolk Archaeological Unit

Healy, F 1997 'Site 3. Flagstones' *in* Smith, R J C, Healy, F, Allen, M J, Morris, E L, Barnes, I and Woodward, P J *Excavations along the route of the Dorchester By-pass, Dorset, 1986–8* (Wessex Archaeol Rep **11**). Salisbury: Trust for Wessex Archaeology, 27–47

Hedges, J and Buckley, D G 1978 'Excavations at a Neolithic Causewayed Enclosure, Orsett, Essex, 1975'. *Proc Prehist Soc* **44**, 219–308

Herring, P 1999 'Trencrom, Lelant: archaeological and historical assessment'. Unpublished report, Cornwall Archaeological Unit

Hey, G 1997 'Neolithic settlement at Yarnton, Oxfordshire' *in* Topping, P (ed), *Neolithic landscapes*. Oxford: Oxbow Books, 99–111

Hingley, R 1996 'Ancestors and identity in the later prehistory of Atlantic Scotland: the reuse and reinvention of Neolithic monuments and material culture'. *World Archaeol* **28**.2, 231–43

Hoare, R C see Colt Hoare, R C

Hodder, I 1984 'Burials, houses, women and men in the European Neolithic' *in* Miller, D and Tilley, C (eds), *Ideology, power and prehistory*. Cambridge: Cambridge University Press, 51–68

Hodder, I 1990 *The Domestication of Europe: structure and contingency in Neolithic societies*. Oxford: Basil Blackwell

Hodder, I 1992 'The Haddenham Causewayed Enclosure – a Hermeneutic Circle' *in* Hodder, I (ed), *Theory and Practice in Archaeology*. London: Routledge, 213–240

Hogg, A H A 1981 'The Causewayed Earthwork and the Elizabethan Redoubt on West Wickham Common'. *Archaeol Cantiana* **97**, 71–78

Hogg, A H A and O'Neil, B H St J 1937 'A Causewayed Enclosure in West Kent'. *Antiquity* **11**, 223–5

Hogg, A H A, O'Neil, B H St J and Stevens, C E 1941 'Earthworks on Hayes and West Wickham Commons'. *Archaeol Cantiana* **54**, 28–34

Holden, E W 1951 'Earthworks on Court Hill'. *Sussex Notes Queries* **13**.8, 183–5

Holgate, R 1981 'The Medway Megaliths and Neolithic Kent'. *Archaeol Cantiana* **97**, 221–34

Holgate, R 1984 'Neolithic settlement in the Upper Thames Valley'. *Curr Archaeol* **8**, 374–5

Holgate, R 1988 *Neolithic settlement of the Thames Basin* (Brit Archaeol Rep, Brit Ser **194**). Oxford: Brit Archaeol Rep

Hughes, G and Crawford, G 1995 'Excavations at Wasperton, Warwickshire, 1980–1985'. *Birmingham Warwickshire Archaeol Soc Trans* **99**, 9–45

Ingold, T 1986 *The appropriation of nature*. Manchester, Manchester University Press

Jessup, R 1970 *South East England*. London: Thames and Hudson

Jewell, P A and Dimbleby, G W (eds), 1966 'The experimental earthwork on Overton Down, Wiltshire, England: the first four years'. *Proc Prehist Soc* **32**, 313–42

Johnson, N and Rose, P 1994 *Bodmin Moor. An Archaeological Survey. Vol 1: the human landscape to c 1800* (Engl Heritage Archaeol Rep **24**. RCHME Supplementary Ser **11**), 46–8. London: Cornwall Archaeological Unit/HBMC/RCHME

Johnston, D E 1955–6 'A Romano-British site near Bedford'. *Bedfordshire Archaeol* **1**, 92–97

Jones, D 1998 'Long barrows and Neolithic Elongated Enclosures in Lincolnshire: An Analysis of the Air Photographic Evidence'. *Proc Prehist Soc* **64**, 83–114

Keeley, L and Cahen, D 1989 'Early Neolithic forts and villages in north-east Belgium: a preliminary report' *J Fld Archaeol* **16**, 157–76

Keevill, G D 1992 'Northampton, King's Heath; Whitelands'. *S Midlands Archaeol* (Newsletter of the Counc Brit Archaeol S Midlands Group) **22**, 42–4

Keiller, A 1932 'The Oldest Dog'. *Country Life* **72** (no. 1861), Saturday September 17th

Keiller, A 1934 'Excavation at Windmill Hill'. *Proc First International Congress of Prehistoric and Protohistoric Sciences*. London, 135–8

Keiller, A 1939 *Guide to the Monuments at Avebury, Wiltshire*. Avebury: Morven Institute of Archaeological Research

Keiller, A and Piggott, S 1939 'Badshot Long Barrow (Report on the Excavations)' *in* Oakley, K P, Rankine, W F and Lowther, A W G (eds), *A Survey of the Prehistory of the Farnham District (Surrey)*. Guildford: Surrey Archaeological Society, 133–52

Kendall, H G O 1914 'Flint Implements from the Surface near Avebury: Their Classification and Dates'. *Proc Soc Antiq London*, **2** ser 26, 73–85

Kendall, H G O 1919a 'Windmill Hill, Avebury and Grimes Graves: Cores and Choppers'. *Proc Prehist Soc E Anglia* **3**, 104–8

Kendall, H G O 1919b 'Windmill Hill, Avebury and Grimes Graves: Cores and Choppers'. *Proc Prehist Soc E Anglia* **3**, 192–9

Kendall, H G O 1922 'Scraper-Core Industries of North Wilts'. *Proc Prehist Soc E Anglia* **3**, 515–41

Kendall, H G O 1923 'Excavations conducted on the NE side of Windmill Hill' *in Report of the Earthworks Committee . . . for 1922*. London: Congress of Archaeological, 25–6 Societies/Society of Antiquaries of London

Kendall, H G O 1927 'Further Excavations at the Graig Lwyd Neolithic Stone Axe Factory, Penmaenmawr'. *Archaeol Cambrensis* **82**, 141–6

Kendrick, T D and Hawkes, C F C 1932 *Archaeology in England and Wales 1914–1931*. London: Methuen

King, C C 1880 'Ancient Earth-Works in Britain'. *Trans Berkshire Archaeol Architect Soc 1879/1880*, 34–48

Kinnes, I 1979 *Round barrows and ring-ditches in the British Neolithic* (Brit Mus Occ Pap **7**). London: British Museum

Kinnes, I 1988 'The Cattleship Potemkin: reflections on the first Neolithic in Britain' *in* Barrett, J C and Kinnes, I (eds), *The archaeology of context in the Neolithic and Bronze Age: recent trends*. Sheffield: J R Collis and Univ Sheffield Dep of Archaeol Prehist, 2–8

Kinnes, I 1994 'The Neolithic in Britain' *in* Vyner, B (ed), *Building on the Past. Papers Celebrating 150 Years of the Royal Archaeological Institute*. London: Royal Archaeological Institute, 90–102

Kinnes, I, Schadla-Hall, T, Chadwick, P and Dean, P 1983 'Duggleby Howe reconsidered'. *Archaeol J* **140**, 83–108

Lane Fox, A H 1869a 'An Examination into the Character and Probable Origins of the Hill Forts of Sussex'. *Archaeologia* **42**, 27–52

Lane Fox, A H 1869b 'Further Remarks on the Hill Forts of Sussex: being an Account of Excavations in the Forts at Cissbury and Highdown'. *Archaeologia* **42**, 53–6

Lane Fox, A H 1876 'Excavations in Cissbury Camp, Sussex; being a report of the Exploration Committee of the Anthropological Institute for the year 1875'. *J Anthropol Inst Great Brit Irel* **5**, 357–90

Last, J 1999 'Out of line: cursuses and monument typology in eastern England' *in* Barclay, A and Harding, J (eds), *Pathways and ceremonies. The cursus monuments of Britain and Ireland* (Neolithic Studies Group Seminar Pap **4**). Oxford: Oxbow Books, 86–97

Leach, P E 1983 'The excavations of a Neolithic causewayed enclosure on Barkhale Down, Bignor Hill, West Sussex'. *Sussex Archaeol Collect* **121**, 11–30

Leech, R 1977 *The Upper Thames Valley in Gloucestershire and Wiltshire*. Bristol: Committee for Rescue Archaeology in Avon, Gloucestershire and Somerset

Leeds, E T 1927 'A Neolithic Site at Abingdon, Berks'. *Antiq J* **7**, 438–64

Leeds, E T 1928 'A Neolithic Site at Abingdon, Berks, second report'. *Antiq J* **8**, 461–77

Legge, A 1981 'Aspects of Cattle Husbandry' *in* Mercer, R (ed), *Farming Practice in British Prehistory*. Edinburgh: Edinburgh University Press, 169–81

Lewes Archaeological Group 1974 'Malling Hill'. *Sussex Archaeol Soc Newsletter* **12**, 47

Lewis, C forthcoming *Settlement and landscape: the the field archaeology of South Wiltshire.* Swindon: English Heritage

Liddell, D 1930 'Report on the Excavations at Hembury Fort, Devon, 1930'. *Proc Devon Archaeol Exploration Soc* **1**, 39–63

Liddell, D 1931 'Report of the Excavations at Hembury Fort, Devon. Second Season 1931'. *Proc Devon Archaeol Exploration Soc* **1**, 90–120

Liddell, D 1932 'Report on the Excavations at Hembury Fort. Third Season 1932'. *Proc Devon Archaeol Exploration Soc* **1**, 162–190

Liddell, D 1935 'Report on the Excavations at Hembury Fort. 4th and 5th Seasons, 1934 and 1935'. *Proc Devon Archaeol Exploration Soc* **2**, 135–175

Lobb, S 1995 'Excavations at Crofton causewayed enclosure'. *Wiltshire Archaeol Nat Hist Mag* **88**, 18–25

Lowther, A W G 1936 'Archaeological Survey of Farnham'. *Surrey Archaeol Collect* **44**, 155

Lubbock, J 1865 *Pre-Historic Times, as illustrated by ancient remains, and the manners and customs of modern savages.* London: Williams and Norgate

McGrail, S 1978 *Logboats of England and Wales* (Brit Archaeol Rep, Brit Ser **51**). Oxford: Brit Archaeol Rep

Madsen T, 1988 ' Causewayed enclosures in south Scandinavia' *in* Burgess, C, Topping, P, Mordant, C and Maddison, M (eds), *Enclosures and defences in the Neolithic of Western Europe.* Oxford: Brit Archaeol Rep, 301–36

Mallory, J P 1993 'A Neolithic ditched enclosure in Northern Ireland'. *Actes du XIIème Congrès International des Sciences Préhistoriques et Protohistoriques* **2** (Bratislava), 415–8

Mallory, J P and Hartwell, B 1984 'Donegore'. *Curr Archaeol* **92**, 271–5

Malone, C 1989 *The English Heritage Book of Avebury.* London: Batsford and English Heritage

Manby, T G (ed) 1988 *Archaeology in eastern Yorkshire: essays in honour of TCM Brewster.* Sheffield: Department of Archaeology and Prehistory, University of Sheffield

Marshall, A 1995 'Salmonsbury' *in* Rawes, B (ed), 'Archaeological Review No. 19, 1994'. *Trans Bristol Gloucestershire Archaeol Soc* **113**, 185–6

Matthews, C L 1976 *Occupation Sites on a Chiltern Ridge: excavations at Puddlehill and sites near Dunstable, Bedfordshire – Part 1: Neolithic, Bronze Age and Early Iron Age* (Brit Archaeol Rep, Brit Ser **29**). Oxford: Brit Archaeol Rep

Megaw, J V S and Simpson, D D A 1979 *Introduction to British prehistory from the arrival of Homo sapiens to the Claudian invasion.* Leicester: Leicester University Press

Mercer, R J 1980a *Hambledon Hill A Neolithic landscape.* Edinburgh: Edinburgh University Press

Mercer, R J 1980b *Hambledon Hill 1980: Interim statement.* Edinburgh: Edinburgh University Press

Mercer, R J 1980c 'The evaluation of modern ploughing threats to prehistoric sites – Hambledon Hill, Iwerne Courtney, Dorset' *in* Hinchcliffe, J and Schadla-Hall, R T, *The Past Under the Plough* (DoE Occas Pap **3**). London: DoE, 105–8

Mercer, R J 1981 'Excavations at Carn Brea, Illogan, Cornwall, 1970–73: a Neolithic fortified complex of the third millennium bc'. *Cornish Archaeol* **20**, 1–204

Mercer, R J 1985 'A Neolithic fortress and funeral center'. *Scientific American* **252** (part 3), 94–101

Mercer, R J 1986a *Excavation of a Neolithic enclosure at Helman Tor, Lanlivery, Cornwall, 1986. Interim report* (Project Paper no. 4). Edinburgh: Dept Archaeology, University of Edinburgh

Mercer, R J 1986b 'The Neolithic in Cornwall'. *Cornish Archaeol* **25**, 35–80

Mercer, R J 1987 'A Flint Quarry in the Hambledon Hill Neolithic Enclosure Complex' *in* Sieveking G de G and Newcomer M H (eds), *The Human Uses of Flint and Chert: Proceedings of the Fourth International Flint Symposium, held at Brighton Polytechnic 10–15 April 1983.* Cambridge: Cambridge University Press, 159–163

Mercer, R J 1988 'Hambledon Hill, Dorset, England' *in* Burgess, C, Topping, P, Mordant, C and Maddison, M (eds), *Enclosures and defences in the Neolithic of Western Europe.* Oxford: Brit Archaeol Rep, 89–106

Mercer, R J 1989a 'The Earliest Defences in Western Europe: part 1–Warfare in the Neolithic'. *Fortress* **2**, 16–22

Mercer, R J 1989b 'The Earliest Defences in Western Europe: part 2–The Archaeological Evidence'. *Fortress* **3**, 2–11

Mercer, R J 1990 *Causewayed Enclosures.* Princes Risborough: Shire

Mercer, R J and Healey, F in preparation *Excavation and Fieldwork on Hambledon Hill*

Moore, J 1997 'The infernal cycle of fire ecology' *in* Topping, P (ed), *Neolithic landscapes.* Oxford: Oxbow Books, 33–40

Mordant, C and Mordant, D 1988 'Les enceintes Néolithiques de la haute-vallée de la Seine' *in* Burgess, C, Topping, P, Mordant, C and Maddison, M (eds), *Enclosures and defences in the Neolithic of Western Europe.* Oxford: Brit Archaeol Rep, 231–54

Mordant, C and Mordant, D 1992 'Noyen-sur-Seine: a Mesolithic waterside settlement' *in* Coles, B (ed), *The wetland revolution in prehistory.* Exeter: WARP and the Prehistoric Society, 55–64

Munro, R 1908 'On the Transition Between the Palaeolithic and Neolithic Civilisations in Europe'. *Archaeol J* **65**, 205–44

Musson, R 1950 'An excavation at Combe Hill camp near Eastbourne, August 1949'. *Sussex Archaeol Collect* **89**, 105–16

Needham, S and Macklin, M (eds) 1992 *Archaeology under alluvium.* Oxford: Oxbow

Newman, T G 1976 'A crop-mark site at Hasting Hill, Tyne and Wear, NZ 355 541'. *Archaeol Aeliana*, 5 ser 4, 183–4

Oxford Archaeological Unit 1974 'Dunsden'. *Oxford Archaeol Unit Newsletter* **7–9** (October), 2

Oxford Archaeological Unit 1982 'Eastleach'. *Oxford Archaeol Unit Newsletter* **9** (part 4, August), 7

Orme, B 1981 *Anthropology for archaeologists: an introduction.* London: Duckworth

Oswald, A 1939 'Some unrecorded earthworks in Nottinghamshire'. *Trans Thoroton Soc Nottinghamshire* **43**, 1–15

Palmer, R 1976 'Interrupted Ditch Enclosures in Britain: the use of Aerial Photography for Comparative Studies'. *Proc Prehist Soc* **42**, 161–86

Parker, A G 1997 'Late Flandrian Palaeoecological History of Daisy Banks Fen' *in* Lewis, S G and Maddy, D (eds), *The Quaternary of the South Midlands & the Welsh Marches: Field Guide.* London: Quaternary Research Organisation

Pathy-Barker, C 1988 'Mayfield Farm, East Bedfont'. *London Archaeol*, **6** (3), 74

Peacock, D P S 1969 'Neolithic Pottery Production in Cornwall'. *Antiquity* **43**, 145–9

Piggott, S 1930 'Butser Hill'. *Antiquity* **4**, 187–200

Piggott, S 1931 'The Neolithic Pottery of the British Isles'. *Archaeol J* **88**, 67–158

Piggott, S 1952 'The Neolithic Camp on Whitesheet Hill, Kilmington Parish'. *Wiltshire Archaeol Nat Hist Mag* **54**, 404–10

Piggott, S 1954 *Neolithic Cultures of the British Isles: a Study of the Stone-using Agricultural Communities of Britain in the Second Millennium BC.* Cambridge: Cambridge University Press

Piggott, S 1955 'Windmill Hill – East or West?'. *Proc Prehist Soc* **21**, 96–101

Piggott, S 1983 'Archaeological Retrospect 5'. *Antiquity* **57**, 28–36

Piggott, S 1985 *William Stukeley: An Eighteenth-Century Antiquary* (2 edn). London: Thames and Hudson

Pluciennik, M 1998 'Deconstructing "The Neolithic"in the Mesolithic–Neolithic Transition' *in* Edmonds, M R and Richards, C (eds), *Understanding the Neolithic of North-Western Europe.* Glasgow: Cruithne Press, 61–83

Pollard, S H M 1966 'Neolithic and Dark Age settlements on High Peak, Sidmouth, Devon'. *Devon Archaeol Exploration Soc* **23**, 35–58

Priddy, D 1988 'Excavations in Essex 1987'. *Essex Archaeol Hist* **19**, 260–71

Pryor, F M M 1987 'Etton 1986: Neolithic metamorphoses'. *Antiquity* **61**, 78–80

Pryor, F M M 1988a 'Etton, near Maxey, Cambridgeshire: a causewayed enclosure on the fen-edge' *in* Burgess, C, Topping, P, Mordant, C and Maddison, M (eds), 1988 *Enclosures and defences in the Neolithic of Western Europe* . Oxford: Brit Archaeol Rep, 107–126

Pryor, F M M 1988b 'Earlier Neolithic organised landscapes and ceremonial in lowland Britain' *in* Barrett, J C and Kinnes, I (eds), *The archaeology of context in the Neolithic and Bronze Age: recent trends*. Sheffield: J R Collis and Univ Sheffield Dep of Archaeol Prehist, 63–72

Pryor, F M M 1998a *Farmers in Prehistoric Britain*. Stroud: Tempus

Pryor, F M M 1998b *Etton: excavations at a neolithic causewayed enclosure near Maxey Cambridgeshire* (Engl Heritage Archaeol Rep **18**). London: English Heritage

Pryor, F M M, French, C A I and Taylor, M 1985 'An Interim Report on Excavations at Etton, Maxey, Cambridgeshire, 1982–1984'. *Antiq J* **65**, 275–311

Pryor, F M M and Kinnes, I A 1982 'A waterlogged causewayed enclosure in the Cambridgeshire Fens'. *Antiquity* **56**, 124–6

Pye, W R 1967–9 Unpublished notes on excavations at Dorstone Hill

Pye, W R 1967 'Dorstone Hill'. *Trans Woolhope Natur Fld Club* **39**, part 1, 157

Pye, W R 1968 'Dorstone Hill'. *Trans Woolhope Natur Fld Club* **39**, part 2, 362

Pye, W R 1969 'Dorstone Hill' *Trans Woolhope Natur Fld Club* **39**, part 3, 475

Radcliffe, F M 1995 'Archaeology and historical landscape in West Dorset from the air'. *Proc Dorset Nat Hist Archaeol Soc* **117**, 51–66

Radley, J 1964 'Occupation remains at Buzbury Rings, Tarrant Keyneston'. *Proc Dorset Nat Hist Archaeol Soc* **86**, 112–14

Raetzel-Fabian, D and Kappel, I 1991 'Erdwerk und Megalithgrab bei Calden. Mittelpunkt einer Region vor 5000 Jahren'. *Archäologische Denkmäler in Hessen* 91. Kassel

Rawlins, M N *et al* forthcoming 'Excavations and survey at Whitesheet Hill, Wiltshire, 1989–90'. *Wiltshire Archaeol Nat Hist Mag*

Ray, K 1998 'Bury Down, Lanreath: investigations in 1994'. *Cornish Archaeol* **33**, 227–8

RCHME 1960 *A Matter of Time: an archaeological survey of the river gravels of England*. London: HMSO

RCHME 1970 *An Inventory of the Historical Monuments of the County of Dorset, Vol 3, Central Dorset (Part 1)*. Edinburgh: HMSO

RCHME 1976 *Ancient and Historical Monuments of the County of Gloucestershire, Vol 1: Iron Age and Romano-British monuments in the Gloucestershire Cotswolds*. London: HMSO

RCHME forthcoming *The field archaeology of the Salisbury Plain Training Area*. Swindon: English Heritage

Renfrew, C 1973 'Monuments, Mobilisation and Social Organisation in Neolithic Wessex' *in* Renfrew, C (ed), *The Explanation of Culture Change: models in prehistory*. London: Duckworth, 539–558

Reynolds, N 1980 'Dark Age timber halls and the background to excavation at Balbridie'. *Scott Archaeol Forum* **10** (1978), 50–2

Richards, C 1996 'Henges and Water'. *J Material Culture* **1**, 313–35

Richards, J 1990 *The Stonehenge Environs Project* (Engl Heritage Archaeol Rep **16**). London: Historic Buildings and Monuments Commission for England

Robertson-Mackay, R 1987 'The Neolithic causewayed enclosure at Staines, Surrey: Excavations 1961–63'. *Proc Prehist Soc* **53**, 23–128

Ross Williamson, R P 1930 'Excavations in Whitehawk Neolithic camp, near Brighton'. *Sussex Archaeol Collect* **71**, 56–96

Rowley-Conwy, P 1996 'Why didn't Westropp's "Mesolithic" catch on in 1872?'. *Antiquity* **70**, 940–4

Russell, M and Rudling, D 1996 'Excavations at Whitehawk Neolithic enclosure, Brighton, East Sussex, 1991–3'. *Sussex Archaeol Collect* **134**, 39–61

Russell, M 1997 'NEO-"Realism?": an alternative look at the Neolithic chalkland database of Sussex' *in* Topping P (ed), *Neolithic landscapes*. Oxford: Oxbow Books, 69–85

St Joseph, J K S 1964 'Air Reconnaissance: Recent Results, 2'. *Antiquity* **38**, 290–2 and plate LIII

St Joseph, J K S 1966 'Air Photography and Archaeology' *in* St Joseph, J K S (ed), *The Uses of Air Photography: nature and man in a new perspective*. London: John Baker, 112–25

St Joseph, J K S 1970 'Air Reconnaissance: Recent Results, 20'. *Antiquity* **44**, 144–5 and plate XXIII

St Joseph, J K S 1973 'Air Reconnaissance: Recent Results, 31'. *Antiquity* **47**, 236–8 and plate XXXI

Savile, A 1978 'Excavations at Icomb Hill, Gloucestershire, 1975'. *Trans Bristol Gloucestershire Archaeol Soc* **96**, 27–31

Schofield, A J 1987 'Putting lithics to the test: non-site analysis and the Neolithic settlement of southern England'. *Oxford J Archaeol* **6**.3, 269–86

Schofield, A J (ed) 1991 *Interpreting artefact scatters: contributions to ploughzone archaeology* (Oxbow monogr **4**). Oxford: Oxbow Books

Semple, S 1998 'A fear of the past: the place of the prehistoric burial mound in the ideology of middle and later Anglo-Saxon England'. *World Archaeol* **30**.1, 109–26

Shand, G 1998 'A Neolithic causewayed enclosure in Kent'. Past: *The Newsletter of the Prehistoric Society* **29**, 1

Sharpe, A 1992 'Treryn Dinas: cliff castles reconsidered'. *Cornish Archaeol* **31**, 65–8

Sharples, N 1985 'Maiden Castle project 1985: an interim report'. *Proc Dorset Nat Hist Archaeol Soc* **107**, 111–9

Sharples, N 1986 'Maiden Castle project 1986: an interim report'. *Proc Dorset Nat Hist Archaeol Soc* **108**, 53–62

Sharples, N 1991a *Maiden Castle: Excavations and Field Survey 1985–6* (Engl Heritage Archaeol Rep **19**). London: Historic Buildings and Monuments Commission for England

Sharples, N 1991b 'Warfare in the Iron Age of Wessex'. Scott *Archaeol Rev* **8**, 79–89

Shennan, S J, Healy, F and Smith, I F 1985 'The excavation of a Ring-Ditch at Tye Field, Lawford, Essex'. *Archaeol J* **142**, 150–215

Sherratt, A 1990 'The genesis of megaliths, monumentality, ethnicity and social complexity in Neolithic north-west Europe'. *World Archaeol* **22**.2, 147–67

Silvester, R J 1979 'The Relationship of First Millennium Settlement to the Upland area of the South West'. *Devon Archaeol Soc Proc* **37**, 176–90

Simpson, D and Gibson, A 1989 'Lyles Hill'. *Curr Archaeol* **114**, 214–5

Smith, I F 1956 'The Decorative Art of Neolithic Ceramics in South Eastern England'. Unpublished PhD thesis, University of London

Smith, I F 1959 'Excavations at Windmill Hill, Avebury, Wilts, 1957–8'. *Wiltshire Archaeol Nat Hist Mag* **57**, 149–62

Smith, I F 1965 *Windmill Hill and Avebury: excavations by Alexander Keiller 1925–1939*. Oxford: Clarendon Press

Smith, I F 1966 'Windmill Hill and its implications'. *Palaeohistoria* **12** (Groningen), 469–81

Smith, I F 1971 'Causewayed Enclosures' *in* Simpson, D D A (ed), *Economy and Settlement in Neolithic and Early Bronze Age Britain and Europe*. Leicester: Leicester University Press, 89–112

Smith, I M 1982 'Sprouston (Sprouston p). Survey'. *Discovery Excav Scotl*, 3

Smith, I M 1991 'Sprouston, Roxburghshire: an early Anglian centre of the eastern Tweed Basin'. *Proc Soc Antiq Scotl* **121**, 261–94

Smith, R A 1912 'On the Date of Grime's Graves and Cissbury Flint-Mines'. *Archaeologia* **63**, 109–58

Smith, W G 1894 *Man the Primeval Savage: his haunts and relics from the hill-tops of Bedfordshire to Blackwall*. London: Edward Stanford

Smith, W G 1904 *Dunstable: its History and Surroundings* (The Homeland Library III). London: The Homeland Association

Smith, W G 1915 'Maiden Bower, Bedfordshire'. *Proc Soc Antiq London*, 2 ser 27, 143–61

Startin, B and Bradley, R J 1981 'Some notes on work organisation and society in Prehistoric Wessex' *in* Ruggles, C L N and Whittle, A W R (eds), *Astronomy and society in Britain during the period 4000 to 1500 BC* (Brit Archaeol Rep, Brit Ser **88**). Oxford: Brit Archaeol Rep, 289–296

Stoertz, C 1997 *Ancient landscapes of the Yorkshire Wolds: aerial photographic transcription and analysis*. Swindon: RCHME

Stopford, J 1987 'Danebury: an alternative view'. *Scott Archaeol Rev* **4**, 70–5

Stukeley, W 1743 *Abury, a Temple of the British Druids, with Some Others, Described*. London, privately published

Sturge, W A 1909 'The Chronology of the Stone Age'. *Proc Prehist Soc E Anglia* **1**, 43–105

Thomas, J 1991 *Rethinking the Neolithic*. Cambridge: Cambridge University Press

Thomas, J 1993 'Discourse, Totalization and "The Neolithic"' *in* Tilley, C (ed), *Interpretative Archaeology*. Oxford: Berg, 357–394

Thomas, J 1996a *Time, Culture and Identity*. London: Routledge

Thomas, J 1996b 'Neolithic Houses in Mainland Britain and Ireland – a sceptical view' *in* Darvill, T and Thomas, J (eds), *Neolithic Houses in Northwest Europe and Beyond* (Neolithic Studies Group Seminar Pap 1; Oxbow Monograph 57). Oxford: Oxbow Books, 1–12

Thomas, K D 1982 'Neolithic enclosures and woodland habitats on the south downs in Sussex, England' *in* Bell, M and Limbrey, S (eds), *Archaeological aspects of woodland ecology* (Brit Archaeol Rep, Int Ser **146**). Oxford: Brit Archaeol Rep, 147–170

Thomas, N 1964 'The Neolithic Causewayed Camp at Robin Hood's Ball, Shrewton'. *Wiltshire Archaeol Nat Hist Mag* **59**, 1–27

Tilley, C 1994 *A phenomenology of landscape: places, paths and monuments*. Oxford: Berg

Tingle, M 1995 'Interim report on excavations at Membury August 1994'. *Devon Archaeol Soc Newsletter* (January) **60**, 7

Todd, M 1984 'Excavations at Hembury (Devon), 1980–83: a summary report'. *Antiq J* **64**, 251–68

Topping P 1996 'Structure and ritual in the Neolithic house: some examples from Britain and Ireland' *in* Darvill, T and Thomas, J (eds), *Neolithic Houses in Northwest Europe and Beyond* (Neolithic Studies Group Seminar Pap **1**; Oxbow Monograph 57), Oxford: Oxbow Books, 157–70

Topping, P 1997a 'Different realities: the Neolithic in the Northumberland Cheviots' *in* Topping P (ed), *Neolithic landscapes*. Oxford: Oxbow Books, 113–23

Topping, P (ed) 1997b *Neolithic landscapes* (Neolithic Studies Group Seminar Pap 2; Oxbow Monograph **86**). Oxford: Oxbow Books

Trigger, B G 1989 *A History of Archaeological Thought*. Cambridge: Cambridge University Press

Trow, S 1985 'An interrupted-ditch enclosure at Southmore Grove, Rendcomb, Gloucestershire'. *Trans Bristol Gloucestershire Archaeol Soc* **103**, 17–22

Tuan, Y-F 1977 *Space and Place: the perspective of experience*. London: Edward Arnold

Ucko, P J, Hunter, M, Clark, A J and David, A 1991 *Avebury Reconsidered from the 1660s to the 1990s*. London: Unwin Hyman

Waddington, C 1996 *The 1995 excavation on the Coupland enclosure and associated 'droveway' in the Milfield Plain, Northumberland* (Univ Durham and Univ Newcastle upon Tyne Archaeol Rep **19**). Durham: University of Durham and the University of Newcastle upon Tyne

Wainwright, G J 1972 'The excavation of a Neolithic settlement on Broome Heath, Ditchingham, Norfolk'. *Proc Prehist Soc* **38**, 1–97

Wainwright, G J 1975 'Religion and settlement in Wessex, 3000–1700bc' *in* Fowler, P J (ed), *Recent work in rural archaeology*. Bradford on Avon: Moonraker Press, 57–71

Warne, C 1872 *Ancient Dorset: The Celtic, Roman, Saxon and Danish Antiquities of the County, including early coinage*. Bournemouth: D Sydenham

Wheeler, R E M 1943 *Maiden Castle, Dorset* (Rep Res Comm Soc Antiq London **12**). London: Society of Antiquaries of London

Whittle, A W R 1977 *The earlier Neolithic of southern England and its continental background* (Brit Archaeol Rep, Supplement Ser **35**). Oxford: Brit Archaeol Rep

Whittle, A W R 1990 'A Pre-Enclosure Burial at Windmill Hill, Wiltshire'. *Oxford J Archaeol* **9**, 25–8

Whittle, A W R 1993 'The Neolithic of the Avebury Area: Sequence, Environment, Settlement and Monuments'. *Oxford J Archaeol* **12**, 29–53

Whittle, A W R 1996 *Europe in the Neolithic. The Creation of New Worlds*. Cambridge: Cambridge University Press

Whittle, A W R 1997 'Moving on and moving around: Neolithic settlement mobility' *in* Topping P (ed), *Neolithic landscapes*. Oxford: Oxbow Books, 15–22

Whittle, A W R and Pollard, J 1995 'Windmill Hill Causewayed Enclosure. The Harmony of Symbols' *in* Edmonds, M R and Richards, C (eds), *Understanding the Neolithic of North-Western Europe*. Glasgow: Cruithne Press, 231–47

Whittle, A W R, Pollard, J and Grigson, C 1999 *The harmony of symbols: the Windmill Hill causewayed enclosure, Wiltshire* (Cardiff Studies in Archaeology). Oxford: Oxford University Press

Williams, A 1952 'Clegyr-Boia, St. David's, Pemb: excavation in 1943'. *Archaeol Cambrensis* **102**, part 1, 20–47

Williams, H 1998 'Monuments and the past in early Anglo-Saxon England'. *World Archaeol* **30**.1, 90–108

Williams-Freeman, J P 1915 *An Introduction to Field Archaeology as Illustrated by Hampshire*. London: Macmillan

Williamson, R P R 1930 'Excavations in Whitehawk Neolithic Camp, Near Brighton'. *Sussex Archaeol Collect* **71**, 56–96

Wilson, D R 1975 '"Causewayed Camps" and "interrupted ditch systems"'. *Antiquity* **49**, 178–86

Woodward, P J 1988 'Pictures of the Neolithic: discoveries from the Flagstones House excavations, Dorchester, Dorset'. *Antiquity* **62**, 266–74

Woodward, A B and Woodward, P J 1996 'The topography of some barrow cemeteries in Bronze Age Wessex'. *Proc Prehist Soc* **62**, 275–91

# Index